Useful Expressions

Hello! Hallo! (_hah_-low)

Hi! Hoi! (_hoy_)/Hi! (_hay_)

Good morning! Goedemorgen! (_khoo-der-mor_-khern)

Good afternoon! Goedemiddag! (_khoo-der-mi_-dakh)

Good evening! Goedenavond! (_khoo-der-aa_-font)

See you later! Bye! Tot ziens! (_toat seens_)/Dag! (_dakh_) Hoi! (_hoai_)

Here you are! Alstublieft (_als-stuw-bleeft_)

Please? Alsjeblieft? (_als-yer-bleeft_)

Thanks! Bedankt! (_ber-dahnkt_)

I am sorry! Neem me niet kwalijk (_naym mer neet kvoa-lerk_)/ sorry! (_sor-ree_)

The Dutch Alphabet

A	ah	**N**	en
B	bay	**O**	oa
C	say	**P**	pay
D	day	**Q**	kuw
E	ay	**R**	ehr
F	ef	**S**	es
G	khay	**T**	tay
H	hah	**U**	uw
I	ee	**V**	fay
J	yay	**W**	way
K	kah	**X**	ix
L	el	**Y**	ehy
M	em	**Z**	zet

Useful Questions

Do you speak English? Spreekt u Engels? (_spraykt uw eng-erls_)

Would you help me please? Kunt u mij helpen? (_kuhnt uw may hel-pern_)

Where are the toilets? Waar is het toilet? (_vaar is het tvaa-let_)

How much is that? Hoeveel kost dat? (_hoo-feyl kost dat_)

Where can I find . . . ? Waar kan ik de . . . vinden? (_vaar kan ik der . . . fin-dern_)

At what time do you open? Hoe laat gaat u open? (_hoo laat khaat uw o-pern_)

What time do you close? Hoe laat gaat u dicht? (_hoo laat khaat uw dikht_)

Could you talk a bit slower? Kunt u wat langzamer praten? (_kuhnt uw vat lankh-sa-mern praatern_)

Could you repeat that please? Kunt u dat herhalen? (_Kuhnt uw dat her-haa-lern_)

Phrases for Emergencies

Help! Help! (_help_)

Hurry up! Schiet op! (_skeet op_)

Please call 112! Bel 112! (_bel ayn ayn tway_)

Police! Politie! (_po-lee-tsee_)

Fire brigade Brandweer (_brant-wayr_)

Get a doctor! Haal een dokter! (_haal ern dok-ter_)

I am ill! Ik ben ziek! (_ik ben seek_)

Somebody has stolen my . . . Iemand heeft mijn . . . gestolen (_ee-mant hayft mayn . . . khe-stoh-lern_)

Where is the hospital? Waar is het ziekenhuis? (_wahr is het see-kern-hoais?_)

Dutch For Dummies®

The Dutch Calendar

Days (de dagen) (*der dah-kern*)

Sunday zondag (*zon-dakh*)

Monday maandag (*maan-dakh*)

Tuesday dinsdag (*dins-dakh*)

Wednesday woensdag (*voons-dakh*)

Thursday donderdag (*don-der-dakh*)

Friday vrijdag (*fray-dakh*)

Saturday zaterdag (*zaa-ter-dakh*)

Months (de maanden) (*der maan-dern*)

January januari (*yan-nuw-aa-ree*)

February februari (*fay-bruw-aa-ree*)

March maart (*maart*)

April april (*a-pril*)

May mei (*may*)

June juni (*yuw-nee*)

July juli (*yuw-lee*)

August augustus (*ow-khuhs-tuhs*)

September september (*sep-tem-ber*)

October oktober (*ok-toa-ber*)

November november (*noa-fem-ber*)

December december (*day-sem-ber*)

The Numbers

0 nul (*nuhl*)

1 één (*ayn*)

2 twee (*tvay*)

3 drie (*dree*)

4 vier (*feer*)

5 vijf (*fayf*)

6 zes (*zes*)

7 zeven (*zay-fern*)

8 acht (*akht*)

9 negen (*nay-khern*)

10 tien (*teen*)

11 elf (*elf*)

12 twaalf (*twaalf*)

13 dertien (*dehr-teen*)

14 veertien (*fayr-teen*)

15 vijftien (*fayf-teen*)

16 zestien (*zes-teen*)

17 zeventien (*say-fern-teen*)

18 achttien (*akh-teen*)

19 negentien (*nay-khern-teen*)

20 twintig (*tvin-tikh*)

21 eenentwintig (*ayn-ern-tvin-tikh*)

22 tweeëntwintig (*tvay-ern-tvin-tikh*)

23 drieëntwintig (*dree-ern-tvin-tikh*)

24 vierentwintig (*feer-ern-tvin-tikh*)

25 vijfentwintig (*fayf-ern-tvin-tikh*)

30 dertig (*dehr-tikh*)

40 veertig (*fayr-tikh*)

50 vijftig (*fayf-tikh*)

60 zestig (*zes-tikh*)

70 zeventig (*zay-fern-tih*)

80 tachtig (*takh-tikh*)

90 negentig (*nay-khern-tikh*)

100 honderd (*hon-dert*)

200 tweehonderd (*tway-hon-dert*)

300 driehonderd (*dree-hon-dert*)

400 vierhonderd (*feer-hon-dert*)

500 vijfhonderd (*fayf-hon-dert*)

1000 duizend (*doai-zernt*)

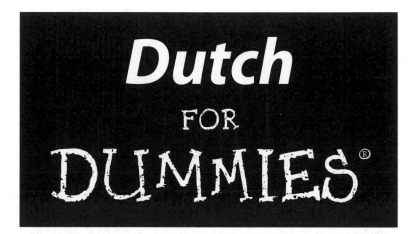

by Margreet Kwakernaak

John Wiley & Sons, Ltd

Dutch For Dummies®

Published by John Wiley & Sons, Ltd
The Atrium
Southern Gate
Chichester
West Sussex
PO19 8SQ
England

E-mail (for orders and customer service enquires): cs-books@wiley.co.uk

Visit our Home Page on www.wiley.com

Copyright © 2006 Pearson Education Benelux edition

UK edition published by John Wiley & Sons, Ltd, March 2008

For general information on our other products and services, please contact our Customer Care Department within the U.S. at 800-762-2974, outside the U.S. at 317-572-3993, or fax 317-572-4002.

For technical support, please visit www.wiley.com/techsupport.

Wiley also publishes its books in a variety of electronic formats. Some content that appears in print may not be available in electronic books.

British Library Cataloguing in Publication Data: A catalogue record for this book is available from the British Library

ISBN: 978-0-470-51986-8

Printed and bound in Great Britain by Bell & Bain Ltd., Glasgow

10 9 8 7 6 5 4 3 2 1

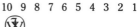

About the Author

Margreet Kwakernaak is a language teacher and the director of the language school *Suitcase talen* in Almere, near Amsterdam, in the Netherlands. She is the producer of courses for Dutch as a Second Language, Dutch as a First Language, German, English, and Spanish. During her many years of teaching students of all ages and nationalities she has learned a lot about the needs of students and how to give them confidence to speak and write.

Author's Acknowledgements

Many people contributed to this book. In the first place I want to thank my brother Huibert Kwakernaak. As an expert in Systems, Signals, and Control he is not only the one who keeps providing me with the latest computer technology, but also my teacher in efficiency and work methodology. My brother Erik Kwakernaak, a foreign language teaching methodologist and author of several books about how to teach languages, has sharpened my eyes and ears for the needs of the language learner. He has made me aware of the patterns of development that language learners have in common. Once I started working with individual students, practice overruled theory and I became an expert in speeding up individual language learning processes. The work with individual students taught me that the most efficient learning process is that in which the teacher allows the student to steer himself while the teacher serves as a guide, looking for more and more difficult roads and providing the student with the practice and theory he needs at a particular moment. During my many years of teaching at secondary school and adult evening classes I have built up a lot of experience. But my learning speed really began to accelerate when I started my own language school, where students and teachers from all over the world come together, sharing experience and methods. When I was writing this book students, teachers and secretaries of *Suitcase talen* were always willing to answer practical and linguistic questions. Sanderina Visser has lent a helping hand during the last three months of the ordering and writing process. Mathijs Petri notated the pronunciation of each Dutch word in this book. My thanks to you all, for your help.

Publisher's Acknowledgements

We're proud of this book; please send us your comments through our Dummies online registration form located at www.dummies.com/register/.

Some of the people who helped bring this book to market include the following:

Acquisitions, Editorial, and Media Development

Project Editor: Simon Bell

Content Editor: Nicole Burnett

Copy Editor: Lesley Green

Publisher: Jason Dunne

Executive Project Editor: Daniel Mersey

Cover Photos: © Nigel Hicks/Alamy

Cartoons: Rich Tennant (www.the5thwave.com)

Composition Services

Project Coordinator: Erin Smith

Layout and Graphics: Reuben W. Davis, Melissa K. Jester, Stephanie D. Jumper, Christine Williams

Proofreader: Susan Moritz

Indexer: Sharon Shock

Publishing and Editorial for Consumer Dummies

Diane Graves Steele, Vice President and Publisher, Consumer Dummies

Joyce Pepple, Acquisitions Director, Consumer Dummies

Kristin A. Cocks, Product Development Director, Consumer Dummies

Michael Spring, Vice President and Publisher, Travel

Kelly Regan, Editorial Director, Travel

Publishing for Technology Dummies

Andy Cummings, Vice President and Publisher, Dummies Technology/General User

Composition Services

Gerry Fahey, Vice President of Production Services

Debbie Stailey, Director of Composition Services

Contents at a Glance

Table of Contents

Introduction

• •

*A*s life becomes more and more global, knowing how to say at least a few words in other languages is becoming increasingly useful. Students do part of their studies abroad, and many businesses not only need overseas communication but travel as well. While English will do for business dealings in the Netherlands, people will open up if you know some words and phrases in Dutch. Wouldn't it be fun to talk to your neighbours, colleagues, and new friends in Dutch and have a good laugh together?

Whatever your motivation is, *Dutch For Dummies* can help. You'll not only find materials for basic communication such as greeting or ordering a meal, but also for telephoning or writing an e-mail. Some basic grammar provides you with the building blocks for your personal communication. *Dutch For Dummies* uses a clear and simple notation system for the pronunciation of each word, while pronunciation and accent come alive on the audio CD that supplements the book.

About This Book

This book is more than just a compilation of practical sentences and words. It will prove useful when your goal is to learn some words and phrases just to get around, but also when you intend to stay longer in the country and want to communicate with neighbours, new friends and colleagues. You can go through the book at your own pace and in your order of preference, reading and skipping as much or as little as you like. *Dutch For Dummies* is your personal guide: always ready for help.

Note: If you're a novice to Dutch, you may want to read the chapters in Part I, before you start talking. This part will give you the basics, such as how to pronounce the various sounds, which will help you to take the next steps.

Conventions Used in This Book

To make this book easier to navigate through, we have set up a set of conventions:

- ✔ Dutch terms are set in **boldface** to make them stand out.
- ✔ Pronunciations are set in *italics*, following the Dutch terms. Stressed syllables are <u>underlined</u>.

Verb conjugations (lists that show you the forms of a verb) are given in tables in this order: the 'I' form, the 'you' (singular, informal) form, the 'you' (singular and plural, formal) form, the 'he/she/it form', the 'we' form, the 'you' (plural, informal) form, and the 'they' form. Pronunciations follow in the second column. Here's an example of the verb **werken** (to work):

Conjugation	Pronunciation
ik werk	ik vehrk
jij werkt	yay vehrkt
u werkt	uw vehrkt
hij/zij/het werkt	hay/zay/het vehrkt
wij werken	vay <u>vehr</u>-kern
jullie werken	<u>yuw</u>-lee <u>vehr</u>-kern
zij werken	zay <u>vehr</u>-kern

Language learning is a specialty, so this book includes a few elements that other *For Dummies* books do not. These are the new elements:

- ✔ **Talkin' the Talk dialogues:** Most language is oral, or spoken, and most speaking is done in dialogues between two persons, so we include dialogues throughout the book. The dialogues come under the heading 'Talkin' the Talk' and show you the Dutch words, their pronunciation and the English translations. A lot of these dialogues can be found on the audio CD that comes with the book.

- ✔ **Words to Know blackboards:** Memorising words and phrases is also important in language learning, so we collect all the new words in the dialogues on a blackboard, under the heading 'Words to Know'. Dutch nouns have a gender, which determines the (definite) article each noun takes. In the Words to Know lists, we include the article for each noun so that you memorise it together with the noun.

Also note that, because each language has its own ways of expressing ideas, the English translation that we provide for the Dutch terms may not be a literal one. We want you to understand the gist of what someone is saying, not just the words that are being said. For example, you can translate the Dutch phrase 'Ik moet nu snel weg' literally as 'I have to leave soon' but the phrase really means 'I have to go now'. This book gives you the 'I have to go now' translation.

Foolish Assumptions

To write his book, we had to make some assumptions about who you are and what you want from a book called *Dutch For Dummies*. Here are some assumptions that we have made about you:

✔ You know little to no Dutch – and if you do know some words and phrases, you don't know how to organise them.

✔ You are not looking for a book that will make you fluent in Dutch: you just want to know some words, phrases and sentence constructions so that you can communicate basic information in Dutch.

✔ You want to learn real-life Dutch for real-life use, in a life that you have already started or will start soon. You make your own choices of the material that the book offers, not only deciding which parts and how much, but also when, where, and how you study.

✔ You want to have fun and learn some Dutch at the same time.

If these statements apply to you, you have found the right book!

How This Book Is Organised

This book is divided by topics into five parts. Each part is divided into chapters. The following sections will show you what types of information you can find in each part.

Part I: Getting Started

This part is not to be missed, as it's like the foundations of a house. As the ground work is never as exciting as what comes later, you might prefer to start with some real communication like greeting. Do as you like, and go back to the basics when you notice that you need them. In Part I you'll find Dutch words that you probably already know, as well as the alphabet, pronunciation and some 'first aid' expressions. It gives you the structure of verbs, tenses and sentences and all you need to know about numbers, time, the days of the week and the different seasons.

Part II: Dutch in Action

In this part you begin learning and using Dutch. Instead of focusing on grammar points, this part focuses on everyday situations, such as talking to people, enjoying a meal, shopping, leisure, and work.

Part III: Dutch on the Go

This part hands you the tools you need to find your way in Dutch in a bank, in a hotel, on the road, on a plane, a train or a taxi. This part covers all aspects of getting around in the Netherlands, and includes a chapter on handling emergencies.

Part IV: The Part of Tens

If you're looking for small, easily digestible pieces of information about Dutch, this part is for you. Here, you can find ten ways to learn Dutch quickly, five things never to say, ten favourite Dutch expressions, 10 public holidays that you should not miss and ten phrases that make you sound professional.

Part V: Appendixes

The last part of the book includes important information which you can use for reference. It starts with verb tables, which show you how to conjugate regular verbs as well as those that don't fit into any pattern. You'll also find a list of the tracks that appear on the audio CD that comes with this book, so that you can find out where in the book those dialogues are and follow along. Finally, you'll find a mini-dictionary with both Dutch to English and English to Dutch formats. If you encounter a Dutch word that you don't understand or if you need to know the specific word in Dutch, you can look it up here.

Icons Used in This Book

You may be looking for particular information while reading this book. To make certain types of information more easily accessible, you'll find the following items in the left-hand margins widely throughout the book:

This icon highlights tips that can make learning Dutch easier.

This icon points to some grammar rules that are not essential but 'nice to know'.

If you're looking for information and advice about culture and how to deal with the Dutch, look for these icons.

The audio CD included in this book gives you the opportunity to listen to native Dutch speakers. This will increase your understanding of spoken Dutch. The icon marks the Talkin' the Talk dialogues which you can find on the CD.

Where to Go from Here

Learning a language is all about jumping in and just trying. So start now! You can start reading at the beginning, pick a chapter that interests you, or play the CD and listen to a few dialogues. Who knows, in a short time you may ask a Dutchman talking to you in English: **Ik studeer Nederlands, wilt u Nederlands praten?** *(ik stuw-dayr nay-der-lans vilt uw nay-der-lans praa-tern* (I'm studying Dutch, would you mind talking Dutch?).

Part I
Getting Started

The 5th Wave   By Rich Tennant

'Learning Dutch should be easy for you. A word sounding a lot like 'duh' seems to appear quite a bit.'

In this part . . .

You have to start somewhere, but we bet that you already jumped in. This part is a lifeboat that you can use whenever you fear that drowning is near. This part contains the alphabet, pronunciation, and some basic grammar – why not check your lifeboat before trying out the rest of the book?

Chapter 1

You Already Know Some Dutch

. . . .

In This Chapter

▶ The Dutch you already know

▶ Useful responses and wishes

▶ Reciting your ABC

▶ Pronouncing vowels

▶ Pronouncing Dutch diphthongs

▶ Trying the 'ch' and the 'g'

▶ Pronunciation and stress

▶ Questioning and exclaiming

. . . .

*T*he best way to learn a language is simply to start. In this chapter you jump into the Dutch language. This chapter shows you the Dutch you probably know already, explains how to pronounce Dutch words and introduces you to some popular Dutch expressions.

The Dutch You Know Already

Dutch is an Indo-European language. Among the families of Indo-European languages, Dutch, like German and English, belongs to the German group. Many words are identical with German words or look-alikes. Though English is not as close a relative as German, English-speaking people will recognise many words as well. These words either have their roots in the same family or belong to the growing group of internationally used words.

Close relatives

The words listed below are the same in Dutch, English, and German and mean the same. The only difference is the pronunciation and the spelling. German nouns start with a capital letter.

Dutch	Pronunciation	German	English
de arm	*der arm*	der Arm	the arm
de bank	*der bank*	die Bank	the bank
fantastisch	*fan-tas-tees*	fantastisch	fantastic
het glas	*het khlas*	der Glas	the glass
de hand	*der hant*	die Hand	the hand
de sport	*der sport*	der Sport	the sport
de tunnel	*der tuw-nerl*	der Tunnel	the tunnel
de wind	*der vint*	der Wind	the wind

Kissing cousins

More and more English words and phrases are used in Dutch, in an area such as sports but also in daily life. The Dutch usually make small adaptations, generally in spelling. Some elderly people and purists dislike the growing influence of English but all those who make use of new products and innovations cannot avoid the English expressions. There are no completely Dutch words for **de digitale tv** (*der dee-khee-taa-ler tay-fay*) (digital TV) or **de megastore** (*der may-khaa-stoar*) (the megastore)! Some more frequently used words with small adaptations are:

> **de supermarkt** (*der suw-per-markt*) the supermarket
>
> **de fitnessclub** (*der fit-ners-klup*) the fitness club

Dunglish

As Dutch-speaking people are internationally orientated, the Dutch use a lot of English verbs and expressions, especially in sports, IT, and business. They adapt the verbs to Dutch rules, which results in a combination of Dutch and English, or Dunglish. For example, you might hear: **Ik ga dat even checken** (*ik khaa dat ay-fern cheh-kern*) (I'm going to check that) or **Het vliegtuig was overboekt** (*het fleekh-toaikh vas oa-fer-bookt*) (The plane was overbooked). The Dutch find it very difficult to write this kind of verb!

Some verbs that are used in sports:

> **fitnessen** (*fit-ner-sern*) to go to a fitness centre
>
> **joggen** (*io-gern*) to jog
>
> **stretchen** (*stret-shern*) to stretch
>
> **trainen** (*tray-nern*) to train, to work out

Some words from the IT world:

deleten (*der-lee-tern*) to delete

downloaden (*down-loa-dern*) to download

inloggen (*in-lo-khern*) to log in/on

printen (*prin-tern*) to print

English is very popular in management and business. Check the following verbs:

coachen (*koa-tchern*) to coach

managen (*meh-ner-gern*) to manage

marketen (*mar-ker-tern*) to market

pushen (*poo-shern*) to push

Find more about the Dutch way of conjugating English verbs in chapter 8.

Talkin' the Talk

Don't think that the following conversation gives you an idea of how the average Dutchman talks. However, you might overhear a similar conversation between two young men in the street:

Marcel: **Hi, hoe is 't? Hoe is je nieuwe job?**
hi hoo is het. hoi is yer nee-wer job
Hi, how are you, how is your new job?

Jacco: **Prima! Ik ben HR manager bij Lease Consult en leasing is een spannende business.**
pree-maa. ik ben haa-ehr meh-ner-ger bay lees kon-suhlt en lee-sing is ern spa-ner-der bis-nis
Fine! I'm a Human Resource manager at Lease Consult and leasing is an exciting business.

Marcel: **Echt waar? Lease Consult is een Major Account van ons!**
ekht vaar? lees kon-suhlt is ern may-ger er-kownt fan ons
Really? Lease Consult is one of our Major Accounts!

Jacco: **Ik kom je dus nog wel eens tegen in de Board Room.**
ik kom yer duhs nokh vel erns tay-khern in der bort room
So we're bound to meet in the Board Room.

Marcel: **Wie weet!**
vee vayt
Who knows!

Jacco: **En ben jij weer happy?**
en ben yay vayr heh-pee

	So, are you happy again?
Marcel:	**Ja, maar Renate zit in een dip. Fulltime werken met een kid is nogal heavy en ze wil graag parttime werken.**
	yaa maar rer-naa-ter zit in ern dip. fool-taim vehr-kern met ern kit is no-khal heh-fee en zer vil khraakh par-taim vehr-kern
	Yes, but Renate is in a dip. Working full-time with a kid is rather heavy and she wants to work part-time.
Jacco:	**Ik begrijp het. Is parttime werken een optie?**
	ik ber-khrayp het. is par-taym vehr-kern ern op-see
	I see. Is working part-time an option?
Marcel:	**Op dit moment niet. Ze zitten midden in een reorganisatie.**
	op dit moa-ment neet. zer zi-tern mi-dern in ern ray-or-kha-nee-saa-see
	Not at the moment. They are in the middle of a reorganisation.

Street language for Dummies

Young people in the street use their own language which changes everyday. This lingo is influenced by languages such as American English, Surinam, Antillean, Turkish, and Moroccan. Street language reflects the multicultural society, while trends from music (hip-hop) and TV give it an international sound. In the big cities you might overhear the following street language words:

Dutch word	Pronunciation	Translation
nakken	na-kern	to nick, to steal
doekoe	doo-koo	money
flex	fleks	OK, good
loesoe	loo-soo	away
een chickie checken	*ernt chi-kee cheh-kern*	to observe a girl

Family members, teachers, and bosses have adopted parts of the language of the youngsters they live and work with. You might hear them saying things like: **Wie is die weirdo?** (*vee is dee vayr-doa*) (Who is that strange person?).

Words from other languages have found their way in the **Van Dale Groot woordenboek van de Nederlandse taal** (the main dictionary of the Dutch language). Some 330,000 Surinam people live in the Netherlands and about 150 phrases from their language have found their way into the dictionary. Some funny ones are: **het okseltruitje** (*het ok-serl-troai- tyer*) (the sleeveless T-shirt) which literally means 'armpit T-shirt'and **de handknie** (*der hant-knee*) (the elbow), literary translated 'the hand knee'. Not only Surinam words, but also words from Japanese, like **tsunami** (*tsoo-naa-mee*) (seaquake), Belgian, like **onthaalouder** (*ont-haal- ow-der*) (host parent), Arabic, like **felouka** (*fer-loo-kaa*) (Egyptian sailboat) and Hebrew, like **bollebof** (*bo-ler-bof*) (chief of police) can be found in a Dutch dictionary.

Useful Responses and Wishes

All language students get into the stage in which they understand a lot, but still speak poorly. People notice that you understand and they start talking to you, expecting a response. But you don't know how to react! Learning by heart at least one positive and one negative response can be helpful in a difficult situation.

Learn a positive term like: **prima** (*pree-maa*) (excellent), a neutral one that you can use in almost any occasion without insulting anybody, like **interessant** (*in-ter-rer-sant*) (interesting), and have one ready in case somebody tells you something negative: **wat jammer** (*vat ya-mer*) (what a pity). Here are some examples of useful responses and when to use them:

- ✔ **Wat vind je van dit restaurant? – Prima!** (*vat fint yer fan dit res-toa-rant. pree-maa*) (How do you like this restaurant? – Excellent!)

- ✔ **Heb je zin om dit weekend mee te gaan zeilen? – Fantastisch!** (*hep yer zin om dit vee-kent may ter khaan zay-lern. fan-tas-ees*) (Would you like to go sailing this weekend? – Great!)

- ✔ **Zullen we even pauzeren? – OK.** (*zuh-lern ver ay-fern pow-zayr-rern. oa-kay*) (Shall we take a short break? – Okay.)

- ✔ **Dit zijn foto's van Amsterdam twintig jaar geleden. – Wat interessant!** (*dit zayn foa-toas fan am-ster-dam tvin-tikh yaar kher-lay-dern. vat in-ter-er-sant*) (These are photographs of Amsterdam 20 years ago. – How interesting!)

- ✔ **Het concert is afgelast. – Wat jammer!** (*het kon-sehrt is af-kher-last. vat ya-mer*) (The concert has been cancelled. – Too bad!)

- ✔ **Mijn auto is stuk. – Wat een pech!** (*mayn ow-toa is stuhk. vat ern pekh*) (My car broke down – Bad luck!)

In case somebody asks you to do something, you may use the next positive answers:

- ✔ **Help je me even? – Natuurlijk.** (*help yer mer ay-fern. naa-tuwr-lerk*) (Can you help me for a moment? – Of course.)

- ✔ **Kunt u mij om 11 uur bellen?** – Geen probleem. (*kuhnt uw may om elf uwr beh-lern. khayn proa-blaym*) (Could you call me at 11 o'clock? – No problem.)

In case you need a negative answer, try the next safe ones:

> ✔ **Bent u morgen op kantoor? – Nee, het spijt me** (*bent uw <u>mor</u>-khern op kan-<u>toar</u>. nay het spayt mer*) (Are you at the office tomorrow? – No, I am sorry.)
>
> ✔ **Gaan jullie met ons mee? – Misschien de volgende keer.** (*khaan <u>yuw</u>-lee met ons may. mi-<u>skheen</u> der <u>fol</u>-khern-der kayr*) (Are you accompanying us? – Maybe next time.)

For special occasions use one of the following wishes:

> ✔ **Fijne avond.** (*<u>fay</u>-ner <u>aa</u>-font*) (Have a nice evening.)
>
> ✔ **Goed weekend.** (*khoot <u>vee</u>-kent*) (Have a nice weekend.)
>
> ✔ **Goede reis.** (*<u>khoo</u>-der rays*) (Have a good trip.)
>
> ✔ **Veel plezier.** (*fayl pler-<u>zeer</u>*) (Have fun.)
>
> ✔ **Beterschap.** (*<u>bay</u>-ter-skhap*) (I wish you a speedy recovery.)
>
> ✔ **Sterkte.** (*<u>stehrk</u>-ter*) (All the best.)

When drinking alcohol in company you can raise your glass, saying:

> **Proost!** (*proast*) (Cheers!)

As your understanding of Dutch grows and you're making friends, conversations may become more personal. In chapter 17 you'll find useful responses to confidential or hilarious stories.

A Mouthful of Pronunciation Rules

The key to pronouncing a new language is overcoming your fear of sounding awkward and never getting it right. Don't be afraid to sound silly and do not think that you will never succeed!

In the beginning you won't understand a word when people are speaking a language you don't know, but after a while you'll start to distinguish sounds and repeating patterns. Later on you will recognise some of the patterns, like greetings and how people start and finish a phone call. Most language learners start imitating the popular patterns, repeating them as well as they can. As soon as they get a reaction, this stimulates them to go ahead and try more complex phrases. At this stage, pronunciation becomes important. The Dutch will not understand you when they don't recognise the words you're trying to say.

When mastering a language it speeds up the process when you learn some basic rules about how to pronounce the written words. On the road, in the streets and in the shops you will not only hear but also read words and when you know how people pronounce them, you can add them to your personal vocabulary. The following sections present you the alphabet and some basic guidelines for proper pronunciation.

Dealing with pronunciation in this book

Throughout this book, you can find the pronunciation of a Dutch word next to it in parenthesis, which we call *pronunciation brackets*. Within the pronunciation brackets, we separate all the words that have more than one syllable with a hyphen, like this: **goedemorgen** (*khoo-der-<u>mor</u>-khern*) (good morning). An underlined syllable within the pronunciation brackets tells you to accent, or stress, that syllable. You'll find more about stress in the section 'Pronunciation and Stress' in this chapter.

In this book the phonetic script (the script that shows you how to pronounce a word) uses letter combinations that are the English equivalents of the Dutch letter's pronunciation.

Reciting Your ABC

The Dutch alphabet has the same number of letters as the English and German alphabets, 26. However, many of the letters are pronounced differently. English-speaking people will find the Dutch G difficult to pronounce. You'll find some extra words to exercise.

Track 1 on the CD gives you the sounds of the Dutch letters.

The Dutch alphabet:

A ah	**H** hah
B bay	**I** ee
C say	**J** yay
D day	**K** kah
E ay	**L** el
F ef	**M** em
G khay	**N** en

O oa	**U** uw
P pay	**V** fay
Q kuw	**W** way
R ehr	**X** ix
S es	**Y** ehy
T tay	**Z** zet

Pronouncing Vowels

Dutch has many vowel and diphthong (combined vowels) sounds, and some will be unfamiliar to your ear. We give the best approximation here, but listening to Dutch speakers will help you to get a more accurate picture. Check out Table 1-1 for the full story.

The vowels **a, e, i, o** and **u** can have both long, drawn-out vowel sounds and shorter vowel sounds. Luckily, there are some general rules that apply:

✔ A vowel is short when it's followed by one or more consonants at the end of a word or a syllable (a part of a word), as in de dag (der dakh) (the day), geld (khelt) (money), ik (ik) (I), kort (kort) (short), druk (druhk) (busy).

✔ A vowel is long when it's doubled, as in gaan (khaan) (to go) geen (khayn) (no), ook (oak) (too) and uur (uwr) (hour).

✔ A vowel is long when it's the last letter of a syllable, as in **dragen** (*draa-khern*) (to carry), **eten** (*ay-tern*) (to eat), **roken** (*roa-kern*) (to smoke), **juni** (*yuw-nee*) (June).

The vowel a

The **a** has a short sound in closed syllables, that is if they are followed by one or more consonants at the end of a word or syllable. Try out the sound of these words:

✔ **de bal** (*der bal*) (the ball)

✔ **de dag** (*der dakh*) (the day)

✔ **het gras** (*het khras*) (the grass)

A single letter **a** in an open syllable, that is at the end of a syllable or word, is pronounced like a long, drawn-out vowel sound. Try out the sound of these words:

- **dragen** (_draa_-khern) (to carry)
- **de dagen** (der _daa_-khern) (the days)
- **de lanen** (der _laa_-nern) (the lanes)

Whether it occurs in a closed syllable or a long syllable, **aa** (double a) always gives that same long, drawn-out sound. Try practising the sound with these words:

- **gaan** (_khaan_) (to go)
- **staan** (_staan_) (to stand)
- **de laan** (der _laarn_) (the lane)

Open and closed syllables

Words can be divided into parts or syllables. Syllables are essential when you are willing to spell and pronounce words well. Knowing how to divide words in syllables will speed up your learning process, as well as knowing how to distinguish an **open syllable** from a **closed syllable**.

A syllable is a part of a word and you can find it by clapping your hands when pronouncing the word. Each clap is a syllable. You can also have a look in your dictionary. A good one will show you the words divided in syllables.

In order to be able to distinguish an open syllable from a closed syllable, you need to remember the difference between **vowels** and **consonants.** Vowels are the letters that form the central sound in a word: **a, e, i, o,** and **u.** The other letters of the alphabet are called **consonants.** These letters accompany the vowels: **b c d f g h j k l m n p q r s t v w x z.**

Syllables that end with one or more consonants are **closed syllables.** For instance, both syllables in the word **paspoort** (_pas_-poart) (passport) are closed syllables.

Syllables that end with a vowel are **open syllables,** as the first syllable in the word **model** (moa-_del_) (model) or the first syllable in the word **euro** (_u_-roa) (euro).

The difference between open and closed syllables is the key to understanding the pronunciation of Dutch words: open syllables have long vowels, and, when only one vowel is written in a closed syllable, the vowel sounds short.

Also, when you start writing Dutch, understanding open and closed syllables helps you to know when to write double vowels and consonants.

The vowel e

When followed by one or more consonants at the end of a word, the **e** has a short sound. Try it out on these words:

- **gek** (*khek*) (mad)
- **het geld** (*het khelt*) (the money)
- **de herfst** (*der hehrfst*) (autumn)

When the **e** is at the end of a syllable you pronounce it like a long, drawn-out vowel sound. Try the sound in these words:

- **geven** (*khay-fern*) (to give)
- **eten** (*ay-tern*) (to eat)
- **beter** (*bay-ter*) (better)

Note that when in an unstressed syllable, the **e** sounds like the English vowel sound in *sister*. It is transcribed *-er*.

Whether or not it's a long syllable or a closed syllable, **ee** always gives a long sound. Try it, practising on these words:

- **geen** (*khayn*) (no)
- **geel** (*khayl*) (yellow)
- **de neef** (*der nayf*) (the nephew/cousin)

The vowel i

When followed by one or two more consonants at the end of a word or syllable, **i** has a short vowel sound. Try it out on these words:

- **ik** (*ik*) (I)
- **het ding** (*het ding*) (the thing)
- **dicht** (*dikht*) (closed)

When you find the **i** at the end of a word or syllable, you pronounce it like a long, drawn-out vowel sound. Try practising the sound on these words:

- ✔ **juni** (*juw-nee*) (June)
- ✔ **de activiteit** (*der ak-tee-vee-tayt*) (the activity)

As we have seen, the four vowels **a, e, u, o** are sometime doubled (**aa, ee, uu, oo**) to spell the long version of the vowel. Now you might suppose that the long **i** will be written as **ii**. Sadly, the Dutch happen to be less rational than you are: they don't spell **ii**, but instead they spell **ie**.

- ✔ **drie** (*dree*) (three)
- ✔ **het bier** (*het beer*) (the beer)
- ✔ **de fiets** (*der feets*) (the bike)

The vowel o

When followed by one, two or more consonants at the end of a syllable the **o** has a short sound. Try to pronounce these words:

- ✔ **op** (*op*) (on)
- ✔ **kort** (*kort*) (short)
- ✔ **de pot** (*der pot*) (the pot)

When you find **o** at the end of a word or a syllable, you pronounce it like a long vowel sound. Try practising the sound on these words:

- ✔ **boven** (*boa-fern*) (above)
- ✔ **roken** (*roa-kern*) (to smoke)
- ✔ **het document** (*het doa-kuw-ment*) (the document)

Oo is always a long vowel, as in the next words:

- ✔ **ook** (*oak*) (also)
- ✔ **mooi** (*mooy*) (beautiful)
- ✔ **de persoon** (*der per-soan*) (the person)

The vowel u

When followed by one more consonants at the end of a syllable or word the **u** has a short sound. Try the next list of examples:

- **dun** (*duhn*) (thin)
- **de hulp** (*der huhlp*) (the help)
- **de club** (*der klup*) (the club)

When you find the **u** in a syllable that ends in a vowel, you pronounce the **u** like a long, drawn-out vowel sound. Try out the sound practising on these words:

- **u** (*uw*) (you, formal)
- **de studie** (*der stuw-dee*) (the studies)
- **juni** (*juw-nee*) (June)

Uu always gives a long vowel sound. Try to pronounce these **uu** words:

- **het uur** (*het uwr*) (the hour)
- **het excuus** (*het ek-skuws*) (the excuse)
- **het kostuum** (*het kos-tuwm*) (the costume)

Pronouncing Dutch Diphthongs

Diphthongs are combinations of two vowels in one syllable. Dutch has a lot of them, and, depending on your native language, some will be difficult for you as you don't know them in your own language. Different sounds create different words, so Dutch people might not understand you if you don't know how to pronounce the sounds. Observe how the Dutch do and ask them to help you!

Pronouncing the diphthongs ei and ij

The diphthong **ei** is a sound which does not occur in English, nor in any other major European language, and it may be a bit hard to pronounce. You will come close if you take the sound of *ay* in English *day*. Try to open your mouth a little bit more than you would do in English. Some examples of this sound:

- **het ei** (*het ay*) (the egg)
- **mei** (*may*) (may)
- **klein** (*klayn*) (small)

The same sound is represented with the letter combination **ij**. At the beginning of a word or in an open syllable, **ij** sounds exactly the same as **ei**:

- ✔ **mij** (*may*) (me)
- ✔ **mijn** (*mayn*) (my)
- ✔ **ijs** (*ays*) (ice)

When **ij** occurs at the end of a word in a closed syllable, the sound is reduced and you pronounce it like *er* in English *her*:

- ✔ **heerlijk** (*hayr-lerk*) (delicious)
- ✔ **makkelijk** (*ma-ker-lerk*) (easy)
- ✔ **moeilijk** (*mooy-lerk*) (difficult)

The diphthong oe

The diphtong **oe** sounds like the letter combination *oo* in English *too*. Try to pronounce these examples of **oe**:

- ✔ **hoe** (*hoo*) (how)
- ✔ **het boek** (*het book*) (the book)
- ✔ **genoeg** (*kher-nookh*) (enough)
- ✔ **de broer** (*der broor*) (the brother)

The diphthongs ou and au

The letter combinations **ou** and **au** are two ways of spelling one and the same sound. This sound is fairly easy to produce: just like *ow* in English *cow*:

- ✔ **gauw** (*khow*) (soon)
- ✔ **blauw** (*blow*) (blue)
- ✔ **lauw** (*low*) (lukewarm)
- ✔ **oud** (*owt*) (old)
- ✔ **bouwen** (*bow-ern*) (to build)
- ✔ **trouwen** (*trow-ern*) (to marry)

The diphthong eu

The diphthong **eu** is another funny Dutch diphtong that doesn't occur in most European languages. It approximates the sound of the letter *u* in English *pure*. Try to pronounce the diphthong **eu** a bit more in the front of your mouth than you would do in English:

- **de keuken** (*der ku-kern*) (the kitchen)
- **de neus** (*der nus*) (the nose)
- **de sleutel** (*der slu-terl*) (the key)

The diphthong ui

Another diphtong belonging to the Dutch language is **ui**. We won't even bother to compare it to any existing sound in English. The sound approximates that of 'eu' in the French 'peu'. Take in mind the letter combination *oai* and don't move your lips while breathing out.

- **buiten** (*boai-tern*) (outside)
- **vuil** (*voail*) (dirty)
- **juist** (*yoaist*) (right)

For many people it's hard to hear the difference between **eu** and **ui**, and it's even harder to actually produce these sounds. Listening intensively to the CD accompanying this book may help. Also, in case you happen to meet the Dutch football legend Johan Cruijff, ask him to demonstrate the **ui**-sound featured in his name:

Johan Cruijff (*yoa-han kroaif*) Johan Cruijff

When you have finally mastered the sound, celebrate it by ordering a hamburger with **ui** (*oai*) (onion) on it.

Table 1-1	Pronouncing Vowels and Diphthongs			
Letter	**Pronunciation**	**Symbol**	**Example**	**Phonetics**
a	between *u* as in c*u*p and *a* as in c*a*t	*a*	**dag**	*dakh*
aa	*ar* as in m*ar*ket	*aa*	**gaan**	*chaan*
i	*i* as in b*i*t	*i*	**in**	*in*
ie	*ee* as in s*ee*n	*ee*	**drie**	*dree*

Letter	Pronunciation	Symbol	Example	Phonetics
e	e as in red	e	**bed**	bet
ee	ay as in say	ay	**bleek**	blayk
ei	ay as in day	ay	**klein**	klayn
ij	er as in mother or ay as in day	er ay	**lelijk** **wij**	lay-lerk way
o	o as in not	o	**pot**	pot
oe	oo as in too	oo	**hoe**	hoo
ou/au	ow as in now	ow	**koud, blauw**	kowt, blow
oo	oa as in boat	oo	**ook**	oak
eu	u as in pure	u	**keuken**	ku-ken
u	u as in fur	uh	**bus**	uhs
u, uu	u as in new	uw	**nu, muur**	nuw, muwr
ui	no English equivalent	oai	**buiten**	boai-ten

Pronouncing Consonants

Consonants tend to sound the same in English and Dutch. You will soon master any few differences that you might find. Table 1-2 gives you the low-down.

Table 1-2	Pronouncing Dutch Consonants			
Letter	Pronunciation	Symbol	Example	Phonetics
b c f h k l m n p q f x y z	as in English			
ch	ch as in loch	kh	**nacht**	nakht
d	d as the English t at the end of a word	d/t	**bed**	bet
g	ch as in loch rarely zh as in pleasure	kh zh	**groot** **genre**	khroat zhen-rer
j	y as in yes	y	**ja**	ya

continued

Letter	Pronunciation	Symbol	Example	Phonetics
Table 1-2 *(continued)*				
r	*r* rolled or in the back of the mouth	*r*	**rijst**	*reyst*
s	always hard as in pa*ss*	*s*	**stop**	*stop*
sch	*s* followed by *ch* as in lo*ch*	*skh*	**schaal**	*skhaal*
v	as an English *f*	*f*	**vader**	*faa*-der
w	as an English *v*	*v*	**water**	*vaa*-ter

There is a great variety in the pronunciation of the letter **r** among Dutch speakers. People from Belgium and the northern provinces use a 'rolling r' like in Italian, others use a 'throat r' like in French, and yet others employ an 'American r'. Many people mix them up, beginning words with a 'rolling r', and ending them with a 'throat r'.

Pronouncing the Dutch 'g'

Now we get to a major obstacle for most foreign language learners: the letter **g**. The corresponding sound doesn't exist in English, although other languages like French and Arab do employ it. Here is the key to the **g**: make it sound like *kh*. Try to prolongue a **k** in order to realise this guttural sound which happens to be a basic characteristic of Dutch.

- **gaan** (*khaan*) (to go)
- **geen** (*khayn*) (no)
- **graag** (*khraakh*) (please)

Don't be afraid if your g doesn't sound quite correct, just remember that some English native speakers call Dutch 'an illness of the throat'. Your neighbour, your boss and your colleagues will appreciate it when you're trying to speak Dutch, and in return they will rasp an admiring **goed gedaan!** (*khoot kherdaan*) (well done!). **G** is a popular letter in Dutch, and to make it even worse, the letter combination **ch** should sound exactly the same. Train them in the next words:

- **slecht** (*slekht*) (bad)
- **wachten** (*vakh*-tern) (to wait)
- **voorzichtig** (*foar-zikh-tikh*) (careful)

Pronunciation and Stress

Can you believe that you're actually looking for stress? In Dutch, the right stress at the right time is a good thing, and fortunately stress in Dutch is easy to control.

The general rule is that Dutch words carry the main stress on the first syllable. Some words, however, don't carry the main stress on the first syllable. For instance, many foreign words (often borrowed from English or French) stress a later syllable.

Try the stress pronunciation of the following words, concentrating on getting the stress right. Pronounce the underlined syllable with more emphasis (i.e. louder) than the others.

- **de vader** (*der faa-der*) (the father)
- **bouwen** (*bow-ern*) (to build)
- **heerlijk** (*hayr-lerk*) (delicious)

Now look at some words that have been borrowed from French, and hence have a different stress:

- **de activiteit** (*der ak-tee-fee-tayt*) (the activity)
- **de persoon** (*der per-soan*) (the person)
- **actief** (*ak-teef*) (active)

Another notable exception to the 'first syllable rule': the prefixes **be-, ge-, her-, er -, ont-** and **ver-** are never stressed. Instead, words with these prefixes, stress the second syllable. Try to pronounce the next list:

- **bestellen** (*ber-steh-lern*) (to order)
- **gelukkig** (*kher-luh-kikh*) (happy)
- **herinneren** (*heh-ri-ner-rern*) (to remember)
- **ervaren** (*ehr-faa-rern*) (to experience)
- **ontmoeten** (*ont-moo-tern*) (to meet)
- **vergeten** (*fer-khay-tern*) (to forget)

Questioning and Exclaiming

Questions start with a verb or a question word, like **wie** (*vee*) (who), **wat** (*vat*) (what), **waar** (*vaar*) (where), **hoe** (*hoo*) (how) or **wanneer** (*va-nayr*) (when?). Even without knowing this, you will notice a question by the way it sounds: at the end of the question the voice rises. In the sentence **Ga je naar huis?** (*khaa yer naar hoais*) (Are you going home?) the voice rises toward the last word. The same, although earlier, happens in the sentence **Hoe heet ze?** (*hoo hayt zer*) (What's her name?).

Sentences that end in an exclamation mark do the same, though the tone is slightly different. In the sentence **Ik ga naar huis** (*ik khaa naar hoais*) (I am going home) the voice goes down with the last word, but in the sentence **Ik ga naar huis!** (*ik khaa naar hoais!*) (I am going home!) all words are pronounced in a higher tone and this tone goes slightly up in the last word. In the sentence **Ze heet Cilla** (*zer hayt si-laa*) (Her name is Cilla) the tone descends in the last word. **Ze heet Cilla!** (*zer hayt si-laa!*) (Her name is Cilla!) sounds totally different: the tone of the whole sentence is higher and it goes up in the last word.

Chapter 2

Low-cal Grammar: Just the Basics

- -

- -

*L*earning a language can be done in many ways. Most people use all of them but some prefer special routines. Do you still remember how you learned your native language? You probably won't, because you were a child. You started listening to your mother. The first sound you made was crying. You cried in response of basic needs: hunger, soiled nappies, and pain. Nobody had to teach you this! Then you started smiling and cooing, a language only your mother understood. But your mum and dad talked to you from the first day on. You listened to them. You started imitating the sounds and one day you said 'dada' – or was it 'mumma'? After that first little word, you used more and more loose words for communication. Your mum and dad repeated your words to make clear that they understood you. When you were a bit older, they helped you when you started making short sentences. They repeated them, saying them in the right way. So you learned talking by imitation, without any grammar!

Now you're no longer a baby. Some grammar might be helpful! Some adults learn faster when they understand the structure of the language. It took you years to learn your native language and perhaps you spent many hours of writing exercises at primary and secondary school. Maybe you had grammar at school. Either it helped you to understand the structure of our own language, or it was of no use for you. As a language teacher I've experienced that the more languages a person knows, the faster he can master another one, having a better understanding of the structures, similarities and differences between languages. Whether or not you want to learn any grammar is up to you: this book offers all opportunities for personal learning.

Parts of Speech

In order to make a simple sentence you need building materials. Nouns, adjectives, prepositions and verbs are the most important parts of speech.

Using the Definite Articles 'de' and 'het'

In English, there is only one definite article: *the*. Unfortunately for you, Dutch has two different definite articles: **de** and **het**:

de fiets the bike

de man the man

de vrouw the woman

het huis the house

het meisje the girl

Not knowing when to use **de** and when **het** makes many students of Dutch unhappy. Take your time! This book offers you some rules that tell you whether to use **de** or **het**, but using the rules will only solve part of the problem. The best way to use the right article is learning by heart the article that goes with each word. In this book most nouns go accompanied by an article. It's a good start, and the rest you'll learn by listening to spoken Dutch, reading or watching TV.

Dutch nouns used to have genders, like French and German still have. But nowadays there's hardly any difference between the feminine and masculine noun. The article **de** goes with most nouns, either masculine or feminine. **De** also goes with all plural nouns.

✔ **de man** (der man) (the man)

  de mannen (der ma-nern) (the men)

✔ **de vrouw** (der frow) (the woman)

  de vrouwen (der frow-ern) (the women)

✔ **de fiets** (der feets) (the bike)

  de fietsen (der feet-sern) (the bikes)

✔ **de trein** (der trayn) (the train)

  de treinen (*der <u>tray</u>-nern*) (the trains)

Although the difference between masculine and feminine words has almost disappeared, the neuter still exists in Dutch. The article **het** goes with neuter nouns. How do you know whether a noun is neuter? It's a great help to know that **het** is always used for a small thing or a small person. In these cases you use a diminutive that ends in **-tje** or **-je**: it always has **het**.

- ✔ **het meisje** (*het mays-yer*) (the girl)
- ✔ **het fietsje** (*het feets-yer*) (the small bike)

Below you will find more rules how to recognise the gender of a word.

Using the Indefinite Article 'een'

The use of the indefinite article **een** will cause you no problems. **Een** is the same as **a** or **an** in English. It has no plural and it never changes!

- ✔ **een man** (*ern man*) (a man)
- ✔ **een vrouw** (*ern frow*) (a woman)
- ✔ **een fiets** (*ern feets*) (a bike)
- ✔ **een trein** (*ern trayn*) (a train)
- ✔ **een jongetje** (*ern yong-er-tyer*) (a little boy)
- ✔ **een meisje** (*ern mays-yer*) (a little girl)

The second thing that is easy to remember: plural neuter nouns get the article **de**, because all plurals have **de**!

Don't panic if you find it difficult to choose between **de** and **het**. Remember that most words have **de**. A Dutchman will understand you when you use the wrong article, and he'll appreciate the fact that you are learning Dutch.

There is a difference in pronunciation between the article **een** (*ern*) (a or an) and the numeral **één** (*ayn*) (one).

For those who feel that rules will help them, here is some information that might assist you in making a choice between **de** and **het**.

De goes with:

- ✔ **all plurals:**
  - • **de mannen** (*der ma-nern*) (the men)
  - • **de bomen** (*der boa-mern*) (the trees)
  - • **de landen** (*der lan-dern*) (the countries)

- ✔ **professions:**
    - **de dokter** (*der dok-ter*) (the doctor)
    - **de bakker** (*der ba-ker*) (the baker)
    - **de slager** (*der slaa-kher*) (the butcher)
- ✔ **vegetables:**
    - **de ui** (*der oai*) (the onion)
    - **de asperge** (*der as-pehr-zher*) (the asparagus)
    - **de sla** (*der slaa*) (the lettuce)
- ✔ **trees:**
    - **de eik** (*der ayk*) (the oak)
    - **de wilg** (*der vilkh*) (the willow)
    - **de den** (*der den*) (the fir)
- ✔ **plants:**
    - **de roos** (*der roas*) (the rose)
    - **de klimop** (*der klim-op*) (the ivy)
    - **de tulp** (*der tuhlp*) (the tulip)
- ✔ **mountains:**
    - **de Sint-Pietersberg** (*der sint-pee-ters-behrkh*)
    - **de Vaalserberg** (the highest 'mountain' in the Netherlands, 322 m.)
- ✔ **rivers:**
    - **de Rijn** (*der rayn*) (the Rhine)
    - **de Maas** (*der maas*) (the Meuse)
    - **de Waal** (*der vaal*) (the Walloon)

Het goes with:

- ✔ **diminutives:**
    - **het jongetje** (*het yong-er-tyer*) (the little boy)
    - **het meisje** (*het mays-yer*) (the little girl)
    - **het stadje** (*het stat-yer*) (the small town)
- ✔ **nouns of two syllables that start with be:**
    - **het begin** (*het ber-khin*) (the beginning)
    - **het belang** (*het ber-lang*) (the importance)
    - **het beleid** (*het ber-layt*) (the policy)

✓ **nouns of two syllables that start with ge-:**

- **het gezin** (*het kher-zin*) (the family)
- **het gevoel** (*het kher-fool*) (the feeling)
- **het geluid** (*het kher-loait*) (the sound)

✓ **nouns of two syllables that start with ver-:**

- **het verkeer** (*het fer-kayr*) (the traffic)
- **het vervoer** (*het fer-foor*) (the transport)
- **het vertrek** (*het fer-trehk*) (the departure)

✓ **nouns of two syllables that start with ont-:**

- **het ontbijt** (*het ont-bayt*) (the breakfast)
- **het ontslag** (*het ont-slakh*) (the dismissal)
- **het ontwerp** (*het ont-vehrp*) (the design)

Relating Adjectives to 'de' and 'het' Words

Words like **mooi** (pretty, beautiful), **groot** (big), and **klein** (small) are adjectives. Adjectives tell something more about an object, a person or an idea: whether he, she or it is pretty, big, good or anything else that characterises the object, person or idea. For most students of Dutch it's not easy to relate adjectives to the nouns they correspond with. The problem is that you sometimes add an **e** to the adjective and sometimes you don't. Check the following examples:

✓ **de mooie man** (*der moa-yer man*) (the handsome man)

✓ **de mooie mannen** (*der moa-yer man-ern*) (the handsome men)

✓ **de mooie vrouw** (*der moa-yer frow*) (the pretty woman)

✓ **de mooie vrouwen** (*der moa-yer frow-ern*) (the pretty women)

✓ **het mooie jongetje** (*het moa-yer yong-er-tyer*) (the pretty little boy)

✓ **de mooie jongetjes** (*der moa-yer yong-er-tyers*) (the pretty little boys)

So far so good. You will have noticed that the adjective has an **e** at the end in all places. This is always the case when you use the adjective in combination with **de** or **het**.

However, using the adjective in combination with **een** is tricky. See what happens:

- ✔ de **mooie** man (*der moa-yer man*) (the handsome man)
- ✔ een **mooie** man (*ern moa-yer man*) (a handsome man)
- ✔ de **mooie** vrouw (*der moa-yer man*) (the pretty woman)
- ✔ een **mooie** vrouw (*ern moa-yer frow*) (a pretty woman)
- ✔ het **mooie** jongetje (*het moa-yer yong-er-tyer*) (the pretty little boy)
- ✔ een **mooi** jongetje (*ern moay yong-er-tyer*) (a pretty little boy)

So when you use **een** instead of **het** the adjective loses the end **e.** In order to do this correctly, you have to know whether a word has **de** or **het**. It's easier to master this when writing than when speaking. Writing gives you more time to think.

Finding Your Way with Prepositions

Students of Dutch often tell me how difficult it is to learn the prepositions, those small words that often come together with nouns and are often used to indicate a place or time. It might comfort you to know that English prepositions are equally difficult for Dutch students of English!

Prepositions are small words of great importance. They tell you whether something is in, on, under or next to the place where you are looking for it. You will use them very often and you will soon learn if something is **in het bed**, **op het bed**, **onder het bed**, or **bij het bed**. Prepositions of place and those of time are used most.

Like in English many Dutch verbs go together with certain prepositions: the so-called phrasal verbs. Sometimes the combination of verb and preposition is logical, sometimes not at all. You will have to learn the verbs together with the prepositions.

Prepositions of place: aan, binnen, buiten, in, langs, op, over, tegen, tot, and tussen

Here are some examples of prepositions that are used to indicate a place.

✔ **aan** (*aan*) (on)

Het schilderij hangt aan de muur. (*het skhil-der-ray hangt aan der muwr*) (The painting is on the wall.)

✔ **binnen** (*bi-nern*) (inside)

Er zijn meer planten buiten dan binnen het huis. (*ehr zayn mayr plan-tern boai-tern dan bi-nern het hoais*) (There are more plants outside than inside the house.)

✔ **buiten** (*boai-tern*) (outside)

Buiten het centrum zijn geen kledingzaken. (*boai-tern het sentruhm zayn khayn klay-dings-zaa-kern*) (There are no clothes shops outside the centre.)

✔ **in** (*in*) (in)

Zij wonen in Amsterdam. (*zay voa-nern in am-ster-dam*) (They live in Amsterdam.)

✔ **langs** (*langs*) (along)

Wij wandelen langs de grachten. (*vay van-der-lern langs der khrakh-tern*) (We are strolling along the canals.)

✔ **op** (*op*) (on)

De vaas staat op de kast. (*der faas staat op der kast*) (The jar is on the cupboard.)

✔ **over** (*oa-fer*) (over)

Hij klimt over de muur. (*hay klimt oa-fer de muwr*) (He's climbing over the wall.)

✔ **tegen** (*tay-khern*) (against)

De fiets staat tegen de muur. (*der feets staat tay-khern der muwr*) (The bike is standing against the wall.)

✔ **tot** (*tot*) (up to)

Ik geef je een lift tot Amsterdam. (*ik khayf yer een lift tot am-ster-dam*) (I will take you up to Amsterdam.)

✔ **tussen** (*tuh-sern*) (in between)

Den Haag ligt tussen Amsterdam en Rotterdam. (*den-haakh likht tuh-sern am-ster-dam en ro-ter-dam*) (The Hague is in between Amsterdam and Rotterdam.)

Prepositions of time: aan, in, na, sinds, tot, voor

The following prepositions are used to indicate time. Note that some of them may also be used for other purposes, for example, to indicate place.

- ✔ **aan** (*aan*) (at)

    Aan het eind van het jaar is het erg druk. (*aan het aynt fan het yaar is het ehrkh druhk*) (At the end of the year it is very busy.)

- ✔ **in** (*in*) (in)

    Ik ben geboren in 1970. (ik ben kher-<u>boa</u>-rern in nay-khern-teen-<u>takh</u>-tikh) (I was born in 1970.)

- ✔ **na** (*naa*) (after)

    Ik zal dat doen na het weekend. (*ik zal dat doon naa het <u>vee</u>-kent*) (I will do it after the weekend.)

- ✔ **sinds** (*sints*) (since)

    Sinds september ben ik in Nederland. (*sints sep-<u>tem</u>-ber ben ik in <u>nay</u>-der-lant*) (I have been in the Netherlands since September.)

- ✔ **tot** (*tot*) (until)

    Ik kan tot 10 uur blijven. (*ik kan tot teen uwr <u>blay</u>-fern*) (I can stay until 10 o'clock.)

- ✔ **voor** (*foar*) (before)

    Wil je deze brief posten voor 5 uur? (*vil yer <u>day</u>-zer breef <u>pos</u>-tern foar fayf uwr*) (Please post this letter before 5 o'clock?)

Phrasal verbs: verbs that go together with a preposition

As in English, hundreds of verbs collocate with a preposition. Here are a few that are commonly used:

- ✔ **bellen naar** (<u>beh</u>-lern naar) (to call somebody)

    Naar wie is hij aan het bellen? (*naar vee is hay aan het <u>beh</u>-lern*) (Whom is he calling?)

- ✔ **denken aan** (<u>den</u>-kern aan) (to think of)

    Ik denk vaak aan mijn moeder. (*ik denk faak aan mayn <u>moo</u>-der*) (I often think of my mother.)

✔ **dromen over** (_droa_-mern _oa_-fer) (to dream about)

Ik droom vaak over je. (_ik droam faak _oa_-fer yer_) (I often dream about you.)

✔ **geven aan** (_khay_-fern aan) (to give)

Cilla geeft de kopieën aan Hans. (_si_-laa khayft der koa-_pee_-yern aan hans) (Cilla gives Hans the copies.)

✔ **houden van** (_how_-dern fan) (to like)

Ik houd van wijn. (_ik howt fan vayn_) (I like wine.)

✔ **kijken naar** (_kay_-kern naar) (to watch, to look at)

Raymond kijkt naar Cilla. (_ray_-mont kaykt naar _si_-laa) (Raymond watches Cilla.)

✔ **luisteren naar** (_loais_-ter-ern naar) (to listen to)

Alan luistert niet naar Cilla. (_a_-lan _loais_-tert neet naar _si_-laa) (Alan is not listening to Cilla.)

✔ **praten met** (_praa_-tern met) (to talk to)

Cilla praat met Hans. (_si_-laa praat met hans) (Cilla is talking to Hans.)

✔ **praten over** (_praa_-tern _oa_-fer) (to talk about)

Hans praat altijd over het werk. (_hans praat _al_-tayt _oa_-fer het vehrk_) (Hans is always talking about work.)

✔ **vragen aan** (_fraa_-khern aan) (to ask)

Hans vraagt dat aan Cilla. (_hans fraakht dat aan _si_-laa) (Hans is asking Cilla for it.)

✔ **wachten op** (_vakh_-tern op) (to wait for)

Raymond wacht op Cilla. (_ray_-mont vakht op _si_-laa) (Raymond is waiting for Cilla.)

The Tenses: Present, Perfect, and Past

When you're talking about using verbs, the word **tense** is indispensable. 99% of the sentences contain one or more verbs and these are in a certain tense: the present tense, the perfect tense, or the past tense.

First, you need to know how to make the various forms of the tenses, and second, whether to use the present, the perfect, or the past. In this chapter, you'll find a concise overview of both: the forms and how to use them.

Some theory, terms, and simple exercises will warm you up before diving into the deep end.

The full form of the verb is called the infinitive. In English, the infinitive starts with 'to': *to work, to hear, to play*. In Dutch the infinitive very often ends in **-en**: **werken**, **horen**, **spelen**.

A verb indicates an action or a situation in a sentence. The person that causes the action or situation is **the subject** of the sentence. The verb adapts to the subject. For example, in the very short sentence **ik werk** (*ik vehrk*) (I work) the form of the verb is different from the form in the sentence **wij werken** (*vay vehr-kern*) (we work). In the first sentence you see **werk**, in the second **werken.**

When the infinitive ends in **-en**, it's easy to find the I-form; just take away **-en**. Another word for the I-form is the stem. For **jij**, **hij**, **zij**, **het** and **u** just add a **t**. For **wij**, **jullie** and **zij** (plural) you can also use the infinitive.

> **ik werk** *ik vehrk* I work
>
> **jij werk-t** *yay vehrkt* you work [singular, informal]
>
> **u werk-t** *uw vehrkt* you work [formal, singular and plural]
>
> **hij/zij/het werk-t** *hay/zay/het vehrkt* he/she/it works
>
> **wij werken** *vay vehr-kern* we work
>
> **jullie werken** *yuw-lee vehr-kern* you work (informal, plural)
>
> **zij werken** *zay vehr-kern* they work

Spelling causes an extra difficulty in some verbs. You have to double the vowel in the first three forms. This spelling problem doesn't trouble you when speaking! A verb of this kind is **slapen:**

> **ik slaap** *ik slaap* I sleep
>
> **jij slaap-t** *yay slaapt* you sleep
>
> **u slaap-t** *uw slaapt* you sleep (formal, singular and plural)
>
> **hij/zij/het slaap-t** *hay/zay/het slaapt* he/she/it sleeps
>
> **wij slapen** *vay slaa-pern* we sleep
>
> **jullie slapen** *yuw-lee slaa-pern* you sleep (informal, plural)
>
> **zij slapen** *zay slaa-pern* they sleep

Why do we have to double the **a** in the first three forms? This is in order to maintain the sound of the long **a** throughout the verb. If we would write: 'ik slap, jij slapt, hij slapt' we would have to pronounce it with a short **a**, and a Dutchman will not understand what you mean.

Irregular verbs have irregularities, either in the present tense or in the other tenses. The most frequent ones are: **willen** (*vi-lern*) (to want to), **kunnen** (*kuh-*nern) (to be able to), **zullen** (*zuh-*lern) (shall, will), **mogen** (*moa-*khern) (to be allowed to), **hebben** (*heh-*bern) (to have), en **zijn** (*zayn*) (to be). You'll find the forms of each of these verbs in the verb table at the end of this book.

You don't appreciate this theoretical explanation, or you don't understand? Just skip the theory and don't panic. Many ways of learning are possible: by listening, by imitating, by reading, by memorising by heart. You can just pick the verbs you need from the verb tables at the end of this book. Also, you'll find hundreds of sentences throughout the book and on the CD. All of them contain ready-made verbs.

Using the present tense

When you know the most important forms of the present tense you can say a lot. The present tense is used to describe what happens now, as you can see in the next phrase:

> **Ik kijk televisie.** (*ik kayk tay-ler-fee-see*) (I am watching TV.)

You can also use the present tense in order to describe what is happening sometimes, generally or always, like in the next two examples:

- ✔ **'s Avonds kijk ik televisie.** (*saa-fonts kayk ik tay-ler-fee-see*) (In the evening I watch TV.)

  Na het werk ga ik naar de supermarkt. (*naa het vehrk khaa ik naar der suw-per-markt*) (After work I go to the supermarket.)

Very often the present tense is used to tell what is going to happen You might overhear some colleagues saying:

- ✔ **Morgen werk ik thuis.** (*mor-khern vehrk ik toais*) (Tomorrow I work at home.)

  Ik bel je morgen. (*ik bel yer mor-khern*) (I'll give you a ring tomorrow.)

Mother's little helper: using the perfect tense

In English there are two ways of describing the past: using the perfect tense (I have worked) and the past tense (I worked). Dutch also has these two tenses, but the Dutch very often use the perfect instead of the past tense. Some English native speakers feel shortcomings when they study Dutch, because it takes time to learn the irregular forms of the Dutch past tense. No need for it: do as the Dutch, and use the perfect tense!

The perfect tense is formed with an auxiliary plus the past participle of the verb. Most verbs take the auxiliary **hebben** (to have), as in the following examples:

> ✔ **Ik heb gestudeerd.** (*ik hep kher-stuw-dayrt*) (I studied/have studied.)
>
> ✔ **Ik heb naar muziek geluisterd.** (*ik hep naar muw-zeek kher-loais-tert*) (I listened/have listened to the music.)
>
> ✔ **Heb je hem gezien?** (*hep yer hem kher-zeen*) (Have you seen him?)

Some verbs use **zijn** (to be) in order to make the perfect. These verbs generally describe a certain process, like **vliegen** (to fly), **aankomen** (to arrive), or **gaan** (to go):

> ✔ **Wij zijn naar Brussel gevlogen.** (*ver zayn naar bruh-serl kher-floa-khern*) (We flew to Brussels.)
>
> ✔ **Tom is nog niet aangekomen.** (*tom is nokh neet aan-kher-koamern*) (Tom has not yet arrived.)
>
> ✔ **Wij zijn naar Amsterdam gegaan.** (*vay zayn naar am-ster-dam kher-khaan*) (We went to Amsterdam.)

Now that you know whether to choose the auxiliary verb **hebben** or **zijn**, you still need to know how to make the past participle in order to be able to use the perfect.

Dutch verbs are divided into three groups:

> ✔ regular verbs,
>
> ✔ irregular verbs, and
>
> ✔ very irregular verbs.

Just as in English, the most frequently used verbs like **hebben** (to have), **zijn** (to be), and **doen** (to do) are the most irregular.

You'll find some regular, irregular, and very irregular verbs in the verb tables at the end of the book.

Making a past participle

So, in order to make the perfect tense, we need to have an auxiliary and a past participle. Past participles of regular verbs generally start with **ge-** and end with **-d** or **-t.** In the middle is the stem of the verb, which is generally equivalent to the I-form of the verb.

past participle: **ge-** + stem + **-d/-t**

verb: **bellen** (to call)

past participle: **ge-bel-d**

perfect tense: **ik heb gebeld**

verb: **werken** (to work)

past participle: **ge-werk-t**

perfect tense: **ik heb gewerkt**

In Chapter 8, you'll find out why some verbs get **-d** at the end of the word, while others get **-t**.

Even young children very quickly recognise patterns in verbs. Of course, they are not able to explain them, but they use them, as you too will do in a short time. The patterns make young children and students say: **Ik heb** *gedrinkt* (mistaken phrase for 'I have drunk'). However, the right phrase is: **Ik heb gedronken** (I have drunk). **Gedronken** is one of the many irregular past participles and the way to learn them is simply by memorising them. Fortunately even the most irregular past participles start with **ge-**, and they often end with **-en**. In the stem of the verb unpredictable vowel changes can take place. Once you've heard and read them several times, you'll remember! Try the following verbs, and their past participles:

verb: **vliegen** (to fly)

past participle: **gevlogen**

perfect tense: ik heb gevlogen

verb: **nemen** (to take)

past participle: **genomen**

perfect tense: ik heb genomen

See Chapter 8 in order to know more about when to use the perfect tense.

Talking about former times: using the past tense

Though the Dutch language prefers the perfect over the past tense, the Dutch use the past tense as well, be it in certain circumstances. Let's first see how to form the past of regular verbs.

Forming the past of regular verbs

In the singular, regular verbs add **-de** or -**te** to the stem, while in the plural, regular verbs add **-den** or **-ten** to the stem.

> past tense singular: stem + **-de** / -**te**

> past tense plural: stem + **-den** / -**ten**

Table 2-1	The Past of Regular Verbs, Adding -de to the Stem
Conjugation	*Pronunciation*
bellen (to make a call)	
ik belde	*ik <u>bel</u>-der*
jij belde	*yay <u>bel</u>-der*
u belde	*uw <u>bel</u>-der*
hij/zij/het belde	*hay/zay/het <u>bel</u>-der*
wij belden	*vay <u>bel</u>-dern*
jullie belden	*<u>yuw</u>-lee <u>bel</u>-dern*
zij belden	*zay <u>bel</u>-dern*

Table 2-2	The Past of Regular Verbs, Adding -te to the Stem
Conjugation	*Pronunciation*
werken (to work)	
ik werkte	*ik <u>vehrk</u>-ter*
jij werkte	*yay <u>vehrk</u>-ter*
u werkte	*uw <u>vehrk</u>-ter*
hij/zij/het werkte	*hay/zay/het vehrk-ter*
wij werkten	*vay <u>vehrk</u>-tern*
jullie werkten	*<u>yuw</u>-lee <u>vehrk</u>-tern*
zij werkten	*zay <u>vehrk</u>-tern*

Irregular verbs make unpredictable changes in the vowel of the stem. You will learn them after hearing and reading them often.

Table 2-3	The Past of an Irregular Verb
Conjugation	*Pronunciation*
beginnen (to begin, to start)	
ik begon	*ik ber-khon*
jij begon	*yay ber-khon*
u begon	*uw ber-khon*
hij/zij/het begon	*hay/zay/het ber-khon*
wij begonnen	*vay ber-kho-nern*
jullie begonnen	*yuw-lee ber-kho-nern*
zij begonnen	zay ber-kho-nern

The third group of verbs, the very irregular verbs follow no rules at all. The verbs **hebben** en **zijn** belong to this group.

Table 2-4	The Past of the Very Irregular Verbs 'zijn' and 'hebben'
Conjugation	*Pronunciation*
zijn (to be)	
ik was	*ik vas*
jij was	*yay vas*
u was	*uw vas*
hij/zij/het was	*hay/zay/het vas*
wij waren	*vay vaa-rern*
julie waren	*yuw-lee vaa-rern*
zij waren	*zay vaa-rern*
hebben (to have)	
ik had	*ik hat*
jij had	*yay hat*
u had	*u hat*
hij/zij/het had	*hay/zay/het hat*
wij hadden	*vay ha-dern*

continued

Table 2-4 *(continued)*	
Conjugation	*Pronunciation*
jullie hadden	_yuw_-lee ha-dern
zij hadden	zay _ha_-dern

Using the past tense

You may need the past tense when talking about the past. However, the Dutch often use the perfect tense when talking about the past. In Dutch, you use the past tense in just three cases. Here they are, followed by examples. Use the past tense:

- ✔ When describing a situation:

  Het regende in Brussel. (*het _ray_-khern-der in _bruh_-serl)* (It was raining in Brussels.)

  Het vliegtuig had vertraging. (*het _fleekh_-toaikh hat fer-_traa_-khing*) (The plane had a delay.)

- ✔ When talking about habits:

  In Brussel dronk ik altijd Belgisch bier. (*in _bruh_-serl dronk ik _al_-tayt _bel_-khees beer*) (In Brussels, I used to drink Belgian beer.)

  De vliegtuigen hadden altijd vertraging. (*der _fleekh_-toai-khern _ha_-dern _al_-tayt fer-_traa_-khing*) (The planes were always delayed.)

- ✔ When enumerating a series of facts:

  Ik nam het vliegtuig in Amsterdam. Wij landden om 9.30 uur in Brussel. Ik nam een taxi en om 10.30 uur begon de vergadering. (*ik nam het _fleekh_-toaikh in am-ster-_dam_. vay _lan_-dern om _nay_-khern uwr in _bruh_-serl. ik nam ern _tak_-see en om half elf ber-_khon_ der fer-_khaa_-der-ring* (I got on the plane in Amsterdam. We landed in Brussels at 9:30. I took a taxi, and at 10:30 the meeting started.)

Find more information about the past tense in Chapter 15.

Talking about the future

In general, Dutch people simply use the present tense in order to tell what is going to happen. You may have heard your colleagues saying:

- ✔ **Morgen werk ik thui.s** (*_mor_-khern vehrk ik toais*) (Tomorrow I will work at home.)
- ✔ **Ik bel je morgen.** (*ik bel yer _mor_-khern*) (I'll give you a ring tomorrow.)

When Dutch-speaking people are making a promise or giving a guarantee, they use the auxiliary verb **zullen** (*zuh-lern*) (will/shall). You might hear them saying:

- ✔ **Ik zal vanavond koken.** (*ik zal fa-naa-font koa-kern*) (I will cook dinner tonight.)
- ✔ **Ik zal de boodschappen doen.** (*ik zal boat-skha-pern-doon*) (I will do the shopping.)
- ✔ **We zullen eens kijken.** (*ver zuh-lern erns kay-kern*) (We will see.)

The next table gives the correct use of the verb **zullen**.

Table 2-5	The Use of the Verb 'zullen'
Conjugation	*Pronunciation*
zullen	
ik zal	*ik zal*
jij zult	*yay zuhlt*
u zult	*uw zuhlt*
hij/zij/het zal	*hay/zay/het zal*
wij zullen	*vay zuh-lern*
jullie zullen	*yuw-lee zuh-lern*
zij zullen	*zay zuh-lern*

When Dutch-speaking people announce something that is certain to happen they use the verb **gaan** (*khaan*) (to go). Count on them when you hear them saying:

- ✔ **Ik ga vanavond koken.** (*ik khaa fa-naa-font koa-kern*) (I'm going to cook tonight.)
- ✔ **Ik ga boodschappen doen.** (*ik khaa boat-skha-pern-doon*) (I'm going to do the shopping.)
- ✔ **Wij gaan morgen tennissen.** (*vay khaan mor-khern teh-ni-sern*) (We are going to play tennis tomorrow.)

Table 2-6	The Use of the Verb 'gaan'
Conjugation	*Pronunciation*
gaan	
ik ga	*ik khaa*
jij gaat	*yay khaat*
u gaat	*uw khaat*
hij/zij/het gaat	*hay/zay/het khaat*
wij gaan	*vay khaan*
jullie gaan	*yuw-lee khaan*
zij gaan	*zay khaan*

Five Basic Sentence Constructions

Dutch word order is logical in simple sentences, containing just one part. Word order is much more complicated in compound sentences: sentences of two or more parts. Compound sentences make use of conjunctions like **en** (*en*) (and), **maar** (*maar*) (but), or **omdat** (*om-dat*) (because). The language material of this book consists mainly of simple sentences and for this reason we limit the theory about word order to the order in simple sentences.

Native speakers of English, however, normally need a lot of time to find out how Dutch word order works, in simple as well as compound sentences. The word order of English is different, and it takes time to get used to the Dutch order. Some people find a little theory helpful.

Construction one: in normal sentences the verb goes second

Dutch normal word order is: the subject first, then the verb, then the rest. A different way of saying the same thing is: the verb comes second. Check the examples in the table.

Table 2-7	In Normal Sentences the Verb Comes Second	
Subject	**Verb**	**The Rest**
Ik	**kom**	**uit Duitsland**
ik	*kom*	*oait <u>doaits</u>-lant*
I	am	from Germany
Ik	**werk**	**bij een bank**
ik	*vehrk*	*bay ern bank*
I	work	in a bank

Construction two: after an expression of time, the verb comes first

In sentences that start with an expression of time, the verb comes first, i.e. before the subject: we call this **inversion**.

Table 2-8	After an Expression of Time the Verb Comes First	
Expression of Time	**Verb**	**The Rest**
Morgen	**gaat**	**mijn partner naar Rotterdam**
<u>mor</u>-khern	*khaat*	*mayn <u>part</u>-ner naar ro-ter-<u>dam</u>*
(Tomorrow	goes	my partner to Rotterdam)
Tomorrow, my partner		
goes to Rotterdam		
Nu	**werk**	**ik bij een bank**
nuw	*vehrk*	*ik bay ern bank*
(Now	work	I with a bank)
Now I work with a bank		
Na het eten	**drink**	**ik koffie**
naa het <u>ay</u>-tern	*drink*	*ik <u>ko</u>-fee*
(After dinner	drink	I coffee)
After dinner, I drink coffee		
Soms	**drink**	**ik bier**
soms	*drink*	*ik beer*
(Sometimes	drink	I beer)
Sometimes I drink beer		

Morgen, nu, na het eten and **soms** are expressions of time. More expressions of time are:

- ✔ **'s ochtends** (_sokh_-terns) (in the morning)
- ✔ **'s middags** (_smi_-dakhs) (in the afternoon)
- ✔ **'s avonds** (_saa_-fonts) (in the evening)
- ✔ **maandagmorgen** (_maan_-dakh-mor-khern) (Monday morning)
- ✔ **na het eten** (naa het _ay_-tern) (after dinner)
- ✔ **soms** (soms) (sometimes)
- ✔ **na** (naa) (after)
- ✔ **altijd** (al-_tayt_) (always)

Construction three: after an expression of place, the verb comes first

Sentences that open with an expression of place have inversion as well. In other words, after an expression of place, the verb comes first.

Table 2-9   After an Expressions of Place, the Verb Comes First

Expr of place	Verb	The Rest
In Amsterdam	**wonen**	**veel mensen**
in am-ster-dam	_voa-nern_	_fayl men-sern_
(In Amsterdam	live	many people)
Many people live in Amsterdam		
Ergens	**moet**	**het liggen**
ehr-kherns	_moot_	_het li-khern_
(Somewhere	should	it be)
It should be somewhere		
Op de fiets	**zie**	**je veel**
op der feets	_zee_	_yer fayl_
(On a bike	see	you a lot)
On a bike, you see a lot		

Some expressions of place are:

- ✔ **daar** (daar) (there)
- ✔ **ergens** (_ehr_-kherns) (somewhere)

    ✔ **nergens** (_nehr_-kherns) (nowhere)

    ✔ **in Amsterdam** (_in am-ster-_dam_) (in Amsterdam)

Construction four: after 'misschien', 'soms' and 'toch', the verb comes first

Some other words in the beginning of the sentence cause inversion. The most important ones are **misschien** (_mi-_skheen_) (perhaps), **soms** (_soms),_ and **toch** (_tokh_) (nevertheless, yet). In other words, after **misschien, soms** and **toch,** the verb comes first. Check the following examples:

    ✔ **Misschien ga ik naar Den Haag.** (_mi-_skheen_ khaa ik naar den-_haakh_) (Perhaps I will go to The Hague.)

    ✔ **Soms drink ik bier.** (_soms drink ik beer_) (Sometimes I have a beer.)

    ✔ **Toch zal ik aan je denken.** (_tokh zal ik aan yer_ den_-kern_) (Nevertheless I'll remember you.)

Construction five: in questions, the verb comes first

Naturally, questions that start with a verb have inversion. In other words, in questions that start with the verb, the verb comes first.

Table 2-10 In Questions that Start with a Verb, the Verb Comes First

Verb	Subject	The Rest
Ga	**je**	**naar huis?**
khaa	yer	naar hoais
(go	you	home)
Are you going home?		
Woon	**je**	**in Amsterdam?**
voan	yer	in am-ster-_dam_
(live	you	in Amsterdam)
Do you live in Amsterdam?		
Spreek	**je**	**Nederlands?**
sprayk	yer	_nay_-der-lants
(speak	you	Dutch)
Do you speak Dutch?		

Questions can also start with a question word. Question words are: **wie** (*vee*) (who), **wat** (*vat*)(what), **waar** (*vaar*) (where), **waarom** (*vaa-rom*) (why), **hoe** (*hoo*) (how), and **wanneer** (*va-nayr*) (when). Check the following sentences to see that the question starts with the question word, followed by the verb and then the rest.

In questions that start with a question word, the verb comes first:

- ✔ **Wie gaat naar Amsterdam?** (*vee khaat naar am-ster-dam*) (Who goes to Amsterdam?)

- ✔ **Wat ga je doen?** (*vat khaa yer doon*) (What are you going to do?)

- ✔ **Waar woon je?** (*vaar voan yer*) (Where do you live?)

- ✔ **Waarom ben je in Nederland?** (*vaa-rom ben yer in nay-der-lant*) (Why are you staying in the Netherlands?)

- ✔ **Hoe ga je naar huis?** (*hoo khaa yer naar hoais*) (How are you going home?)

- ✔ **Wanneer gaan we tennissen?** (*va-nayr khaan ver teh-ni-sern*) (When are we going to play tennis?)

Chapter 3

Number Magic: All Kinds of Counting

. . . .

In This Chapter

▶ Mastering cardinal numbers

▶ Knowing when to use ordinal numbers

▶ Telling time

▶ Days, months, seasons

. . . .

*T*ime, money, travelling, business – you need numbers! This chapter gives you the number phrases that you need to get around your world. It also shows you how to tell time and navigate the months of the year.

1, 2, 3 – Cardinal Numbers

For English-speaking people Dutch numbers have some tricky aspects. German-speaking people, however, will have no problems: they will recognise most of them. Here are the numbers until 20:

0 nul (nuhl)	**10 tien** (teen)
1 een (ayn)	**11 elf** (elf)
2 twee (tvay)	**12 twaalf** (tvaalf)
3 drie (dree)	**13 dertien** (<u>dehr</u>-teen)
4 vier (feer)	**14 veertien** (<u>fayr</u>-teen)
5 vijf (fayf)	**15 vijftien** (<u>fayf</u>-teen)
6 zes (zes)	**16 zestien** (<u>zes</u>-teen)
7 zeven (<u>zay</u>-fern)	**17 zeventien** (<u>zay</u>-fern-teen)
8 acht (akht)	**18 achttien** (<u>akh</u>-teen)
9 negen (<u>nay</u>-khern)	**19 negentien** (<u>naykh</u>-ern-teen)

As in almost any language you'll have to simply learn the numbers until 10 by heart: sometimes you recognise elements of other languages, sometimes not. Then, starting with 13, you'll get some help from your memory: in the numbers until 13 to 20 you'll recognise the word **tien**.

Now we're arriving at 20 and more: for English-speaking people these are tricky. Take it easy and start learning the tens:

20 twintig (_tvin_-tikh)

30 dertig (_dehr_-tikh)

40 veertig (_fayr_-tikh)

50 vijftig (_fayf_-tikh)

60 zestig (_zes_-tikh)

70 zeventig (_zay_-fern-tikh)

80 tachtig (_takh_-tikh)

90 negentig (_nay_-khern-tikh)

After 20 you would expect something like: 'twintig-en-één', twintig-entwee'. However, Dutch starts with **één** en then adds **en twintig**. Try it yourself and start saying **twee** and then add the rest: **en twintig**. Continue until 30 and repeat the same proceedings: **één,** add **en,** add **dertig.** After that continue until one hundred and you'll soon get used to the Dutch habit of starting with **een, twee, drie, vier, vijf, zes, zeven, acht** and **negen** and ending with the tens. Here are some examples:

21 eenentwintig (_ayn_-ern-tvin-tikh)

22 tweeëntwintig (_tvay_-ern-tvin-tikh)

23 drieëntwintig (_dree_-ern-tvin-tikh)

24 vierentwintig (_feer_-ern-tvin-tikh)

25 vijfentwintig (_fayf_-ern-tvin-tikh)

26 zesentwintig (_zes_-ern-tvin-tikh)

27 zevenentwintig (_zay_-fern-ern-tvin-tikh)

28 achtentwintig (_akh_-tern-tvin-tikh)

29 negenentwintig (_nay_-khern-ern-tvin-tikh)

30 dertig (_dehr_-tikh)

31 eenendertig (_ayn_-ern-dehr-tikh)

40 veertig (_fayr_-tikh)

44 vierenveertig (_feer_-ern-fayr-tikh)

50 vijftig (_fayf_-tikh)

55 vijfenvijftig (*fayf*-ern-fayf-tikh)

60 zestig (*zes*-tikh)

66 zesenzestig (*zes*-ern-zes-tikh)

77 zevenenzeventig (*zay*-fern-ern-zay-fern-tikh)

80 tachtig (*takh*-tikh)

88 achtentachtig (*akh*-tern-takh-tikh)

90 negentig (*nay*-khern-tikh)

99 negenennegentig (*nay*-kher-nern-nay-khern-tikh)

Have you got children? I'll bet they'll get the hang of Dutch numbers first! It could be a nice pastime when you're in a traffic jam to read the number plates of the cars aloud, including the letters.

The hundreds are no surprise: they are built up identically to English and German. Here are some:

100 honderd (*hon*-dert)

200 tweehonderd (*tvay*-hon-dert)

300 driehonderd (*dree*-hon-dert)

400 vierhonderd (*feer*-hon-dert)

500 vijfhonderd (*fayf*-hon-dert)

1000 duizend (*doai*-zernt)

Over 1000

Some languages say: a thousand one hundred, a thousand two hundred etc. Dutch is different: after a thousand it starts with **elf, twaalf, dertien, veertien, vijftien, zestien, zeventien, achttien, negentien** and then adds **-honderd**. See the following examples:

1100 elfhonderd (*elf*-hon-dert)

1200 twaalfhonderd (*tvaalf*-hon-dert)

1300 dertienhonderd (*dehr*-teen-hon-dert)

1400 veertienhonderd (*fayr*-teen-hon-dert)

1500 vijftienhonderd (*fayf*-teen-hon-dert)

1600 zestienhonderd (*zes*-teen-hon-dert)

1700 zeventienhonderd (<u>zay</u>-fern-teen-hon-dert)

1800 achttienhonderd (<u>akh</u>-teen-hon-dert)

1900 negentienhonderd (<u>nay</u>-khern-teen-hon-dert)

After saying elfhonderd, twaalfhonderd, dertienhonderd etcetera, you just add the rest, as you can see in the following examples:

1101 elfhonderdeen (elf-hon-dert-<u>ayn</u>)

1210 twaalfhonderdtien (tvaalf-hon-dert-<u>teen</u>)

As soon as you have mastered these numbers start with the thousands. The structure of the Dutch numbers with the thousands is the same as in English or German. Here are the thousands:

2000 tweeduizend (<u>tvay</u>-doai-zernt)

3000 drieduizend (<u>dree</u>-doai-zernt)

4000 vierduizend (<u>feer</u>-doai-zernt)

5000 vijfduizend (<u>fayf</u>-doai-zernt)

6000 zesduizend (<u>zes</u>-doai-zernt)

7000 zevenduizend (<u>zay</u>-fern-doai-zernt)

8000 achtduizend (<u>akht</u>-doai-zernt)

9000 negenduizend (<u>nay</u>-khern-doai-zernt)

10.000 tienduizend (<u>teen</u>-doai-zernt)

After **tweeduizend**, however, some Dutch-speaking persons continue the system that is used from **duizend** to **tweeduizend**. This means that they start with **eenentwintighonderd, tweeëntwintighonderd, drieëntwintighonderd.** When necessary they add the rest in the usual way, as you can see in the following examples:

2101 eenentwintighonderdeen (ayn-ern-tvin-tikh-hon-dert-<u>ayn</u>)

2444 vierentwintighonderdvierenveertig (feer-ern-tvin-tikhhon-dert-<u>feer</u>-ern-<u>fayr</u>-tikh)

However, most people prefer saying the numbers over 2000 in this way:

2101 tweeduizendhonderdeen (tvay-doai-zernt-hon-dert-<u>ayn</u>)

2444 tweeduizendvierhonderdvierenveertig (tvay-doai-zernt-feer-hon-dert-<u>feer</u>-ern-fayrtikh)

Doing sums

Would you like to teach Dutch math to your children? Here are the basics of **optellen** (*op-teh-lern*) (to add):

- ✔ 4 + 4 = 8 **vier plus vier is acht** (*feer pluhs feer is akht*)
- ✔ 8 + 8 = 16 **acht plus acht is zestien** (*akht pluhs akht is <u>zes</u>-teen*)

Now that you know how to add, you might want to know how to **aftrekken** (*af-treh-kern*) (to subtract):

- ✔ 8 – 4 = 4 **acht min vier is vier** (*akht min feer is feer*)
- ✔ 24 – 8 = 16 **vierentwintig min acht is zestien** (*feer-ern-<u>twin</u>-tikh min akht is <u>zes</u>-teen*)

Vermenigvuldigen (*fehr-may-nikh-fuhl-di-khern*) (multiplication) goes like this:

- ✔ 2 x 2 = 4 **twee maal twee is vier** (*tvay maal tvay is feer*)
- ✔ 4 x 16 = 64 **vier maal zestien is vierenzestig** (*feer maal <u>zes</u>-teen is feer-ern-<u>zes</u>-tikh*)

In order to be able to help your children, you might want to learn to **delen** (*<u>day</u>-lern*) (do divisions) as well:

- ✔ 4 ÷ 2 = 2 **vier gedeeld door twee is twee** (*feer kher-<u>daylt</u> doar tvay is tvay*)
- ✔ 16 ÷ 4 = 4 **zestien gedeeld door vier is vier** (*<u>zes</u>-teen kher-<u>daylt</u> doar feer is feer*)

Playing with fractions, per cents, and metres

Daily life offers you a lot of challenges, be it in the house or at work. You'll not need only the usual numbers, but fractions as well. Here are some that are frequently used:

- ✔ ½ **een half** (*ern half*)
- ✔ 1½ **anderhalf** (*<u>an</u>-der-half*)
- ✔ ¼ **een kwart** (*ern kvart*)
- ✔ ¾ **driekwart** (*<u>dree</u>-kvart*)

As soon as you start interchanging facts with friends or colleagues, you'll need to know how to use the percentages. They're not very different from English or German, except that Dutch and English use of commas and stops are inversed. So Dutch says two comma six percent where English says two point six percent, as you can see in the following examples:

- ✔ 2,6% **twee komma zes procent** (*tvay ko-maa zes proa-sent*)
- ✔ 3,8% **drie komma acht procent** (*dree ko-maa akht proa-sent*)
- ✔ 50% **vijftig procent** (*fayf-tikh proa-sent*)
- ✔ 100% **honderd procent** (*hon-dert proa-sent*)

When you're busy with relocation and housing you might hear the following expressions:

- ✔ 1,67 m **een meter zevenenzestig** (*ayn may-ter zay-fern-ern-zes-tikh*)
- ✔ 3,5 m **drieëneenhalve meter** (*dree-ern-hal-fer may-ter*)

The Dutch average house measures:

- ✔ 125 m^2 **honderdvijfentwintig vierkante meter** (*hon-dert-fayf-erntvin-tikh feer-kan-ter may-ter*)

Distances are measured in parts of a thousand metres, **een kilometer** (*ern kee-loa-may-ter*). When you use this word in combination with a number, you always use the singular:

- ✔ **twee kilometer** (*tvay kee-loa-may-ter*) (two kilometres)
- ✔ **duizend kilometer** (*doai-zernt kee-loa-may-ter*) (a thousand kilometres)
- ✔ **Hoeveel kilometer is het van Amsterdam naar Den Haag?** (*hoo-fayl kee-loa-may-ter is het fan am-ster-dam naar den-haakh*) (How many kilometres is it from Amsterdam to The Hague?)
- ✔ **Van Amsterdam naar Den Haag is 59 km.** (*fan am-ster-dam naar den-haakh is het nay-khern-ern-fayf-tikh kee-loa-may-ter*) (From Amsterdam to The Hague is 59 km.)

However, in combination with a word like **veel** (*fayl*) (a lot of), you use the plural: **We hebben veel kilometers gereden** (*ver heh-bern fayl kee-loa-may-ters kher-ray-dern*) (We covered a lot of kilometres).

Discovering Ordinal Numbers

Ordinal numbers put something in a certain order: first, second, third. It might please you that the three ordinal numbers **eerste, tweede, derde,** are frequently used in Dutch, and the higher ordinal numbers **twintigste, tachtigste** (20th, 80th) less: the latter are difficult to pronounce for English native speakers. Here are the most frequently used ordinals:

1e   **eerste** (_ayr_-ster)

2e   **tweede** (_tvay_-der)

3e   **derde** (_dehr_-der)

4e   **vierde** (_feer_-der)

5e   **vijfde** (_fayf_-der)

6e   **zesde** (_zes_-der)

7e   **zevende** (_zay_-fern-der)

8e   **achtste** (_akh_-ster)

9e   **negende** (_nay_-khern-der)

10e   **tiende** (_teen_-der)

Using ordinal numbers

In all languages, ordinal numbers are useful when you are discussing and enumerating arguments. In these cases you precede them by the word **ten**. The following expressions may prove very handy:

ten eerste: (_ten ayr-ster_) in the first place

ten tweede: (_ten tvay-der_) in the second place

ten derde: (_ten dehr-der_) in the third place

Here's an example of somebody who is very angry, using an enumeration:

Ten eerste heb ik dat niet gezegd, ten tweede is het niet waar en ten derde wil ik er niet over praten!

(_ten ayr-ster hep ik dat neet kher-zekht ten tvay-der is het neet vaar en ten dehr-der vil ik er neet oa-fer praa-tern_)

(In the first place, I didn't say that; in the second place it's not true; and in the third place, I don't want to talk about it!)

The expression **eerst** (*ayrst*) (first) is not really an ordinal but it is used as well when mentioning a sequence of things, often in combination with the words **dan** (*dan*) (than) and **daarna** (*daar-naa*) (after that). See the following example of a boss talking over with his secretary the program for that morning:

Eerst ga ik mijn e-mail checken. Dan heb ik een bespreking met Raymond van Dieren. Daarna wil ik even wat dingen voor de meeting van morgen doorpraten.

(*ayrst khaa ik mayn ee-mayl cheh-kern. dan hep ik ern ber-spray-king met ray-mont fan dee-rern. daar-naa vil ik ay-fern vat ding-ern foar der mee-ting fan mor-khern doar-praa-tern*)

(First I am going to check my e-mail. Then I have a meeting with Raymond van Dieren and after that I would like to talk over some things for tomorrow's meeting).

Ordinal numbers may go together with the word **keer** (*kayr*) (time):

- **de eerste keer** (*der ayr-ster kayr*) (the first time)
- **de vierde keer** (*der feer-der kayr*) (the fourth time)

A sequence of ordinal numbers may be finished by the expression **de laatste keer** (*der laat-ster kayr*) (the last time). See also the following examples:

- **Ik gebruik deze creditcard voor de eerste keer.** (*ik kher-broaik day-zer kreh-dit-kart foar der ayr-ster kayr*) (I am using this credit card for the first time.)
- **Uitgeverij Pearson organiseert voor de vierde keer een auteursborrel.** (*oait-khay-fer-ray peer-sern or-khaa-nee-sayrt foar der feer-der kayr ern ow-turs-bo-rerl*) (Pearson Editors is organising for the fourth time a drink for the authors.)
- **Het North Sea Jazzfestival is voor de laatste keer in Den Haag.** (*het nort-see jes-fes-tee-fal is foar der laat-ster kayr in den-haakh*) (The North Sea Jazz Festival is held for the last time in The Hague.)

Ordinal numbers are of great use in all other cases in which you are enumerating, like in sports and when giving directions.

- **Hij behaalde de eerste plaats.** (*hay ber-haal-der der ayr-ster plaats*) (He won first place.)
- **Hij finishte als derde.** (*hay fi-nish-ter als dehr-der*) (He finished third.)
- **Het is de tweede straat rechts.** (*het is der tvay-der straat rekhts*) (It's the second street on the right.)

You use ordinals when counting days, weeks, months or years in which you have been doing things:

- ✔ **Dit is mijn eerste dag in Amsterdam.** (*dit is mayn ayr-ster dakh in am-ster-dam*) (This is my first day in Amsterdam.)

- ✔ **Dit is mijn tweede week in Nederland.** (*dit is mayn tvay-der vayk in nay-der-lant*) (This is my second week in the Netherlands.)

- ✔ **Dit is mijn derde maand in dit appartement.** (*dit is mayn dehr-der maant in dit a-par-ter-ment*) (This is my third month in this apartment.)

- ✔ **Dit is mijn vierde jaar bij Lease Consult.** (*dit is mayn feer-der yaar bay lees kon-suhlt*) (This is my fourth year with Lease Consult.)

Telling Time: Klokkijken

Are you new to the Netherlands? Everybody will understand you when you use the digital system. But you will not understand the Dutch when they use their own system. It is very different from that of other countries.

You can tell time

First, the digital system. You know it, because it's international. Using the digital system you say: its two o'clock, it's two fifteen, it's two thirty, its two forty-five, it's three o'clock. **Het is twee uur, het is twee uur vijftien, het is twee uur dertig, het is twee uur vijfenveertig, het is drie uur.**

TIP

Birthdays and ages

Unlike in English, in Dutch you often use an ordinal when talking about age:

- **Op mijn achttiende heb ik een Citroën CX gekocht.** (*op mayn akh-teender hep ik ern see-troo-ehn say-iks kher-kokht*) (At the age of 18, I bought a Citroën CX.)

- **Op zijn achtenveertigste werd hij ontslagen.** (*op zayn akh-tern-fayr-tikh-ster vehrt hay ont-slaa-khern*) (He was 48 when he was fired.)

In case a friend invites you over for his birthday, he might say: **Kom je zaterdag?**

- **Ik vier mijn dertigste verjaardag.** (*kom yer zaa-ter-dakh ik feer mayn dehr-tikhster fer-yaar-dakh*) (Are you joining us Saturday night? I'm celebrating my 30th birthday.)

When directly asked about age you generally use a numeral:

- **Mijn dochter is dertien.** (*mayn dokh-ter is dehr-teen*) (My daughter is 13 years old.)

- **Ik ben achtendertig.** (*ik ben akh-tern-dehr-tikh*) (I'm 38.)

Rock around the clock

The analogue system in Dutch is rather complicated. Most languages divide the clock in two halves. In the right half, they look backwards to the last hour, in the left they look forwards to the next hour. Take a look at Figure 3–1 to see what I mean.

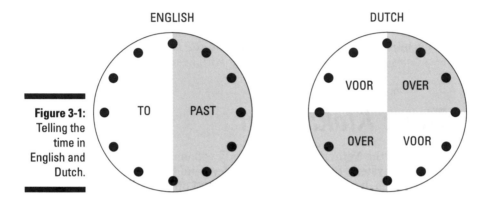

Figure 3-1: Telling the time in English and Dutch.

In English, you start saying: 'It is two o'clock.' After that you are entering the right half of the clock and you say: 'It's five past two, ten past two, a quarter past two, twenty past two, twenty-five past two, half past two.'

After 'half past' you enter the left half of the clock. You start looking forward to the next hour. In English you say: 'It's twenty-five to three, twenty to three, a quarter to three, ten to three, five to three, three o'clock.'

In Dutch, however, the clock is divided in four parts. The first quarter, right above, is easy. It's just like in English: you look back to the past hour and you say in Dutch:

> ✔ **Het is twee uur.** (*het is tvay uwr*) (It's two o'clock.)
>
> ✔ **Het is vijf over twee.** (*het is fayf oa-fer tvay*) (It's five past two.)
>
> ✔ **Het is tien over twee.** (*het is teen oa-fer tvay*) (It's ten past two.)
>
> ✔ **Het is kwart over twee.** (*het is kvart oa-fer tvay*) (It's a quarter past two.)

Now you are entering the second part. You start looking forward to the next half hour and say:

> ✔ **Het is tien voor half drie.** (*het is teen foar half dree*) (It's twenty past two.)
>
> ✔ **Het is vijf voor half drie.** (*het is fayf foar half dree*) (It's twentyfive past two.)
>
> ✔ **Het is half drie.** (*het is half dree*) (It's half past two.)

Then you come into the third quarter. You keep in mind the half hour and start looking backwards to it.

- ✔ **Het is vijf over half drie.** (*het is fayf oa-fer half dree*) (It's twentyfive to three.)

- ✔ **Het is tien over half drie.** (*het is teen oa-fer half dree*) (It's twenty to three.)

Finally you enter the last quarter and you look forward to the next hour.

- ✔ **Het is kwart voor drie.** (*het is kvart foar dree*) (It's quarter to three.)

- ✔ **Het is tien voor drie.** (*het is teen foar dree*) (It's ten to three.)

- ✔ **Het is vijf voor drie.** (*het is fayf foar dree*) (it's five to three.)

- ✔ **Het is drie uur.** (*het is dree uwr*) (It's three o'clock.)

In the morning, in the evening?

You've just met your new neighbour and she invites you over for coffee. She is very busy at the moment, so she does not invite you right away, but for the next day. She says: come and have a cup of coffee at nine o'clock tomorrow! But still you don't know when to come, so you ask:**'s ochtends of 's avonds?** (*sokh-terns of saa-fonts*) (In the morning or in the evening?). A very normal question because Dutchmen traditionally have coffee in the morning as well as in the evening. Here are some more expressions to indicate which part of the day you are talking about.

- ✔ 9–12 a.m.: **'s ochtends** (*sokh-terns*) (in the morning)

- ✔ 12–1 p.m. (13.00 hrs): **tussen de middag** (*tuh-sern der mi-dakh*) (around noon)

- ✔ 12.30–1.30 p.m.: **lunchtijd** (*lunsh-tayt*) (lunch time)

- ✔ 12–6 p.m.: **'s middags** (*smi-dakhs*) (in the afternoon)

- ✔ 4–6 p.m.: **in de namiddag** (*in der naa-mi-dakh*) (the late afternoon)

Days, Months, Seasons

You will learn days and months without even studying them. They are every-where: on your tickets, in the papers, on TV, and in the e-mails you receive. Getting used to Dutch seasons might take some years: just try their names first.

CULTURAL WISDOM

Just in time but are you in time?

Your neighbours have invited you over for coffee at 9.30 in the morning. At what time should you be there? Between 9.30 and 9.40. At what time should you leave? After two cups of coffee.

Your neighbours have invited you and your partner over for coffee at 8.30 in the evening. At what time should you be there? Between 8.30 and 8.40. At what time should you leave? It depends on the situation and whether you all feel at ease. If you get along very well, after coffee your neighbours probably will offer you a drink. At what time should you leave now?

When your neighbours are getting impatient or tired, or maybe when you or your partner are getting impatient or tired. What could you say when you leave? **Bedankt, het was gezellig** (ber-<u>dankt</u> het vas kher-<u>zeh</u>-likh) (Thanks, we had good time). Should you invite them over to your house? You can if you feel like it and when you feel your neighbours would like it. Many neighbours prefer to just chat for some minutes over the fence (each in their own garden), over the balcony, in the lift, or when meeting in the street or in the supermarket.

Making them small

In Dutch the days of the week are written in small letters:

✔ **zondag** (*<u>zon</u>-dakh*) (Sunday)

✔ **maandag** (*<u>maan</u>-dakh*) (Monday)

✔ **dinsdag** (*<u>dins</u>-dakh*) (Tuesday)

✔ **woensdag** (*<u>voons</u>-dakh*) (Wednesday)

✔ **donderdag** (*<u>don</u>-der-dakh*) (Thursday)

✔ **vrijdag** (*<u>fray</u>-dakh*) (Friday)

✔ **zaterdag** (*<u>zaa</u>-ter-dakh*) (Saturday)

You write the names of the months in lower case as well:

✔ **januari** (*ya-nuw-<u>aa</u>-ree*) (January)

✔ **februari** (*fay-bruw-<u>aa</u>-ree*) (February)

✔ **maart** (*maart*) (March)

✔ **april** (*a-<u>pril</u>*) (April)

✔ **mei** (*may*) (May)

✔ **juni** (*<u>yuw</u>-nee*) (June)

✔ **juli** (*<u>yuw</u>-lee*) (July)

✓ **augustus** (*ow-khuhs-tuhs*) (August)

✓ **september** (*sep-tem-ber*) (September)

✓ **oktober** (*ok-toa-ber*) (October)

✓ **november** (*noa-fem-ber*) (November)

✓ **december** (*day-sem-ber*) (December)

Getting used to the Dutch seasons

Using Dutch climate as a source of inspiration for social talk is the best way to tackle it. You might be grateful for the quick changing of weather conditions: it gives you something to talk about! Besides, for those who are fond of change, the four seasons offer opportunities for different wardrobes: every season invites a suitable outfit. Here are the names and the dates of the seasons:

✓ 21 maart – 21 juni: **de lente** (*der len-ter*) (spring)

✓ 21 juni – 21 september: **de zomer** (*der zoa-mer*) (summer)

✓ 21 september – 21 december: **de herfst** (*der hehrfst*) (autumn/fall)

✓ 21 december – 21 maart: **de winter** (*der vin-ter*) (winter)

Dutch seasons

As it borders on the North Sea, the Netherlands enjoys a sea climate. This means both moderate summers and winters. Spring starts in March, but there is a saying: **maart roert zijn staart** (*maart roert sun staart)* (March has a sting in its tail). This month is generally chilly, with some days of sunshine. But May normally has 200 hours of sunshine. In May the air is still clear, and you'll notice the effect of the sun on your skin immediately. Enjoy May like the Dutch do! The **meivakantie** (*may-fa- kan-see*) (May Holiday) is becoming more and more popular to try out tents and caravans and for other outings. But beware: until May 13th, a date called **IJsheiligen** (*ays-hay-li-khern*) (Ice Saint), it might freeze during the night.

June, July, and August each have an average of 190 hours of sun. Temperatures vary between 15 and 33 °Celsius (59 and 91 °Fahrenheit). Dutch summers have a lot of days around 20 degrees Celsius (68 °F), some of 25 degrees (77 °F) and more, and some exceptionally hot days of 30 °C (86 °F) or more. A period of five consecutive days of 30+ degrees is called **een hittegolf** (*ern hi-ter-kholf*) (a heat wave)!

However, you never can be sure. Because of the rising temperatures clouds are formed quickly. If you're going somewhere for the weekend, remember to take a raincoat and something warm! There is usually more rainfall during June, July, and August than during any of the other months of the year. And the Dutch use various names for different types of rain. It can **stortregenen** (*stort-ray-kher-nern*), **hozen** (*hoa-zern*), **plenzen** (*plen-zern*), and **gieten** (*khee-tern*) (all meaning 'to pour down'), and somewhat vulgar, **zeiken** (*zay-kern*) (to piss down), or just **motregenen** (*mot-ray-kher-nern*), **druilen** (*droai-lern*), and **miezeren** (*mee-zer-ern*) (all meaning 'to drizzle').

Onweer (*on-vayr*) (storms) tend to happen during periods of hot weather. They have dangerous **bliksem** (*blik-serm*) (lightning) and **donder** (*don-der*) (thunder), but above all **harde wind** (*har-der vint*) (strong winds): from **windkracht** (*vint-krakht*) (wind force) 6 to 9.

How are Dutch winters? They are not really cold. From December to February temperatures between 0 °C (32 °F) and 10 °C (50 °F) are normal, sometimes sub-zero at night. Sometimes it's raining, and during the three months there will be 38 days without any **zonneschijn** (*zo-nerskhayn*) (sunshine).

A Dutch winter should have about 10 **ijsdagen** (*ays-daa-khern*) (Ice days): periods of 24-hour **vorst** (*forst*) (freezing). Over the past five years or so Dutch periods of freezing have been very short. Most children born in the late nineties have hardly known, let alone skated on, natural ice. They only know thick layers of **sneeuw** (*snayw*) (snow) from **wintersport** (*vin-ter-sport*) (winter sports) in Austria, France, or Switzerland.

Talking about the weather

To complain about the weather is a national pastime in the Netherlands. Dutchmen, especially older people, very often start the day with a comment about the weather. When you ask a 60-year old: 'How are you?', the answer could be: 'It's chilly today.'

Young people talk less about the weather. They just leave the country two or three times a year to warm up on some sunny beach. It's getting more and more popular among Dutch builders and building contractors in their 30s to emigrate to Spain. They fix and sell houses for all those elderly people who spend the last part of their lives in a warm country, escaping the North European gloomy winters.

Understanding weather-inspired expressions

Being an important factor in life, the climate inspires Dutchmen to use weather-based expressions, such as the following ones:

- ✔ **De mist ingaan** (*der mist in khaan*). This means literally 'to enter the fog'. In English, you would say: to fail completely.

- ✔ **Van de regen in de drup komen** (*fan der ray-khern in der druhp koa-mern*). This expression means to come from the rain in the drip and is equivalent to the British: To jump out of the frying pan into the fire.

- ✔ **Niet over één nacht ijs gaan** (*neet oa-fer ayn nakht ays khaan*), literally meaning: not to tread the (thin) ice of one night. English-speaking people might say: Look before you leap.

- ✔ **Ondergesneeuwd raken** (*on-der-kher-snaywt raa-kern*) is not uniquely Dutch. It means 'being snowed under'.

- ✔ **In de wolken zijn** (*in der vol-kern zayn*) means 'being in the clouds' or to be very happy.

CULTURAL WISDOM

Skating on canals and lakes

Dutch people like to skate: after three days of –5 °C frost young children and their parents can be found on the ice after school and in the weekend, sometimes even getting the day off to go skating.

After five days of frost, ice committees and clubs will organise trips of up to 60 kilometres on canals and lakes in the western and northern part of the Netherlands. On those rare occasions thousands of families and friends tread the frozen canals during sunny weekends, mostly in January or February.

The most famous tour is **de Elfstedentocht** (der elf-stay-dern-tokht) in the northern province of Friesland, a skating marathon, as the name tells us, along canals between eleven Frisian towns. Between 1909 and now 15 times the ice has been strong enough to organise this 'tour of tours'. In 1997, 16,000 skaters started in the darkness very early in the morning and every one who reached the finish after 220 long kilometres will forever be a hero to his family and friends. You can find them on the skating rinks: those who train for years, dreaming their dreams: to pass the finishing line in this big event that the Dutch climate so seldom permits.

Part II
Dutch in Action

The 5th Wave · By Rich Tennant

'Next time, I'd prefer you perfect your Dutch pronunciation of the words, 'eel', 'cabbage', and 'vinegar' in the hotel room and not in a restaurant.'

In this part . . .

This part contains all the language tools for daily life. You'll find Dutch for ordering in a restaurant or finding your favourite food in the supermarket, shopping terminology, vocabulary to make the most of your leisure time, and essential phrases for work.

Chapter 4

Greetings and Introductions

- -

In This Chapter

▶ Being formal and informal

▶ Introducing yourself

▶ Introducing others

▶ Chatting about towns, nationalities, and languages

▶ Asking where somebody is from

▶ Learning something about nationalities

- -

*M*eeting new people and getting to know them can be stressful, especially when you don't know their language. This chapter helps you to have a chat with Dutch-speaking people when you meet them for the first time.

Dutchmen consider that keeping a certain distance is best when starting a relationship. They consider it appropriate to use friendlier and informal phrases only after knowing each other better.

Being Formal and Informal

In Dutch there is a difference between the formal **u** (*uw*) and the informal **jij** (*yay*) or **je** (*yer*). It depends on the person and the occasion which form you will be using. This chapter will help you to figure out when to use the informal **jij** or **je**.

Young personnel in supermarkets and cheap restaurants automatically will address anybody with **jij** or **je**. Unless you are one of them, say **u** to an older person, an official or superior. When you get to know each other better, the older of the two or the female person can propose: **Laten we 'je'zeggen, ik heet Petra** *(lah-tern weh jer zeh-khern, ik hayt pay-trah)* (Let's say 'je', my name is Petra). If the other person is of your own age and says **je** to you, you do the same. If he or she is a superior or older and you feel at ease, you could ask: **Mag ik 'je' zeggen?** *(Makh ik yer zeh-khern?)* (May I talk informally to you?).

If you are under 20 or so you may persist in **u** in combination with the first name of the superior or older person. Elderly people often like to be addressed in this way! If they want you to say **je** in combination with their first name, they will tell you to do so.

If you start using the safe and formal **u** for anyone who is a superior or older than 30, you will be seen as a polite person. When you make your first Dutch friends, try using **je**.

Hallo! Greetings

The first part of a greeting usually includes a general phrase. Which greeting you should use depends on the person and time of day. Most popular are, in a range from formal to informal:

- ✔ **goedemorgen** (*khoo-der-mor-khern*) (good morning) (You can use this greeting in the morning, until noon)

- ✔ **goedemiddag** (*khoo-der-mi-dakh*) (use from 12–6 p.m.)

- ✔ **goedenavond** (*khoo-dern-aa-font*) (use from 6–10 p.m.)

- ✔ **dag** (*dakh*) (neutral: hello/goodbye)

- ✔ **hallo** (*ha-loa*) (informal: hello)

- ✔ **hoi** (*hoy*) (used a lot in the northern parts of the Netherlands, informal: hi)

You are being very correct when using **dag** in combination with the surname of the person you address to: **Dag mevrouw Harskamp** (*dakh mer-frow hars-kamp*).

You are a bit less formal using **hallo** in combination with the surname of the person: **Hallo mevrouw Harskamp** (*ha-loa mer-frow hars-kamp*).

You are correct and informal using **dag** in combination with the first name of the person you speak to: **Dag Petra** (*dakh pay-tra*).

You are less formal using **hallo** and the first name of this person: **Hallo Petra** (*ha-loa pay-tra*).

Whenever informality is suitable, just say **hallo** or **hoi** (hi).

Personal pronouns and prepositions

The personal pronouns *I, you, he, we,* and *they* change form, depending on their role in the sentence. Pronouns do this in English as well as in Dutch.

When the personal pronouns play the role of the subject in the sentence they have the forms **ik** (*ik*) (I), **jij** (*yay*) (you, informal, singular) or the unstressed form **je** (*yer*), **hij** (*hay*) (he), **zij** (*zay*) (she) or the unstressed **ze** (*zer*) (she), **wij** (*vay*) (we) or the unstressed form **we** (*wer*) (we), **jullie** (*yuw-lee*) (you informal, plural), **zij** (*zay*) (they) or the unstressed **ze** (*zer*) (they). You use these pronouns to make sentences like: **Ik werk in Rotterdam** (*ik verk in ro-ter-dam*) (I work in Rotterdam) and **Zij werkt in Den Haag** (*zay verkt in dehn-haakh*) (She works in The Hague).

Personal pronouns change form if their role in the sentence is other than that of the subject. This happens, for instance, when the pronoun follows a preposition. After a preposition pronouns have special forms.

Prepositions are words like **met** (*met*) (with), **naar** (*naar*) (to), **op** (*op*) (on), **naast** (*naast*) (next to), **voor** (*foar*) (before), and **na** (*naa*) (after). For more information about prepositions, see Chapter 2.

Pronoun as a subject	Preposition	Pronoun after preposition
ik	**met** (with)	**mij/me** (me)
jij	**naar** (to)	**jou/je** (you)
u	**voor** (for)	**u** (you)
hij	**op** (on)	**hem** (him)
zij/ze	**naast** (next to)	**haar** (her)
wij	**over** (about)	**ons** (us)
jullie	**in** (in)	**jullie** (you)
zij/ze	**tot** (to, until)	**hen** (them)

Here you find some examples of prepositions in combination with pronouns. In the sentence **Met mij gaat het goed en met jou?** (*met may khaat het khoot en met yow?*) (I am all right and how are you?) you notice that the pronoun **mij** has been used and not the form **ik** (ik).

The same happens in **Ik kijk naar jou** (*ik kayk naar yow*) (I look at you): instead of **jij** the word **jou** is used. Some more examples of prepositions followed by pronouns are:

✔ **Zij** or **ze** changes into **haar**: **Hij zit naast haar** (*hay zit naast haar*) (He is sitting next to her).

✔ **U** does not change form after a preposition. In the sentence: **Dit is voor u** (*dit is foar uw*) (This is for you, formal, singular/plural) **u** has the same form as it has in the sentence: **U bent laat** (*uw bent laat*) (You are late), where **u** is the subject in the sentence and does not follow a preposition.

✔ In **Zij praten over ons** (*zay praa-tern oa-fer ons*) (They are talking about us) you will notice that **ons** is a special form of **wij**.

✔ **Jullie** does not change. It always keeps the same form as you can see in the sentence: **Wij geloven in jullie** (*way khe-loa-fern in yuw-lee*) (We believe in you, informal, plural).

✔ **De rechter sprak tot hen** (*der rekh-ter sprak tot hen*) (The judge spoke to them) shows you that instead of **zij** or **ze** the word **hen** is used after a proposition.

✔ A lot of Dutch-speaking people do not know well how to use **hen**: you will often hear them using **hun** instead.

The how question: how are you?

You are at a birthday party and you are introduced to an elderly Dutch person. The hostess introduces you and mentions your name. Some elderly Dutch people will then say something like: **Dag meneer Plooij, hoe maakt u het?** (_dakh mer-nayr ploay, hoo maakt uw het_) (Hello Mr Plooij, how are you?).

Most younger Dutchmen will just say **Hallo** to you. You will repeat your name and say: **Hallo, ik ben Jacco** (_ha-loa ik ben ya-koa_). The question, **Hoe maakt u het?** (_hoo maakt uw het_) (How are you?) when you meet someone for the first time, is getting outdated. However, people you met before do appreciate it very much when you ask them how they are. You will leave a good impression when you listen to the answer and even better when you remember the next time what you have been told. Here are the forms that you can use, in a range from formal to informal:

- ✔ **Hoe maakt u het?** (_hoo maakt uw het_) (How do you do?) (very formal and a bit old-fashioned)

- ✔ **Hoe gaat het met u?** (_hoo khaat het met uw_) (How are you doing?) (formal)

- ✔ **Hoe gaat het ermee?** (_hoo khaat het er-may_) (How are things going?)

- ✔ **Hoe gaat het met jou?** (_hoo khaat het met yow_) (How are you doing?)

- ✔ **Hoe gaat het?** (_hoo khaat het_) (How's it going?)

Greeting and meeting are accompanied by forms of physical contact. To shake hands is the most usual form. In the Netherlands kissing is only for friends and family. Women who know each other well kiss each other on the cheek. Kissing three times (right, left, right) is usual. Dutch males usually don't kiss each other and don't hug. They shake hands. Men who are friends or want to show friendship shake hands and pat their male friend on the back. A man who is a good friend of the woman he meets, kisses her. Men do not kiss their female superiors!

On most informal occasions Dutchmen don't shake hands or touch each other: they just say **Hallo.** Handshaking takes place mostly on formal occasions: when meeting each other for the first time or at special occasions like birthdays or whenever there's a reason for congratulations. Nor do Dutchmen shake hands with neighbours: they just say **dag** (_dakh_), **hallo** (_ha-loa_) or **hoi** (_hoy_). At work colleagues who meet each other daily or weekly don't shake hands. In the office they greet each other by saying: **goedemorgen** (_khoo-der-mor-khen_) (good morning) or **goedemiddag** (_khoo-der-mi-dakh_) (good afternoon). Business partners shake hands a lot. They do so when they arrive and after their business is concluded, when they leave. Influenced by other cultures Dutch youngsters often adopt international greetings, like the rapper's greeting or shaking hands every time they meet.

Giving the right answer

In English 'How are you?' is a greeting and nobody waits for an answer. In Dutch business situations you answer the question but nobody really listens to it: your answer is always **prima** (*pree-ma*) (fine). In more personal situations the question is meant to be answered seriously and in this case you could use one of the next range of answers:

- ✔ **Uitstekend.** (*oait-stay-kernt*) (Excellent.)
- ✔ **Prima.** (*pree-maa*) (Fine.)
- ✔ **Goed, dank je.** (*khoot, dank yer*) (OK, thank you.)

When you are among real friends, you could say:

- ✔ **Het gaat wel.** (*het khaat vel*) (Not too bad.)
- ✔ **Niet zo goed.** (*neet zoa khoot*) (Not very well.)

A good friend will, later in the conversation, ask you for more details! He will ask you what's wrong, if you have answered **Het gaat wel** or **Niet zo goed**.

In formal situations, after replying you ask at your turn: **En met u?** (*en met uw*) (And how are you?) Elderly people will like your manners when you ask them this question in return and you take your time to listen to the answer. In informal situations it will be appreciated when you return the question **Hoe gaat het?** (*hoo khaat het*) (How are you?) with: **Met mij prima en met jou?** (*met may pree-maa en met yow*) (I am fine and how are you?).

Talkin' the Talk

 In the next dialogue you hear some sentences that elderly people will use in a formal setting:

Chris Vreugdenhil:	**Goedenavond mevrouw De Hoogh.**
	khoo-dern-aa-font mer-frow der hoakh
	Good evening, Mrs De Hoogh.
Margriet de Hoogh:	**Goedenavond meneer Vreugdenhil, hoe gaat het met u ?**
	khoo-dern-aa-font mer-nayr frukh-tern-hil
	Good evening Mr Vreugdenhil, how are you?
Chris Vreugdenhil:	**Prima, dank u. En met u?**
	pree-maa dank uw. en met uw
	Fine, thank you. And how are you?
Margriet de Hoogh:	**Ook goed, dank u.**
	oak khoot dank uw
	Fine as well, thank you.

Talkin' the Talk

 Now you hear a dialogue between Jacco and Marcel. They are former colleagues who meet in the supermarket.

Jacco: **Hallo Marcel!**
ha-loa mar-sel
Hello Marcel!

Marcel: **Jacco, hallo, hoe gaat het?**
ya-koa ha-loa hoo khaat het
Jacco, hello, how are you?

Jacco: **Met mij prima en met jou?**
met may pree-ma en met yow
Fine and how are you?

Marcel: **Wat doe je tegenwoordig?**
vat doo yer tay-khern-voar-dikh
What are you doing nowadays?

Jacco: **Ik werk bij Lease Consult op personeelszaken. En jij?**
ik vehrk bay lees con-suhlt op pehr-soa-nayls-zaa-kern. en yay
I am doing HR with Lease Consult. And you?

Marcel: **Ik werk als accountant bij Biz Accountants. Woon je nog steeds in Amsterdam- Noord?**
ik vehrk als er-kown-ternt bay biz er-kown-terns. voan yer nokh stayts in am-ster-dam-noart
I am working as an accountant at Biz Accountants. Do you still live in the northern part of Amsterdam?

Marcel: **Nee, ik woon tegenwoordig in Lelystad. Maar ik moet nu snel weg, mijn vrouw en kinderen staan buiten te wachten. Ik bel je.**
nay ik voan tay-khern-voar-dikh in lay-lee-stat. maar ik moot nuw snel vekh mayn frow en kin-der-ern staan boai-tern ter wakh-tern. Ik bel yer
No, I am living in Lelystad now. But I have to go now, my wife and kids are waiting outside. I will call you!

Jacco: **OK, hoi!**
oa-kay hoy
Okay, bye!

Marcel: **Hoi!**
hoy
Bye!

Words to Know

met mij prima	*met may <u>pree</u>-ma*	I am fine
tegenwoordig	*tay-khern-<u>voar</u>-dikh*	nowadays
Personeelszaken	*pehr-soa- <u>nayls</u>-zaa-kern*	Human Resources
de accountant	*der er-<u>kown</u>-ternt*	the accountant /auditor
snel	*snel*	rapidly

Introducing Yourself

In some situations you have to introduce yourself. Many people introduce themselves by just saying their name, including in more formal settings. In Dutch people generally introduce themselves by saying:

Hallo, ik ben Jessica de Rover. (*ha-<u>loa</u> ik ben <u>yeh</u>-see-kaa der <u>roa</u>-ver*) (Hello, I am Jessica de Rover.)

or

Ik zal me even voorstellen, ik ben Jacco Plooij. (*ik zal may <u>ay</u>-vern <u>foar</u>-steh-lern ik ben <u>ya</u>-koa ploay*) (Let me introduce myself, my name is Jacco Plooij.)

Talkin' the Talk

 In the next conversation Jacco Plooij arrives at his first meeting with some colleagues that he has never met before. He is looking for a seat.

Jacco Plooij: **Goedemorgen, zit hier iemand?**
khoo-dern-<u>mor</u>-khern zit heer <u>ee</u>-mant
Good morning, is anyone sitting here?

Cilla Vermeent: **Nee hoor, ga je gang.**
nay hoar kha yer khang
No, just sit down.

Jacco Plooij:	**Dank je. Ik ben Jacco Plooij van personeelszaken.**
	dank yer. ik ben <u>ya</u>-koa ploay fan pehr-soa-<u>nayl</u>-saa-kern
	Thank you, I am Jacco Plooij of HR.
Cilla Vermeent:	**Hallo, ik ben Cilla Vermeent, de secretaresse van Hans van der Jagt.**
	ha-<u>loa</u> ik ben <u>si</u>-laa fer-<u>maynt</u> der si-krer-taa-<u>rehs</u>-ser fan hans fan der yakht
	Hello, I am Cilla Vermeent, secretary of Hans van der Jagt

Introducing Others

When you meet people, you will want to know how to introduce people other than yourself. This is very easy. You start with: **Dit is ...** (dit is) (This is...) Then you say the name of the person you introduce. You can clarify the relation by saying: **Dit is Cilla Vermeent, de secretaresse van Hans van der Jagt** (*dit is si-la fer-<u>maynt</u> si-krer-taa-<u>res</u>-ser fan hans fan der yakht*) (This is Cilla Vermeent, the secretary of Hans van der Jagt), or **Dit is mijn collega Jessica de Rover** (*dit is mayn ko-<u>lay</u>-khaa <u>yeh</u>-see-kaa der <u>roa</u>-ver*)(This is my colleague Jessica de Rover).

If you are introduced to an English-speaking person you probably will say: **Nice to meet you**. Elderly Dutch people will appreciate your using the sentence: **Prettig met u kennis te maken**. (*<u>preh</u>-tikh met uw <u>keh</u>-nis ter <u>maa</u>-kern*) (Nice to meet you). When you are among younger and more informal people and you are introduced you just say **Hallo** and, while shaking hands, repeat your own name. Immediately after doing this you ask a question, for instance: **Bent u een collega van Jacco Plooij ?** (*bent uw ern ko-<u>lay</u>-khaa fan <u>ya</u>-koa ploay*) or, in more personal situations: **Bent u een kennis van Jacco Plooij?** (*bent uw ern <u>keh</u>-nis fan <u>ya</u>-koa ploay*) (Are you an acquaintance of Jacco Plooij?). You address the person to whom you are introduced. Frequently the question regards the relation that the introduced person has to the person who introduced you to each other, but it can also concern the person you are introduced to: **Bent u hier voor het eerst?** (*bent uw heer foar het ayrst*) (Is this the first time that you are here?).

Introductions at special occasions

Occasionally you are in a situation where introducing and meeting are very formal. There are some sentences that work well:

- ✔ **Mag ik u voorstellen: Jessica de Rover.** (*makh ik uw <u>foar</u>-stehlern yeh-see-ka der <u>roa</u>-ver*) (May I introduce to you: Jessica de Rover.)

- ✔ **Prettig met u kennis te maken.** (<u>*preh*</u>-*tikh met uw <u>keh</u>-nis ter <u>maa</u>-kern*) (Nice to meet you.)

- ✔ **Insgelijks.** (*ins-kher-<u>layks</u>*) (Likewise.)

Talkin' the Talk

 In this dialogue a young director, Raymond van Dieren, meets an older director, Hans van der Jagt, on a formal occasion. They know each other well from the business community. Hans van der Jagt introduces his wife.

Raymond van Dieren: **Goedenavond Hans.**
khoo-dern-<u>aa</u>-font hans
Good evening, Hans.

Hans van der Jagt: **Goedenavond Raymond, hoe gaat het! Mag ik je mijn vrouw Rita voorstellen?**
khoo-dern-<u>aa</u>-font <u>ray</u>-mont hoo khaat het.
makh ik yer mayn frow <u>ree</u>-taa <u>foar</u>-steh-lern
Good evening Raymond, how are you? May I introduce my wife Rita to you?

Raymond van Dieren: **Goedenavond mevrouw Van der Jagt, ik ben Raymond van Dieren van Biz Accountants. Prettig met u kennis te maken!**
khoo-dern-<u>aa</u>-font mer-<u>frow</u> fan der yakht, ik ben <u>ray</u>-mont fan <u>dee</u>-rern fan biz er-<u>kown</u>-ternts, <u>preh</u>-tikh met uw <u>keh</u>-nis ter <u>maa</u>-kern
Good evening Mrs Van der Jagt, I am Raymond van Dieren of Biz Accountants. Nice to meet you!

Rita van der Jagt: **Insgelijks. Hans heeft mij al veel over u verteld. Woont u nog steeds in Amsterdam–Noord?**
ins-kher-<u>layks</u>. hans hayft may al fayl oa-fer uw fer-<u>telt</u>. voant uw nokh stayts in am-sterdam–<u>noart</u>
Likewise. My husband has told me a lot about you. Do you still live in the northern part of Amsterdam?

Raymond van Dieren: **Nee, ik woon nu op het Java-eiland.**
nay ik voan nuw op <u>jaa</u>-faa-ay-lant
No, I am now living on the Java-eiland.

Saying Goodbye

When it's time to say goodbye, you can say (both formal and informal) **Tot ziens** (*tot zeens*) or **Dag!** (*dakh*) or (very informal) **Doei!** (*dooy*), or **Doeg!** (*dookh*). If it was an informal meeting with friends, you say **Het was gezellig** (*het vas kher-<u>zeh</u>-likh*) (We had a nice time). If people have been speaking about their plans or are working on something, you often end with a wish: **Veel succes!** (*fayl suwk-<u>ses</u>*) (Good luck!).

In business, when leaving, you generally mention things to be done, like **Ik stuur u zo spoedig mogelijk het voorstel** (*ik stuwr uw zoa snel <u>moa</u>-kher- lerk het <u>foar</u>-stel*) (I'll send you our proposal as soon as possible) or **Ik wacht uw verslag af** (*ik vakht uw fer-<u>slakh</u> af*) (I'll wait for your report).

Talkin' the Talk

Cilla Vermeent and Gerda Jongsma have met at Mike Johnson's party in Laren. They say goodbye.

Gerda:	**Het is al laat, ik moet naar huis. Het was leuk om je te leren kennen.**
	het is al laat ik moot naar hoais. het vas luk om yer ter <u>lay</u>-rern <u>keh</u>-nern
	It is late, I have to go home now. It was nice meeting you.
Cilla:	**Ja, het was gezellig. Veel succes met je plannen.**
	yaa het vas kher-<u>zeh</u>-likh. fayl suwk-<u>ses</u> met yer <u>pla</u>-nern
	Yes, we had a nice time. Lots of luck with your plans.
Gerda:	**Bedankt en tot ziens.**
	ber-<u>dankt</u> en tot zeens
	Thanks, bye.

Chatting about Towns, Countries, and Languages

Introducing is a good start, but how to start a conversation? In this section you learn how to say where you are from, how to ask from where the other person is and which languages he or she speaks.

Telling where you are from

All you need are the words:

Ik kom uit . . . (*ik kom oait*) (I am from ...)

When saying this, most people refer to the place where they are living at that moment. This is seldom the place where they were born. When people think it is important to mention their birthplace, they say: **Ik kom uit Amsterdam, maar ik ben geboren op Curaçao.** (*ik kom oait am-ster-dam maar ik ben kher-boa-rern op kuw-raa-sow*) (I am from Amsterdam, but I was born on the island Curaçao). Normally they stick to: **Ik kom uit...** Using this expression, you can refer to a village, town, region or country. Here are some examples:

- ✔ **Ik kom uit Kortenhoef.** (*ik kom oait kor-tern-hoof*) (I am from Kortenhoef.)
- ✔ **Ik kom uit Maastricht.** (*ik kom oait maa-strikht*) (I am from Maastricht.)
- ✔ **Ik kom uit Friesland.** (*ik kom oait frees-lant*) (I am from Friesland.)
- ✔ **Ik kom uit Duitsland.** (*ik kom oait doaits-lant*) (I am from Germany.)

Do you know the following European capitals and countries? Table 4-1 shows you how to pronounce them.

Table 4-1	European Capitals and Countries		
Capital		*Country*	
Bern (*bern*)	Bern	**Zwitserland** (*svit-ser-lant*)	Switzerland
Boedapest (*boo-daa-pest*)	Budapest	**Hongarije** (*hon-khaa-ray-er*)	Hungary
Brussel (*bruh-serl*)	Brussels	**België** (*bel-khee-yer*)	Belgium
Dublin (*duh-blin*)	Dublin	**Ierland** (*eer-lant*)	Ireland
Kopenhagen (*koa-pern-haa-khern*)	Copenhagen	**Denemarken** (*day-ner-mar-kern*)	Denmark
Luxemburg (*luw-ksem-buhrkh*)	Luxembourg	**Luxemburg** (*luw-ksem-buhrkh*)	Luxemburg
Lissabon (*li-saa-bon*)	Lisbon	**Portugal** (*por-tuw-khal*)	Portugal

(continued)

Table 4-1 *(continued)*

Capital		Country	
Londen (*lon*-dern)	London	**Engeland** (*eng*-er-lant)	England
Madrid (maa-*drit*)	Madrid	**Spanje** (*span*-yer)	Spain
Oslo (*os*-loa)	Oslo	**Noorwegen** (*noar*-vay-khern)	Norway
Parijs (paa-*rays*)	Paris	**Frankrijk** (*frank*-rayk)	France
Praag (praakh)	Prague	**Tsjechië** (*tsyeh*-khee-yer)	Czech Republic
Rome (*roa*-mer)	Rome	**Italië** (ee-*taa*-lee-yer)	Italy
Stockholm (*stok*-holm)	Stockholm	**Zweden** (*svay*-dern)	Sweden
Warschau (*var*-show)	Warsawa	**Polen** (*poa*-lern)	Poland
Wenen (*vay*-nern)	Vienna	**Oostenrijk** (*oa*-stern-rayk)	Austria

To be: the verb 'zijn'

One of the most important verbs in all languages is **to be**, in Dutch **zijn** (*zayn*). Just like in English this verb is used in order to describe something: from moods as in **verdrietig zijn** (*fer-dree-tikh zayn*) (to be sad) or **blij zijn** (*blay zayn*) (to be happy) to physical characteristics like **groot zijn** (*khroat zayn*) (to be tall) and **slank zijn** (*slank zayn*) (to be slim). **Zijn** is a very irregular verb.

Conjunction	Pronunciation
ik ben	*ik ben*
jij bent	*yay bent*
u bent	*uw bent*
hij/zij/het is	*hay/zay/het is*
wij zijn	*vay zayn*

jullie zijn	*yuw-lee zayn*
zij zijn	*zay zayn*

Asking Where Somebody Is From

When you want to ask a person where they are from, you first have to decide if you want to be formal or informal with them. If you want to be informal you have to make a choice between singular (if you address one person) or plural (if you address two or more persons). So you choose one of these three:

✔ **Waar komt u vandaan?** (formal, singular, and plural)

(*vaar komt uw fan-daan*)

✔ **Waar kom je vandaan?** (informal, singular)

(*vaar kom yer fan-daan*)

✔ **Waar komen jullie vandaan?** (informal, plural)

(*vaar koa-mern yuw-lee fan-daan*)

Talkin' the Talk

Sytske and Kirstin meet each other on a canal trip in Amsterdam.

Kirstin:	**Waar kom jij vandaan?**
	vaar kom yay fan-daan
	Where are you from?
Sytske:	**Uit Sneek, dat is in Friesland**
	oait snayk dat is in frees-lant
	From Sneek, that is in Friesland
Kirstin:	**Waar ligt Friesland?**
	vaar likht frees-lant
	Where is Friesland?
Sytske:	**In het noorden van Nederland. En waar kom jij vandaan?**
	in het noar-dern fan nay-der-lant. en vaar kom yay fan-daan
	In the north of the Netherlands. And where are you from?
Kirstin:	**Ik kom uit Duitsland. Ik kom uit Berlijn.**
	ik kom oait doaits-lant. ik kom oait behr-layn
	I am from Germany. I am from Berlin.

To come: komen

You'll meet this Dutch verb often. It is a regular verb.

Conjunction	Pronunciation
ik kom	*ik kom*
jij komt	*yay komt*
u komt	*uw komt*
hij/zij/het komt	*hay/zay/het komt*
wij komen	*vay koa-mern*
jullie komen	*yuw-lee koa-mern*
zij komen	*zay koa-mern*

Learning Something about Nationalities

While chatting about the country where you are from, the person you are talking to might ask you which nationality you are and which is your own language.

In Table 4-2 you'll find several countries, the right words to tell your nationality as well as the Dutch words for the languages that are spoken in those countries.

Table 4-2	Country Names, Male and Female Nouns, and Adjectives			
English	*Dutch*	*Male noun*	*Female noun*	*Adjective*
The Netherlands	**Nederland** *nay-der-lant*	**Nederlander** *nay-der-lan-der*	**Nederlandse** *nay-der-lan-ser*	**Nederlands** *nay-der-lans*
Austria	**Oostenrijk** *oa-stern-rayk*	**Oostenrijker** *oa-stern-ray-ker*	**Oostenrijkse** *oa-stern-rayk-ser*	**Oostenrijks** *oa-stern-rayks*
Belgium	**België** *bel-khee-yer*	**Belg** *belkh*	**Belgische** *bel-khee-ser*	**Belgisch** *bel-khees*
England	**Engeland** *eng-er-lant*	**Engelsman** *eng-erls-ma*	**Engelse** *eng-erl-ser*	**Engels** *eng-erls*
France	**Frankrijk** *frank-rayk*	**Fransman** *frans-man*	**Française** *fran-seh-ser*	**Frans** *frans*

English	Dutch	Male noun	Female noun	Adjective
Germany	**Duitsland** *doaits-lant*	**Duitser** *doait-ser*	**Duitse** *doait-ser*	**Duits** *doaits*
Italy	**Italië** *ee-taa-lee-yer*	**Italiaan** *ee-tal-yaan*	**Italiaanse** *ee-tal-yaan-ser*	**Italiaans** *ee-tal-yaans*
Switzerland	**Zwitserland** *svit-ser-lant*	**Zwitser** *svit-ser*	**Zwitserse** *svit-ser-ser*	**Zwitsers** *svit-sers*
United States	**Verenigde Staten** *fer-ray-nikh-ter staa-tern*	**Amerikaan** *a-may-ree-kaan*	**Amerikaanse** *amay-ree-kaan-ser*	**Amerikaans** *a-may-ree-kaans*

Using these terms in a sentence

- **Cilla Vermeent komt uit Nederland.** (*si-laa fer-maynt komt oait nay-der-lant*) (Cilla Vermeent is from the Netherlands.)

- **Cilla is Nederlandse.** (*si-laa is nay-der-lan-ser*) (Cilla is Dutch.)

- **Cilla heeft de Nederlandse nationaliteit.** (*si-laa hayft der nay-derlan-ser na-shoa-naa-lee-tayt*) (Cilla has the Dutch nationality.)

- **Mike Johnson komt uit de Verenigde Staten.** (*mike john-son komt oait der fer-ray-nikh-ter staa-tern*) (Mike Johnson is from the US.)

- **Mike is Amerikaan.** (*mike is a-may-ree-kaan*) (Mike is an American.)

- **Mike heeft de Amerikaanse nationaliteit.** (*mike hayft der a-mayree-kaan-ser na-shoa-naa-lee-tayt*) (Mike has the American nationality.)

- **Kirstin Liebherr komt uit Duitsland.** (*kir-stin leep-hehr komt oait doaits-lant*) (Kirstin Liebherr is from Germany.)

- **Kirstin is Duitse.** (*kir-stin is doait-ser*) (Kirstin is German).

- **Kirstin heeft de Duitse nationaliteit.** (*kir-stin hayft der doait-ser na-shoa-naa-lee-tayt*) (Kirstin has the German nationality.)

Chatting about languages

You use the verb **spreken** (to speak) in order to chat about languages.

Conjunction	*Pronunciation*
ik spreek	*ik sprayk*
jij spreekt	*yay spraykt*
u spreekt	*uw spraykt*
hij/zij/het spreekt	*hay/zay/het spraykt*
wij spreken	*vay spray-kern*
jullie spreken	*yuw-lee spray-kern*
zij spreken	*zay spray-kern*

Talkin' the Talk

Kirstin and Sytske are on a canal tour in Amsterdam. The guide speaks English, German, and Spanish. Kirstin notices that Sytske understands Spanish.

Kirstin: **Spreek je ook Spaans?**
sprayk yer oak spaans
Do you speak Spanish as well?

Sytske: **Ja, ik spreek Spaans. En jij?**
yaa, ik sprayk spaans. en yay
Yes, I do speak Spanish. And you?

Kirstin: **Nee, ik spreek alleen Duits en een beetje Nederlands. Spreek jij Duits?**
nay ik sprayk a-layn doaits
No, I just speak German and some Dutch. Do you speak German?

Sytske: **Nee, ik spreek geen Duits. Ik spreek Fries, Nederlands, Engels en Spaans.**
nay ik sprayk khayn doaits. ik sprayk frees nay-der-lants eng-erls en spaans
No, I don't speak German. I speak Frisian, Dutch, English and Spanish.

Kirstin: **Spreken alle Nederlanders zoveel talen?**
spray-kern a-ler nay-der-lan-ders zoa-fayl taa-lern
Do all Dutch people speak so many languages?

Sytske: **Alle Nederlanders leren op school Nederlands en nog twee talen. Alleen Friezen spreken Fries.**

a-ler <u>nay</u>-der-lan-ders <u>lay</u>-rern op skhoal nay-der-lans en nokh tvay <u>taa</u>-lern. A-<u>layn</u> <u>free</u>-zern <u>spray</u>-kern frees

All Dutch learn Dutch and two more languages at school. Only Frisians speak Frisian.

Words to Know

Engels	<u>eng</u>-erls	English
Duits	doaits	German
Spaans	spaans	Spanish
Fries	frees	Frisian
Nederlands	<u>nay</u>-der-lans	Dutch
de taal	der taal	the language
de school	der skhoal	the school

Chapter 5

Getting to Know Each Other Better

• •

In This Chapter

▶ Inviting the other to talk

▶ Telling about yourself

▶ Talking about the weather

• •

*I*f you really want to know somebody you have to talk with him. Using the social talk of this chapter, you will not only make new contacts, but also learn to talk Dutch. Whether you are talking on the train or on a bus, on a plane or at a party: there are always things you can talk about. Ask questions, talk about yourself or about the weather.

When people really get interested in you, they might ask questions about your family. You will find useful words for family talk in the last but one part of this chapter. In case you want to stick to more neutral subjects, a chat about the weather will help you to break the ice.

Inviting the Other to Talk

Do you find it difficult to make contact? Use questions for an opening. Ask people whether they know the place where you are going to or where you are. They will answer you and if they are interested in you, they will ask you a question in return. At a later stage you can ask more personal questions. The following opening sentences might be useful:

▸ **Bent u hier bekend** (*bent uw heer ber-<u>kent</u>*) (Do you know this place?) (formal)

▸ **Ben je hier bekend?** (*ben yer heer ber-<u>kent</u>*) (Do you know this place?) (informal)

▸ **Bent u hier voor de eerste keer?** (*bent uw heer foar der <u>ayr</u>-ster kayr*) (Is this the first time you're here?) (formal)

✔ **Ben je hier voor de eerste keer?** (*ben yer heer foar der ayr-ster kayr*) (Is this the first time you're here?) (informal)

✔ **Komt u hier wel vaker?** (*komt uw heer vel faa-ker*) (Do you come here often?) (formal)

✔ **Komen we binnenkort aan?** (*koa-men ver bi-nern-kort aan*) (Are we going to arrive soon?)

✔ **Moeten we lang wachten?** (*moo-tern ver lang vakh-tern*) (Will we have to wait a long time?)

All questions that start with a verb are 'closed questions'. The person you're talking to might answer them with a simple 'yes' or 'no'.

Open questions start with a question word. Question words are words such as **wie** (*vee*) (who?), **wat** (*vat*) (what?), **waar** (*vaar*) (where?), **hoe** (*hoo*) (how?) and **wanneer** (*va-nayr*) (when?). If you ask an open question the person you're talking to will give a longer answer than only **ja** (*yaa*) (yes) or **nee** (*nay*) (no). Here are some suitable open questions that start with a question word:

✔ **Wanneer komen we aan?** (*va-nayr koa-mern ver aan*) (When will we arrive?)

✔ **Waar gaat u naartoe?** (*vaar khaat uw naar too*) (Where are you going to?) (formal)

✔ **Waar ga je naartoe?** (*vaar khaa yer naar too*) (Where are you going to?) (informal)

✔ **Wat is dit voor soort restaurant?** (*vat is dit foar soart res-to-rant*) (What kind of restaurant is this?)

✔ **Wie is dat?** (*vee is dat*) (Who is that person?)

When you are at a party, you can ask the other person about his relationship with the host:

Hoe lang kent u de familie Sturmey al? (*hoo lang kent uw der faa-mee-lee stuhr-may al*) (How long have you known the Sturmey family?)

People will talk longer when you ask them questions that also require a personal statement. See what happens when you ask one of the following questions:

Kent u Allan Sturmey goed? (*kent uw a-lan stur-may khoot*) (Do you know Allan Sturmey well?)

See for more information about questions the section on asking questions Chapter 2.

Talking about Yourself

When you talk about yourself, tell the person you are speaking to the things you would like to know about him or her! You may say what kind of work you do and where you are from. Perhaps at the end of the conversation you want to give them your telephone number.

Talking about your work

Generally you can tell what kind of work you do, using the words **'I am'** in combination with your profession or function. You don't use an article. Some professions have masculine and feminine forms.

> ✔ **Ik ben secretaris.** (*ik ben sek-rer-<u>taa</u>-ris*) (I am a secretary, male.)
>
> ✔ **Ik ben secretaresse.** (*ik ben sek-rer-taa-<u>reh</u>-ser*) (I am a secretary, female.)
>
> ✔ **Ik ben student.** (*ik ben stuw-<u>dent</u>*) (I am a student.)
>
> ✔ **Ik ben hoogleraar.** (*ik ben hoakh-<u>lay</u>-raar*) (I am a professor.)

A lot of professions once had a feminine form and have now lost that. In this case, you always use the masculine form. Women generally say **Ik ben directeur** (*ik ben di-rek-<u>tur</u>*) (I am a director) instead of the old-fashioned **Ik ben directrice** (*ik ben di-rek-<u>tree</u>-ser*) (I am a director). Young teachers will say **Ik ben docent Nederlands.** (*ik ben doa-<u>sent</u> <u>nay</u>-der-lans*) (I am a teacher of Dutch) Only elderly women still use the feminine form **Ik ben docente Nederlands.** (*ik ben doa-<u>sen</u>-ter <u>nay</u>-der-lans*) (I am a teacher of Dutch).

More and more professions have English names. You'll find the the next professions among your Dutch business partners:

> ✔ **Ik ben accountmanager.** (*ik ben account manager*) (I am an account manager.)
>
> ✔ **Ik ben general manager.** (*ik ben general manager*) (I am a general manager.)
>
> ✔ **Ik ben HR-assistent.** (*ik ben HR-assistant*) (I am a human resource assistant.)
>
> ✔ **Ik ben supervisor.** (*ik ben supervisor*) (I am a supervisor.)

If you don't find the word for your profession, check the dictionary or a dictionary on the Internet. You can also opt for another possibility and mention the place where you work:

> ✔ **Ik werk op de universiteit.** (ik verk op der uw-nee-fer-see-<u>tayt</u>) (I work at the University.)
>
> ✔ **Ik werk bij een internationaal bedrijf.** (ik verk bay ern in-ter-nashoa-<u>naal</u> ber-<u>drayf</u>)) (I work in an international company.)
>
> ✔ **Ik werk in een ziekenhuis.** (*ik verk in ern <u>zee</u>-kern-hoais*) (I work in a hospital.)

When you're a student, you may want to mention what you study. Just start saying: **Ik studeer** (*ik stuw-<u>dayr</u>*) (I study) and then add:

> ✔ **wiskunde** (<u>*vis*</u>-*kuhn-der*) (mathematics)
>
> ✔ **literatuur** (*lee-ter-raa-<u>tuwr</u>*) (literature)
>
> ✔ **internationaal recht** (*in-ter-na-shoa-<u>naal</u> rekht*) (international law)
>
> ✔ **medicijnen** (*may-dee-<u>say</u>-nern*) (medicine)

In case you're doing something else, the following sentences might come in handy:

> ✔ **Ik ben op reis.** (*ik ben op rays*) (I am travelling.)
>
> ✔ **Ik ben op zakenreis.** (*ik ben op <u>zaa</u>-kern-rays*) (I'm on a business trip.)
>
> ✔ **Ik ben hier op tijdelijke basis.** (*ik ben heer op <u>tay</u>-der-ler-ker <u>baa</u>-sis*) (I'm here temporarily.)

Asking and giving a telephone number

When you first offer to give your telephone number, the other person will probably give his telephone number in return. So if you're interested in staying in touch, you might say: **Ik geef je mijn telefoonnummer in geval je contact met me wilt opnemen** (*ik khayf yer mern tay-ler-<u>foa</u>-nuh- mer in kher-<u>fal</u> dat yer con-<u>takt</u> met mer vil <u>op</u>-nay-mern*) (I'll give you my telephone number in case you want to get in touch with me). Generally you'll write down your number or you'll give you business card. After handing over the card, you can add: **Dit is mijn mobiele nummer** (*dit is mern moa-<u>bee</u>-ler <u>nuh</u>-mer*) (This is my mobile number), or **het netnummer is . . .** (*het <u>net</u>-nuh-mer is*) (the dialing/area code is . . .), en **het abonneenummer is . . .** (*het a-bo-<u>nay</u>-nuh-mer is*) (the subscriber's number is . . .). A good sentence to end the exchange of telephone numbers is: **Je kunt me altijd bellen** (*yer kunt mer <u>al</u>-tayt <u>beh</u>-lern*) (You can always call me).

Dutch telephone numbers always have ten digits. The first two, three or four digits stand for the dialing/area code: 06 for cell phones, 0 plus two digits for the major cities, and 0 plus three digits for the smaller towns.

- ✔ **06** (mobile) **nul zes** (*nuhl zes*) (o/zero six)
- ✔ **010** (Rotterdam) **nul tien** (*nuhl teen*) (zero ten)
- ✔ **020** (Amsterdam) **nul twintig** (*nuhl tvin-terkh*) (zero twenty)
- ✔ **030** (Utrecht) **nul dertig** (*nuhl dehr-terkh*) (zero thirty)
- ✔ **070** (The Hague) **nul zeventig** (*nuhl zay-vern-terkh*) (zero seventy)

In the phone book the subscriber's number starts with three digits and then is divided in groups of two.

020–679 04 28: **nul twintig, zes zeven negen, nul vier, twee acht** (*nuhl tvin-tikh, zes zay-vern nay-khern, nuhl feer, tvay akht*) (zero twenty, zero seven nine, zero four, two eight)

In Web sites, on business cards and on official papers you'll find telephone numbers divided like this. When you ask a private person for his telephone number, he will give it the way it sounds best to him: very often in separate figures, but other combinations are also possible. You can even hear partners mentioning their common telephone number in different ways! One partner will say:

036–532 532 1: **nul zesendertig, vijf drie twee, vijf drie twee, één** (*nuhl zes-ern-dehr-tikh, fayf dree tvay, fayf dree tvay, ayn*) (zero thirty six, five three two, five two three, one)

The other partner will tell you:

036–53 25 321: **nul zesendertig, drieënvijftig, vijfentwintig, drie twee één** (*nuhl zes-ern-dehr-terkh, dree-ern-fayf-terkh, fayf-ern-tvin-terkh, dree tvay ayn*) (zero thirty-six, fifty-three, twenty-five, three two one)

Cold comfort: Dutch people generally agree about the dialling code: It always starts with zero and the tens are pronounced as tens, so **nul tien** (*nuhl teen*) (zero ten) and **nul twintig** (*nuhl tvin-terkh*) (zero twenty). In case the dialling code has four figures, is is pronounced as 0320 **nul drie twee nul** (*nuhl dree tvay nuhl*), like separate figures.

Talkin' the Talk

Cilla Vermeent is at a party. She is having her first glass of wine when she meets Mike Johnson. She immediately notices that he is not a Dutchman, though he speaks Dutch rather well.

Cilla Vermeent: **Wat heeft u naar Nederland gebracht?**
vat hayft uw naar <u>nay</u>-der-lant kher-brakht
What brought you to the Netherlands?

Mike Johnson: **Ik ben hier op tijdelijke basis. Ik werk voor een internationaal bedrijf.**
ik ben heer op tay-der-ler-ker <u>baa</u>-sis. ik verk foar ern in-ter-naa-shoa-<u>naal</u> ber-<u>drayf</u>
I am here temporarily. I work for an international company.

Cilla Vermeent: **En welk bedrijf is dat, als ik het vragen mag?**
en velk ber-<u>drayf</u> is dat, als ik <u>fraa</u>-khern makh
And which company is that, if I may ask?

Mike Johnson: **Ik werk voor Golfwagen Duitsland en ben nu in Amsterdam gestationeerd.**
ik verk foar <u>kholf</u>-vaa-khern <u>doaits</u>-lant en ben nuw in am-ster-<u>dam</u> kher-staa-sho-<u>nayrt</u>
I'm with Golfwagen Germany and I'm now stationed in Amsterdam.

Cilla Vermeent: **Bent u dan Duits?**
bent uw dan doaits
In that case, are you German?

Mike Johnson: **Mijn moeder is Duits en mijn vader is Amerikaans.**
mayn <u>moo</u>-der is doaits en en mayn <u>faa</u>-der is a-may-ree-<u>kaans</u>)
My mother is German and my father is American.

Cilla Vermeent: **Waar woont u?**
vaar voant uw
Where do you live?

Mike Johnson: **Doordeweeks woon ik in een hotel in Naarden. In het weekend ga ik naar Keulen, naar mijn vrouw. Dat is maar een paar uur rijden. En waar woon jij?**
doar-der-<u>vayks</u> voan ik in ern hoa-<u>tel</u> in <u>naar</u>-dern. in het <u>vee</u>-kent khaa ik naar <u>ku</u>-lern naar mayn frow. het is maar ern paar uwr <u>ray</u>-dern. en vaar voan yay
During the week, I live in a hotel in Naarden. In the weekends I go to Cologne, to my wife. It's only a couple of hours' driving. Where do you live?

Cilla Vermeent:	**Hier vlakbij, in Kortenhoef. Blijft u vanavond in Nederland?**
	heer vlak-bay in kor-tern-hoof. blayft uw faa-naa-font in nay-der-lant
	Nearby, in Kortenhoef. Are you staying in the Netherlands tonight?
Mike Johnson:	**Nee, ik rijd straks naar huis.**
	nay ik ray straks naar hoais
	No, I will drive home soon.
Cilla Vermeent:	**O, dus daarom drinkt u geen alcohol. Ik wens u een goeie reis!**
	oa, duhs daa-rom drinkt uw kheen al-koahol. Ik vens uw ern khoo-yer rays)
	So that's why you don't drink alcohol. I wish you a good trip!

Telling about your family

When you are getting to know each other better you may talk about your family. In non-business circumstances, women talk to other women about their children. This is very natural after work and when you're in child-friendly surroundings, such as schools, sports fields and swimming pools. Be careful in businesslike situations: Dutch bosses want you to stick to your work when you're working! Talking about your family is something you do when you get confidential with people or when they ask questions about it. You can use the following words:

- ✔ **de ouders** (*der ow-ders*) (the parents)
- ✔ **de vader** (*der faa-der*) (the father)
- ✔ **de moeder** (*der moo-der*) (the mother)
- ✔ **de kinderen** (*der kin-der-ern*) (the children)
- ✔ **de zoon** (*der zoan*) (the son)
- ✔ **de jongen** (*der yong-er*) (the boy)
- ✔ **de dochter** (*der dokh-ter*) (the daughter)
- ✔ **het meisje** (*het may-sher*) (the girl)
- ✔ **de broers en zussen** (*der broors en zuh-sern*) (the brothers and sisters)
- ✔ **de grootvader** (*der khroat-faa-der*) (the grandfather)

> ✔ **de opa** (*der <u>oa</u>-paa*) (the grandpa)
>
> ✔ **de grootmoeder** (*der <u>khroat</u>-moo-der*) (the grandmother)
>
> ✔ **de oma** (*der <u>oa</u>-maa*) (the grandma)
>
> ✔ **de oom** (*der oam*) (the uncle)
>
> ✔ **de tante** (*der <u>tan</u>-ter*) (the aunt)
>
> ✔ **de neef** (*der nayf*) (the cousin, male)
>
> ✔ **de neef, het neefje** (*het <u>nayf</u>-jer*) (the nephew)
>
> ✔ **de nicht** (*der nikht*) (the cousin, female)
>
> ✔ **de nicht, het nichtje** (*der nikht*) (the niece)
>
> ✔ **de schoonfamilie** (*der <u>skhoan</u>-fa-mee-lee*) (the in-laws)
>
> ✔ **de schoonvader** (*der <u>skhoan</u>-faa-der*) (the father-in-law)
>
> ✔ **de schoonmoeder** (*der <u>skhoan</u>-moo-der*) (the mother-in-law)
>
> ✔ **de schoonzoon** (*der <u>skhoan</u>-zoan*) (the son in law)
>
> ✔ **de schoondochter** (*der <u>skhoan</u>-dokh-ter*) (the daughter-in-law)
>
> ✔ **de schoonzus** (*der <u>skhoan</u>-zuhs*) (the sister-in-law)
>
> ✔ **de zwager** (*der <u>svaa</u>-kher*) (the brother-in-law)

Divorce is almost as popular as family life in the Netherlands. In the larger cities you'll meet a lot of **alleenstaanden** (*a-layn-<u>staan</u>-dern*) (singles). Some of them stay single, others have relationships but keep away from marriage.

Dutch has many words for the people you are related to. A man who mentions **mijn vriend Marcel** (*mayn freent <u>mar</u>-sel*), probably met Marcel at school or when studying. They have kept in touch. Whenever a woman talks about **mijn vriend** (*mayn freent*) (without mentioning the name) she is probably refers to her partner in life. When she mentions **mijn vriendin Gerda** (*mayn freen-<u>din</u> <u>khehr</u>-daa*), she probably refers to a school or study friend with whom she kept in touch. Conversely, when a man talks about **mijn vriendin** (*mayn freen-<u>din</u>*), he is probably referring to his life partner.

As the words **mijn vriend** and **mijn vriendin** may cause confusion it's safer to use **mijn partner** (*mayn <u>part</u>-ner*) when talking about your life partner.

A married man says **mijn vrouw** (*mayn frow*) when referring to his wife. Elderly men or younger men who want to indicate a certain distance to their partner call her **mijn echtgenote** (*mayn <u>ekht</u>-kher-noa-ter*) (my spouse). A married woman says **mijn man** (*mayn man*) when referring to her husband. Elderly women or younger women who want to indicate a certain distance to their partner refer to her him as **mijn echtgenoot** (*mayn ekht-kher-noat*).

Talkin' the Talk

 Cilla has met Gabriele Neuland from München at the election ceremony of Secretary of the Year in Amsterdam. Gabriele is an executive secretary working with Golfwagen in Amsterdam. When Cilla and Gabriele meet for the second time they talk about their families.

Cilla: **Heb je broers en zussen?**
hep yer broors en zuh-sern
Have you got any brothers and sisters?

Gabriele: **Ik heb één zus in Duitsland.**
ik hep ayn zuhs in doaits-lant
I've got one sister in Germany.

Cilla: **Wat toevallig, ik heb ook één zus.**
vat too-fa-likh ik hep oak ayn zuhs
What a coincidence, I have one sister as well!

Gabriele: **Is ze ouder of jonger dan jij?**
is zer ow-der of yong-er dan yay
Is she older or younger than you are?

Cilla: **Ze is ouder. En die van jou?**
zer is ow-der. en dee fan yow
She's older. And yours?

Gabriele: **De mijne ook, wat toevallig!**
der may-ner oak vat too-fa-likh
Mine is older as well, what a coincidence!

Cilla: **Heeft jouw zus kinderen?**
hayft yow zuhs oak kin-der-ern
Has your sister got any children?

Gabriele: **Ja, twee: een jongen en een meisje.**
ya tvay ern yong-ern en ern may-sher
Yes, two, a boy and a girl.

Cilla: **Nou, dan hebben we nu een verschil gevonden: mijn zus is niet getrouwd en heeft geen kinderen.**
now dan heh-bern ver nuw ern fer-skhil kher-fon-dern mayn zus is neet kher-trowt en hayft khayn kin-der-ern)
Well then, we've found a difference now: my sister is not married and has no children.

Words to Know

ouder	<u>ow</u>-der	older
jonger	<u>yong</u>-er	younger
toevallig	too-<u>fa</u>-likh	by coincidence
en die van jou?	en dee fan yow	and yours?
een verschil	ern fer-<u>skhil</u>	a difference
getrouwd	kher-<u>trowt</u>	married

Negating: 'niet' and 'geen'

Dutch has two ways of negating. The first is by combining **niet** (*neet*) with a verb.

- ✔ **Mijn zus is niet getrouwd.** (*mayn zuhs is neet kher-<u>trowt</u>*) (My sister is not married.)
- ✔ **Ik ben niet rijk.** (*ik ben neet rayk*) (I am not rich.)
- ✔ **Ik woon niet in Amsterdam.** (*ik voan neet in am-ster-<u>dam</u>*) (I don't live in Amsterdam.)
- ✔ **Ik luister niet naar jou.** (*ik <u>loai</u>-ster neet naar yow*) (I don't listen to you.)

The second is by combining **geen** with a noun: either a person or a thing.

- ✔ **Mijn zus heeft geen kinderen.** (*mayn zuhs hayft khayn <u>kin</u>-derern*) (My sister has no children.)
- ✔ **Ik heb geen geld.** (*ik hep khayn khelt*) (I have no money.)
- ✔ **Ik heb geen auto.** (*ik hep khayn <u>ow</u>-tow*) (I have no car.)

Between **geen** (*khayn*) and the person or thing you may place an adjective that tells something about the person or thing.

- ✔ **Mijn zus heeft geen kleine kinderen.** (*mayn <u>zus</u>-ter hayft khayn <u>klay</u>-nern <u>kin</u>-der-ern*) (My sister has no small children.)
- ✔ **Ik heb geen Engelse ponden.** (*ik hep khayn <u>eng</u>-erl-ser <u>pon</u>-dern*) (I have no English pounds.)
- ✔ **In heb geen zwarte auto.** (*ik hep khayn <u>svar</u>-ter <u>ow</u>-tow*) (I have no black car.)

CULTURAL WISDOM

Dealing with your neighbours

The Dutch spend a lot of time in and around the house, especially in winter. Their house is their castle, and generally they don't like people to drop in uninvited unless they're very good friends. When they ask you: **Kom eens langs** (kom aynslangs) (Drop by one day) you should respond: **Wanneer komt dat uit?** (va-<u>nayr</u> komt dat oait) (What is convenient for you?). They will have a look in their diary or first have to check with their partner. Then they will tell you when: in the morning or in the evening, for coffee, before dinner or just for a drink. If you are very familiar with your neighbours and sometimes just walk in, don't do that during dinner time, which is between 6 and 7 p.m. Your neighbours will feel embarrassed. Similarly, your neighbours will avoid visiting you while you are having dinner.

Talking about the Weather

The Dutch like to talk about the weather. Even when you work and live in a town, the weather is important: what are you going to wear, what are you going to do, are you going to walk, cycle, or take the bus to work, and even how moody will your colleagues be today? Talking about the weather is a favourite pastime among the Dutch. Here are some phrases to join them:

How's the weather?

Start your sentence with **het is** (*het is*) (it is):

- **Het is fris.** (*het is fris*) (It's chilly.)
- **Het is koud.** (*het is kowt*) (It's cold.)
- **Het is mooi weer.** (*het is moay vayr*) (It's nice weather.)
- **Het is warm.** (*het is varm*) (It's warm.)
- **Het is heet.** (*het is hayt*) (It's hot.)

Note that Dutchmen start their chat about the weather mentioning things that the person with whom they're talking will probably have noticed too! In order to share your feelings about the weather (happiness, disappointment or anger) you can add the word **hè** (*heh*) and then make your sentence a question by raising the tone at the end of the sentence. For instance, **Het is koud hè?** (*het is kowt heh*) (It's cold, isn't it?) or **Het is heet hè?** (*het is hayt heh*) (It's hot, isn't it?). This remark in the form of a question will cause a reaction, probably something like: **Ik moest krabben** (*ik moost <u>kra</u>-bern*)

(I had to scrape the ice off my car windows) or **Ja, hadden we maar airco** (*yaa ha-dern ver maar air-co*) (Yes, I wish we had air conditioning).

As Dutch weather can be very changeable, the following weather descriptions will come in handy:

- ✔ **Het is zonnig.** (*het is zo-nikh*) (It is sunny.)
- ✔ **Het is bewolkt.** (*het is ber-volkt*) (It's cloudy.)
- ✔ **Het is mistig.** (*het is mis-tikh*) (It's misty.)
- ✔ **Het is regenachtig.** (*het is ray-khern-akh-tikh*) (It's rainy.)
- ✔ **Het is buiig.** (*het is boai-ikh*) (It's showery.)
- ✔ **Het is winderig.** (*het is vin-der-ikh*) (It's windy.)
- ✔ **Het vriest.** (*het freest*) (It's freezing.)

Watching the weather forecast on TV, you might hear some of the next sentences:

- ✔ **Het gaat regenen.** (*het khaat ray-kher-nern*) (It's going to rain.)
- ✔ **Het klaart op.** (*het klaart op*) (The sky is clearing up.)
- ✔ **We krijgen zonnige perioden.** (*wer kray-gern zon-ner-ger peh-ri-oh-dern*) (There will be sunny spells.)
- ✔ **Het houdt op met regenen.** (*het howt op met ray-kher-nern*) (It will stop raining.)
- ✔ **Het gaat onweren.** (*het khaat on-vay-rern*) (There will be thunder.)
- ✔ **Het gaat vriezen.** (*het khaat free-zern*) (It's going to freeze.)
- ✔ **'s Ochtends is er kans op mist.** (*sokh-terns is ehr kans op mist*) (In the morning it might be foggy.)
- ✔ **'s Ochtends is er kans op gladheid.** (*sokh-terns is ehr kans op khlat-hayt*) (In the morning it might be slippery.)

Talking about the temperature

When the person you talk to about the weather has said something in reaction to your remark, you might confirm your shared observations by adding some detail, like the temperature, saying:

- ✔ **Het is min 10.** (*het is min teen*) (It's minus ten degrees.)
- ✔ **Het is 10 graden onder nul.** (*het is teen khraa-dern on-der nuhl*) (It's 10 °C below zero.)

▮ ✔ **Het is 30 graden in de schaduw.** (*het is <u>dher</u>-tikh <u>khraa</u>-dern in der <u>skhaa</u>-duw*) (It's thirty degrees in the shade.)

And finish the chat saying:

Morgen wordt het nog kouder. (<u>mor</u>*-khern vort het nokh <u>kow</u>-der*) (Tomorrow it will be even colder.)

or:

Morgen wordt het nog warmer. (<u>mor</u>*-khern vort het nokh <u>var</u>-mer*) (Tomorrow it will be even hotter.)

Talkin' the Talk

Gerda and Jessica are members of the same gym. In summer they do some open-air sports as well, such as biking or running. They have agreed on running on Saturday morning, 10 o'clock. They meet in the gym.

Gerda: **Hallo Jessica, hoe gaat het?**
ha-<u>loa</u> yeh-see-kaa hoo khaat het
Hi Jessica, how are you?

Jessica: **Hallo Gerda, met mij gaat het prima, maar ik ben bang dat het gaat regenen!**
ha-<u>loa</u> <u>kher</u>-daa met may khaat het <u>pree</u>-maa maar ik ben bang dat het khaat <u>ray</u>-kher-nern
Hi Gerda, I am fine, but I'm afraid it's going to rain!

Gerda: **Denk je dat echt? Het weerbericht zegt dat het vanmiddag gaat regenen.**
denk yer dat ekht. het <u>veer</u>-ber-rikht zekht dat het fan-<u>mi</u>-dakh khaat <u>ray</u>-ker-nern
Do you really think so? The weather forecast says that it is going to rain this afternoon.

Jessica: **Nou, het is nu al erg bewolkt. We hebben gepland om de lange route te lopen, maar misschien is het beter om de korte te nemen.**
now het is nuw al erkh ber-<u>volkt</u>. ver <u>heh</u>-bern kher-<u>plehnt</u> om der <u>lang</u>-er <u>roo</u>-ter ter <u>loa</u>-pern, maar mi-<u>skheen</u> is het <u>bay</u>-ter om der <u>kor</u>-ter ter <u>nay</u>-mern
Well, it's very cloudy already. We planned to run the long course, but maybe it's better to take the short one.

Gerda:	**Ik wil dolgraag de lange lopen. Kijk, de lucht klaart op, laten we nu gaan! In het park kunnen we nog besluiten of we de lange of de korte route nemen.**
	ik vil dol-khraakh der lang-er loa-pern. Kayk der luhkht klaart op laa-tern wer nuw khaan. in het park kuh-nern ver nokh ber-sloai-tern of ver der lang-er of der kor-ter roo-ter nay-mern
	I would love to run the long one. Look, the sky is clearing up, let's go now! In the park we can still decide whether to take the long or the short course.
Jessica:	**OK, laten we dan gaan!**
	oa-kay laa-tern ver dan khaan
	Okay, let's go then.

Words to Know

bang zijn	*bang zayn*	to be afraid
het weerbericht	*het veer-ber-rikht*	the weather forecast
een route lopen	*ern roo-ter loa-pern*	to walk/run a course
laten we gaan	*laa-tern ver khaan*	let's go
het park	*het park*	the park

Chapter 6

Enjoying a Meal and Eating Out

· ·

In This Chapter

▶ Enjoying your meal

▶ Setting the table

▶ Essential verbs at the table

▶ Choosing your restaurant

▶ Entering a restaurant and sitting down

▶ What's on the menu?

▶ Taking your time for dinner

▶ The take-away food verb: *meenemen*

▶ Shopping for food

▶ Finding what you're looking for

▶ Shopping for food at the traditional market

· ·

*F*ood, eating habits, and eating out are some of the best ways to get to know a country. Whether you are cooking yourself and having dinner with friends or having a business lunch: it's always useful to know how to talk about food.

Enjoy Your Meal

Eating out in the Netherlands is an international experience. Especially in the western part of the Netherlands it's difficult to find restaurants with 'typical' Dutch food: it's easier to find restaurants with non-Dutch food!

Until some 30 years ago the traditional Dutch meal consisted of (boiled) potatoes, vegetables and meat. After 1950, when many people came back from the former Dutch Indies, 'Chinese food' became popular for eating out. It was not actually food from China, but the food Chinese people prepared in the Indies for their masters: spicy and sweet-and-sour. After 1960, Italian food entered the Dutch kitchen. It was mostly considered fast food. Travelling abroad became more and more popular and so did food that people got to know on

their

holidays, such as Spanish and Greek. This process went on in the 1970s and 1980s. Hamburger chains introduced fast food, and in the 1990s supermarkets started to sell fast food too. As a counterbalance to all this high-calorie food the 'nouvelle cuisine' became popular in the more expensive restaurants: refined international food. You can recognise this kind of restaurant by the carefully set tables with lots of wine glasses and white tablecloths.

The big cities offer a large variety of restaurants to choose from, from virtually every country. Of course, you'll also find these elsewhere in Europe, except for the Chinese-Indonesian ones from the former Dutch Indies. You'll recognise the Chinese-Indonesian restaurants by their traditional look: generally they are decorated with red and gold or green and gold. Try one of them! As an exception to most other restaurants, they also serve hot lunches, and their service is quick.

For expensive business lunches and dinners 'nouvelle cuisine' is still popular. Ask your colleagues for the names of good restaurants! In the bookshops near stations, you'll find all kinds of restaurant guides.

Is it time to eat?

Traditionally, the Dutch had three meals: breakfast, lunch and dinner. Breakfast is losing its popularity in many Dutch homes, but hotels will serve it in the morning in between 7 and 10. The hotel breakfast is generally international. It has juice, cereals, milk products, bread, butter, marmalade, cheese, sliced cold meat, and fruit.

Dutch breakfast at home is modest: a glass of juice, a cup of tea or coffee, maybe some cereals. The traditional slice of bread with cheese, marmalade or **chocoladehagel** (*shoa-koa-laa-der-haa-kherl*) (chocolate sprinkling) is disappearing. In the western part of Holland many commuters take their breakfast in their car while in the traffic jam: a breakfast drink or some coffee from home and a wrapped snack or candy bar. Train stations offer breakfast drinks, hot coffee, and snacks.

Lunch is somewhere between 12 o'clock and 12.30. If you are from the southern part of Europe, you will be disappointed! Dutch lunch is plain: some bread rolls with ham or cheese and a glass of milk. People often bring their own lunch from home: a sandwich or some fruit. Having lunch takes them just 10 minutes. As the law obliges employers to organise a one-hour lunch break, people spend the rest of the time on their mobiles, browsing the Internet or going out for a walk.

Lunches are more elaborate when taken in a restaurants. Restaurants offer something warm in combination with bread rolls: soup, a slice of pizza or a **kroket** (croquette). As nowadays only farmers and shift workers have their main meal at noon, a business lunch, even when it is taken in a starred restaurant, will always be a light meal.

Dinner is the main meal. You have it somewhere between 6 and 8 at home or between 7 and 10 o'clock in a restaurant. The dinner at home can be anything. A small group of Dutch people stick to their traditional potatoes, meat, and vegetables. Processed food and fast food are becoming popular. The supermarkets offer a wide range of prepared food that can be heated in the oven or microwave. At home dinner consists of a main dish and some dessert. The dessert may be fruit, but it generally is one of the hundreds of dairy products offered in supermarkets, such as **vla** (custard).

In restaurants, three dishes are offered: a first course, a main course. and dessert. Coffee or tea are served as well, or you go to some other place to have them there. Many people, especially women, skip one of the dishes, either first course or dessert. They wait for the others to finish their course – the main course is eaten by all guests at the same time.

Setting the Table

When you're eating in a restaurant you'll find on your table the following items:

- ✔ **het glas** (*het khlas*) (the glass)
- ✔ **het bord** (*het bort*) (the plate)
- ✔ **het soepbord** (*het soop-bort*) (the soup bowl)
- ✔ **het servet** (*het sehr-fet*) (the napkin)
- ✔ **het mes** (*het mes*) (the knife)
- ✔ **de vork** (*der fork*) (the fork)
- ✔ **de lepel** (*der lay-perl*) (the spoon)
- ✔ **het lepeltje** (*het lay-perl-tyer*) (the small spoon)
- ✔ **het kopje** (*het kop-yer*) (the cup)

When something is missing on the table, you can ask the waiter:

> **Mag ik een lepel alstublieft?** (*makh ik ern lay-perl als-tuw-bleeft*) (May I have a spoon, please?)

When eating at home you might use the same items for setting the table in the traditional way, either with **een tafellaken** (*ern taa-ferl-laa-kern*) (a table-cloth) or with **placemats** (*plays-mats*) (place-mats). Or you can join most young Dutch people and have dinner seated on **de bank** (*der bank*) (the couch) while watching TV.

Using more of them: plurals

You can divide the plurals of Dutch nouns (nouns are words that can be preceded by **de** (*der*), **het** (*het*) or **een** (*ern*)) in two main groups. The biggest group has a plural ending in **-en**: **de borden** (*der bor-dern*) (the plates), **de vorken** (*der for-kern*) (the forks).

The second group has a plural ending in **-s**, such as **de lepels** (*der lay-perls*) (the spoons), **de kopjes** (*der kop-yers*) (the cups).

How can you know whether the plural suffix is **-en** or **-s**? Words that end in **-el**, **-en**, **-er**, **-em**, **-erd**, **-e**, **-ie** or **-aar**, get an **-s**. It may be difficult to remember this long row, but there is some logic to it: all the mentioned suffixes of these words are unstressed. So words that end in an unstressed syllable, often get **-s**:

- **de tafel** (*der taa-ferl*) (the table)

  de tafels (*der taa-ferls*) (the tables)
- **de jongen** (*der yong-ern*) (the boy)

  de jongens (*der yong-ers*) (the boys)
- **de moeder** (*der moo-der*) (the mother)

  de moeders (*der moo-ders*) (the mothers)
- **de bezem** (*der bay-zerm*) (the broom)

  de bezems (*der bay-zerms*) (the brooms)
- **de lieverd** (*der lee-fert*) (the darling)

  de lieverds (*der lee-ferts*) (the darlings)
- **de secretaresse** (*der seh-crer-taa-reh-ser*) (the secretary)

  de secretaresses (*der seh-crer-taa-reh-sers*)
- **de vakantie** (*der faa-kan-see*) (the holiday)

  de vakanties (*der faa-kan-sees*) (the holidays)
- **de winnaar** (*der vi-naar*) (the winner)

  de winnaars (*der vi-naars*) (the winners)

Almost all diminutives (words that are used to indicate small things or small persons) end in an unstressed **-je** or **-tje**, such as **het kopje** (*het kop-yer*) (the little cup) en **het lepeltje** (*het lay-perl-tyer*). Following the general rules for plurals they get an **-s**: **de kopjes** (*der kop-yers*) (the little cups) en **de lepeltjes** (*der lay-perl-tyers*) (the little spoons).

The second, far bigger, group consists of words that do not end in an unstressed **-el**, **-en**, **-er**, **-em**, **-erd**, **-e**, **-ie** or **-aar**. They get **-en** for the plural.

> ✔ **het bord** (*het bort*) (the plate)
>
> **de borden** (*der bor-dern*) (the plates)
>
> ✔ **het land** (*het lant*) (the country)
>
> **de landen** (*der lan-dern*) (the countries)
>
> ✔ **de deur** (*der dur*) (the door)
>
> **de deuren** (*der du-rern*) (the countries)
>
> ✔ **de fiets** (*der feets*) (the bike)
>
> **de fietsen** (*der feet-sern*) (the bikes)

So far so good. When you are speaking, you won't have too many difficulties with the plurals, because you won't have time to think of the rules. Very often you will just imitate other people. After some time, you will know most plurals by intuition. However, when you start writing, there are complications in the spelling of the words.

It's beyond the reach of this book to treat them all, but here are some examples:

> ✔ **de kat** (*der kat*) (the cat)
>
> **de katten** (*der ka-tern*) (the cats)
>
> ✔ **het mes** (*het mes*) (the knife)
>
> **de messen** (*der meh-sern*) (the knives)
>
> ✔ **de pil** (*der pil*) (the pill)
>
> **de pillen** (*der pi-lern*) (the pills)
>
> ✔ **de rok** (*der rok*) (the skirt)
>
> **de rokken** (*der ro-kern*) (the skirts)
>
> ✔ **de rug** (*der ruhkh*) (the back)
>
> **de ruggen** (*der ru-khern*) (the backs)

In each of these words a doubling occurs of the consonant at the end of the first syllable, in order to keep the vowel sound short. Consonants are all letters that are not a, e, i, o, or u.

In other cases you'll have to employ a trick in order write the long vowels (a, e, i, o and u) correctly. Compare the spelling of the singulars with that of the plurals:

✔ **de baan** (*der baan*) (the job)

   de banen (*der baa-nern*) (the jobs)

✔ **het been** (*het bayn*) (the leg)

   de benen (*der bay-nern*) (the legs)

✔ **de boom** (*der boam*) (the tree)

   de bomen (*der boa-mern*) (the trees)

✔ **de muur** (*der muwr*) (the wall)

   de muren (*der muw-rern*) (the walls)

For more information about short and long vowels see Chapter 1.

Most important changes in the spelling of the consonants take place in words that end in -f or -s. The singular **de brief** (*der breef*) (the letter) is written as **de brieven** (*der bree-fern*) in plural. The singular **het huis** (*het hoais*) (the house) becomes **de huizen** (*der hoai-zern*).

You are ready to use more of them now!

Essential Verbs at the Table

Drinken (*drin-kern*) (to drink) and **eten** (*ay-tern*) (to eat) are essential to stay alive and so it's important to be able to use them when you're living in the Netherlands.

To drink: the verb 'drinken'

The verb **drinken** is regular. Take off the **-en** and you have the first person. For the second (you informal) and the third (he, she and you formal) person just ad -t! For the plurals (we, you plural informal and they) you can take the whole verb or infinitive: **drinken**.

Conjugation	Pronunciation
ik drink	*ik drink*
jij drinkt	*yay drinkt*
u drinkt	*uw drinkt*
hij/zij/het drinkt	*hay/zay/het drinkt*
wij drinken	*vay drin-kern*
jullie drinken	*yuw-lee drin-kern*
zij drinken	*zay drin-kern*

To eat: the verb 'eten'

The verb **eten** (ay-tern) is regular as well. However, it has some complications when spelling it. In order to make the **e** (*ay*) sound like a long vowel you have to double it in the first, second and third person. (I, you, he, she, and you formal).

Conjugation	Pronunciation
ik eet	*ik ayt*
jij eet	*yay ayt*
u eet	*uw eet*
hij/zij/het eet	*hay/zay/het ayt*
wij eten	*vay ay-tern*
jullie eten	*yuw-lee ay-tern*
zij eten	*zay ay-tern*

At the Restaurant

Eating out is popular for singles and couples. A lot of Dutch people consider eating out a luxury – people go to restaurants on holidays such as Boxing Day or when they have something to celebrate. Families with young children will visit hamburger chains and pancake houses on family outings. Grill restaurants are popular when the children grow older.

Choosing your restaurant

Big towns have a large choice of restaurants. An **Argentijns grillrestaurant** (*ar-khern-tayns khril-res-to-rant*) (an Argentinian grill restaurant) offers you large and low-priced meat dishes.

In seaport towns such as Amsterdam and Rotterdam you may find a genuine **Chinees restaurant** (*shee-nays res-to-rant*) (a Chinese restaurant). The food in Chinese restaurants is very different from the Chinese-Indonesian restaurants. Dutch people erroneously call the traditional Chinese-Indonesian restaurants **de Chinees** (*der shee-nays*) (The Chinese). Chinese food from China is not spicy and not sweet and sour like the Chinese-Indonesian from the former Dutch East Indies colony, the present Indonesia.

- ✔ **Eten bij de Chinees** (*ay-tern bay der shee-nays*) (to have Chinese-Indonesian food) has always been popular among those who want large meals for a reasonable price.

- ✔ **Frans eten** (*frans ay-tern*) (to go to a French restaurant) is possible in the big towns. **Franse restaurants** (*fran-ser res-to-rants*) (restaurants offering French cuisine) generally are exclusive and expensive.

- ✔ You will find **Indiase restaurants** (*in-deey-aa-ser res-to-rants*) (Indian food restaurants) in the larger towns.

- ✔ **Nederlandse restaurants** (*nay-der-lan-ser res-to-rants*) (Dutch restaurants) hardly exist and are very difficult to find. Only a few restaurants specialise in traditional Dutch food such as pancakes and peasoup, mostly for the tourists.

- ✔ **Thais** or **Vietnamees eten** (*tais/vyet-naa-mays ay-tern*) (to have Thai/Vietnamese food) is possible in a lot of restaurants in the big towns.

- ✔ **Visrestaurants** (*fis-res-to-rants*) (fish restaurants) can be found in larger towns and those with a harbour.

- ✔ **Internationaal eten** (*in-ter-na-shoa-naal ay-tern*) (to have international food, in the categories Cajun or fusion, Greek, Italian, Mexican, Spanish, and so on) is possible in almost every town.

- ✔ If you want to find a **vegetarisch restaurant** (*fay-kher-taa-rees resto-rant*) (vegetarian restaurant), buy a good guide in a bookshop or look at www. iens.nl.

- ✔ **Zakenrestaurants** (*zaa-kern-res-to-rants*) (Business restaurants with three or more stars) are generally expensive and not necessarily in the city centre. You can find them in special guides or by recommendation of your colleagues. You generally go to them by car and they have good parking facilities.

Places for lunch

Dutch lunches are plain and generally not hot.

- ✔ If you're not too hungry, try a **haringkraam** (*haa-ring-kraam*) (a seafood car) for a **haring** (*haa-ring*) (herring) or **een lekkerbekje** (*ern leh-ker-beh-kyer*) (deep-fried fish fillet).

- ✔ If you don't mind calories, try a **patatkraam** (*pa-tat-kraam*) (a fries/chips stall) for a **patatje** (*pa-ta-tyer*) (portion of fries/chips) or **frikadel** (*free-kan-del*) (minced-meat hotdog).

- ✔ If you prefer something healthier, go for a **broodje gezond** (*broa-tyer kher-zont*) (a CLT roll with cheese, egg, tomato, and some lettuce or cucumber) in a **croissanterie** (*kra-san-ter-ree*) (a croissant shop) or **een broodjeszaak** (*ern broa-tyers-zaak*) (a sandwich bar).

- ✔ In a **snackbar** (*snehk-bar*) (a snack bar) or a **cafetaria** (*ka-fer-taa-ree-yaa*) (a cafeteria) you can have a lot of the things mentioned above plus soup or an **uitsmijter** (*oait-smay-ter*) (fried eggs and ham on two slices of bread).

- ✔ In some towns you may find a **poffertjeskraam** (*po-fer-tyerskraam*). These traditional tiny pancakes are eaten with sugar and butter. Children like them very much.

- ✔ **Een pannenkoek** (*ern pa-nern-kook*) (a pancake) in a **pannenkoekenhuis** (*pa-nern-koo-kern-hoais*) (pancake house) is a substantial lunch, especially when you take the traditional **spekpannenkoek** (*spek-pa-nern-kook*). This pancake is a curious mix of sweet and salty: it has a lot of bacon on it and is eaten with syrup.

At the end of the afternoon, you may long for an alcoholic beverage and something salty. If you want to go international, find a tapas bar and accompany a glass of wine with small portions of olives, fish, or meat.

In case you are looking for something really Dutch, enter a **bruin café** (*ern broain ka-fay*) (a 'brown café' or pub) and have **een biertje** (*ern beer-tyer*) (a beer) or **een borrel** (*ern bo-rerl*) (a drink). In the traditional brown café, snacks are limited to **een portie kaas** (*ern por-see kaas*) (a portion of cheese) or **een portie leverworst** (*ern por-see lay-fer-vorst*) (a portion of liver sausage).

In a **café** (*ka-fay*) (a café, pub, or bar) alcohol is the main thing you will find. Some cafés serve **een portie saté** (*ern por-see saa-tay*) (a portion of satay), pieces of pork meat on a stick, served with a warm, spicy peanut sauce, or perhaps **een portie bitterballen** (*ern por-see bit-ter-bah-lern*) (a type of croquette, served as an appetiser). There are many different kinds of **cafés**, mostly with their own group of clients, but they will not be as old and brown as the **bruin café**.

Eating herring

The older generation loves herring. Though many young people are horrified by the thought of eating raw fish, the salty herring, garnished with onions, is offered as an exquisite bite at parties and receptions. Especially, the first young herring of the season, **nieuwe haring** (_nee_-wer _haa_-ring) (new herring), sold in May, is exquisite and expensive. However, in the big towns and on traditional markets fish shops sell this Dutch specialty to those who love it. Try one when you have drunk a lot of beer the night before. They say herring is a cure for hangovers!

When you're really hungry, long for a beer or glass of wine and you don't want to spend too much on food, try an **eetcafé** (_ern ayt_-ka-fay) (bar/pub serving meals). The owners will serve you simple food in a relaxed ambiance.

Coffeeshops (_ko_-fee-shops) (coffee shops) are places to buy and enjoy marihuana legally. See a guide for a selection!

Making a reservation

For some restaurants you can make a reservation on the Internet. You can also call after three in the afternoon and make a reservation for the night or for the weekend. Make sure to put in a reservation for trendy and business restaurants! The following sentences will be helpful:

- ✔ **Ik wil graag een tafel reserveren.** (_ik vil khraakh ern taa-ferl rayser-vay-rern_) (I would like to reserve a table.)

- ✔ **Ik wil een tafel reserveren voor vier personen om zeven uur. Is dat mogelijk?** (_ik vil ern taa-ferl ray-ser-vay-rern foar feer per-soa-nern om zay-fern uwr. is dat moa-kher-lerk_) (I would like to reserve a table for four at 7 p.m. Is that possible?)

In order to be specific, you have to mention the time and day. For example:

- ✔ **voor vanavond** (_foar fa-naa-font_) (for tonight)

- ✔ **voor morgenavond** (_foar mor-khern-aa-font_) (for tomorrow night)

- ✔ **voor zaterdagavond** (_foar zaa-ter-dakh-aa-font_) (for Saturday night)

- ✔ **voor zondagavond** (_foar zon-dakh-aa-font_) (for Sunday night)

The following complete sentences might come in handy:

- **Ik wil graag een tafel voor vanavond reserveren.** (*ik vil khraakh ern taa-ferl foar fa-naa-font ray-ser-fay-rern*) (I would like to reserve a table for tonight.)

- **Heeft u een vrije tafel voor morgenavond om zeven uur?** (*hayft uw ern fray-yer taa-ferl foar mor-khern-aa-font om zay-fern uwr*) (Have you got a free table for tomorrow night, 7 p.m.?)

Talkin' the Talk

Raymond van Dieren and his colleague Marcel Westendorp want to try out the Restaurant Newton. Marcel calls the restaurant, in order to make a reservation.

Restaurant:	**Newton, met René.**
	nyoo-tern, met rer-nay
	Newton, René speaking.
Marcel:	**Hoi, ik wil graag een tafel reserveren voor vanavond.**
	hoy ik vil khraakh ern taa-ferl ray-ser-vay-rern foar fa-naa-font
	Hi, I would like to make a reservation for tonight.
Restaurant:	**Voor hoeveel personen?**
	foar hoo-fayl per-soa-nern
	For how many persons?
Marcel:	**Voor twee personen graag. Heb je een tafel vrij om acht uur?**
	foar tvay per-soa-nern khraakh. hep yer ern taa-ferl fray om akht uwr
	For two persons please. Have you got a free table at 8 o'clock?
Restaurant:	**Het spijt me, om acht uur zijn we volgeboekt. Er is een tafel vrij om half negen.**
	het spayt mer om akht uwr zayn ver fol-kherbookt. er is ern taa-ferl fray om half nay-khern
	I'm sorry, we are fully booked for 8 o'clock. There is a table free at 8.30.
Marcel:	**Nou, half negen is ook goed.**
	now, half nay-khern is oak khoot
	Well, 8.30 is all right.
Restaurant:	**Mag ik uw naam misschien?**
	makh ik uw naam mis-kheen
	What's your name, please?
Marcel:	**Westendorp.**
	ves-tern-dorp
	Westendorp.

Restaurant:	**OK, ik heb een tafel voor u gereserveerd om half negen vanavond.**
	oa-kay ik hep ern taa-ferl foar uw kher-ray-ser-fayrt om half nay-khern fa-naa-font
	Okay, I have reserved a table for you at 8.30 tonight.
Marcel:	**Bedankt. Tot vanavond.**
	ber-dankt. tot fa-naa-font
	Thank you. See you tonight.

Entering a Restaurant and Sitting Down

If you go into a restaurant without a reservation, the following sentences might be useful:

- **Heeft u plaats voor twee personen?** (*hayft uw plaats foar tvay persoa-nern*) (Have you got place for two persons?)

- **Nee, het spijt me, we zijn volgeboekt voor vanavond.** (*nay het spayt mer ver zayn fol-kher-bookt foar fa-naa-font*) (No, I'm sorry, we are fully booked for tonight.)

- **Kunt u wachten bij de bar? Over 10 minuten komt een tafel vrij.** (*kunt uw vakh-tern bay der bar. oa-fer teen mi-nuw-tern komt ern taa-ferl fray*) (Could you wait at the bar? There will be a table free in ten minutes.)

As soon as you sit down at your table the waiter will come and bring your menu. In case you haven't got anything to drink yet, he will ask you first what you would like. While you are studying the menu, you'll get your drink.

Talkin' the Talk

Marcel and Raymond enter the new restaurant where Marcel has reserved a table.

Marcel:	**Goedenavond, mijn naam is Westendorp.Ik heb een tafel gereserveerd voor twee personen.**
	khoo-dern-aa-font mayn naam is ves-terndorp. ik hep ern taa-ferl kher-ray-ser-fayrt foar tvay per-soa-nern
	Good evening, my name is Westendorp. I reserved a table for two persons.

Waiter:	**Goedenavond, gaat u hier zitten. Kan ik uw jassen aannemen?**
	khoo-dern-aa-font khaat uw heer zi-tern. Kan ik uw ya-sern aan-nay-mern
	Good evening. Please sit down here. Can I take your coats?
Marcel:	**Kunnen we misschien die tafel naast het raam krijgen?**
	kuh-nern ver mis-kheen dee taa-ferl naast het raam kray-khern
	Could we have that table near the window please?
Waiter:	**Jazeker, geen probleem. Gaat u zitten en ik breng u de menukaart.**
	yaa-zay-ker, kheen pro-blaym. khaat uw zi-tern en ik breng uw der mer-nuw-kaart
	Yes, of course, no problem. Please sit down and I'll bring you the menu.

Words to Know

gereserveerd	kher-ray-ser-_fayrt_	reserved
gaan zitten	khaan _zi_-tern	to sit down
jassen aannemen	_ya_-sern _aan_-nay-mern	to take coats
krijgen	_kray_-khern	to get
het menu	het mer-_nuw_	the menu

Getting what you want: the verb 'willen'

The easiest way to tell what you want is to say: **ik wil** (I want). The present tense of **willen** is regular.

Conjugation	_Pronunciation_
ik wil	_ik vil_
jij wilt/wil	_yay vilt/vil_
u wilt	_uw vilt_
hij/zij/het wil	_hay/zay/het vil_

Conjugation	Pronunciation
wij willen	*vay vi-lern*
jullie willen	*yuw-lee vi-lern*
zij willen	*zay vi-lern*

Ordering something special: 'graag'

It's okay to say **ik wil** (*ik vil*) (I want). However, you are much more polite when you add the word **graag** (*khraakh*) (it means something like 'please' or 'would like'). So you could say **Ik wil tomatensoep** (*ik vil toa-maa-tern-soo*p) but the waiter will be more helpful when you say **Ik wil graag tomatensoep** (*ik vil kraakh toa-maa-tern-soop*) (I would like tomato soup). **Ik wil graag een biertje** (*ik vil khraakh ern beer-tyer*) (I want a beer, please) is a good start to a nice evening!

A way to order urgently but politely is: **Geeft u mij alstublieft eerst een biertje** (*khayft uw may al-stuw-bleeft ayrst ern beer-tyer*) (Please, give me a beer first).

> **Geeft u mij alstublieft advies.** (*khayft uw may al-stuw-bleeft at-fees*)
> (Please, give me advice.)

Do you want to be even more polite? In this case, don't say **Ik wil** in the present tense, but use the same verb in the past tense together with please: **ik wilde graag** (*ik vil-der khraakh*).

- ✔ **Ik wilde graag tomatensoep.** (*ik vil-der khraakh toa-maa-tern-soop*) (I would like tomato soup please.)

- ✔ **Ik wilde graag gemengde salade.** (*ik vil-der khraakh kher-meng-der sa-laa-der*) (I would like the mixed salad please.)

Beware! Some joker might answer you **En nu niet meer?** (*en nuw neet mayr*) (And now you don't want it any more?)

What's on the Menu?

Now the time has come to choose. What is on the menu depends of course on the kind of restaurant that you have chosen.

As the Netherlands is a small country with many means of communication, not many regional dishes are left. You'll find more regional specialties in sweet stores than in restaurants!

Having breakfast or not: that's the question

Dutch hotels will always offer you a breakfast. You might be offered the following things:

- ✔ **de boterham** (*der boa-ter-ram*) (the slice of bread)
- ✔ **het broodje** (*het broa-tyer*) (the bread roll)
- ✔ **de croissant** (*der kra-sant*) (the croissant)
- ✔ **de toast** (*der toast*) (the toast)
- ✔ **de kaas** (*der kaas*) (the cheese)
- ✔ **de vleeswaren** (*der flays-vaa-rern*) (sliced cold meat/cold cuts)
- ✔ **de boter** (*der boa-ter*) (the butter)
- ✔ **de granen** (*der khraa-nern*) (the cereals)
- ✔ **het sap** (*het sap*) (the juice)
- ✔ **de melk** (*der melk*) (the milk)
- ✔ **het sinaasappelsap** (*het see-naa-sa-perl-sap*) (the orange juice)
- ✔ **het ei** (*het ay*) (the egg)

Dutch breakfast is generally a light meal. Your egg will be boiled, unless you ask for **een omelet** (*ern oa-mer-let*) (an omelet) or **roerei** (*roor-ay*) (scrambled eggs).

Lunch strolling: to catch a flying bird

As soon as you're going to work in the Netherlands you will get acquainted with Dutch lunch habits. For most Dutch people lunch means nothing else but a simple bread roll and a short break. In towns a lunch stroll may be attractive. Big companies have canteens and if not, spending the lunch break is a personal thing – some people play a computer game, others make an urgent call home. In business working lunches may provide good food, but no relaxation. Canteens at companies, schools, and hospitals serve:

- ✔ **de soep** (*der soop*) (the soup)
- ✔ **het broodje kaas** (*het broa-tyer kaas*) (the cheese roll)
- ✔ **het broodje ham** (*het broa-tyer ham*) (the ham roll)
- ✔ **het broodje kroket** (*het broa-tyer kroa-ket*) (the croquette roll)
- ✔ **de uitsmijter** (*der oait-smay-ter*) (fried bacon and eggs served on slices of bread)

- **de tosti** (*der <u>tos</u>-tee*) (the toasted ham and cheese sandwich)
- **de melk** (*der melk*) (the milk)
- **de karnemelk** (*der <u>kar</u>-ner-melk*) (the buttermilk)
- **de appel** (*der <u>a</u>-perl*) (the apple)
- **de sinaasappel** (*der <u>see</u>-naa-sa-perl*) (the orange)
- **de banaan** (*der ba-<u>naan</u>*) (the banana)

Taking Your Time for Dinner

While breakfast and lunch are meals of minor importance for most Dutch people, dinner is not. Though dinner at home could be simple, when you're going to a restaurant you should take your time: one hour and a half or two hours at least, depending on the number of staff, the day of the week, and the kind of restaurant that you're visiting.

In countries such as France and Spain dinners always consist of three or more dishes. In the Netherlands, when you have dinner in a restaurant, you can take two or three courses: either a starter and the main dish, or the main dish, and a dessert. In most restaurants the main dish will not come before your companions have finished their starters, but generally, you can already have coffee or tea while the others are still having dessert. Coffee and tea for the others will come very soon after their desserts.

Starters

Soups and salads serve as starters. Here is a selection of Dutch soups that you can find on the menus:

- **tomatensoep** (*toa-<u>maa</u>-tern-soop*) (tomato soup)
- **kippensoep** (*<u>ki</u>-pern-soop*) (chicken soup)
- **groentesoep** (*<u>khroon</u>-ter-soop*) (vegetable soup)
- **champignonsoep** (*sham-peen-<u>yon</u>-soop*) (mushroom soup)
- **ossenstaartsoep** (*<u>o</u>-sern-staart-soop*) (oxtail soup)
- **aspergesoep** (*as-<u>pehr</u>-sher-soop*) (asparagus soup)
- And in winter, when it's cold: **erwtensoep** (*<u>ehr</u>-tern-soop*) or **snert** (*snehrt)* (pea soup).

Other popular starters are:

- **meloen met ham** (*mer-loon met ham*) (melon with ham)

- **haring met toast** (*haa-ring met toast*) (herring on toast)

- **Hollandse garnalen met citroenmayonaise** (*ho-lan-tser khar-naa-lern met see-troon-ma-yoa-neh-ser*) (Dutch shrimps and lemon mayonnaise)

- **gestoomde makreel met toast** (*kher-stoam-der ma-krayl met toast*) (steamed mackerel on toast)

- **gerookte paling met toast** (*kher-roak-ter paa-ling met toast*) (smoked eel on toast)

- **gemengde salade** (*kher-meng-der sa-laa-der*) (mixed salad)

- **groene salade met geitekaas** (*khroo-ner sa-laa-der met khay-terkaas*) (green salad with goat cheese)

- **gevulde aubergine** (*kher-fuhl-der oa-ber-zyeen*) (stuffed aubergine)

Main dishes

Traditional Dutch dishes consist of meat and boiled or fried potatoes. Additional vegetables will be served. Sometimes, salad is included, but generally salad has to be ordered separately. In the Netherlands, green salads are eaten after the main dish or as a side dish, unless they are offered as a starter. Here are some meat dishes:

- **biefstuk** (*beef-stuhk*) (steak)

- **kalfsentrecote** (*kalfs-an-trer-koat*) (veal prime rib)

- **kalfslever met madera** (*kalfs-lay-fer met ma-day-ra*) (calf's liver with Madeira)

- **lamskoteletten** (*lams-koa-ter-leh-tern*) (lamb chops)

Here is some **gevogelte** (*kher-foa-kherl-ter*) (poultry):

- **gevulde kalkoen** (*kher-fuhl-der kal-koon*) (stuffed turkey)

- **eendenborst** (*ayn-der-borst*) (duck breast)

- **kip met dragon** (*kip met draa-khon*) (chicken with tarragon)

- **kipfilet** (*kip-fee-lay*) (chicken breast)

Fish and seafood lovers will find:

- ✔ **gekookte mosselen** (*kher-koa-kter mo-ser-lern*) (boiled mussels)
- ✔ **gebakken tong** (*kher-ba-ker tong*) (fried sole)
- ✔ **gegrilde tonijn** (*kher-khril-der toa-nayn*) (grilled tuna fish)
- ✔ **gerookte zalm** (*kher-roak-ter zalm*) (smoked salmon)
- ✔ **zeebaars** (*zay-baars*) (bass)

Most dishes will be served with either:

- ✔ **gekookte aardappelen** (*kher-koak-ter aar-da-per-lern*) (boiled potatoes)
- ✔ **gebakken aardappelen** (*kher-ba-kern aar-da-per-lern*) (fried potatoes) or
- ✔ **(patat) frites** (*pa-tat freet*) (chips/fries)

Desserts

Dutch restaurants commonly offer many dishes as **nagerecht** (*naa-kherrekht*) including the following:

- ✔ **fruitsalade** (*froait-sa-laa-der*) (fruit salad)
- ✔ **aardbeien met ijs en slagroom** (*aart-bay-yern met ays en sla-khroam*) (strawberries with ice cream and whipped cream)
- ✔ **warme appeltaart met ijs en slagroom** (*var-mer a-perl-taart met ays en sla-khroam*) (warm apple pie with ice cream and whipped cream)
- ✔ **griesmeelpudding met bessensap** (*khrees-mayl-puh-ding met beh-sern-sap*) (semolina pudding with currant juice)
- ✔ **flensjes** (*flen-syers*) (crêpes)
- ✔ **chocolademousse** (*shoa-koa-laa-der-moos*) (chocolate mousse)

Another possibility is to have pastry with coffee or tea.

Drinks

When it comes to ordering **water** (*vaa-ter*) (water), **spa** or **mineraalwater** (*mee-ner-raal-vaa-ter*) (mineral water) you have the choice between the carbonated or non-carbonated water. The waiter of waitress will ask you: **Met of zonder koolzuur?** (*met of zon-der koal-zuwr*) (carbonated or non-carbonated water?) or **Met of zonder prik?** (*met of zon-der prik*) (with or without bubbles?).

Wine is usually offered by **een fles** (*ern fles*) (a bottle), **een karaf** (*ern kaa-raf*) (a carafe) or **een glas** (*ern khlas*) (a glass).

In the following list, you find a couple of common drinks, **dranken** (*dran-kern*), that you might find on the menu card:

✔ **het bier** (*het beer*) (the beer)

✔ **het tapbier** (*het tap-beer*) (the draft beer)

✔ **het pils** (*het pils*) (the bitter, lager beer)

✔ **de wijn** (*der vayn*) (the wine)

✔ **de rode wijn** (*der roa-der vayn*) (the red wine)

✔ **de witte wijn** (*der vi-ter vayn*) (the white wine)

✔ **de rosé** (*der roa-zay*) (the rosé wine)

✔ **de huiswijn** (*der hoais-vayn*) (the wine of the house, lowest quality)

✔ **de koffie** (*der ko-fee*) (the coffee)

✔ **de thee** (*der tay*) (the tea)

Talkin' the Talk

Marcel and Raymond have just sat down. The waiter brings them the menu and says:

Waiter:	**Kan ik u iets te drinken brengen terwijl u uw keuze maakt?**
	kan ik uw eets ter drin-kern breng-ern tehr-vayl uw uw ku-zer maakt
	Can I bring you something to drink while you are making your choice?
Marcel:	**Ja, ik wil graag een glas bier.**
	yaa ik vil khraakh ern khlas beer.
	Yes please, I would like a glass of beer
Waiter:	**Bier van de tap? We hebben gewoon bier en witbier.**
	beer fan der tap? ver heh-bern kher-voan beer en vit-beer
	Draft beer? We have lager and white beer.
Marcel:	**Witbier graag.**
	vit-beer khraakh
	White beer, please.
Waiter:	**En wat mag het voor u zijn?**
	en vat makh het foar uw zayn?
	What would you like?

Raymond: **Ik wil graag een glas droge rode wijn.**
             ik vil khraakh ern khlas <u>droa</u>-kher <u>roa</u>-der vayn
             I would like a glass of dry red wine.

Words to Know

een glas bier	ern khlas beer	a glass of beer
bier van de tap	beer fan der tap	draft beer
het witbier	het <u>vit</u>-beer	the white beer
een glas droge rode wijn	ern khlas <u>droa</u>-kher <u>roa</u>-der vayn	a glass of dry red wine

Ordering something unusual

You may need the following phrases to order something a little out of the ordinary:

- ✔ **Heeft u vegetarische schotels?** (*hayft uw fay-kher-<u>taa</u>-ree-ser <u>skhoa</u>-terls*) (Have you got vegetarian dishes?)

- ✔ **Heeft u iets zonder varkensvlees?** (*hayft uw eets <u>zon</u>-der <u>far</u>-kerns- flays*) (Have you got something without pork?)

- ✔ **Heeft u schotels voor diabetici?** (*hayft uw <u>skhoa</u>-terls foar dee-aa-<u>bay</u>-tee-see*) (Have you got dishes for diabetics?)

- ✔ **Heeft u porties voor kinderen?** (*hayft uw <u>por</u>-sees foar <u>kin</u>-derern*) (Have you got portions for children?)

Handling the routine question

Halfway through dinner the waiter will come to you and ask: **Is alles naar wens?** (*is <u>a</u>-lers naar vens*) (Is everything to your liking?). If you wish for anything special this is the moment to say what you want. If everything is to your liking the routine answer is: **Dank u, alles is in orde** (*dank uw alers is in <u>or</u>-der*) (Thank you, everything is fine).

Being polite: the verb 'mogen'

Mogen (to be allowed) is a verb that makes you sound more polite. In the single forms of the present tense the **o** changes to an **a**.

Conjugation	*Pronunciation*
ik mag	*ik makh*
jij mag	*yay makh*
hij/zij/het mag	*hay/zay/het makh*
wij mogen	*vay moa-khern*
jullie mogen	*yuw-lee moa-khern*
zij mogen	*zay moa-khern*

You can use this verb to ask the following questions:

✔ **Mag ik een glas bier?** (*makh ik ern khlas beer*) (May I have a glass of beer?)

✔ **Mag ik een glas wijn?** (*makh ik ern khlas vayn*) (May I have a glass of wine?)

✔ **Mag je hier roken?** (*makh yer heer roa-kern*) (Is it allowed to smoke here?)

After you have finished the main dish, the waiter may drop by again and ask: **Heeft het gesmaakt?** (*hayft het kher-smaakt*) (Did you enjoy your meal?). Now is the moment to be critical if you feel you need to be and you might say: **Nou, het vlees was een beetje aan de rauwe kant**. (*now het flays vas ern bay-tyer aan der row-ver kant*) (Well, the meat was a bit rare). The waiter may react: **Dat had u eerder moeten zeggen, dan hadden we u een medium gebracht!** (*dat hat uw ayr-der moo-tern zeh-khern dan ha-dern ver uw ern may-dee-uhm kher-brakht*) (You should have told us before, we would have brought you a medium!). If you are happy with the meal or don't want to make any fuss, you say: **Dank u, goed** (*dank uw khoot*) (Thank you, good), or, a bit stronger: **Dank u, erg goed** (*dank uw ehrkh khoot*) (very well) or, even more enthusiastic: **Dank u, uitstekend** (*dank uw oait-stay-kernt*) (excellent). You can also fit these words in a sentence: **Dank u, het heeft erg goed gesmaakt** (*dank uw het hayft ehrkh khoot kher-smaakt*) (Thank you, we enjoyed it a lot).

Smoking in restaurants

Under Dutch law, you are no longer allowed to smoke in public buildings. In train stations you are only allowed to smoke near special poles, to be used as ashtrays, on the platform. In offices and industrial buildings, smoking is only allowed outside or, when inside, in a special room with an extractor fan. Restaurants and some bars have a smoking and non-smoking part. In most smaller bars you can light up anywhere.

The bill, please

The waiters in Dutch restaurants don't want you to stand up and go to the cash register and pay. You should ask the waiter for **de rekening** (the bill) and you can do that in the following ways:

✔ **Ik wil graag afrekenen.** (*ik vil khraakh <u>af</u>-ray-ker-nern*) (I would like to pay.)

✔ **De rekening alstublieft.** (*der <u>ray</u>-ker-ning*) (The bill please.)

You can pay together – **Alles bij elkaar graag** (*<u>a</u>-les bay el-<u>kaar</u> khraakh*) (Everything together, please.) – or you can go Dutch and pay separately – **Wij willen graag apart afrekenen.** (*vay <u>vi</u>-lern khraakh a-<u>part</u> af-ray-ker-nern*) (We would like to pay separately).

Talkin' the Talk

Marcel and Raymond have enjoyed their meal. They are ready for the bill and they plan to tip the waiter.

Marcel: **Ober, de rekening graag.**
           <u>oa</u>-ber der <u>ray</u>-ker-ning khraakh
           Waiter, the bill please.
Waiter: **Alstublieft.**
           al-stuw-<u>bleeft</u>
           Here you are.
           Marcel takes the bill and has a glance. It is € 82.
           Marcel lays down € 90. on the saucer and says: **Het is OK zo** (That's all right).
Waiter: **Dank u, een fijne avond nog.**
           dank uw ern <u>fay</u>-ner <u>aa</u>-font nokh
           Thank you, and have a nice evening.

Tipping

While tipping was abolished by law many years long ago, most people will feel the need to leave a tip. After you have made clear to the waiter that you want to pay, you will have to wait. Very often the bill still has to be made and the waiter will serve some other tables before he brings you the bill, laying carefully folded on a saucer. If you are paying cash and the waiter has to go for change, you can say: **Maak er . . . van** (*maak ehr ... fan*) (Make it ...), offering him a tip of 8 to 10 percent. If you have the exact money, just round up the sum of money you are paying with 8 to 10 per cent. The phrase **Zo is het goed** (*zoa is het khoot*) or **Het is OK zo** (*het is oa-kay zoa*) (Keep the change) lets the waiter know that the sum added on to the bill is his tip. When you are paying with a credit card, you have to sign for the amount that is on your cash register slip. In case you have no cash, you should tell the waiter the total amount of the cash register slip before he makes it, saying: **Maak er € ... van** (*maak ehr ... u-roa fan*) (Make it € . . .). Otherwise you can leave your tip on the saucer.

Your Own Restaurant at Home: Take-away Food

If you don't feel like cooking, look for an **afhaalchinees** (*af-haal-sheenays*) (Chinese takeaway). Almost all Chinese-Indonesian restaurants offer the opportunity to take out food. You can have your restaurant meal at home! Did you miss the train station supermarket or is the **avondwinkel** (*aa-font-vink-erl*) (night shops in some big towns that offer snacks and fastfood) closed tonight? Call **een pizzakoerier** (*ern pee-tsaa- koo-reer*) (a pizza deliverer) for a **pizza** (*peet-saa*) (pizza) or **spare ribs** (*spehr-rips*) (spare ribs).

Separating your verbs. The take-away food verb: 'meenemen'

When you've made your choice in a restaurant you might say to your partner, while studying the menu: **Ik neem tomatensoep** (*ik naym toa-maa- tern-soop*) (I'll take tomato soup). You can use the same phrase telling the waiter what you want to have: **Ik neem tomatensoep and mijn partner neemt meloen met ham** (*ik naym toa-maa-tern-soop en mayn part-ner naymt mer-loon met ham*) (I'll take tomato soup and my partner melon with ham).

The verb **nemen** (*nay-mern*) means to take. When preceded by the little word or prefix **mee** (*may*) (along), you get the verb **meenemen** (*may-nay-mern*) (to take away, but also: to bring along). Dutch has a lot of verbs that start with a stressed syllable, generally a preposition such as **op-** (*op*), **aan-** (*aan*), **uit-** (*oait*): **opbellen** (*op-beh-lern*) (to give a ring), **aanraken** (*aan-raa-kern*) (to touch), **uitkleden** (*oait-klay-dern*) (to undress). In the present tense, these separable verbs are divided in two parts. Here is **meenemen:**

Conjugation	Pronunciation
ik neem mee	*ik naym may*
jij neemt mee	*yay naymt may*
u neemt mee	*uw naymt may*
hij/zij/het neemt mee	*hay/zay/het naymt may*
wij nemen mee	*way nay-mern may*
jullie nemen mee	*yuw-lee nay-mern may*
zij nemen mee	*zay nay-mern may*

Another example is the verb **aanraken** (*aan-raa-kern*) (to touch):

Conjugation	Pronunciation
ik raak aan	*ik raak aan*
jij raakt aan	*yay raakt aan*
hij/zij/het raakt aan	*hay/zay/het raakt aan*
wij raken aan	*vay raa-kern aan*
jullie raken aan	*yuw-lee raa-kern aan*
zij raken aan	*zay raa-kern aan*

Sometimes interposing can be complicating. When you call your partner and tell him that after work you intend to go to the **afhaalchinees** (*af-haal-shee-nays*) (Chinese takeaway) in order to get some **bami** (fried noodles), you say: **Ik neem bami mee** (*ik naym baa-mee may*) (I'll bring noodles [with me]). You ask your partner to bring something from the station store: **Neem jij een toetje mee?** (*naym yay ern too-tyer may*) (Will you bring a dessert [with you]?).

Scheidbare werkwoorden (*skhayt-baa-rer verk-voar-dern*) (separable verbs) are separated in the present tense and in the past tense. However, you don't separate them in the present perfect. For separable verbs in the past tense see chapter 13, for separable verbs in the present perfect see chapter 8.

Shopping for Food

Sometimes you might not feel like eating out and might prefer to do the cooking yourself. The first thing to know is where to go for shopping.

Where to get your food?

The following is a list of stores where you might want to shop:

- **de supermarkt** (*der suw-per-markt*) (the supermarket)

- **de markt** (*der markt*) (the market)

- **de slager** (*der slaa-kher*) (the butcher's)

- **de bakkerij** (*der ba-ker-ray*) (the baker's)

- **de slijterij** (*der slay-ter-ray*) (the liquor store/wine shop)

- **de banketbakkerij** (*der ban-ket-ba-ker-ray*) (the patisserie)

- **de groenteboer/de groentewinkel** (*der khroon-ter-boor/der khroon-ter-vin-kerl*) (the greengrocer's)

- **de viswinkel** (*der fis-vin-kerl*) (the fish shop)

 You will find supermarkets anywhere – every **buurt** (*buwrt*) (neighbourhood) has one. When you are in the centre of a large city such as Amsterdam, Rotterdam or The Hague you won't find many of them. Look for them at the train stations!

Finding what you are looking for

The following is a list of typical foods you might buy.

- **het brood** (*het broat*) (the bread)

- **het broodje** (*het broa-tyer*) (the bread roll)

- **het bruinbrood** (*het broain-broat*) (the brown bread)

- **het witbrood** (*het vit-broat*) (the white bread)

- **de cake** (*der kayk*) (the cake)

- **het gebak** (*het kher-bak*) (the pastry)

✔ **de koekjes** (*der kook-yers*) (the cookies)

✔ **de boter** (*der boa-ter*) (the butter)

✔ **de margarine** (*der mar-kher-ree-ner*) (the margarine)

✔ **de kaas** (*der kaas*) (the cheese)

✔ **de karnemelk** (*der kar-ner-melk*) (the buttermilk)

✔ **de melk** (*der melk*) (the milk)

✔ **de room, de slagroom** (*der roam, der slakh-roam*) (the cream, the whipping cream)

✔ **het rundvlees** (*het ruhnt-flays*) (the beef)

✔ **het varkensvlees** (*het far-kerns-flays*) (the pork)

✔ **het spek** (*het spek*) (the bacon)

✔ **de ham** (*der ham*) (the ham)

✔ **de worst** (*der vorst*) (the sausage)

✔ **de kip** (*der kip*) (the chicken)

✔ **de forel** (*der fo-rel*) (the trout)

✔ **de kabeljauw** (*der ka-berl-yow*) (the codfish)

✔ **de tonijn** (*der toa-nayn*) (the tuna)

✔ **de zalm** (*der zalm*) (the salmon)

✔ **de garnalen** (*der khar-naa-lern*) (the shrimps)

✔ **de kreeft** (*der krayft*) (the lobster)

✔ **de mossel** (*der mo-serl*) (the mussel)

✔ **de aardbei** (*der aart-bay*) (the strawberry)

✔ **de appel** (*der a-perl*) (the apple)

✔ **de banaan** (*der ba-naan*) (the banana)

✔ **de peer** (*der payr*) (the pear)

✔ **de sinaasappel** (*der see-naa-sa-perl*) (the orange)

✔ **de aardappel** (*der aar-da-perl*) (the potato)

✔ **de broccoli** (*der bro-koa-lee*) (the broccoli)

✔ **de champignon** (*der sham-peen-yon*) (the mushroom)

- ✔ **de komkommer** (*der kom-ko-mer*) (the cucumber)

- ✔ **de knoflook** (*der knof-loak*) (the garlic)

- ✔ **de kropsla** (*der krop-slaa*) (the lettuce)

- ✔ **de paprika** (*der pa-pree-kaa*) (the sweet pepper)

- ✔ **de sperzieboon** (*der sper-zee-boan*) (the green bean)

- ✔ **de spinazie** (*der spee-naa-zee*) (the spinach)

- ✔ **de tomaat** (*der toa-maat*) (the tomato)

- ✔ **de ui** (*der oai*) (the onion)

- ✔ **de wortel** (*der vor-terl*) (the carrot)

- ✔ **de zuurkool** (*der zuwr-koal*) (the sauerkraut)

- ✔ **de macaroni** (*der ma-kroa-nee*) (the macaroni)

- ✔ **de rijst** (*der rayst*) (the rice)

- ✔ **de spaghetti** (*der spa-kheh-tee*) (the spaghetti)

- ✔ **de salade** (*der sa-laa-der*) (the salad)

Paying and getting change back

In supermarkets, the most usual way of paying is **pinnen** (*pi-nern*) (to pay by switch or debit card). You will see the signs **PIN** everywhere. Only switch cards of Dutch banks are valid! Credit cards are accepted only by very big supermarkets. In case you pay cash, the cashier might ask you:

- ✔ **Heeft u het gepast?** (*hayft uw het kher-past*) (Do you have the exact amount ready?)

- ✔ **Heeft u er misschien een euro bij?** (*hayft uw er mis-kheen ern uroa bay*) (Have you got an extra euro?)

And you could answer:

- ✔ **Het spijt me, ik heb niet kleiner.** (*het spayt mer ik hep neet klay-ner*) (I'm sorry, I haven't got any change.)

- ✔ **Het spijt me, ik heb helemaal geen kleingeld.** (*het spayt mer ik hep hay-ler-maal khayn klayn-gelt*) (I am sorry, I haven't got any change at all.)

Cashing the question: bonnetje erbij?

Then, after you have paid, the cashier will ask you one of the following questions: **Wilt u de bon erbij?** (*vilt uw der bon er-<u>bay</u>*) or more informal **Bonnetje erbij?** (*<u>bo</u>-ner-tyer er-<u>bay</u>*) (Do you want to have the receipt?)

As Dutch people are very fond of **zegels sparen** (*<u>zay</u>-kherls <u>spaa</u>-rern*) (to collect trade stamps for money or goods) the cashier might ask you: **Spaart u zegels?** (*spaart uw <u>zay</u>-kherls*) (Do you collect trade stamps?) or **Zegels erbij?** (*<u>zay</u>-kherls er-<u>bay</u>*) (Do you want trade stamps?).

A lot of shops and gas stations ask their clients for a plastic card in order to collect points that are good for money or goods. One of the most famous is the Air Miles Card. The cashier will ask you: **Wilt u airmiles?** (*vilt uw <u>ehr</u>-miles*) (Do you want Air Miles?).

Shopping for Food at the Traditional Market

Traditional markets are held once or twice a week on the marketplaces of the smaller towns. Amsterdam has some everyday markets: the **Albert Cuyp** (*<u>al</u>-bert koaip*) is the most famous of them. It has many stalls with Dutch and exotic food and clothes.

In supermarkets, most of the food is pre-packed and pre-priced. Bigger supermarkets do have specialty shops for bread, cheese and sliced cold meat products. In the specialty shops and markets you'll need to ask for a certain amount or weight.

You start with: **Ik wil graag** (*ik vil khraakh*) (I would like) and then, you mention one of the following measures and weights:

- ✔ **een ons** (*ern ons*) (100 grams)
- ✔ **een half pond** (*ern half pont*) (250 grams)
- ✔ **een pond** (*ern pont*) (500 grams, half a kilo)
- ✔ **anderhalf pond** (*<u>an</u>-der-half pont*) (750 grams)
- ✔ **een kilo** (*ern <u>kee</u>-loa*) (1000 grams, a kilogram)
- ✔ **één stuk, twee stuks** (*ayn stuhk, tvay stuhks*) (one piece, two pieces)
- ✔ **een plak, twee plakken** (*ayn plak / tvay pla-kern*) (one slice, two slices)

After the quantity you mention the kind of food you want, without any extra words in between the quantity and the food):

✔ **Ik wil graag een kilo appels.** (*ik vil khraakh ern <u>kee</u>-loa <u>a</u>-perls*) (one kilogram of apples, please.)

✔ **Ik wil graag een pond kaas.** (*ik vil khraakh ern pont kaas*) (500 grams of cheese, please.)

✔ **Twee plakken ham graag.** (*tvay <u>pla</u>-kern ham khraakh*) (Two slices of ham, please.)

Handling the question: mag het ietsje meer zijn?

Market sellers will often try to sell you a bit more than what you ask for. This concerns especially fresh food that has to be sold out before the end of the market day. The question **Mag het ietsje meer zijn?** (*makh het <u>eet</u>-syers mayr zayn*) means: 'Do you mind if it's a little bit more?' Generally the seller will not mention the new price together with the overweight. If not, just ask him: **Hoeveel kost het dan?** (*<u>hoo</u>-fayl kost dat dan*) (How much will it cost?). If you agree, you could answer: **Dat is goed** (*dat is khoot*) (That's OK).

Bargaining about the price of food is not usual among Dutch people. Markets that are visited mostly by non-Dutch, for instance the Sunday **Zwarte markt** (*<u>svar</u>-ter markt*) ('black market' or bazaar) in Beverwijk, not far from Amsterdam, have their own rules.

Talkin' the Talk

Petra Harskamp buys her fruits, cheese, fish, and flowers at the market. Today she's buying some cheese.

Market vendor:	**Goedemorgen, waarmee kan ik u helpen?** *khoo-der-<u>mor</u>-khern <u>vaar</u>-may kan ik uw <u>hel</u>-pern* Good morning. Can I help you?
Petra Harskamp:	**Een pond belegen Goudse kaas graag.** *ern pont ber-<u>lay</u>-khern <u>khow</u>-tser kaas khraakh* Half a kilo semi-matured cheese from Gouda, please.
Market vendor:	**Ik heb hier een mooi stuk. Mag het een ietsje meer zijn? Het is 600 gram.** *ik hep heer ern moay stuhk. makh het ern <u>eet</u>-syer mayr zayn? het is <u>zes</u>-hon-dert khram* I have a nice piece here. Do you mind if it's a little bit more? It's 600 grams.

Petra Harskamp:	**Dat is goed. Wat voor soort oude kaas heeft u?**
	dat is khoot. vat foar soart <u>ow</u>-der kaas hayft uw?
	That's okay. What kind of old cheese have you got?
Market vendor:	**Ik heb Edammer en Maaslander. Wilt u proeven?**
	ik hep ay-<u>da</u>-mer en <u>maas</u>-lan-der. vilt uw <u>proo</u>-fern?
	I have got Edam and Maasland cheese. You want to try some?
Petra Harskamp:	**Ja graag. Ik vind de Maaslander lekker. Hoeveel kost die?**
	yaa khraakh. ik fint der <u>maas</u>-lan-der <u>leh</u>-ker. <u>hoo</u>-fayl kost dee?
	Yes please. I like the Maasland cheese. How much does it cost?
Market Vendor:	**U mag dit stuk van anderhalf pond hebben voor € 8,50.**
	uw makh dit stuhk fan <u>an</u>-der-half pont <u>heh</u>-bern foar akht <u>u</u>-roa <u>fayf</u>-tikh
	You can have this piece of one pound and a half for eight and a half euros.
Petra Harskamp:	**Oké, dank u.**
	oa-<u>kay</u> dank uw
	Okay, thank you.
Market vendor:	**Anders nog iets?**
	<u>an</u>-ders nokh eets
	Anything else?
Petra Harskamp:	**Nee, dank u. Dat is het.**
	nay dank uw. dat is het
	No, thank you, that's it.

Words to Know

een stuk	*ern stuhk*	a piece
een soort	*ern soart*	a kind
proeven	*<u>proo</u>-fern*	to try/taste
lekker vinden	*<u>leh</u>-ker fin-dern*	to like
kosten	*kos-tern*	to cost

Say cheese

Dutch cheese is famous for its rich variety. Most cheeses bear the names of the regions they are from. **Edammer** (*ay-da-mer*) (cheese from the village Edam, just north of Amsterdam) is a small round cheese that is wrapped in red paper. **Maaslander** (*maas-lan-der*) is milder cheese, less salty. **Oud Amsterdam** (*owt am-ster-dam*) is strong and salty. Most cheeses are sold in three varieties: **jong** (*yong*) (new), **belegen** (*ber-lay-khern*) (matured) and **oud** (*owt*) (fully matured).

The varieties depend on the time that cheese has riped in the **kaasboerderij** (*kaas-boor-der-ray*) (cheese farm) or **kaasfabriek** (*kaas-fa-breek*) (cheese factory). Though cheese is a traditional product because it has been made for hundreds of years in the Netherlands, every year new kinds of cheeses are produced: especially kinds that have less fat than the traditional 40 per cent or even 60 per cent.

Chapter 7

Shopping 'til You Drop

● ●

In This Chapter

▶ Finding the best places

▶ Getting around the store

▶ Buying clothes

▶ Pointing: *deze, die, dit* and *that*

▶ Comparing better or best: the degrees of comparison

▶ Shopping at the traditional market

● ●

*S*hopping in another country can be a fun part of diving into the culture and a great opportunity for rubbing elbows with the locals. If you are in the mood for one-stop shopping, you can head into the major department stores found in all the larger cities.

Most town centres are compact. You will find all the shops together in a couple of the streets, generally in a pedestrian area. A parking garage will be nearby.

Specialty shops are sometimes difficult to find: if you are looking for something very special have a look at the Internet first.

Finding the Best Places

In the larger cities are several kinds of shops, such as:

✔ **het warenhuis** (*het <u>vaa</u>-rern-hoais*) (the department store)

✔ **de speciaalzaak** (*der spay-<u>shaal</u>-zaak*) (the specialty store)

Specialty shops might include:

- **de antiquair** (*der an-tee-<u>kehr</u>*) (the antique shop)

- **de bloemenwinkel** (*der <u>bloo</u>-mern-vin-kerl*) (the flower shop)

- **de boekwinkel** (*der <u>book</u>-vin-kerl*) (the book shop)

- **de computerwinkel** (*der com-pyoo-ter-vin-kerl*) (the computer shop)
- **de delicatessenwinkel** (*der day-lee-kaa-teh-sern-vin-kerl*) (the delicatessen)
- **de dierenwinkel** (*der dee-rern-vin-kerl*) (the pet shop)
- **de drogisterij** (*der droa-khis-ter-ray*) (the chemist's)
- **de juwelier** (*der yuw-er-leer*) (the jeweller)
- **de kledingzaak** (*der klay-ding-zaak*) (the dress shop)
- **de leerwinkel** (*der layr-vin-kerl*) (the leather shop)
- **de notenbar** (*der noa-tern-bar*) (the nut shop)
- **de parfumerie** (*der par-fuh-mer-ree*) (the perfumery)
- **de poelier** (*der poo-leer*) (the poulterer's)
- **de schoenenzaak** (*der skhoo-nern-zaak*) (the shoe shop)
- **de sportzaak** (*der sport-zaak*) (the sport shop)
- **de telefoonwinkel** (*der tay-ler-foan-vin-kerl*) (the telephone shop)

Note that most shops have the suffix **-winkel** or **-zaak**. Both words mean shop.

Most shops are open from 9 a.m. to 6 p.m. Supermarkets are open from 9 a.m. to 8 p.m. One evening a week, often on Thursday or Friday, shops may stay open until 9 p.m.: **koopavond** (*koap-aa-font*) (late opening). On Saturdays shops close at 5 p.m. In larger towns some shops are open on Sundays (generally once a month). Among them are department stores and garden centres: places where you need time to make your choice. Outside the towns, often near the main road, you'll find **de meubelboulevard** (*mu-berl-boo-ler-faar*) (furniture strip): furniture shops together with do-it-yourself shops and kitchen or bathroom showrooms. These kind of shops are not only open on Sundays, but also on public holidays. Have a look on their websites!

In very touristy places like seaside resorts, shops remain open in the evenings and the weekends during the holiday season.

When you want to know a shop's opening hours, you can ask:

- ✔ **Wanneer is deze winkel open?** (*va-nayr is day-zer vin-kerl oa-pern*) (When is this shop open?)
- ✔ **Wanneer bent u gesloten?** (*va-nayr bent uw kher-sloa-tern*) (When are you closed?)
- ✔ **Hoe laat sluit u vanavond?** (*hoo laat sloait uw fa-naa-font*) (At what time do you close tonight?)
- ✔ **Bent u open op zondag?** (*bent uw oa-pern op zon-dakh*) (Are you open on Sundays?)

Using the shopping verb: kopen

The verb **kopen** (*koa-pern*) is essential. Many words are linked with it, like **te koop** (*ter koap*) (for sale/to buy) and **uitverkoop** (*oait-fer-koap*) (sale). The verb **kopen** is regular, but its spelling has to be adapted in order to make sure that the **o** remains a long vowel in all the forms of the verb.

Conjugation	Pronunciation
ik koop	*ik koap*
jij koopt	*yay koapt*
u koopt	*uw koapt*
hij/zij/het koopt	*hay/zay/het koapt*
wij kopen	*vay koa-pern*
zij kopen	*zay koa-pern*

Getting Around the Store

If you need help in finding a certain item or section in a department store, you can consult **Inlichtingen** (*in-likh-ting-ern*) (the information desk). They have all the answers, or at least some of them.

If you're searching for a certain item, you can ask for it using either of the following phrases. At the end of the phrase, just fill in the plural form of the item you are looking for.

- ✔ **Waar zijn de . . .?** (*vaar zayn der*) (Where are the . . .?)
- ✔ **Waar zijn de badjassen?** (*vaar zayn der bat-ya-sern*) (Where are the bathrobes?)

You also could use the next phrase fitting in either a plural or a singular word:

- ✔ **Waar kan ik . . . vinden?** (*vaar kan ik . . . fin-dern*) (Where can I find . . .?)
- ✔ **Waar kan ik de badjassen vinden?** (*vaar kan ik der bat-ya-sern fin-dern*) (Where do I find the bathrobes?) or:
- ✔ **Waar kan ik een badjas vinden?** (*vaar kan ik ern bat-yas fin-dern*) (Where do I find a bathrobe?)

The salesperson will either say **Die verkopen we niet** (*dee fer-koa-pern ver neet*) (We don't sell those), or send you to the right department using one of the following sentences:

- **op de parterre** (*op der par-teh-rer*) (on the ground floor)

- **in het souterrain** (*in het soo-ter-rehn*) (In the basement)

- **op de eerste verdieping** (*op der ir-ster fer-dee-ping*) (on the first floor, American: second floor)

- **een verdieping hoger** (*ern fer-dee-ping hoa-kher*) (one floor higher)

- **een verdieping lager** (*ern fer-dee-ping laa-kher*) (one floor down)

When you want to nose around in a special department, you can use the phrase: **Waar kan ik . . . vinden?** (*vaar kan ik . . . fin-dern*) (Where can I find . . .?) ending it with one of the following department or feature names:

- **huishoudelijke artikelen** (*hoais-how-der-ler-ker ar-tee-ker-lern*) (domestic appliances)

- **herenkleding** (*hay-rern-klay-ding*) (men's clothes)

- **dameskleding** (*daa-mers-klay-ding*) (women's clothes)

- **kinderkleding** (*kin-der-klay-ding*) (children's clothes)

- **de schoenenafdeling** (*der skhoo-nern-af-day-ling*) (the shoe department)

- **de parfumerie** (*der par-fuh-mer-ree*) (the perfumery)

- **de lift** (*der lift*) (the elevator/lift)

- **de roltrap** (*der rol-trap*) (the escalator)

Finding out politely

When asking somebody for help, it pays to do so politely.

The most simple way of asking, is **Kunt u mij vertellen waar de badjassen zijn?** (*kuhnt uw may fer-teh-lern vaar der bat-ya-sern zayn*) (Could you tell me where the bathrobes are?).

You can include the word **misschien** (*mi-skheen*). The phrase **Kunt u mij misschien vertellen waar de badjassen zijn?** (*kuhnt uw may mi-skheen fer-teh-lern vaar der bat-ya-sern zayn*) (Please, could you tell me where the bathrobes are?) is a very polite one.

In case you feel you're really disturbing somebody, say when he is talking to somebody else, you can start by excusing yourself: **Sorry, kunt u mij vertellen waar de badjassen zijn?** (*so-ree kuhnt uw may fer-teh-lern vaar der bat-ya-sern zayn*) (Sorry, could you tell me where the bathrobes are?).

Just looking around

Sometimes you just want to browse without anybody's assistance. However, store assistants may want to make sure you don't need help by saying something like:

- ✔ **Wilt u geholpen worden of rondkijken?** (*vilt uw kher-hol-pern vor-dern of ront-kay-kern*) (Do you want help or do you just want to browse?)

- ✔ **Kan ik u misschien helpen?** (*kan ik uw mi-skheen hel-pern*) (Can I offer you any help?)

Your answer could be:

Ja graag, dank u. (*ya khraakh dank uw*) (Yes please, thank you.)

In some small shops, sellers don't like you to nose around. They'll want to help you and they ask: **Zoekt u iets speciaals?** (*zookt uw eets spayshaals*) (Are you looking for anything special?).

When all you want to do is browse, this phrase can help you politely turn down help:

Ik wil graag rondkijken. (*ik vil khraakh ront-kay-kern*) (I just want to look around.)

The seller will let you know:

- ✔ **Natuurlijk. Zegt u het maar als u een vraag heeft.** (*na-tuwr-lerk. zekht uw het maar als uw ern fraakh hayft*) (Of course. Just let me know if you need help.)

- ✔ **Roept u me als u een vraag heeft.** (*roopt uw mer als uw ern fraakh hayft*) (Call me if you have a question.)

Getting help

In some situations you may want or need some assistance. In this case you may say:

Kunt u mij alstublieft helpen? Ik zoek. . . (*kuhnt uw may als-tuw-bleeft hel-pern. ik zook*) (Could you help me please? I'm looking for. . .)

You may hear the following phrases:

- ✔ **Welke maat zoekt u?** (*vel-ker maat zookt uw*) (What size are you looking for?)

- ✔ **Welke kleur zoekt u?** (*vel-ker klur zookt uw*) (What colour do you want?)

- ✔ **Hoe vindt u deze kleur?** (*hoo fint uw day-zer klur*) (How do you like this colour?).

Buying Clothes

What's your heart's desire? Many terms for clothing are unisex, but some are usually reserved for one gender.

Some items usually meant for women include the following:

- ✔ **de blouse/bloes** (*der bloos*) (the blouse)
- ✔ **de jurk** (*der yuhrk*) (the dress)
- ✔ **het pak, het mantelpak** (*het pak, het man-terl-pak*) (the (woman's) suit)
- ✔ **het broekpak** (*het brook-pak*) (the trouser suit)
- ✔ **de rok** (*der rok*) (the skirt)

The following words usually apply to clothing for men:

- ✔ **het overhemd** (*het oa-fer-hemt*) (the shirt)
- ✔ **het kostuum** (*het kos-tuwm*) (formal), **het pak** (*het pak*) (the suit)
- ✔ **de das** (*der das*) (the tie)

The following clothes are worn by both men and women:

- ✔ **the pullover** (*der pool-oa-fer*) (formal), **de trui** (*der troai*) (informal) (the pullover)
- ✔ **het sweatshirt** (*het sveht-shirt*) (the sweatshirt)
- ✔ **het jasje** (*het yas-yer*) (the jacket)
- ✔ **de blazer** (*der blay-zer*) (the blazer)
- ✔ **het vest** (*het fest*) (the cardigan)
- ✔ **de jas** (*der yas*) (the coat)
- ✔ **de pantalon** (*der pan-taa-lon*) (formal), **de broek** (*der brook*) (the trousers)
- ✔ **het T-shirt** (*het tee-shirt*) (the T-shirt)

These items can be made of all kinds of material and styles. Here are the words to describe them:

- **de zijde** (*der zay-der*) (the silk)
- **de wol** (*der vol*) (the wool)
- **de katoen** (*der ka-toon*) (the cotton)
- **het linnen** (*der li-nern*) (the linen)
- **het leer** (*het layr*) (the leather)
- **gestreept** (*kher-straypt*) (striped)
- **geruit** (*kher-roait*) (checked)
- **gebloemd** (*kher-bloomt*) (flowered)
- **met stippen** (*met sti-pern*) (dotted)
- **effen** (*eh-fern*) (solid colour)
- **sportief** (*spor-teef*) (sporty, casual)
- **gekleed/netjes** (*kher-klayt/neth-yers*) (elegant)

Requesting colour and size

Do you have a preference for a special colour? The names of the basic colours are:

- **zwart** (*svart*) (black)
- **wit** (*vit*) (white)
- **rood** (*roat*) (red)
- **geel** (*khayl*) (yellow)
- **blauw** (*blow*) (blue)
- **groen** (*khroo*n) (green)

These words are all used as adjectives, which means that they say something about the word they belong to. In **de zwarte jas** (*der svar-ter yas*) (the black coat) **zwarte** says something about the coat. In **het blauwe T-shirt** (*het blow-ver tee-shirt*) the adjective **blauwe** tells you that the T-shirt is blue. If you want to find out more about how to fit adjectives into phrases and sentences, see Chapter 2.

Knowing your size

It will help you to find the right size when you know that in a lot of clothes you will find labels with different European and British sizes. Are the sizes unfamiliar to you? The next list might help you to find out the right size.

Women's Clothing		Men's Shirts	
UK	NL	UK	NL
8	34	14½	37
10	36	15	38
12	38	15½	39.5
14	40	16	41
16	42	16½	42
18	44	17	43
20	46	17½	44
22	48		

Talkin' the Talk

Petra Harskamp is in a ladies' fashion store. She wants to buy a blouse and is talking to the shop assistant.

Shop assistant:	**Kan ik u helpen?**
	kan ik uw <u>hel</u>-pern
	Can I help you?
Petra Harskamp:	**Ja graag, ik zoek een blouse.**
	ya khraakh ik zook ern bloos
	Yes please, I'm looking for a blouse.
Shop assistant:	**Welke kleur moet het zijn?**
	<u>vel</u>-ker klur moot het zayn
	Which colour would you like?
Petra Harskamp:	**Wit.**
	vit
	White.
Shop assistant:	**Zoekt u naar iets sportiefs?**
	zookt uw naar eets spor-<u>teefs</u>
	Are you looking for something sporty?
Petra Harskamp:	**Nee, ik zoek een geklede blouse.**
	nay ik zook ern khe-klay-der bloos
	No, I am looking for an elegant blouse.

Shop assistant:	**Prima. Welke maat heeft u?**
	pree-ma vel-ker maat hayft uw
	I see. Which size are you?
Petra Harskamp:	**Maat 40.**
	maat fayr-tikh
	Size 12/14.
Shop assistant:	**Hoe vindt u dit model?**
	hoo fint uw dit moa-del
	How do you like this model?
Petra Harskamp:	**Ik vind het erg mooi.**
	ik fint het erkh moay
	I like it very much.

Pointing: 'Deze', 'Die', 'Dit', 'Dat'

In almost all dress shops you can take items off the rack yourself. In other shops, like a jeweller's, you'll have to point to the thing you want. In that case you need the right words: this, these, that and those. What makes it difficult is that you have to know whether the indicated word is a **de** or a **het** word.

If the indicated word has the article **de**, you always use **deze** (_day-zer_) or **die** (_dee_). So:

- **de**→**deze** (this, nearby) or **die** (that, a bit farther)

- **de pullover** (_der pool-oa-fer_) (the pullover)→**deze pullover** (_day-zer pool-oa-fer_) (this pullover), **die pullover** (_dee pool-oa-fer_) (that pullover)

- **de rok** (_der rok_) (the skirt)→**deze rok** (_day-zer rok_) (this skirt), **die rok** (_dee rok_) (that skirt)

- **de sok** (_der sok_) (the sock)→**deze sok** (_day-zer sok_) (this sock), **die sok** (_dee sok_) (that sock)

Words to Know

gekleed	khe-klayd	elegant
de maat	der maat	the size
het model	het moadel	the model

If the indicated word has the article **het**, you always use **dit** or **dat**.

- ✔ **het→dit** (this, nearby) or **dat** (that, a bit farther)

- ✔ **het overhemd** (*het oa-fer-hemt*) (the shirt)→**dit overhemd** (*dit oa-fer-hemt*) (this shirt) **dat overhemd** (*dat oa-fer-hemt*) (that shirt)

- ✔ **het T-shirt** (*het tee-shirt*) (the T-shirt)→**dit T-shirt** (*dit tee-shirt*) (this T-shirt) **dat T-shirt** (*dat tee-shirt*) (that T-shirt)

- ✔ **het vest** (*het fest*) (the cardigan)→**dit vest** (*dit fest*) (this cardigan) **dat vest** (*dat fest*) (that cardigan)

Plurals will cause no problems: all plurals always have **de.** The plural **de** changes into **deze** (these, nearby) or **die** (those, farther off).

- ✔ **de→deze** (these, nearby) or **die** (those, a bit farther)

- ✔ **de pullovers→deze pullovers** (*day-zer pool-oa-fers*) (these pullovers)

- ✔ **die pullovers** (*dee pool-oa-fers*) (those pullovers)

- ✔ **de overhemden→deze overhemden** (*day-zer oa-fer-hem-dern*) (these shirts) **die overhemden** (*dee oa-fer-hem-dern*) (those shirts)

Note: In English you use the plural for various singular items like trousers. In Dutch you use the singular: **de broek** (*der brook*). So when pointing at it you say:

- ✔ **de broek→deze broek** (*day-zer brook*) (these trousers)

- ✔ **de broek→die broek** (*dee brook*) (those trousers)

When you point at two or more of them you say:

- ✔ **de broeken→deze broeken** (*day-zer broo-kern*) (these trousers)

- ✔ **de broeken→die broeken** (*dee broo-kern*) (those trousers)

The same is the case with glasses and sunglasses:

- ✔ **de zonnebril→deze zonnebril** (*day-zer zo-ner-bril*) (this pair of sunglasses)

- ✔ **de zonnebril→die zonnebril** (*dee zo-ner-bril*) (that pair of sunglasses)

- ✔ **de zonnebrillen→deze zonnebrillen** (*day-zer zo-ner-bri-lern*) (these pairs of sunglasses)

- ✔ **de zonnebrillen→die zonnebrillen** (*dee zo-nern-bri-lern*) (those pairs of sunglasses)

Using **deze, die, dit,** and **dat** like Dutch-speaking people do, will take some time! This little trick may help you:

- ✔ **d e**
- ✔ **d eze**
- ✔ **d ie**

all start with a **d**. This will help you to remember that **d**e words (**de auto**) are replaced by **d**eze (**deze auto**) or **d**ie (**die auto**) when pointing at them. **D**eze and **d**ie start with a **d** as well.

- ✔ **he t**
- ✔ **di t**
- ✔ **da t**

all end with a **t.** This will help you to rember that he**t** words (**het fietsje**) are replaced by di**t** (**dit fietsje**) or da**t** (**dat fietsje**) when pointing at them. Di**t** and da**t** end with a **t** as well.

Getting the right fit and trying things on

When you see something that looks promising, you may wish to try it on. You can ask the sales assistant the following question in supplying the name of the article that you want to try on:

- ✔ **Kan ik dit/deze . . . passen?** (*kan ik dit/<u>day</u>-zer <u>pa</u>-sern*) (Can I try this . . . on?)
- ✔ **Kan ik dit shirt passen?** (*kan ik dit shirt <u>pa</u>-sern*) (Can I try this shirt on?)
- ✔ **Kan ik deze broek passen?** (*kan ik <u>day</u>-zer brook <u>pa</u>-sern*) (Can I try these trousers on?)

The next phrase will come in handy in order to find your way:

Waar zijn de paskamers? (*vaar zayn der <u>pas</u>-kaa-mers*) (Where are the fitting rooms?)

If the sales assistant helps you, he or she might use the following sentence:

Wilt u dat passen? (*vilt uw dat pa-sern*) (Would you like to try that on?)

After trying your item the sales assistant may ask you any of the following questions to find out if you like what you saw in the dressing room:

✔ **Past het?** (*past het*) (Does it fit?)

✔ **Hoe is het?** (*hoo is het*) (How is it?)

✔ **Wat vindt u ervan?** (*vat fint uw er-fan*) (How do you like it?)

You can answer with any of the following, depending on how you like the item:

✔ **Het is te lang.** (*het is ter lang*) (It's too long.)

✔ **Het is te kort.** (*het is ter kort*) (It's too short.)

✔ **Het is te groot.** (*het is ter khroat*) (It's too large.)

✔ **Het is te klein.** (*het is ter klayn*) (It is too small.)

✔ **Het is te wijd.** (*het is ter vayt*) (It's too loose.)

✔ **Het is te strak.** (*het is ter strak*) (It's too tight.)

✔ **Het zit hier niet goed.** (*het zit heer niet khoot*) (It doesn't fit well here.)

✔ **Ik denk dat ik een grotere maat nodig heb.** (*ik denk dat ik ern khroa-ter-er maat noa-dikh hep*) (I think I need a larger size.)

✔ **Ik denk dat ik een kleinere maat nodig heb.** (*ik denk dat ik ern klay-ner-er maat noa-dikh hep*) (I think I need a smaller size.)

✔ **Kunt u mij een andere maat brengen?** (*kuhnt uw may ern an-derer maat breng-ern*) (Could you bring me a different size?)

✔ **Ik denk dat het prima past.** (*ik denk dat het pree-maa past*) (I think it fits me very well.)

✔ **Ik vind het leuk staan.** (*ik fint het luk staan*) (I think it looks good.)

✔ **Ik vind het niet leuk staan.** (*ik fint het neet luk staan*) (I think it doesn't look good.)

✔ **Ik vind het niet mooi.** (*ik fint het neet moay*) (I don't like it.)

✔ **Ik heb liever de andere kleur.** (*ik hep lee-fer der an-der-er klur*) (I'd prefer the other colour.)

✔ **Het spijt me, maar ik kan niet vinden wat ik zoek.** (*het spayt mer maar ik kan neet fin-dern vat ik zook*) (I'm sorry, I can't find what I'm looking for.)

✔ **Ik neem dit.** (*ik naym dit*) (I'll take this.)

✔ **Ik koop dit.** (*ik koap dit*) (I'll buy this one.)

Comparing Better or Best: The Degrees of Comparison

When selecting things to buy and talking about them with the salesperson, you need words to express what you like and what you like more and most.

- ✔ **Dit is mooi.** (*dit is moay*) (This is beautiful.)
- ✔ **Dit is mooier.** (*dit is <u>moa</u>-yer*) (This is more beautiful.)
- ✔ **Dit is de mooiste.** (*dit is der <u>moay</u>-ster*) (This is the most beautiful.)

When talking about the quality of things, you could say: **Dit is goed** (*dit is khoot*) (This is good), **Dit is beter** (*dit is <u>bay</u>-ter*) (This is better) or **Dit is de beste** (*dit is der <u>bes</u>-ter*) (This is best).

- ✔ **goed** (*khoot*) (good)
- ✔ **beter** (*<u>bay</u>-ter*) (better)
- ✔ **de beste** (*dit is der <u>bes</u>-ter*) (best)

The regular way to make comparisons is as follows:

- ✔ **leuk** (*luk*) (nice)
- ✔ **leuker** (*<u>lu</u>-ker*) (nicer)
- ✔ **de leukste** (*der <u>luk</u>-ster*) (the nicest)

So, the first step is using the regular adjective, for the second you add **-er**, and for the superlative you add **-ste** plus **het**.

- ✔ **klein** (*klayn*) (small)
- ✔ **kleiner** (*<u>klay</u>-ner*) (smaller)
- ✔ **de kleinste** (*der <u>klayn</u>-ster*) (smallest)

As in many words, you sometimes need to adapt the spelling to make sure that the sound of the vowel stays the same in all forms. In the next example the **l** in the word **sneller** (*<u>sneh</u>-ler*) has to be doubled to make sure that the short vowel **e** remains a short vowel. If you do not double the **l**, the word would sound quite different and nobody would understand what you mean: **sneler** (*<u>snay</u>-ler*) (which is a non-existing word).

- ✔ **snel** (*snel*) (fast)
- ✔ **sneller** (*<u>sneh</u>-ler*) (faster)
- ✔ **de snelste** (*der <u>snel</u>-ster*) (fastest)

Another spelling adaptation is necessary in order to keep the original vowel sounds. In the following example the second form is written with just one **o**, but the next one needs two **o**'s in order to remain sounding like a long vowel:

✔ **groot** (*khroat*) (big)

✔ **groter** (*khroa-ter*) (bigger)

✔ **de grootste** (*der khroat-ster*) (biggest)

When talking about quantities you can use this very irregular and unique grade of comparison:

✔ **Dit is veel.** (*dit is fayl*) (This is much.)

✔ **Dit is meer.** (*dit is mayr*) (This is more.)

✔ **Dit is het meeste.** (*dit is het mayst*) (This is the most.)

Talkin' the Talk

 Petra Harskamp likes the blouse the sales assistant has shown her and wants to try it on.

Petra Harskamp:	**Ik wil de blouse graag passen. Waar zijn de paskamers?** *ik vil der bloos khraakh pa-sern. vaar zayn der pas-kaa-mers* I would like to try on the blouse. Where are the fitting rooms?
Shop assistant:	**Deze kant op graag.** *day-zer kant op khraakh* This way please.

A few minutes later Petra comes out of the fitting room.

Shop assistant:	**Past hij?** *past hay* Does it fit?
Petra Harskamp:	**Hij is te groot.** *hay is ter khroat* It's too large.
Shop assistant:	**Ik heb hem ook kleiner, in maat 38.** *ik hep erm oak klay-ner in maat akh-tern-dehr-tikh* I have a smaller one as well, in size 10/12. **Wilt u die passen?** *vilt uw dee pa-sern* Do you want to try it on?

Petra Harskamp:	**Ja, ik wil graag een maat kleiner in het blauw.**
	yaa ik vil khraak ern maat klay-ner in het blow
	Yes, I would like a smaller size in blue.
While Petra is trying it on the sales assistant asks:	
	Is deze beter?
	is day-zer bay-ter
	Is this one better?
Petra Harskamp:	**Ja, hij past beter en blauw is leuker.**
	yaa hay past bay-ter en blow is lu-ker
	Yes, it fits better and blue is much nicer.

Asking for the price

Petra Harskamp has made her choice, but she does not yet know the price of the blouse. She will ask:

Hoeveel kost hij? (*hoo-fayl kost hay*) (How much does it cost?)

Words to Know

passen	*pas-sern*	to try on
de paskamer	*der pas-kaa-mer*	the fitting room
deze kant op	*day-zer kant op*	this way
past hij?	*past hay*	does it fit?
in het blauw	*in het blow*	in blu

Replacing 'de' and 'het' words

When you are talking about **de**-things and you don't mention the thing itself, you replace the **de**-thing by **hij**.

- ✔ **De blouse kost €45,–.** (*der bloos kost <u>fayf</u>-ern-fayr-tikh <u>u</u>-roa*) (The blouse costs €45.)

- ✔ **Hij kost €45,–.** (*hay kost <u>fayf</u>-en-fayr-tikh <u>u</u>-roa*) It costs €45.)

When you are talking about **het**-things and you don't mention the thing itself, you replace the **het**-thing by the word **het**.

- ✔ **Het shirt kost €20,–.** (*het shirt kost <u>tvin</u>-tikh <u>u</u>-roa*) (The shirt costs €20.)

- ✔ **Het kost €45,–.** (*het kost <u>fayf</u>-en-fayr-tikh <u>u</u>-roa*) (It costs €45.)

Talkin' the Talk

Petra Harskamp decides to buy the blouse. She and the shop assistant go to the cash desk. The shop assistant folds the blouse and puts it in a bag. The cashier standing there says:

Cashier:	**Dat is dan €45, alstublieft. Wilt u pinnen?**
	dat is dan <u>fayf</u>-en-fayr-tikh <u>u</u>-roa als-tuw-<u>bleeft</u>.
	vilt uw <u>pi</u>-nern
	That's 45 euros please. Do you want to pay by switch card?
Petra Harskamp:	**Graag.**
	khraakh
	Yes, please.
Cashier	**Een ogenblikje alstublieft.**
	ern oa-khern-<u>blik</u>-yer als-tuw-<u>bleeft</u>
	One moment, please.

(Petra puts in her card the wrong way.)

Cashier:	**De strip aan deze kant alstublieft.**
	der strip aan <u>day</u>-zer kant als-tuw-<u>bleeft</u>.
	The strip on this side please.
	Zo is het goed, dank u. En hier is uw bon.
	zoa is het khoot dank uw. en heer is uw bon
	That's right, thank you. And here is your receipt.

(Hands over the bag with the blouse)

Sales assistant:	**Veel plezier ermee!**
	fayl pler-<u>zeer</u> er-<u>may</u>
	I hope you'll enjoy it!
Petra Harskamp:	**Dank u, tot ziens.**
	dank uw tot zeens
	Thank you, goodbye.

Words to Know

pinnen or switch card	*<u>pi</u>-nern*	to pay by PIN card
een ogenblikje	*ern oa-khern-<u>blik</u>-yer*	one moment
aan deze kant	*aan <u>day</u>-zer kant*	on this side
de bon	*der bon*	the receipt
veel plezier ermee	*fayl pler-<u>zeer</u> er-<u>may</u>*	I hope you'll enjoy it

Bargaining and negotiating

The Dutch have a long tradition of bargaining when it comes to buying and selling houses. However, elderly Dutch citizens will usually not negotiate over items like food or clothes, not even on the traditional market. They will only **afdingen** (*<u>af</u>-ding-ern*) (to bargain) and **onderhandelen** (*on-der-<u>han</u>-der-lern*) (to negotiate) when purchasing a house. Dutch people who buy their weekly fruit, cheese, flowers, or fish on the market, just pay the price asked. Since the Netherlands is becoming more and more **multiculti** (*luhl-tee-<u>kuhl</u>-tee*) (multicultural) and many people from other countries in Dutch bring their own traditions, **afdingen en onderhandelen** at the market and even in shops is no longer seen as unusual among the newest generation of Dutch-speaking people.

Shopping at the Traditional Market

Traditional or week markets mostly offer food and cheap clothes like T-shirts and jeans. Some markets in the big towns offer exotic food and clothes. When you are looking for something special you can use the following sentences:

- ✔ **Heeft u . . .?** (*hayft uw. . .*) (Do you have . . .?)

- ✔ **Waar kan ik . . . vinden?** (*vaar kan ik . . . fin-dern*) (Where can I find . . .?)

- ✔ **Verkopen ze . . . op deze markt?** (*fer-koa-pern zer . . . op day-zer markt*) (Do they sell . . . at this market?)

You could hear one of the following replies:

- ✔ **Nee, dat heb ik niet.** (*nay dat hep ik neet*) (No, I don't have that.)

- ✔ **Nee, dat verkopen we niet.** (*nay dat fer-koa-pern ver neet*) (No, we don't sell that.)

Chapter 8

Making Leisure a Top Priority

. . . .

In This Chapter

▶ The days of the week

▶ Having a good time at shows and events

▶ Enjoying a concert

▶ Going to a party

▶ Being invited

▶ Going out of town

▶ Sports, sports, sports

. . . .

*T*his chapter is all about having a good time, whether that means going out to see a movie, visiting a museum, or going to a party.

Every large town has a concert hall, some cinemas, museums, festivals, and events. While having a good time, you get to know the Dutch culture and the Dutch people. In local papers, you can read every week's programme. You can also find it on the Internet.

Before heading out for a day of fun or a night on the town, you need to know the days of the week. After all, you need to know when the fun starts.

The Days of the Week

In a paper and on the Internet you can read which movies or shows you can visit. If you don't know the names of the days of the week it will be difficult to find out. Some names will be familiar to you, others not, depending on your native language. All days of the week have **de**, but we hardly use the article. Yes, you've noticed correctly, in Dutch the days of the week (as well as months) are written in lower case!

▶ **zondag** (*zon-dakh*) (Sunday)

▶ **maandag** (*maan-dakh*) (Monday)

✔ **dinsdag** (_dins-dakh_) (Tuesday)

✔ **woensdag** (_woons-dakh_) (Wednesday)

✔ **donderdag** (_don-der-dakh_) (Thursday)

✔ **vrijdag** (_fray-dakh_) (Friday)

✔ **zaterdag** (_zaa-ter-dakh_) (Saturday)

When talking about something that always happens on the same day of the week, you use the following words:

✔ **op zondag, 's zondags** (_op zon-dakh, zon-dakhs_) (on Sundays, every Sunday)

✔ **op maandag, 's maandags** (_op maan-dakh, smaan-dakhs_) (on Mondays, every Monday)

✔ **op dinsdag, dinsdags** (_op dins-dakh, dins-dakhs_) (on Tuesdays, every Tuesday)

✔ **op woensdag, 's woensdags** (_op woons-dakh, svoons-dakhs_) (on Wednesdays, every Wednesday)

✔ **op donderdag, donderdags** (_op don-der-dakh, don-der-dakhs_) (on Thursdays, every Thursday)

✔ **op vrijdag, vrijdags** (_op fray-dakh, fray-dakhs_) (on Fridays, every Friday)

✔ **op zaterdag, zaterdags** (_op zaa-ter-dakh, zaa-ter-dakhs_) (on Saturdays, every Saturday)

✔ **Zaterdags ga ik altijd voetballen.** (_zaa-ter-dakhs khaa ik al-tayt foot-ba-lern_) (On Saturdays I always play football.)

Specifying when

When you want to talk about the next day or the day before, you use the following words:

✔ **vandaag** (_fan-daakh_) (today)

✔ **gisteren** (_khis-ter-ern_) (yesterday)

✔ **eergisteren** (_ayr-khis-ter-ern_) (the day before yesterday)

✔ **morgen** (_mor-khern_) (tomorrow)

✔ **overmorgen** (_oa-fer-mor-khern_) (the day after tomorrow)

When you want to know whether something happens on a special part of the day you can combine this with the words **morgen** or **ochtend** (_mor-khern, okh-ternt_) (morning), **middag** (_mi-dakh_) (afternoon), and **avond** (_aa-font_) (evening).

✔ **vanmorgen**, **vanochtend** (*fa-<u>mor</u>-khern, fa-<u>nokh</u>-ternt*) (this morning)

✔ **vanmiddag** (*fa-<u>mi</u>-dakh*) (this afternoon)

✔ **vanavond** (*fa-<u>naa</u>-font*) (this evening)

So you start with the word 'van', when talking about today. When you're talking about tomorrow, just start with 'morgen'.

✔ **morgenochtend** (*mor-khern-<u>okh</u>-ternt*) (tomorrow morning)

✔ **morgenmiddag** (*mor-khern-<u>mi</u>-dakh*) (tomorrow afternoon)

✔ **morgenavond** (*mor-khern-<u>aa</u>-font*) (tomorrow night)

✔ **Morgenavond kijk ik naar** *de Soprano's* (*mor-khern-<u>aa</u>-font kayk ik naar der soa-<u>praa</u>-noas*) (Tomorrow night I'll be watching *The Sopranos*).

City Life: A Never-ending Offer

Whatever you're looking for, the larger towns will reveal their secrets to you the longer you live in them. If you want to avoid having to search all over town, use the Net when you're looking for something very special. Just walking around at night you might find **loungebars** (*<u>lounge</u>-bars*) (lounge bars) and **discotheken** (*dis-koa-<u>tay</u>-kern*) (discotheques).

Every large town has **een schouwburg** (*ern <u>skhow</u>-buhrkh*) (a theatre) or **theater** (*tay-<u>yaa</u>-ter*) (theatre) showing **een toneelstuk** (*ern toa-<u>nayl</u>-stuhk*) (a play), **een musical** (*ern <u>myoo</u>-ser-kerl*) (a musical) or **variété** (*va-ree-yay-<u>tay</u>*) (a variety show).

Popconcerten (*<u>pop</u>-kon-sehr-tern*) (rock concerts) are organised in **een concerthal** (*ern kon-<u>sehrt</u>-hal*) (a concert hall). In summer **openluchtconcerten** (*oa-pern-<u>luhkht</u>-kon-sehr-tern*) (open-air concerts) will take place in **een voetbalstadion** (*ern <u>foot</u>-bal-staa-dee-yon*) (a football stadium) generally on the outskirts of town.

In the next part of its chapter you will find more expressions dealing with all that cities offer you for going out. Now you'll find some phrases that will help you to make your choice.

What shall we do?

When discussing what to do, you can say: **Wat zullen we gaan doen?** (*vat <u>zuh</u>-lern ver khaan doon*) (What shall we do?).

Here are some sentences that you can use when you want to know what somebody's plans are. You can also use these sentences when you want to know if they have time.

- **Heb je iets te doen?** (*hep yer eets ter doon*) (Have you got something to do?)

- **Heb je speciale plannen voor morgenavond?** (*hep yer spay-shaa-ler pla-nern foar mor-khern-aa-font*) (Have you got special plans for tomorrow night?)

- **Heb je vanavond tijd?** (*hep yer fa-naa-font tayt*) (Have you got time tonight?)

Using the going out verb: uitgaan

Uitgaan (*oait-khaan*) (going out) is the separable verb for doing something nice, generally in town. Depending on your age and preferences, it may be **uit eten gaan** (*oait ay-tern khaan*) (eating out), **naar de bioscoop gaan** (*naar der bee-yos-koap khaan*) (going to the movies), **naar het theater gaan** (*naar het tay-yaa-ter khaan*) (going to the theater), **een festival bezoeken** (*ern fes-tee-val ber-zoo-kern*) (to visit a festival) and **iets drinken in een café** (*eets drin-kern in ern kaa-fay*) (to have a drink in a bar) or **een terrasje pakken** (*ern tras-yer pa-kern*) (to have a drink on a pavement café). Next time when you are discussing what to do, just ask:

- **Zullen we vanavond uitgaan?** (*zuh-lern ver fa-naa-font oait-khaan*) (Shall we go out tonight?)

- **Waar zullen we vanavond uitgaan?** (*vaar zuh-lern ver fa-naa-font oait-khaan*) (Where shall we go out tonight?)

Using the verb 'stappen'

The informal verb for going out is **stappen** (*sta-pern*) (to go out on the town). You use it when drinking or dancing is the most important activity planned for the night. When you're going to **stappen**, you will definitely not stay in one place: you're going to visit more places, possibly on a **kroegentocht** (*krookh-ern-tokht*) (pub-crawl/bar-hopping). With the phrase **vanavond ga ik stappen** (*fa-naa-font khaa ik sta-pern*) (tonight I'll go out on the town) you mean that you won't be alone, because **stappen** is always with some friends.

- **Ik heb zin om vanavond te stappen.** (*ik hep zin om fa-naa-font te khaan sta-pern*) (I feel like going out tonight.)

✔ **Waar zullen we vanavond gaan stappen?** (*vaar <u>zuh</u>-lern ver fa-<u>naa</u>- font khaan <u>sta</u>-pern*) (Where shall we go out tonight?)

✔ **Als ik ga stappen, ga ik naar het Leidseplein.** (*als ik khaa <u>sta</u>-pern khaa ik naar het lay-tser-<u>playn</u>*) (When I am going out, I go to the Leidseplein.)

Going to the movies

Larger towns offer plenty of choice when you want to see a movie. You will find big cinemas, with a choice of four or five different movies every night, be it **een sciencefictionfilm** (*ern <u>sa</u>-yerns <u>fik</u>-shern film*), (a science fiction film), **een misdaadfilm** (*ern <u>mis</u>-daat-film*) (a crime/action film), **een psychologisch drama** (*ern psee-khoa-<u>loa</u>-khees <u>draa</u>-maa*) (a psychological drama), **een romantische film** (*ern roa-<u>man</u>-tee-ser film*) (a romantic movie), **een thriller** (*ern <u>tri</u>-ler*) (a thriller), or **een drama** (*ern <u>draa</u>-maa*) (a drama). Are you accompanying your kid? Choose **een kinderfilm** (*ern <u>kin</u>-der-film*) (a children's film), **een tekenfilm** (*ern <u>tay</u>-kern- film*) (a cartoon), **een avonturenfilm** (*ern aa-fon-<u>tuw</u>-rern-film*) (an adventure film), or **een komedie** (*ern koa-<u>may</u>-dee*) (a comedy).

Next time when you are discussing the movies, try these phrases:

✔ **Ik wil graag naar de bioscoop.** (*ik vil khraakh naar der bee-yos-<u>koap</u>*) (I would like to go to the cinema.)

✔ **Ik wil graag een film zien.** (*ik vil khraakh ern film zeen*) (I would like to see a film.)

When you have agreed about going to the movies and you've made your choice, you can use one of the following sentences:

✔ **In welke bioscoop draait . . . ?** (*in <u>vel</u>-ker bee-yos-<u>koap</u> draayt ...*) (Which cinema features . . .?)

✔ **Hoe laat begint de voorstelling?** (*hoo laat ber-<u>khint</u> der <u>foar</u>-stehling*) (At what time does the show start?)

In the Netherlands, both on TV and in the cinema, all films keep the original language in which they are spoken. They are subtitled in Dutch. This offers you a great opportunity to learn new words and to see how Dutch words are written. In the Hollywood-dominated film world, Dutch films tend to get snowed under, but there's no need to be sorry about that – it's very difficult to understand spoken Dutch in films. Generally you can't look at people's faces, the actors use colloquialisms or speak jargon, or the **geluidstechniek** (*kher-<u>loaits</u>-tekh-neek*) (the sound engineering) fails. Don't blame yourself for not understanding a Dutch spoken movie!

Buying tickets

For many cinemas, you'll have to reserve your tickets and you'll have to be there before a certain time in order to pick them up. When you want to buy your tickets just before **de voorstelling begint** (*der foar-steh-ling ber-khint*) (the show starts) tickets might be **uitverkocht** (*oait-fer-kokht*) (sold out).

In case you make a reservation by phone, try the next sentence:

> **Ik wil graag kaartjes reserveren voor...** (*ik vil khraakh kaar-tyers ray-ser-fay-rern foar*) (I would like to reserve tickets for ...)

In de rij staan voor een kaartje (*in de ray staan foar ern kaar-tyer*) (standing in line for a ticket) is another possibility. When you have arrived at the box office you might hear one of the next phrases:

- ✔ **De voorstelling is al begonnen.** (*der foar-steh-ling*) (The show has already started.)
- ✔ **De voorstelling is uitverkocht.** (*der foar-steh-ling is oait-fer-kokht*) (The show is sold out.)
- ✔ **We hebben nog kaartjes voor de voorstelling van 9.00 uur.** (*ver heh-bern nokh kaar-tyers foar der foar-steh-ling fan nay-khern uwr*) (We still have tickets for the nine o'clock show.)

You can use these phrases not only for the movies, but for any kind of show or concert.

Talkin' the Talk

 Sandra is talking to her friend, René. She wants to go to the movies.

Sandra:	**Ik heb gehoord dat *Pride and Prejudice* een hele mooie film is en ik wil hem graag zien.** *ik hep kher-hoart dat praayt en preh-juh-dis ern hay-ler moa-yer film is ern ik vil hem khraakh zeen* I have been told that *Pride and Prejudice* is a very fine movie and I would like to see it.
René:	**Waar draait hij?** *vaar draayt hay* Where is it on?
Sandra:	**Hij draait op het ogenblik in Cinescope.** *hay draayt op het oa-khern-blik in see-ner-skoap* It's on at Cinescope at the moment.

René:	**Wanneer wil je gaan?** *va-nayr vil yer khaan* When do you want to go?
Sandra:	**Morgenavond, want dan ben jij vrij.** *mor-khern-aa-font vant dan ben yay fray* Tomorrow night, because then you're off.
René:	**OK, morgenavond is goed. Hoe laat is de voorstelling?** *oa-kay, mor-khern-aa-font is khoot. hoo laat is der foar-steh-ling* OK, tomorrow night is all right. What time is the show?
Sandra:	**De voorstelling begint om kwart over zeven, maar we moeten de kaartjes om kwart voor zeven afhalen.** *der foar-steh-ling ber-khint om kvart oa-fer zay-fern maar ver moo-tern der kaar-tyers om kvart foar zay-fern af-haa-lern* The show starts at a quarter past seven, but we have to pick up the tickets at a quarter to seven.
René:	**Da's erg vroeg, je zult geen tijd hebben om te eten.** *das erkh frookh yer zuhlt khayn tayt heh-bern om ter ay-tern* That's very early, you won't have any time for dinner.
Sandra:	**Ik koop wel iets op het station voor in de trein en we kunnen koffie drinken voordat de film begint.** *ik koap vel eets op het staa-shon foar in der trayn en ver kuh-nern ko-fee drin-kern foar-dat der film ber-khint* I will buy something to have on the train and we can have some coffee before the movie starts.
René:	**OK, ik haal de kaartjes en daarna drinken we koffie.** *oa-kay ik haal der kaar-tyers en daar-naa drin-kern ver ko-fee* Okay, I'll get the tickets and after that we'll have coffee.
Sandra:	**Ik heb er zin in. Iedereen praat over die film!** *ik hep er zin in. ee-der-rayn praat oa-fer dee film* I'm looking forward to it. Everybody is talking about that film!

Words to Know

een film	ern film	a film
zien	zeen	to see
de koffie	der _ko_-fee	the coffee
de tijd	der tayt	the time
vroeg	frookh	early
de trein	der trayn	the train
praten	_praa_-tern	to talk

Having a Good Time at Festivals and Events

Most towns, not only the larger ones, have their own **festivals** (_fes_-teevals) (festivals) and **evenementen** (ay-ver-ner-_mehn_-tern) (events), generally during summer terms. The festivals have all kinds of cultural themes.

Amsterdam starts the summer with the **Holland Festival**. It has **muziek** (_muw-zeek_) (music), **dans** (_dans_) (dance), **opera** (_oa-per-raa_) (opera) and **theater** (_tay-yaa-ter_) (theater). This festival is international, so the spoken language of the theater is not necessarily Dutch. The festival is indoors.

Amsterdam has some free open air concerts, like in August the famous **Prinsengrachtconcert** (prins-ern-_khrakht_-kon-sehrt) of classical music. The concert takes place on a stage on the water of **de gracht** (_der khrakht_) (the canal). Hundreds of lovers of classical music huddle together in boats on the canal to enjoy the concert, which always ends with a mass singing of an old Amsterdam tear jerker: _Tulips in Amsterdam_. This concert is entirely broadcasted on television.

Also in August, Rooterdam hosts the **North Sea Jazz Festival**, drawing singers and bands from all of the world to the Netherlands. The festival lasts several days and offers many concerts. The music is no longer the traditional pure jazz, but in some cases a mix of jazz, pop and ethnic music. TV offers a selection of the concerts every night during the Festival.

In January Rotterdam offers the **International Film Festival**. Filmmakers and film lovers from all over the world come to Rotterdam to see and comment on the newest films, most of them art movies meant for the **filmhuizen** (*film-hoai-zern*) (the cinema clubs).

Utrecht has, in the second half of May, the **Festival aan de Werf** (*fes-teeval aan der vehrf*), an outdoor festival of theater, music and plastic arts along the canals and in a big party tent in the centre of town. Utrecht also hosts the **Festival van de Oude Muziek** (Festival of Old Music).

Too many events are organised to mention them all: just keep your eyes and ears open and grab your chance whenever you can.

Enjoying a Concert

Large and smaller towns have one or more **muziekzalen** (*muw-zeek-zaa- lern*) (music halls). Otherwise, concerts are given in churches and other places that can seat an audience. Concerts, generally of classical music, are announced on the Internet, in the local paper and on billboards.

Some music loving Dutchmen **zingen in een koor** (*zing-ern in ern koar*) (sing in a choir) where they study for their annual concert, very often with religious music, in the local church. Others practice and perform **zeemansliedjes** (*zay-mans-lee-tyers*) (shanties). Though the members of the choirs are amateurs, the professional conductor and accompanying musicians are professionals in order to guarantee a good quality. Posters in libraries and other places where people gather, announce concerts and the place where tickets can be bought.

Visiting the Museum

Museums of any kind can be found in every town. Lovers of art will find museums of classical and modern arts in all large cities. Smaller towns and even villages offer a wide variety of other museums that show items of local traditions or celebrate a local or national hero.

Het Rijksmuseum (*het rayks-muw-zay-uhm*) (the Rijksmuseum) in Amsterdam has a large collection **schilderijen** (*skhil-der-ray-ern*) (paintings) of the famous Dutch painters of the **Gouden Eeuw** (*khow-dern ayw*) (Golden Age) such as Rembrandt and contemporaries. The nearby **Van Gogh Museum** (*fan-khokh muw-zay-uhm*) (Van Gogh Museum) contains the largest collection of paintings by Van Gogh. **Het Stedelijk Museum** (*het stay-der-lerk muw-zay-uhm*) is a museum of **moderne kunst** (*moa-dehr-ner kuhnst*) (modern art).

Het Centraal Museum (*het sen-traal muw-zay-uhm*) (the Central Museum) of Utrecht is the oldest municipal museum in the Netherlands, containing work from **beroemdheden** (*ber-roomt-hay-dern*) (celebrities) from Utrecht from the **oude meester** (*ow-der may-ster*) (old master) Saenredam to **de ontwerper** (*der ont-ver-per*) (the designer) Gerrit Rietveld.

Het Mauritshuis (*het mow-rits-hoais*) (the Mauritshuis) in **Den Haag** (*den haakh*) (The Hague) is a unique 17th century **paleis** (*pa-lays*) (palace) and one of the most beautiful examples of Dutch classicist **architectuur** (*ar-shee-tek-tuwr*) (architecture). Most of the paintings on display are by artists who were popular in the 18th century, such as Jan Steen, who lent his name to the popular Dutch expression: **een huishouden van Jan Steen** (*ern hoais-how-dern fan jan stayn*) (a household of Jan Steen, being a very disorganised household).

Museum Boijmans van Beuningen in Rotterdam not only displays **meester-werken** (*may-ster-wehr-kern*) (masterpieces) in the category of classical and modern paintings, but also **beeldhouwkunst** (*baylt-how-kunst*) (sculpture).

De museumjaarkaart (*der muw-zay-uhm-yaar-kaart*) (the annual season ticket for museums) costs only €25, can be bought online or in the museum and allows free or reduced entrance to more than 400 museums in the Netherlands.

Giving Your Opinion

When it comes to entertainment, everybody seems to have an opinion. So why miss out on the fun?

Asking your opinion

Someone might ask you one of the following questions, or you might pose one of them to someone else, in order to start a conversation about a film, an exhibition, concert or a performance:

> **Hoe vond je de film/tentoonstelling/het concert/de opera?** (*hoo font yer der film/der ten-toan-steh-ling/het kon-sehrt/der oa-per-raa*) (How did you like the movie/exposition/concert/opera?)

Telling people what you think

Now comes the fun part: telling someone what you think about a film or show you've just seen. For starters, you can say whether or not you liked the entertainment. Try one of the following phrases:

- ✔ **Ik vond de film/de tentoonstelling/het concert de opera erg mooi.** (*ik font der film/der ten-toan-steh-ling/het kon-sehrt/der oa-per- raa ehrkh moay*) (I liked the exposition/concert/opera very much.)

- ✔ **Ik vond de film/de tentoonstelling/het concert/de opera niet erg mooi.** (*ik font der film/der ten-toan-steh-ling/het kon-sehrt/der oa-per-raa neet ehrkh moay*) (I didn't like the exposition/the concert/ opera very much.)

You may want to follow up on that statement. Start out by saying:

> **De film/de tentoonstelling/het concert/de opera was ...** (*der film/der ten-toan-steh-ling/het kon-sehrt/der oa-per-raa vas ...*) (The movie/ exposition/ concert/ opera really was...)

Then, you can finish the thought with any of the following adjectives that might apply. You can always string a few of these adjectives together with **en**.

- ✔ **echt mooi** (*ekht moay*) (really beautiful)

- ✔ **opwindend** (*op-vin-dernt*) (exciting)

- ✔ **fantastisch** (*fan-tas-tees*) (fantastic)

- ✔ **te gek** (*ter khek*) (great)

- ✔ **interessant** (*in-ter-rer-sant*) (interesting)

- ✔ **de moeite waard** (*der mooy-ter vaart*) (worthwhile)

- ✔ **teleurstellend** (*ter-lur-steh-lent*) (disappointing)

- ✔ **saai** (*saay*) (dull)

- ✔ **De film/de tentoonstelling/het concert/de opera viel tegen.** (*der film/ der ten-toan-steh-ling/het kon-sehrt/der oa-per-raa feel tay-khern*) (the film/ the exhibition/the concert/the opera/disappointed me.)

- ✔ **Het was een hele zit.** (*het vas ern hay-ler zit*) (It was a long sit.)

- ✔ **Opera is niets voor mij.** (*oa-per-raa is neets foar may*) (Opera is not my cup of tea.)

- ✔ **Een opera is niet aan mij besteed.** (*ern oa-per-raa is neet aan may ber-stayt*) (An opera is wasted on me.)

Talkin' the Talk

Petra Harskamp went to a show in the weekend. Now, her boss at the office is asking her about it.

Raymond van Dieren: **Hoe was je musical zaterdagavond?**
hoo vas yer myoo-ser-kerl zaa-ter-dakh-aa-font
How was your musical Saturday night?

Petra Harskamp: **Ik heb er erg van genoten**
ik hep er ehrkh fan kher-noa-tern
I enjoyed it very much.
De dansers waren te gek, de kostuums fantastisch en de muziek was fantastisch, erg ritmisch en opwindend.
der dan-sers vaa-rern ter khek der kos-tuwms fan-tas-tees en der muw-zeek vas fan-tas-tees erkh rit-mees en op-vin-dernt
The dancers were great and the music was fantastic, very rhythmic and exciting.
Je kon je het bijna niet voorstellen dat dansers het zolang volhielden. De hele voorstelling duurde drie uur.
yer kon yer het bay-naa neet foar-steh-lern dat dan-sers het zoa-lang fol-heel-dern. Der hay-ler foar-steh-linh duwr-der dree uwr
You hardly could understand that the dancers had so much endurance. The performance lasted three hours.

Raymond van Dieren: **Was het makkelijk om aan kaartjes te komen?**
vas het ma-ker-lerk om aan kaar-tyers ter koa-mern
Was it easy to get tickets?

Petra Harskamp: **Het was heel makkelijk, we hebben ze via internet gekocht. Je kunt op de site kijken naar Hot Tickets, dat zijn kaartjes die nog over zijn.**
het was hayl ma-ker-lerk ver heh-bern zer vee-aa in-ter-net kher-kokht. yer kunt op der sayt kay-kern naar hot ti-kets dat zayn kaar-tyers dee nokh oa-fer zayn
It was very easy, you can buy them on the Internet. Just look on the website for Hot Tickets: leftover tickets for the next few weeks.

Raymond van Dieren:	**Nou, een voorstelling van drie uur is me veel te lang. Ik heb vroeger de musical *Tommy* gezien, dat was ook een hele zit.**
	now ern <u>foar</u>-steh-ling fan dree uwr is mer fayl ter lang. ik hep <u>froo</u>-kher der <u>myoo</u>-serkerl <u>to</u>-mee kher-<u>zeen</u> dat vas oak ern <u>hay</u>-ler zit
	Well, a performance lasting three hours is far too long for me. I saw the musical *Tommy* once, that was also a long sit.
Petra Harskamp:	**Ik hoor het al. Een musical is gewoon niks voor jou.**
	ik hoar het al. ern <u>myoo</u>-ser-kerl is kher-<u>voan</u> niks foar yow
	I know what's coming. Musicals are not your cup of tea.
Raymond van Dieren:	**Nee, een musical is aan mij niet besteed.**
	nay ern <u>myoo</u>-ser-kerl is aan may neet may ber-<u>stayt</u>
	No, musicals are wasted on me.

Words to Know

de musical	der <u>myoo</u>-ser-kerl	the musical
ik heb genoten	ik hep kher-<u>noa</u>-tern	I enjoyed it
de dansers	der <u>dan</u>-sers	the dancers
het kostuum	het kos- <u>tuwm</u>	the costume
ritmisch	<u>rit</u>-mees	rhythmic
zich voorstellen	sikh <u>foar</u>-steh-lern	to imagine
volhouden	<u>fol</u>-howl-dern	to endure

Going to a Party

Different people have different ideas about what makes a good party.

Some people like to plan months ahead, and they work hard to make sure that everything falls neatly into place. Others prefer their parties to be very spontaneous. On that kind of party everybody is welcome: family, friends, friends of friends and neighbours.

In case you're invited to a rather formal gathering at somebody's private residence it would be polite to bring a gift, such as a bottle of wine or a bouquet of flowers.

If you receive a written **uitnodiging** (*oait-noa-der-khing*) (invitation), make sure to check if you are expected to RSVP. This abbreviation originally is a French expression and means that you're expected to respond to the invitation.

If you're asked to an informal party your host may ask you to contribute something: a bottle of wine, a six-pack of beer, a salad or a tart. You can also take the initiative and ask if you should bring anything: **Moet ik wat meenemen?** (*moot ik vat may-nay-mern*) (Do you want me to bring anything?).

Birthdays generally give occasion for a small informal party: **een verjaardagsfeestje** (*ern fer-yaar-dakh-fays-tyer*) or **een verjaardag** (*ern fer-yaar- dakh*). You will receive your invitation orally, a week or some days in advance, or even on the day itself.

A birthday party

Traditional Dutch birthdays follow the same pattern: you start with **koffie** (*ko-fee*) (coffee), **thee** (*tay*) (tea) and **gebak/taart** (*kher-bak/taart*) (pastry/ pie). After that you will be offered **een biertje** (*ern beer-tyer*) (a beer) or some other drink. A birthday is very often celebrated in the weekend, on Saturday night. If your Dutch friend has a big family and a lot of friends, he will reserve a whole day for his birthday party, probably Sunday. He does not mind at what time you arrive unless he tells you otherwise. You stay for one, two or three hours, and you can have whatever is offered: tea, coffee, soup, salads or (alcoholic or non-alcoholic) drinks, depending on the time of day.

Very often the birthday party has **zelfbediening** (*zelf-ber-dee-ning*) (selfservice), and you'll find anything you need in the kitchen or on a table.

At a traditional birthday you'll notice that Dutchmen not only congratulate the person who is having his birthday, but also his or her relatives: brothers and sisters, parents, and sometimes even the best friends.

Birthday objection: the alternatives

When it's a Dutchman's birthday, he is under no obligation to give a birthday party. But people will ask him: **Doe je iets met je verjaardag?** (*doo yer eets met yer fer-yaar-dakh*) (Are you doing something on your birthday?) He might respond with one of the following sentences:

✔ **Nou, er komt wat familie, zaterdagavond.** (*now er komt vat fa-mee- lee zaa-ter-dakh-aa-font*) (Well, some relatives are coming Saturday night.)

✔ **Ja, er komen vanavond wat mensen. Als je ook wilt komen, ben je welkom.** (*yaa er koa-mern fa-naa-font vat men-sern. als yer oak vil koa-mern ben yer vel-kom*) (Yes, some people are coming tonight. You're welcome to come as well.)

✔ **Nee, ik doe niets speciaals, ik hoop dat mijn dochter vanavond komt.** (*nay ik doo neets spay-shaals ik hoap dat mayn dokh-ter fa-naa-font komt*) (No, I am doing nothing special, I hope that my daughter will be coming tonight.)

✔ **Ja, ik ga vanavond uit eten met mijn partner.** (*yaa ik khaa fa-naa- font oait ay-tern met mayn part-ner*) (Yes, I'll be eating out tonight with my partner.)

✔ **Ja, ik heb zaterdagavond een etentje met wat goede vrienden.** (*yaa ik hep zaa-ter-dakh aa-font ern ay-tern-tyer met vat khoo-der freen-dern*) (Yes, I'm having dinner with a few close friends on Saturday night.)

✔ **Nee, ik doe dit jaar niets. Ik ben niet in de stemming.** (*nay ik doo dit yaar neets. ik ben neet in der steh-ming*) (No, I'm doing nothing this year. I'm not in the mood for it.)

As a response, one of the following sentences might be helpful:

✔ **OK, veel plezier!** (*oa-kay, fayl pler-zeer*) (Okay, have a nice party!)

✔ **Dank je, ik kom vanavond langs.** (*dank yer ik kom fa-naa-font langs*) (Thank you, I might drop by tonight.)

✔ **OK, veel plezier in ieder geval!** (*oa-kay fayl pler-zeer in ee-der kher-fal*) (Okay, have a good time anyhow!)

Don't feel insulted if you're not invited. A birthday is a private and not a public matter!

Being Invited

You may hear any of the following common phrases when receiving **een uitnodiging voor een feestje** (*ern oait-noa-der-khing foar ern fays-tyer*) (an invitation to a party):

> ✔ **Ik wil je graag uitnodigen voor een feestje.** (*ik vil yer khraakh oait-noa-der-khern foar ern fayst-yer*) (I would like to invite you for a party.)
>
> ✔ **Ik geef een feestje, vind je het leuk om te komen?** (*ik khayf ern fays-tyer fint yer het luk om ter koa-mern*) (I'm having a party, would you like to come?)

You may need to ask when and where the parting is going to take place before you can accept or decline the invitation. These simple phrases can get to the information you need:

> ✔ **Wanneer is het feest?** (*va-nayr is het fays-tyer*) (When is the party?)
>
> ✔ **Waar is het feest?** (*vaar is het fayst*) (Where is the party?)

Declining an invitation

If you can't make it or if for some reason you don't want to go, you can politely turn down the invitation by saying the following:

> ✔ **Nee, het spijt me, ik kan niet komen.** (*nay het spayt mer ik kan neet koa-mern*) (No, I'm sorry, I'm not able to come.)
>
> ✔ **Nee, ik kan niet komen, ik heb al iets anders.** (*nay ik kan neet koa-mern ik hep al eets an-ders*) (I won't be able to come, as I already have something else planned.)

Accepting

If the time and place are right and the mood strikes you, you can accept an invitation with the following phrases:

> ✔ **Dank je. Ik neem de uitnodiging graag aan.** (*dank yer. ik naym der oait-noa-der-khing khraakh aan*) (Thank you. I gladly accept the invitation.)
>
> ✔ **OK, ik vind het leuk om te komen. Moet ik iets meenemen?** (*oakay ik fint het luk om ter koa-mern*) (Sure, I would like to come. Do you want me to bring something?)

To the question of whether you can bring something with you, your host may respond:

- ✔ **Nee, het is niet nodig om iets mee te nemen. Voor eten en drinken wordt gezorgd.** (*nay het is neet noa-dikh om eets may ter nay-mern. foar ay-tern en drin-kern vort kher-zorkht*) (No, it is not necessary to bring something. Food and drinks are taken care of.)

- ✔ **Het zou leuk zijn als je een salade meenam.** (*het zow luk zayn als yer ern sa-laa-der may-nam*) (It would be nice if you brought a salad.)

- ✔ **Ja graag. Ik weet dat je heerlijke appeltaart bakt. Neem er eentje mee.** (*yaa khraakh. ik vayt dat yer hayr-ler-ker a-perl-taart bakt. naymn er aynt-yer may*) (Yes please. I know that you bake great apple pies. Please bring one.)

Talking about a party

When somebody asks you **Hoe was het feest?** (*hoo vas het fayst*) (What was the party like?), here are some possible responses:

- ✔ **Leuk, we zijn daar heel lang gebleven.** (*luk ver zayn daar hayl lang kher-blay-fern*) (Fine, we stayed there a long time.)

- ✔ **Wij hebben het erg leuk gehad.** (*vay heh-bern het ehrkh luk kher-hat*) (We had a great time.)

- ✔ **Het feestje was...** (*het fays-tyer vas*) (The party was...)

  - **erg gezellig** (*ehrkh kher-zeh-likh*) (very pleasant)

  - **leuk** (*luk*) (fine)

  - **te gek** (*ter khek*) (great)

  - **fantastisch** (*fan-tas-tees*) (fantastic)

  - **opwindend** (*op-vin-dernt*) (exciting)

  - **nogal saai** (*no-khal saay*) (rather dull)

  - **erg vermoeiend** (*erkh fer-mooy-ernt*) (exhausting)

Going Out of Town

In this chapter, we look at the fun things people do when they are not working. Dutchmen are entitled to an average of 20 to 30 vacation days per year – in addition to national holidays – and they like to make the most of them. Some people prefer to have two or three short holidays during the year: they fly to a warm beach, take another week for diving, and go skiing for another week.

Others save their holidays up for longer, exotic and sometimes extreme, travel to some country in a different continent.

In the weekends some Dutchmen spend their time renovating their houses, others just relax to recover from the week. Part of the inhabitants of the western part of the Netherlands go to a camping or holiday park every weekend. Water sports and boating are very popular in the Netherlands. In this chapter you'll find some language material to keep you busy, even when relaxing.

Talking about Hobbies and Interests

During the course of conversations, the topic often turns to various interests and hobbies. In this section, you'll find what you need to know to join in the conversation.'

Verzamelen' (collecting)

Some people like to **sparen** (*spaa-rern*) (to collect) things. To tell people about your particular area of interest, say:

Ik verzamel . . . (*ik fer-zaa-merl*) (I collect . . .)

At the end of this phrase, you name the object of your collection.

- ✔ **bierviltjes** (*beer-vilt-yers*) (coasters)
- ✔ **antieke poppen** (*an-tee-ker po-pern*) (antique dolls)
- ✔ **koekblikken** (*kook-bli-kern*) (biscuit boxes)
- ✔ **munten** (*muhn-tern*) (coins)
- ✔ **postzegels** (*post-zay-kherls*) (stamps)

Telling people about your hobby

Some people enjoy making things with their hands. Just use this simple phrases to introduce the topic:

Mijn hobby is . . . (*mayn ho-bee is . . .*)

At the end of this phrase, you supply the necessary information. For example:

- ✔ **koken** (*koa-kern*) (cooking)
- ✔ **tuinieren** (*toai-nee-rern*) (gardening)

    ✔ **doe-het-zelven** (*doo-ert-<u>zel</u>-fern*) (to do-it-yourself)

    ✔ **tekenen** (*<u>tay</u>-ker-nern*) (drawing)

    ✔ **schilderen** (*<u>skhil</u>-der-ern*) (painting)

Jonge gezinnen (*<u>yong</u>-er kher-zi-nern*) (young families) and **drukke mensen** (*<u>druh</u>-ker <u>men</u>-sern*) (busy people) have little time for hobbies. When you ask them how they they spend their leisure time, they might answer:

    ✔ **Ik onstpan ik me met televisiekijken.** (*ik ont-<u>span</u> mer met tay-ler-<u>fee</u>-see <u>kay</u>-kern*) (I relax watching TV.)

    ✔ **Ik vermaak me met de kinderen.** (*ik fer-<u>maak</u> mer met der <u>kin</u>-der-ern*) (I make fun with the kids.)

    ✔ **Ik verwen mezelf met een sauna.** (*ik fer-<u>ven</u> mer-<u>zelf</u> met ern <u>sow</u>-naa*) (I pamper myself with a sauna.)

    ✔ **Ik veroorloof me een ochtend op het voetbalveld.** (*ik fer-<u>oar</u>-loaf mer ern <u>okh</u>-ternt op het <u>foot</u>-bal-felt*) (I allow myself a morning on the football pitch.)

In all the answers a reflexive verb is used. See below.

Reflexive Verbs: 'Zich ontspannen'

Some verbs in Dutch are always accompanied by an extra personal pronoun such as **zich** (*zikh*) (oneself), **me** (*mer*) (myself), **je** (*yer*) (yourself), **zich** (*zikh*) (himself, herself, or yourself formal), **ons** (*ons*) (ourselves), **je** (*yer*) (yourselves), and **zich** (*zikh*) (yourselves). We call them **wederkerende werkwoorden** or reflexive verbs. Here is **zich ontspannen** (*zikh ont-<u>span</u>-nern)* (to relax).

Conjugation	*Pronunciation*
ik ontspan me	*ik ont-<u>span</u> mer*
jij ontspant je	*yay ont-<u>spant</u> yer*
u ontspant u/zich	*uw ont-<u>spant</u> uw/zikh*
hij ontspant zich	*hay ont-<u>spant</u> zikh*
zij ontspant zich	*zay ont-<u>spant</u> zikh*
het ontspant zich	*het ont-<u>spant</u> zikh*
wij ontspannen ons	*way ont-<u>span</u>-nern ons*
jullie ontspannen je	*<u>yuw</u>-lee ont-<u>span</u>-nern yer*
zij ontspannen zich	*zay ont-<u>span</u>-nern zikh*

The most frequent reflexive verbs in Dutch are: **zich schamen** (*zikh skhaa-mern*) (to feel ashamed), **zich vergissen** (*zikh fer-khi-sern*) (to make a mistake), **zich vervelen** (*zikh fer-fay-lern*) (to be bored), **zich herinneren** (*zikh heh-ri-ner-rern*) (to remember), **zich bemoeien met** (*zikh ber-mooy-ern met*) (to meddle in), and **zich gedragen** (*zikh kher-draa- khern*) (to behave oneself).

- ✔ **Ik schaam me vreselijk.** (*ik skhaam mer fray-ser-lerk*) (I am terribly ashamed.)

- ✔ **Je vergist je.** (*yer fer-khist yer*) (You are making a mistake.)

- ✔ **Ik herinner me zijn naam.** (*ik her-ri-ner mer zayn naam*) (I remember his name.)

- ✔ **Ik verveel me nooit.** (*ik fer-fayl mer nooyt*) (I am never bored.)

- ✔ **Ik bemoei met niet met haar zaken.** (*ik ber-mooy mer neet met haar zaa-kern*) (I don't meddle in her affairs.)

- ✔ **Gedraag je!** (*kher-draakh yer*) (Behave yourself!)

Other verbs can be used in two different ways: as a normal verb or as a reflexive one. **Ik was mijn haar** (*ik vas mern haar*) (I'm washing my hair), is as correct as **Ik was me** (*ik vas mer*) (I wash myself), but means something different. It's possible to say **De verpleegkundige scheert de patiënt** (*der fer-playkh-kuhn-der-kher skhayrt der pa-shehnt*) (The nurse shaves the patient) but also **Ik scheer me twee keer per dag** (*ik skayr mer tvay kayr per dakh*) (I shave twice a day). **Ergeren** (*ehr-kher-ern*) can be used as **Die man ergert me** (*dee man ehr-khert mer*) (That man irritates me) but also as a reflexive verb: **Ik erger me aan die man** (*ik ehr-kher- mer aan dee man*) (I feel irritated by that man). **Het kind vermaakt me** (*het kint fer-maakt mer*) (The child amuses me) means something different from **Ik vermaak me met mijn kind** (*ik fer-maak mer met mern kint*) (I amuse myself with my child). Here is the complete conjugation of **zich vermaken** (*zikh fer-maa-kern)* (to amuse oneself).

Conjugation	Pronunciation
ik vermaak me	*ik fer-maak mer*
jij vermaakt je	*jay fer-maakt jer*
u vermaakt u/zich	*uw fer-maakt uw/zikh*
hij/zij/het vermaakt zich	*hay/zay/het fer-maakt zikh*
wij vermaken ons	*vay fer-maa-kern ons*
jullie vermaken je	*yuw-lee fer-maa-kern yer*
zij vermaken zich	*zay fer-maa-kern zikh*

Leaving Town

Are you longing to leave hectic city life behind and breathe some fresh air? Even in the **Randstad** (*rant-stat*) (the urbanised western part of the Netherlands) you'll find patches of nature for a walk. You'll find a wood or lake near every town, big enough to get a breath of fresh air.

Going for a walk

Een eindje wandelen (*ern ayn-tyer van-der-lern*) (to take a short walk) is the most popular pastime in the Netherlands during the weekend. Most people go for a short walk in a park or wooded area nearby or they take the car to drive to some place for a walk of an hour or longer.

Woods for a hiking of a day can be found in a few places in the Netherlands. The largest of these areas is **de Veluwe** (*der fay-luw-er*) in the central part of the country. Though the woods are extensive, they are very cultivated. You'll find footpaths and bicycle tracks everywhere. In all parks and woods you'll meet Dutchman walking their dogs: generally **aangelijnd** (*aan-kher-laynt*) (kept on a leash).

Lovers of hiking will find a historical path connecting the south and north of the country: **het Pieterpad**. This historical route has been cultivated and protected and leads along some of the most beautiful and quiet parts of the Netherlands. Dutchmen take the time to walk it: they do it in parts, in the weekends and during holidays. You'll find the route along with Bed and Breakfast places on the Net.

Biking: 'fietsen'

Second-best in popularity is **een eind fietsen** (*ern aynt feet-sern*) or **een fiet-stocht maken** (*ern feets-tokht maa-kern*) (to go for a biking trip). Holland boasts more bikes than inhabitants (18 million compared to 16 million) and 40% of the bikes are used for recreation. Each year over a million bikes are sold – and 750,000 stolen. So keep your bike well locked when you're having a rest, especially in town! **Een fietstocht** (*ern feets-tokht*) (a biking trip) is an interesting pastime on Sundays in summer. You will see parts of the Netherlands that cannot be reached by car.

Dutchmen make the tour in the region where they live, or they load the bikes onto their car in order to explore some different region. People take their bikes to the camp site as well. Thousands of **fietspaden** (*feets-paa- dern*) (bicycle tracks) and **paddenstoelen** (*pa-der-stoo-lern*) (small white signposts in the form of a mushroom, called 'mushrooms') make it easy to find your way.

To rent a bike is possible at almost all train stations. Be aware: don't hit the road if you've never been on a bike. Though biking looks very easy, it's difficult to get the hang of at a later age.

Going to an amusement park

Speeltuinen (_spayl_-toai-nern) (playgrounds) and **pretparken** (_pret_-parkern) (amusement parks) are popular for families. You'll find them on the Internet.

Going to the beach

The Netherlands have hundreds of kilometers of sandy beach along the North Sea. Some people love to go to the beach and book a two-week holiday in a sea resort every year. If the sun shines, you can sunbathe and have a swim in the sea. Scheveningen near Den Haag and Zandvoort boast a casino, as well as terraces, bars, restaurants, and discos for those who prefer to spend their money otherwise. Those who love **het strandleven** (het _strant_-lay-fern) (the beach life) hire **een strandhuisje** (ern _strant_-hois-yer) (a beach cabin) for some weeks and enjoy **zwemmen** (_sveh_-mern) (swimming) and **zonnebaden** (_zo_-ner-baadern) (sunbathing). The children love **pootjebaden** (_poa_-tyer-baa-dern) (to paddle), **schelpen zoeken** (_skhel_-pern _zoo_-kern) (to collect shells), and **zandkastelen bouwen** (_zant_-kas-tay-lern _bow_-ern) (to build sandcastles) when it's **eb** (ep) (low tide). The castle will be washed away by the **vloed** (floot) (rising tide) that comes up twice **per etmaal** (pehr _eht_-maal) (per twenty-four-hour period).

Be prepared that in June, July, and August the temperature of the North Sea water is still a mere 17 °C!

Surfen (_sur_-fern) (wave surfing) and **vliegeren** (_flee_-kher-rern) (to fly kites) are possible only in special places.

On sunny days with temperatures over 25 °C the roads to the coast will be crowded. Well-informed Dutchmen take the bike, the bus or the train to go to the beach, just carrying **een handdoek** (ern _han_-dook) (a towel), **zwembroek** (_svem_-brook) (swimming trunks), **bikini** (bee-_kee_-nee) (bikini), and **zonnebrandcrème** (_zo_-ner-brant-crehm) (sun cream) in their **strandtas** (_stran_-tas) (beach bag).

The beach is **openbaar** (oa-pern-_baar_) (open to the public) and it's possible to hire **een strandstoel** (ern _strant_-stool) (a deck chair) at one of the many **strandpaviljoens** (_strant_-paa-verl-yoons) (beach pavilions). Sometimes, **kleedhokjes** (_kleet_-hok-yers) (changing cubicles) are available. Most people change on the beach, some of them already wearing their bathing trunks and bikinis underneath their clothes. **Toiletten** (*tvaa-leh-tern*) (toilets), **douches** (*doo-shers*) (showers), **een kinderbadje** (*ern kin-der-ba-tyer*) (children's pool) **met of zonder toezicht** (*met of zon-der too-zikht*) (with or without attendance) are available in all beach resorts, as well as **de reddingsbrigade** (*der reh-dings-bree-khaa-der*) (lifeguards). **De reddingsbrigade** will try to save your life if you are dragged along by a **gevaarlijke stroming** (*kher-faar-ler-ker stroa-ming*) (dangerous current). Even if you are **een goede zwemmer** (*ern khoo-der sveh-mer*) (a good swimmer), be sure to keep the ground under your feet. Especially **oostenwind** (*oas-tern-vint*) (east wind, off the coast) is very dangerous, and it also brings **kwallen** (*kva-lern*) (jellyfish). When you want know more about **het strandleven** (*het strant-lay-fern*) (beach life), the next phrases might come in handy:

- ✔ **Is hier een zwembad?** (*is heer ern svem-bat*) (Is there a swimming pool here?)

- ✔ **Is hier een overdekt zwembad?** (*is heer ern oa-fer-dekt svem-bat*) (Is there an indoor swimming pool here?)

- ✔ **Is hier een nudistenstrand in de buurt?** (*is heer ern nuw-dis-ternstrant in der buwrt*) (Is there a nudist beach nearby?)

- ✔ **Wanneer wordt het eb?** (*va-nayr vort het ep*) (When is the low tide coming?)

- ✔ **Wanneer wordt het vloed?** (*va-nayr vort het floot*) (When will it be high tide?)

- ✔ **Mag je hier zwemmen?** (*makh yer heer sveh-mern*) (Is swimming allowed here?)

- ✔ **Zijn hier gevaarlijke stromingen?** (*zayn heer kher-faar-ler-ker stroa-ming-ern*) (Are there dangerous currents?)

You might hear one of the following answers:

- ✔ **De zee is rustig/de zee is woest.** (*der zay is ruhs-tikh/der zay is voost*) (The sea is calm/turbulent.)

- ✔ **De golven zijn hoog.** (*der khol-vern zayn hoakh*) (The waves are high.)

- ✔ **Er komt storm.** (*er komt storm*) (There is a storm coming up.)

- ✔ **Het water is te koud.** (*het vaa-ter is ter kowt*) (The water is too cold.)

- ✔ **Je mag hier niet zwemmen.** (*yer makh heer neet sveh-mern*) (Swimming is not allowed here.)

CULTURAL WISDOM

Walking to a Frisian island

July and August can be pretty rainy. The sunniest places in the Netherlands during summer are the Frisian Islands in the north. They offer a nice opportunity for walking and biking, though in summer, you will not be the only one! If you want to do something more adventurous, walk from Friesland to Schiermonnikoog or to one of the other islands at low tide, and travel back by boat. It's dangerous to do that by yourself and unprepared. You'll have to hire a guide. This **wadlopen** (*vat-loa-pern*) (walking across the mud flats) can be an unforgettable Dutch experience.

Watching the sea

Never mind the weather, the North Sea beach and the dunes are always good for **een strandwandeling** (*ern strant-van-der-ling*) (a walk along the beach). Some people and their dogs love the beach most when it's stormy! Don't try to go for a walk when it's more than 25 °C: roads, dunes, and beaches will be overcrowded. In that case, better try a swim in the early morning or in the late evening.

Sport, Sports, Sports

Sports are a favourite form of amusement. Many people stick to **de sportschool** (*der sport-skhoal*) (the gym) that they visit once, twice or three times a week. Football is very popular among both boys and men. One million Dutchmen are members of the Dutch football league, the KNVB. Second and third Dutch sports are tennis and hockey, with some 750,000 participants each. Volleyball and beach volleyball go for the fifth place among the club sports.

The most popular ball game: 'voetbal'

Men not only love **voetbal kijken** (*foot-bal kay-kern*) (to watch football/soccer) but they also **voetballen** (*foot-ba-lern*) (to play football) themselves. Dutch youngsters start with **voetbal spelen** when they are four, with their parents standing at the sideline. Watching football on TV during **de Europese kampioenschappen** (*der u-roa-pay-ser kam-pee-yoon-skha- pern*) (European Championships) or **de Wereldkampioenschappen** (*der vay-rerlt- kam-pee-yoon-skha-pern*) (World Championships) is massive and during such events many women will join their partners. Up to two and a half million Dutchmen watch the matches on TV and football sometime deregulates working life. **Een prachtige bal** (*ern* <u>*prakh*</u>*- ti-kher bal*) (a sublime shot), **een doelpunt maken** (*ern* <u>*dool*</u>*-puhnt* <u>*maa*</u>*-kern*) (to score a goal) in **de eerste/tweede helft** (*der* <u>*ayr*</u>*-ster/*<u>*tvay*</u>*-der helft*) (the first/the second leg), **een misser** (*ern* <u>*mi*</u>*-ser*) (a poor shot) of **de linksvoor** (*der links-*<u>*foar*</u>) (the left-winger), **de rechtsvoor** (*der rekhts-*<u>*foar*</u>) (the right-winger), **de middenvelder** (*der* <u>*mi*</u>*-dern-felder*) (the midfield player) or **de doelman** (*der* <u>*dool*</u>*-man*) (the goalkeeper) and **strafschoppen** (<u>*peh*</u>*-nal-tees*) (penalties) **voor de rust** (*foar der ruhst*) (before half-time) and **na de rust** (*naa der ruhst*) (after half-time), are the talk of the day. In anticipation people decorate houses and even whole streets with lines of orange flags. When an important match is played, almost everybody will be watching and the streets are deserted. If you are the partner or colleague of a football lover, you might need the following sentences:

- ✔ **Wie spelen er vanavond?** (*vee spay-lern er fa-*<u>*naa*</u>*-font*) (Who are playing tonight?)

- ✔ **Wie zitten er in de finale?** (*vee* <u>*zi*</u>*-tern er in der fee-*<u>*naa*</u>*-ler*) (Who are in the finals?)

When, the day after, you ask how it was, you can hear the next opinions:

- ✔ **De wedstrijd was** (*der* <u>*vet*</u>*-strayt vas*) (The match was):

    - **spannend** (<u>*spa*</u>*-nernt*) (tense)

    - **waardeloos** (<u>*vaar*</u>*-der-loas*) (hopeless)

- ✔ and the favourite club:

    - **. . . heeft gewonnen** (*... hayft kher-*<u>*vo*</u>*-nern*) (... won)

    - **. . . heeft verloren** (*...hayft fer-*<u>*loa*</u>*-ren*) (... lost)

    - **. . . gaat door naar de finale** (*... khaat doar naar der fee-*<u>*naa*</u>*-ler*) (... goes on to the finals).

Skating: 'schaatsen'

Only when the weather gods are with us, is it possible to skate on natural ice. It has to **vriezen** (<u>*free*</u>*-zern*) (to freeze) moderately for three or four days or severely for two 24-hour periods and Dutch **sloten en kanalen** (<u>*sloa*</u>*-tern en ka-*<u>*naa*</u>*-lern*) (ditches and canals) are full of kids and adults that spend every minute of daylight on the ice. If there's no caring mother or father to keep the child from falling on the ice, an old chair will do as support for the first few days and when the frost period stretches for some weeks, the learning period is over and the child, later on, might become a winner of the **Elfstedentocht** (*elf-*<u>*stay*</u>*-dern-tokht*). For more information about skating see Chapter 3.

Nederland heeft gewonnen: Using the present perfect

English-speaking people use the past tense a lot: 'Manchester United started a new era. They entered a brand new competition. They achieved ...'. Therefore English-speaking people tend to use the past tense in Dutch as well. Dutch, however, uses the present perfect much more than the simple past. Some simple rules and a lot of listening to Dutch people and watching Dutch TV will help you to get the necessary experience that permits you to replace rules by intuition. Dutch has several names for this tense. The most simple and meaningful name is **de voltooide tijd** (*der fol-tooy-der tayt*) (the perfect). **Voltooid** means finished. You use the perfect most often when talking about events which started in the past and have already finished: they no longer continue in the present. **Nederland heeft gewonnen.** (*nay-der-lant hayft khe-won-nern*) means that the match is over and that this time the Netherlands won. You also use the perfect to introduce a story about the past: **Nederland heeft gewonnen.** (*nay-der-lant hayft khe-wonnern*) (The Netherlands won). After this introduction you might continue the story in the past tense: **In de tweede helft scoorde ...** (*in der tway-der helft ... scoar-der*) (In the second leg ... scored). You can read more about the forms and help verbs of the perfect and in Chapter 2. You can read more about the past tense and it's use in the chapters 2 and 15.

Boating: 'varen' and 'zeilen'

Varen (*faa-rern*) (boating), and specifically **zeilen** (*zay-lern*) (sailing), demands **inzicht** (*in-zikht*) (insight), **vooruitzien** (*foar-oait-zeen*) (planning ahead), and **reactiesnelheid** (*ray-ak-see-snel-hayt*) (speed of reaction). Lots of people have **een boot** (*ern boat*) (a boat) or **een schip** (*ern skhip*) (a ship) that they use every **weekeinde/weekend** (*vayk-ayn-der/ veek-ent*) (weekend) from April to September. During **het weekend** the ships sail the waters near **de haven** (*der haa-fern*) (the harbour), in holidays the owners of the taller ships explore Dutch, Belgian and French and UK **wateren** (*vaa-ter-ern*) (waters) and **zeeën** (*zay-ern*) (seas).

Most **zeilschepen** (*zayl-skhay-pern*) (sailing ships) do have **een motor** (*ern moa-ter*) (a motor) that is used **in geval van nood** (*in kher-fal fan noat*) (in case of emergency), on **drukke vaarroutes** (*druh-ker faar-rooters*) (busy courses of navigation) and **bij windstilte** (*bay vint-stil-ter*) (when it's windless). **Motorboten** (*moa-ter-boa-tern*) (motorboats) just have a motor. **Watersporters** (*vaa-ter-spor-ters*) (lovers of aquatic sports) love to see Holland from the water and they are fond of the life that belongs to boating. The atmosphere in the harbour and the cheerfull outings **op de wal** (*op der val*) (on the shore) are the reward for a rough day on the water.

Playing golf: 'golfen'

Golf (*kolf/golf*) (golf) is popular for businessmen, pensioners and increasingly young people too. In most regions, you'll find some golf courses.

The playing verb: 'spelen'

Spelen (*spay-lern*) (to play) is a regular verb. In order to pronounce it well, you double the **ee** in the stem (the I-form) and the second and third person (you singular and he, she and you formal).

Conjugation	Pronunciation
ik speel	*ik spayl*
jij speelt	*yay spaylt*
u speelt	*uw spaylt*
hij/zij/het speelt	*hay/zay/het spaylt*
wij spelen	*vay spay-lern*
jullie spelen	*yuw-lee spay-lern*
zij spelen	*zay spay-lern*

The verb **spelen** can be combined with all kinds of sports: **Ik speel voetbal** (*ik spayl foot-bal*), **ik speel tennis** (*ik spayl teh-nis*), **ik speel hockey** (*ik spayl ho-kee*), **ik speel volleyball** (*ik spayl fo-lee-bal*).

Sporting verbs: false friends

The Dutch use a lot of English words, and a lot of English sporting verbs. They will seem easy for you, but in reality they often differ from the English verbs, so these false friends have to be considered carefully. In the following examples you see that Dutch-speaking people conjugate them in their own way, which is perfectly regular (stem, stem plus **-t**, and the infinitive for the plural forms) but different from the English way. Here an example of the verb **racen** (*ray-sern*) (to race).

Conjugation	*Pronunciation*
racen	*ray-sern*
ik race	*ik rays*
jij racet	*yay rayst*
u racet	*uw rayst*
hij/zij/het racet	*hay/zay/het rayst*
wij racen	*vay rays-ern*
jullie racen	*yuw-lee ray-sern*
zij racen	*zay ray-sern*

Instead of **hockey spelen** (*ho-kee spay-lern*) (to play hockey) you will also use the verb **hockeyen** (*ho-kee-yern*), which follows the same routine as all English verbs that are used in Dutch:

Conjugation	*Pronunciation*
hockeyen	*ho-kee-yern*
ik hockey	*ik ho-kee*
jij hockeyt	*yay ho-keet*
u hockeyt	*uw ho-keet*
hij/zij/het hockeyt	*hay/zay/het ho-keet*
wij hockeyen	*vay ho-kee-yern*
jullie hockeyen	*yuw-lee ho-kee-yern*
zij hockeyen	*zah ho-kee-yern*

Golfen (*khol-fern*) (to play golf), **tennissen** (*teh-ni-sern*) (to play tennis) and **joggen** (*yo-gern/jo-gern*) (to jog) are all used in the same way. At the end of your sports hour your coach might say:

> **Nu gaan we stretchen.** (*nuw khaan ver stret-shern*) (Now you're going to stretch.)

and afterwards you might say:

> **Ik voel me heel relaxed.** (*ik fool mer hayl ree-lekst*) (I feel very relaxed.)

Chapter 9

When You Have to Work

. . . .

In This Chapter

▶ Telephone talk

▶ Inside the office

▶ Dealing with the Dutch

. . . .

*T*alking to people in person is just one aspect of communication. You also want to be able to handle everything in telecommunications, be it talking to people on the phone or sending e-mails. Telephone talk involves quite a lot of topics, and so do e-mails.

Telephone Talk

Mobieltjes (*moa-beel-tyers*) or **GSM's** (*khay-es-ems*) (mobile or cell phones) have changed telephone manners. As they have a personal number, cell phone users generally just mention their first name when they **een telefoontje krijgen** (*ern tay-ler-foan-tyer kray-khern*) (receive a call). When you want to say you're going to call someone, or somebody called you, all you need is the verb **bellen** (*beh-lern*) or the more formal verb **opbellen** (*op-beh-lern*) (to call). **Ik bel je** (*ik bel yer*) (I will call you) or **we bellen** (*ver beh-lern*) (we will call each other) is a common informal way of saying goodbye.

Conjugation	Pronunciation
ik bel	*ik bel*
jij belt	*yay belt*
u belt	*uw belt*
hij/zij/het belt	*hay/zay/het belt*
wij bellen	*vay beh-lern*
jullie bellen	*yuw-lee beh-lern*
zij bellen	*zay beh-lern*

Opbellen (*op-beh-lern*) (to call) is a so-called separable verb, a verb that splits into two parts in the present and past tense. The word order of some words may come between the two parts of the verb:

> ✔ **Ik bel hem op.** (*ik bel hem op*) (I'm calling him.)

> ✔ **Jij belt haar vaak op.** (*yay belt haar faak op*) (You call her often.)

GRAMMATICALLY SPEAKING

The personal pronoun as an object

The most common form of the personal pronouns are those we use as a subject, that is in the beginning of the sentence and together with a verb: **ik** (*ik*) (I), **jij/je** (*yay/yer*) (you, informal singular), **hij** (*hay*) (he), **zij/ze** (*zay/zer*) (she), **u** (*uw*) (you, formal singular and plural), **wij/we** (*vay/ver*) (we), **jullie** (*yuw-lee*) (you, informal plural), **zij/ze** (*zay/zer*) (they). However, personal pronouns play different roles in the sentence and Dutch has a specific form for each role, just like English. Here you see what happens when the personal pronoun is not the subject, but the object, in the sentence. Personal pronouns in the role of the object are used in the last part of the sentence. Here are the changes and their examples:

Subject Form	Object Form	
ik	mij, me	**Cilla belt me.** (*si-laa belt mer*) (Cilla calls me.)
jij/ je	jou, je	**Cilla belt je.** (*si-laa belt yer*) (Cilla calls you.)
u	u	**Cilla belt u.** (*si-laa belt uw*) (Cilla calls you.)
hij	hem	**Cilla belt hem.** (*si-laa belt hem*) (Cilla calls him.)
zij	haar	**Cilla belt haar.** (*si-laa belt haar*) (Cilla calls her.)
wij	ons	**Cilla belt ons.** (*si-laa belt ons*) (Cilla calls us.)
jullie	jullie, je	**Cilla belt jullie.** (*si-laa belt yuw-lee*) (Cilla calls you.)
zij/ze	hen, ze	**Cilla belt hen/Cilla belt ze.** (*si-laa belt hen/si-laa beltzer*) (Cilla calls them.)

The pronouns used as an object are equivalent to the pronouns that are used after a preposition. See Chapter 4 for more on this.

Opening lines

Many people have a **mobieltje van de zaak** (*moa-beel-tyer fan der zaak*) (a cell phone provided by the boss) that they use both for business and personal purposes. When they are at work and expect inbound calls, they should answer the phone mentioning the name of the firm, followed by their first and last name: **Biz Accountants, Raymond van Dieren** (*biser-kowntents ray-mont fan dee-rern*) (Biz Accountants, Raymond van Dieren). Elderly people and people in high places just use their last name: **Lease Consult, Van der Jagt** (*lees kon-suhlt fan der yakht*) (Lease Consult, Van der Jagt). Some (elderly) ladies call themselves **mevrouw** (*mer-frow*) (Mrs) and mention this title in combination with their last name: **Biz Accountants, mevrouw Harskamp** (*bis er-kowntents mer-frow hars-kamp*) (Biz Accountants, Mrs Harskamp).

Receptionists and secretaries always start with **Goedemorgen** (*khooder-mor-khern*) (good morning) or **goedemiddag** (*khoo-der-mi-dakh*) (good afternoon): **Goedemorgen, Lease Consult, Cilla Vermeent** (*khooder-mor-khern lees kon-suhlt si-laa fer-maynt*) (Good morning, Lease Consult, Cilla Vermeent).

In smaller or more informal and personal companies, such as beauty salons, hairdressers' and gyms, people often just use their first names: **Beautysalon Welling, met Sonja** (*byoo-tee-sa-lon weh-ling met son-yaa*) (Beauty salon Welling, Sonja speaking).

Calling

When you are calling someone at a private house and the person you wish to speak to doesn't pick up the phone himself, it's up to you to ask for your party. First you have to announce yourself:

> **Hallo, met René.** (*ha-loa met rer-nay*) (Hello, René speaking.)

Then you ask for your party:

- ✔ **Is Sandra thuis?** (*is san-draa toais*) (Is Sandra at home?)
- ✔ **Kan ik Sandra spreken?** (*kan ik san-draa spray-kern*) (Can I speak to Sandra?)

In business situations you are expected to be more formal. You announce yourself wishing a good morning or a good afternoon:

> **Goedemorgen, met Raymond van Dieren.** (*khoo-dern-mor-khern met ray-mont fan dee-rern*) (Good morning, Raymond van Dieren speaking.)

The most widely used options in business when it comes to expressing that you want to speak to somebody, are:

> ✔ **Is de heer . . . aanwezig?** (*is de hayr ... aan-vay-zikh*) (Is Mr ... in?)

> ✔ **Is mevrouw . . . bereikbaar?** (*is mer-frow ... ber-rayk-baar*) (Can Mrs ... be reached by phone?)

Prompting the person you're talking to

When somebody talks too fast, and you can't understand them, the following phrases might be useful:

> ✔ **Kunt u wat langzamer praten?** (*kuhnt uw vat lang-zaa-mer praa-tern*) (Would you mind speaking more slowly, please?)

> ✔ **Kunt u dat herhalen?** (*kuhnt uw dat hehr-haa-lern*) (Could you repeat that, please?)

Many Dutch people will answer by speaking English to you. Lots of Dutchmen like to practise their English talking to foreigners! If you don't want them to speak English, just ask them:

> **Ik ben Nederlands aan het leren, wilt u Nederlands praten?** (*ik ben nay-der-lants aan het lay-rern vilt uw nay-der-lants praa-tern*) (I am learning Dutch, could you speak Dutch, please?)

Making the connection

After you've called a company or an organisation and you have asked to speak to a specific person, you can receive a number of responses depending on who you want and where they are:

> ✔ **Daar spreekt u mee.** (*daar spraykt uw may*) (Speaking.)

> ✔ **Ik verbind u door.** (*ik fer-bint uw doar*) (I'll put you through.)

> ✔ **Een momentje alstublieft, ik verbind u door.** (*ern moa-men-tyer als-tuw-bleeft ik fer-bint uw doar*) (One moment please, I'll put you through.)

> ✔ **De lijn is bezet.** (*der layn is ber-zet*) (The line is engaged.)

Not being there: the routine

Unfortunately, you often don't get through to the person you're trying to reach. You can then hear one of the following phrases:

- ✔ **Mevrouw . . . is op dit moment aan de telefoon, wilt u wachten?** (*mer-frow ... is op dit moa-ment aan der tay-ler-foan vilt uw wakhtern*) (Mrs . . . is on the phone now, do you want to wait?)

- ✔ **Mevrouw . . . is telefonisch in gesprek.** (*mer-frow ... is tay-ler-foanees in kher-sprek*) (Mrs ... is on the phone right now.)

- ✔ **Mevrouw . . . is in bespreking. Kunt u over een uur terugbellen?** (*mer-frow . . . is in ber-spray-king. kuhnt uw oa-ver ern uwr ter-ruhk-beh- lern*) (Mrs . . . is in a meeting. Could you call her back in an hour?)

- ✔ **Mevrouw . . . is in bespreking. Kan zij u terugbellen?** (*mer-frow . . . is in ber-spray-king. kan zay uw ter-rukh-beh-lern*) (Mrs ... is in a meeting. Could she call you back?)

- ✔ **Het spijt me, mevrouw . . . is niet op haar plek.** (*het spayt mer mer-frow ... is neet op haar plek*) (I am sorry, Mrs ... is not at her desk.)

- ✔ **Mevrouw . . . neemt niet op.** (*mer-frow . . . naymt neet op*) (Mrs . . . isn't answering the phone.)

- ✔ **Zou u later terug kunnen bellen?** (*zow uw laa-ter ter-ruhk kuh-nern beh-lern*) (Could you call again later?)

- ✔ **Mag ik uw telefoonnummer?** (*makh ik uw tay-ler-foan-nuh-mer*) (Could I have your phone number please?)

The next expression might be helpful if something is wrong with the connection:

- ✔ **Het is een slechte lijn.** (*het is ern slekh-ter layn*) (It's a bad line.)

- ✔ **Ik versta u slecht.** (*ik fer-staa uw slekht*) (I can't hear you very well.)

Making an appointment

More and more business is done by e-mail and telephone, but in some cases you need to make an appointment for a personal meeting. Here are some introductory remarks:

- ✔ **Ik wil graag een afspraak maken.** (*ik vilh khraakh ern af-spraak maa-kern*) (I would like to make an appointment.)

- ✔ **Kan ik mijn afspraak verzetten?** (*kan ik mayn af-spraak fer-zeh-tern*) (Can I reschedule my appointment?)

And here are some possible answers:

- **Wanneer komt het u uit?** (*va-nayr komt het uw oait*) (When does it suit you?)

- **Wat denkt u van woensdag elf uur?** (*vat denkt uw fan voons-dakh elf uwr*) (What about Wednesday eleven o'clock?)

- **Er is deze week geen ruimte meer voor een afspraak.** (*ehr is day-zer vayk khayn roaim-ter mayr foar ern af-spraak*) (There is no more room for an appointment this week.)

- **De eerste gelegenheid is volgende week.** (*der ayr-ster kher-lay-khern-hayt is fol- khern-der vayk*) (The first opportunity will be next week.)

Talkin' the Talk

Petra Harskamp wants to make an appointment with the beauty parlour. She is talking to the assistant.

Sonja:	**Beautysalon Welling, met Sonja.**
	byoo-tee-saa-lon veh-ling met son-yaa
	Beauty parlour Welling, Sonja speaking.
Petra Harskamp:	**Goedemorgen Sonja, ik wil een afspraak maken voor een behandeling. Heb je plek op zaterdag-middag?**
	khoo-der-mor-khern son-yaa ik vil ern af-spraak maa-kern foar ern ber-han-der-ling. hep yer plek op zaa-ter-dakh-mi-dakh
	Good morning Sonja, I wish to make an appointment for a beauty treatment. Have you got time on Saturday afternoon?
Sonja:	**Goedemorgen mevrouw Harskamp. Wat voor behandeling wilt u: zoals gebruikelijk?**
	khoo-der-mor-khern mer-frow hars-kamp. Vat foar ber-han-der-ling vilt uw. zoa-als kher-broai-ker- lerk
	Good morning Mrs Harskamp. What kind of treatment do you want – as usual?
Petra Harskamp:	**Ja, en ik wil ook een uitgebreide make-up. Ik heb die avond een feest.**
	yaa en ik vil oak ern oait-kher-bray-der mayk-uhp. ik hep dee aa-font ern fayst
	Yes, and I'd like an extensive make-up as well. I have a party that night.
Sonja:	**U bedoelt niet komende zaterdag, hoop ik?**
	uw ber-doolt neet koa-mern-der zaa-ter-dakh hoap ik
	You don't mean next Saturday, I hope?

Petra Harskamp:	**Nee, het is zaterdag de 14de.**
	nay het is zaa-ter-dakh der fayr-teen-der
	No, it's Saturday the 14th.
Sonja:	**OK, we hebben nog een plekje. Komt half drie goed uit?**
	oa-kay ver heh-bern nokh ern plek-yer. komt half dree khoot oait
	Okay, we still have some room. Half past two, is this all right?
Petra Harskamp:	**Dat is goed.**
	dat is khoot
	That will be fine.
Sonja:	**Ik noteer een afspraak van twee uur voor u. Dus zaterdag 14 september, half drie.**
	ik noa-tayr ern af-spraak fan tvay uwr foar uw. dus zaa-ter-dakh fayr-teen sep-tem-ber half dree
	I am noting down an appointment for two hours for you. So that's Saturday, September 14th, half past two.
Petra Harskamp:	**Dank je. Tot dan.**
	dank yer. tot dan
	Thank you. See you then!
Sonja:	**Nog een prettige dag, mevrouw Harskamp.**
	nokh ern preh-ti-kher dakh mer-frow hars-kamp
	Have a nice day, Mrs Harskamp!

Words to Know

een behandeling	ern ber-han-der-ling	a treatment
zoals gebruikelijk	zoa-als kher-broai-ker-lerk	as usual
uitgebreid	oait-kher-brayt	extensive
noteren	noa-tay-rern	to note down

Some special verbs: 'kunnen' and 'zullen'

Kunnen (_kuh_-nern) (to be able to) and **zullen** (_zuh_-lern) (shall, will) are irregular. As these are very popular verbs, you will soon know their forms:

kunnen	_zullen_
ik kan	_ik zal_
jij kunt/kan	_jij zult/zal_
u kunt	_u zult_
hij/zij/het kan	_hij/zij/het zal_
wij kunnen	_wij zullen_
jullie kunnen	_jullie zullen_
zij kunnen	_zij zullen_

These verbs are very often, but not always, used with another 'full verb' or infinitive:

> ✔ **Kan ik mijn afspraak verzetten?** (_kan ik mayn af-spraak fer-zeh-tern_) (Can I reschedule my appointment?)
>
> ✔ **Ik zal eens kijken.** (_ik zal ayns kay-kern_) (I'll see.)

This may also happen with the verbs **willen** (_vi-lern_) (to want to) and **mogen** (_moa-khern_) (to be allowed to).

> ✔ **Ik wil een afspraak maken.** (_ik vil ern af-spraak maa-kern_) (I want to make an appointment.)
>
> ✔ **Mag ik u iets vragen?** (_makh ik uw eets fraa-khern_) (May I ask you something?)

In the above sentences, the infinitives are: **verzetten, kijken, maken,** and **vragen,** and they are at the end of the sentence.

You'll find the conjugation of the verbs **willen** en **mogen** in Chapter 6.

Talkin' the Talk

 Here is a call from Raymond van Dieren to the receptionist of Lease Consult:

Receptionist: **Goedemorgen, Lease Consult, receptie.**
khoo-der-<u>mor</u>-khern lees kon-<u>sult</u> rer-<u>sep</u>-see
Good morning, Lease Consult, reception

Raymond van Dieren: **Goedemorgen, is de heer Van der Jagt telefonisch bereikbaar?**
khoo-der-<u>mor</u>-khern is der hayr fan der yakht tay-ler-<u>foa</u>-nees ber-<u>rayk</u>-baar
Good morning, could I speak to Mr Van der Jagt?

Receptionist: **Het spijt me, maar de heer Van der Jagt zit in een bespreking. Kan ik u doorverbinden met zijn secretaresse?**
het spayt mer maar der hayr fan der yakht zit in ern ber-<u>spray</u>-king. kan ik uw <u>doar</u>-fer-bindern met zayn sek-rer-taa-<u>reh</u>-ser
I'm sorry, but Mr Van der Jagt is in a meeting. Can I put you through to his secretary?

Raymond van Dieren: **Ik wil hem graag zelf spreken.**
ik vil hem khraakh zelf <u>spray</u>-kern
I would like to talk to him personally.

Receptionist: **Kan hij u terugbellen?**
kan hay uw ter-<u>ruhkh</u>-beh-lern
Can he call you back?

Raymond van Dieren: **Ja, als dat voor twee uur is, want ik ben er vanmiddag niet.**
yaa als dat foar tvay uwr is vant ik ben er fa-<u>mi</u> dakh neet
Yes, if possible before two o'clock, since I won't be there this afternoon.

Receptionist: **Ik zal dat aan zijn secretaresse doorgeven. Wat zijn uw naam en telefoonnummer?**
ik zal dat aan zayn sek-rer-taa-<u>reh</u>-ser <u>doar</u>-khay-fern. vat zayn uw naam en tay-ler-<u>foan</u>-nuh- mer
I'll tell his secretary. Could you give me your name and number, please?

Raymond van Dieren: **Raymond van Dieren. Mijn nummer is 020 654 32 10.**
<u>ray</u>-mont fan <u>dee</u>-rern. mayn <u>nuh</u>-mer is nuhl <u>tvin</u>-tikh zes fayf feer dree tvay ayn nuhl
Raymond van Dieren. My number is: 020 654 32 10.

Receptionist: **Dank u, mijnheer Van Dieren en nog een prettige dag.**
dank uw mer-<u>nayr</u> fan <u>dee</u>-rern en nokh ern <u>preh</u>-ti-kher dakh
Thank you, Mr Van Dieren, and have a nice day.

Saying goodbye on the phone

When leaving a shop, it is very normal to say **tot ziens** (*tot zeens*) (see you), even if you know that you'll never be back in that shop. On the phone, it's different. You could say **tot horens** (I'll hear from you) of **dag** (*dakh*) (bye). Both greetings sound pretty informal. In business, other phrases are usual. If you have made an appointment with the person himself, you could say: **tot woensdag** (*tot voons-dakh*) (see you on Wednesday). In other cases, it is always safe to end with a neutral wish, like: **goedemiddag** (*khoo-der-mi-dakh*) (good afternoon) or, a bit more personal, **prettige dag nog** (*preh-tikher dakh nokh*) (have a nice day).

Leaving a message

In large companies, you have to call back if you don't get through to the person you're trying to reach. In smaller companies, you can leave a message. In this case, some of the following expressions might come in handy:

- ✔ **Kan ik een bericht aan u doorgeven?** (*kan ik ern ber-rikht aan uw doar-khay-fern*) (Can I pass a message on to you?)

- ✔ **Kan ik een bericht voor haar achterlaten?** (*kan ik ern ber-rikht foar haar akh-ter-laa-tern*) (Can I leave a message for her?)

- ✔ **Mevrouw ... kan me bereiken op nummer ...** (*mer-frow ... kan mer ber-ray-kern op nuh-mer*) (Mrs ... can call me on number ...)

Talkin' the Talk

Here is a call from Hans van der Jagt to the reception of Biz Accountants:

Receptionist:	**Goedemorgen, Biz Accountants, receptie.**
	khoo-der-mor-khern bis er-kown-ternts rersep-see
	Good morning, Biz Accountants, reception.
Hans van der Jagt:	**Goedemorgen, met Van der Jagt. Kunt u mij doorverbinden met de heer Van Dieren?**
	khoo-der-mor-khern met fan der yakht. Kuhnt uw mer door-fer-bin-dern met der hayr fan dee-rern
	Good morning, Van der Jagt speaking. Could you put me through to Mr Van Dieren?

Receptionist:	**Het spijt me, maar de heer Van Dieren zit in een bespreking. Wilt u een boodschap achterlaten?**
	het spayt mer maar der hayr fan <u>dee</u>-rern zit in ern ber-<u>spray</u>-king. vilt uw ern <u>boat</u>-skhap <u>akh</u>-ter- laa-tern
	I'm sorry, Mr Van Dieren is in a meeting. Would you like to leave a message?
Hans van der Jagt:	**Ja, of hij me terug wil bellen. Mijn naam is Van der Jagt en mijn telefoonnummer is 020 631 66 00.**
	yaa of hay mer ter-<u>rukh</u> vil <u>beh</u>-lern. Mayn naam is fan der yakht en mayn tay-ler-<u>foan</u>-nuh- mer is nuhl <u>tvin</u>-tikh zes dree ayn zes zes nuhl nuhl
	Yes, to call me back. My name is Van der Jagt and my telephone number is 020 631 66 00.
Receptionist:	**OK, dank u. Ik zal mijnheer Van Dieren vragen of hij u terugbelt.**
	oa-<u>kay</u> dank uw. ik zal mer-<u>nayr</u> fan <u>dee</u>-rern <u>fraa</u>-khern of hay uw ter-<u>rukh</u>-belt
	OK, thank you, I'll ask Mr Van Dieren to call you back.
Hans van der Jagt:	**Dank u, goedemiddag.**
	dank uw khoo-der-<u>mi</u>-dakh
	Thank you, good afternoon.
Receptionist:	**Goedemiddag meneer Van der Jagt.**
	khoo-der-<u>mi</u>-dakh mer-<u>nayr</u> fan der yakht
	Good afternoon, Mr Van der Jagt.

Spelling your name: the Dutch telephone alphabet

International companies, where English is the common language, will use the international telephone alphabet. Most Dutch people use the Dutch one when they are asked **Kunt u dat spellen?** (*kuhnt uw dat <u>speh</u>-lern*) (Could you spell that?). The Dutch telephone alphabet might serve you well:

- ✔ **de a van Anton** (*der aa fan <u>an</u>-ton*)
- ✔ **de b van Bernard** (*der bay fan <u>behr</u>-nart*)
- ✔ **de c van Cornelis** (*der say fan cor-<u>nay</u>-lis*)
- ✔ **de d van Dirk** (*der day fan dirk*)
- ✔ **de e van Eduard** (*der ay fan <u>ay</u>-duw-vart*)

- ✔ **de f van Ferdinand** (*der ef fan <u>fehr</u>-dee-nant*)
- ✔ **de g van Gerrit** (*der khay fan <u>kheh</u>-rit*)
- ✔ **de h van Hendrik** (*der haa fan <u>hen</u>-drik*)
- ✔ **de i van Isaac** (*der ee fan <u>ee</u>-saak*)
- ✔ **de j van Johan** (*der yay fan <u>yoo</u>-han*)
- ✔ **de k van Karel** (*der kaa fan <u>kaa</u>-rerl*)
- ✔ **de l van Lodewijk** (*der el fan <u>loa</u>-der-vayk*)
- ✔ **de m van Marie** (*der em fan maa-<u>ree</u>*)
- ✔ **de n van Nico** (*der en fan <u>nee</u>-ko*)
- ✔ **de o van Otto** (*der oa fan <u>o</u>-toa*)
- ✔ **de p van Pieter** (*der pay fan <u>pee</u>-ter*)
- ✔ **de q van Quotiënt** (*der kuw fan koa-<u>shent</u>*)
- ✔ **de r van Rudolf** (*der ehr fan <u>ruw</u>-dolf*)
- ✔ **de s van Simon** (*der es fan <u>see</u>-mon*)
- ✔ **de t van Theodoor** (*der tay fan <u>tay</u>-oa-doar*)
- ✔ **de u van Utrecht** (*der uw fan <u>uw</u>-trekht*)
- ✔ **de v van Victor** (*der fay fan <u>fik</u>-tor*)
- ✔ **de w van Willem** (*der vay fan <u>vi</u>-lerm*)
- ✔ **de x van Xantippe** (*der iks fan ksan-<u>ti</u>-per*)
- ✔ **de ij van IJmuiden** (*der ay fan ay-<u>moai</u>-dern*)
- ✔ **de y van Ypsylon** (*der ay fan <u>ip</u>-see-lon*)
- ✔ **de z van Zaandam** (*der zet fan zaan-<u>dam</u>*)

Better Send an E-Mail

It depends on the kind of company how much e-mail is used. In some lines of business like the building industry, the telephone is used in order to make appointments and the fax in order to confirm orders. In many lines of business the Internet serves as a main source of information. The phone is used for personal and detailed information.

In Dutch business, e-mail is used for almost everything: asking questions, simple consultations, making appointments and even sending agreements. Working at home one day a week instead of in the office, is becoming more and more popular. Busy people have a lot of meetings, so if you want to reach somebody, send them an e-mail!

The traditional paperwork is used for sales and advertising. Paper is suitable for all messages that should be read carefully or have a legal status.

Dutch business e-mails are short and to the point.

You're always safe with the following brief introduction:

> **Geachte heer Van Dieren/Geachte mevrouw Vermeent,** (*kher-akh- ter hayr fan dee-rern/kher-akh-ter mer-frow fer-maynt*) (Dear Mr Van Dieren/Dear Mrs Vermeent,)

If you don't know the person, use:

> **Geachte heer/mevrouw,** (*kher-akh-ter hayr mer-frow*) (Dear Sir/ Madam,)

Being too informal could spoil your business contacts. Though the Dutch seem to be informal in business, they always keep a certain distance in order to be businesslike when necessary. In a lot of business contacts people are on first-name terms and address each other with **je** (*yer*) (you, informal). When it comes to official written business papers like offers and contracts, the style is formal and the business partner is addressed with the surname and **u** (*uw*) (you, formal). For this reason offers and contracts are not in the e-mail itself, but attached to it.

If you are on first-name terms with your business partner, but want to keep a certain distance, the following phrasing is suitable:

> **Raymond,** (*ray-mont*) (Raymond,)

If you have the courage to come nearer of when the addressed person is a friend or an acquaintance you can use the following phrasing:

> **Beste Raymond,/Beste Cilla,** (*bes-ter ray-mont/bes-ter si-laa*) (Dear Raymond,/Dear Cilla,)

E-mails are generally very short (two to six lines). The Dutch, other than English-speaking people, often leave extra space between each part of the subject. The next e-mail is typical for a Dutch business e-mail. The form is informal with restraint, the message is businesslike.

> to: info@author.nl
>
> from: Wardy@theEditor.com
>
> **Margreet,**
>
> **Je hebt beloofd iedere week twee hoofdstukken op te sturen. In de maand november hebben we slechts vier hoofdstukken ontvangen. Ik maak me zorgen of het boek wel op tijd af komt.**

Ik wil nu sluitende afspraken maken over de deadline.

Ik hoor graag van je,

Wardy

mar-<u>khrayt</u>

yer hept ber-<u>loaft</u> <u>ee</u>-der-er vayk tvay <u>hoaft</u>-stuh-kern op ter <u>stuw</u>-rern. in der maant noa-<u>fem</u>-ber <u>heh</u>-bern ver slekhts feer <u>hoaft</u>-stuh-kern ont-<u>fang</u>-ern. ik maak mer <u>zor</u>-khern of het book vel op tayt <u>af</u>-komt.

ik vil nuw <u>sloai</u>-ten-der <u>af</u>-spraa-kern <u>maa</u>-kern <u>oa</u>-fer der <u>det</u>-lain

ik hoar khraakh fan yer

<u>var</u>-dee

Margreet,

You promised to send me two chapters a week. Yet in November, we just received four chapters. I'm afraid that the book will not be ready in time.

I want to come to an agreement on the deadline now.

I look forward to your reply,

Wardy

The introduction of most business e-mails is an explanation of the situation, very often a summary of what happened until now or a few words of thanks for what the other person did. In the middle part of the e-mail, you lay down the problem that has to be solved or ask the question that has to be answered. In the last sentence you make clear what you expect of the other person. If you need a response the following phrases will be useful:

- ✔ **Ik kijk uit naar uw antwoord.** (*ik kayk oait naar uw <u>ant</u>-voart*) (polite and formal: I'm looking forward to your answer.)

- ✔ **Ik hoor graag van u.** (*ik hoar khraakh fan uw*) (formal: I look forward to your reply.)

- ✔ **Ik wacht uw antwoord af.** (*ik vakht uw <u>ant</u>-voart af*) (formal: I am awaiting your reaction.)

- ✔ **Ik hoor graag van je.** (*ik haor khraakh fan yer*) (informal and business like: I look forward to your reply.)

- ✔ **Graag een reactie.** (*khraakh ern ray-<u>ak</u>-see*) (formal but quite unfriendly: Please reply.)

Not all e-mails need a reply. If not, a lot of business people use the option **leesbevestiging** (*<u>lays</u>-ber-fes-ti-khing*) (notification) of their e-mail program. When the receiver uses this option, the sender know his email has been read.

In case there's no need for an answer, you can make use of one of the following last lines:

- **Met vriendelijke groet,** (*met <u>freen</u>-der-ler-ker khroot*) (Kind regards)

- **Vriendelijke groeten,** (*<u>freen</u>-der-ler-ker <u>khroo</u>-tern*) (Kind regards)

- **Groeten,** (*<u>khroo</u>-tern*) (Regards)

- **Groetjes,** (*<u>khroot</u>-yers*) (Love,) is only for good friends and relatives.

Inside the Office

Most companies have **een kantoor** (*ern kan-<u>toar</u>*) (an office). When you leave your house to go to it, you can say: **Ik ga naar kantoor** (*ik khaa naar kan-<u>toar</u>*). When asked what you are going to do, you might say: **Ik ben tot vanavond negen uur op kantoor** (*ik ben tot fa-<u>naa</u>-font <u>nay</u>-khern uwr op kan-<u>toar</u>*) (I'll be at the office until nine o'clock this evening).

Dutch offices have to be well organised. As a lot of office work is done by part-time workers, the organisation of the work has to be well in place. Most work will be done in the morning: after lunchtime or around three o'clock part-timers will start to leave. In order to avoid the morning or evening traffic and to help out mothers or fathers who have to take or pick up their children to or from daycare or school, a lot of offices offer flexible working hours: office staff can enter or leave between certain time limits.

Mastering your desk and supplies

Typically, you might find the following items on or around **het bureau** (*buw-<u>roa</u>*) (the desk):

- **de computer** (*der kom-<u>pyoo</u>-ter*) (the computer)

- **papieren en mappen** (*paa-<u>pee</u>-rern en <u>ma</u>-pern*) (papers and files)

- Generally some people share **de printer** (*der <u>prin</u>-ter*) (the printing machine)

Don't forget to ask, **Waar is/zijn ...?** (*vaar is*) (Where is/are ...?) if you need to ask someone for help finding something around the office.

- **de balpen** (*der <u>bal</u>-pen*) (the ballpoint)

- **het potlood** (*het <u>pot</u>-loat*) (the pencil)

✔ **de nietmachine** (*der neet-ma-shee-ner*) (the stapler)

✔ **het printpapier** (*het print-paa-peer*) (printing paper)

✔ **de cartridges** (*der kar-tri-tshyers*) (the cartridges)

Computerisation speeds up office work, but if the system fails, it might take a lot of time and patience to get things working again. In large companies there is no personal contact with the helpdesk, so problems have to be solved on the phone. Your English might come in handy, as many IT workers are not Dutch!

In a lot of Dutch offices, you can't miss the coffee machine. This is where you meet your colleagues and have a chat. It's at the coffee machine that you start the day with fresh courage and will come back smiling several times a day. You don't like coffee? Try the water cooler! In some offices your colleagues might like it when you ask them:

> **Zal ik u/je een kopje koffie brengen?** (*zal ik uw/yer ern kop-yer ko-fee breng-ern*) (Shall I bring you a cup of coffee?)

Small is beautiful: the diminutive

Coffee stands for a pleasant moment in the day, a break and a chat with colleagues. The Dutch have a special word for such pleasant moments: **gezellig** (*kher-zeh-likh*). Not only a moment, but almost anything can be **gezellig**: an evening (out) may be **een gezellige avond** (*ern kher-zeh-likher aa-font*) (an enjoyable evening), a person may be **een gezellige prater** (*ern kher-zeh-li-kher praa-ter*) (an entertaining talker), the coffee lady may be **een gezellige vrouw** (*ern kher-zeh-li-kher frow*) (a sociable woman), and the room could be **een gezellige kamer** (*ern kher-zeh-li-kher kaa-mer*) (a cosy room). People might even say it about their new lover: **We hebben het zo gezellig samen** (*wer heh-bern het zoa kher-zeh-likh saa-mern*) (We are having such a good time together).

The Dutch like to chat away pleasantly with a cup of coffee: **gezellig kletsen met een kopje koffie** (*kher-zeh-likh klet-sern met ern kop-yer ko-fee*). In order to emphasise **gezelligheid** the Dutch use a lot of diminutives:

✔ **het kopje koffie** (*het kop-yer ko-fee*) (the cup of coffee)

✔ **het leuke feestje** (*het lu-ker feest-yer*) (the enjoyable party)

✔ **het gezellige hoekje** (*het kher-zeh-li-kher hook-yer*) (the cosy corner)

✔ **een ritje in uw nieuwe auto** (*ern rit-yer in uw neew-er ow-tow*) (a ride in your new car)

Generally, you just add **-je** to a word that ends with a consonant:

- ✔ **de kop** (*der kop*) (the cup)

  het kopje (*het <u>kop</u>-yer*) (the little cup)
- ✔ **het feest** (*het fayst*) (the party)

  het feestje (*het <u>fayst</u>-yer*) (the little party)
- ✔ **de hoek** (*der hook*) (the corner)

  het hoekje (*het <u>hook</u>-yer*) (the little corner)
- ✔ **de rit** (*der rit*) (the ride)

  het ritje (*het <u>rit</u>-yer*) (the little ride)

Words that end in **l**, **n**, **w**, **r**, or a vowel (**a, e, i, o, u**) need something extra: **-tje**. Adaptations in the spelling may be necessary.

- ✔ **het ei** (*het ay*) (the egg)

  het eitje (*het <u>ay</u>-tyer*) (the little egg).
- ✔ **de la** (*der laa*) (the drawer)

  het laatje (*het <u>laa</u>-tyer*) (the little drawer)
- ✔ **de auto** (*der <u>ow</u>-tow*) (the car)

  het autootje (*het <u>ow</u>-tow-tyer*) (the little car)

after **m** comes **-pje**:

- ✔ **de boom** (*der boam*) (the tree)

  het boompje (*het <u>boam</u>-pyer*) (the little tree)
- ✔ **het raam** (*het raam*) (the window)

  het raampje (*het <u>raam</u>-pyer*) (the little window)

You will be surprised to hear some special diminutives, which are irregular:

- ✔ **de brug** (*der bruhkh*) (the bridge)

  het bruggetje (*het <u>bruh</u>-kher-tyer*) (the little bridge)
- ✔ **de weg** (*der vekh*) (the road)

  het weggetje (*het <u>veh</u>-kher-tyer*) (the little road)

Notice that all diminutives are **het** words!

Dealing with the Dutch

Knowing how to deal with the Dutch is not a question of language, but a question of culture. When you are in the Netherlands on a temporary basis, your working language may be English. Most Dutch speak English and some of them speak another language such as German, French or Spanish. Here are a few tips for those who are not on a business trip, but live in the Netherlands and are trying to fill cultural gaps.

When you have a business meeting with a Dutchman, arrive just in time, not too early, not too late. When you're early, wait outside or in your car or somewhere else.

Make sure that you can finish your appointment within an hour. If you come from far away and have to talk over important things, tell your host how much time you think you need. Avoid embarrassment and talk this over. Dutch secretaries are used to book one-hour appointments in the agendas of their bosses!

Know how to meet and greet formally. Read the section about talking about your work in chapter 4.

Are you coming during the daytime? Only if you are a Very Important Person you will be taken out for a hot lunch! A normal Dutch lunch consists of some bread rolls and milk. In most situations, you will be offered this while business goes on: **een werklunch** (*ern werk-luhnsh*) (a working lunch).

Doen: the doing verb

Work means doing things. Like most popular verbs, **doen** (*doon*) (to do) is an irregular one.

Conjugation	Pronunciation
ik doe	*ik doo*
jij doet	*yay doot*
u doet	*uw doot*
hij/zij/het doet	*hay/zay/het doot*
wij doen	*vay doon*
jullie doen	*yuw-lee doon*
zij doen	*zay doon*

Here are some phrases that show you how to use the verb:

- ✔ **Zij doet haar e-mail twee keer per dag.** (*zay doot haar <u>ee-mail</u> tvay kayr per dakh*) (She handles her e-mail twice a day.)

- ✔ **Ik doe 's ochtends het meest.** (*ik doo <u>sokh</u>-ternts het mayst*) (I do most in the mornings.)

- ✔ **Wil je dat alsjeblieft voor me doen?** (*vil yer dat a-sher-<u>bleeft</u> foar mer doon*) (Please, do this for me)

Maken: the making verb

Though communication is becoming more and more important in offices, production keeps playing an important role. In order to talk about production, you need the verb **maken** (*<u>maa</u>-kern*) (to make). It's a regular verb, but needs some changes in the spelling in order to make the **a** sound like a long vowel.

Conjugation	*Pronunciation*
ik maak	*ik maak*
jij maakt	*yay maakt*
u maakt	*uw maakt*
hij/zij/het maakt	*hay/zay/het maakt*
wij maken	*vay <u>maa</u>-kern*
jullie maken	*<u>yuw</u>-lee <u>maa</u>-kern*
zij maken	*zay <u>maa</u>-kern*

CULTURAL WISDOM

Vakantiedagen

Holidays are very important for Dutch employees. As there are many part-timers and most of them are women with children, school holidays cause problems for them because the parents have to take extra measures for their children when school is closed. Increasingly, more young fathers stay at home one day a week for **pappadag** (*pa-paa-dakh*) (dad's day, a day in the week on which dad takes care of the children). **Tweeverdieners** (*-fer-dee-ners*) (double income families) depend on the number of holidays the employer offers them. The legal minimum is 20 days a year, the average 23, but people in the civil services enjoy extra holidays, especially the elderly. Large companies make working with them more attractive by offering flexibility and sabbaticals. School teachers have the longest holidays: they teach forty weeks a year.

Automation not only influences all the processes in the office, it also influences the Dutch language. Increasingly more verbs originating from English have found their way in Dutch: **printen** (_prin_-tern) (to print), **faxen** (_fak_-sern) (to fax), **plannen** (_pleh_-nern) (to plan). Here are some useful phrases that show you how to use these English verbs in Dutch:

✔ **Ik print mijn rapport wel op de printer boven.** (_ik print mayn raport vel op der _prin_-ter _boa_-fern_) (I'll print my report on the printer upstairs.)

✔ **Cilla faxt de getekende overeenkomst naar Nadine van Lease Consult.** (_si_-laa fakst der kher-_tay_-kern-der oa-fer-_ayn_-komst naar naa-_dee_-ner fan lees kon-_suhlt_) (Cilla will fax the signed agreement to Nadine of Lease Consult.)

✔ **Cilla plant de bespreking van Hans van der Jagt met Raymond van Dieren.** (_si_-laa plent der ber-_spray_-king fan hans fan der yakht met _ray_-mont fan _dee_-rern_) (Cilla plans the meeting of Hans van der Jagt and Raymond van Dieren.)

Saying hello and goodbye

How to say hello or goodbye in a company depends on the company culture and your social status. When you are among colleagues of the same level, you can say anything to them: **hallo** (ha-_loa_) (hallo), **hoi**(hoy) (hi), **dag** (dakh) (hallo) or **goeiemorgen** (khoo-yer-_mor_-khern) (good morning). When you need to be more formal, you say: **goedemorgen** (khoo-der-_mor_-khern) (good morning) and you mention the name of the person that you greet: **Goedemorgen, Petra** (khoo-der-_mor_-khern _pay_-traa) or **Goedemorgen, mevrouw Harskamp** (khoo-der-_mor_-khern mer-_frow_ _hars_-kamp).

When you leave you can say, informally, **dag!** (dakh) (bye!). Or, very informal, **doei!** (dooy) (bye!) and in some regions even **doei doei** (dooy dooy) (bye bye) which is very, very informal. Many greetings are either local or just used by certain social groups, like the intimate **doeg** (dookh), which is only used among friends. Also, in the northern part of the country, people say **hoi** when they leave, while **hoi** means 'hello' in the rest of the country. In some southern parts **houdoe** (how-_doo_) is popular. Listen carefully to what other people say and adapt to the circumstances! **Tot morgen** (tot _mor_-khern) and **prettig weekend** (_preh_-tikh _vee_-kent) will be appreciated anywhere.

When you need to be formal, friendly and personal at once, **Dag, Cilla** (dakh _si_-laa), **Dag, mevrouw Vermeent** (_dakh_ mer-_frow_ fer-_maynt_), **Tot morgen, Cilla** (tot _mor_-khern _si_-laa) and **Tot morgen, mevrouw Vermeent** (tot _mor_-khern mer-_frow_ fer-_maynt_) are suitable.

Dealing with Your Colleagues

Dutch companies are not very hierarchical compared to American, Japanese, German, or French companies. In case you don't work in an international company but in a Dutch one, you may observe that manners are loose and the dress code is casual. Whether you work in a Dutch company or in an international one with Dutch colleagues, remember: Dutch people don't like to be commanded! It's a deeply rooted Dutch conviction that all people are equal, even if the other wears an expensive suit and drives a beautiful car. Dutch secretaries consider themselves as the advisers of their bosses and they will be of much better help when you treat them with respect. Instead of saying: **Kopieer dat voor mij** (*koa-pee-yayr dat foar may*) (Copy that for me), you should say: **Wil je dat alsjeblieft voor me kopiëren?** (*vil yer dat als-yer-bleeft foar mer koa-pee-yay-rern*) (Could you please copy this for me?). When you've got a good secretary, she plans her day herself. In this case it's even better to say: **Wil je dit op een geschikt moment voor me kopiëren?** (*vil yer dit op ern kher-skhikt moa-ment foar mer koa-pee-yay-rern*) (Could you copy this for me at a convenient moment, please?).

People will work much harder when you add **alsjeblieft** and **wil je**!

Talkin' the Talk

Here is a conversation between Hans van der Jagt and his secretary Cilla Vermeent. Today Hans van der Jagt is at the office early because he has an important meeting.

Hans van der Jagt:	**Goedemorgen, Cilla.** *khoo-der-mor-khern si-laa* Good morning, Cilla.
Cilla Vermeent:	**Goedemorgen, Hans.** *khoo-der-mor-khern hans* Good morning, Hans.
Hans van der Jagt:	**Is Allan Sturmey al binnen?** *is eh-lern stuhr-mee al bi-nern* Do you know if Allan Sturmey is in already?
Cilla Vermeent:	**Ja, hij staat bij de koffiemachine.** *yaa hij staat bay der ko-fee-ma-shee-ner* Yes, he is standing at the coffee machine.
Hans van der Jagt:	**Ik moet dringend met hem praten.** *ik moot dring-ernt met hem praa-tern* I have to talk to him urgently.

Cilla Vermeent:	**OK. En Raymond van Dieren van Biz Accountants heeft net gebeld.**
	oa-<u>kay</u>. en <u>ray</u>-mont fan <u>dee</u>-rern fan bis er-<u>known</u>- ternts hayt net kher-<u>belt</u>
	Okay. And Raymond van Dieren from Biz Accountants just called.
Hans van der Jagt:	**Dank je, ik ga hem meteen bellen. Heb je tijd om deze documenten te kopiëren?**
	dank yer. ik khaa hem mer-<u>tayn</u> <u>beh</u>-lern. Hep yer tayt om <u>day</u>-zer doa-kuw-<u>men</u>-tern ter koa-pee-<u>yay</u>-rern
	Thank you, I'll call him immediately. Have you got time to copy these documents?
Cilla Vermeent:	**Heb je ze nu of zometeen nodig?**
	yaa hep yer zer nuw mer-<u>tayn</u> <u>noa</u>-dikh
	Do you need them now or later?
Hans van der Jagt:	**Ik heb ze om vier uur nodig, dus er is geen haast bij.**
	ik hep zer om feer uwr <u>noa</u>-dikh, dus er is khayn haast bay
	I need them at four o'clock, so no hurry.
Cilla Vermeent:	**OK, geen probleem. Ze liggen om vier uur op je bureau.**
	oa-<u>kay</u> khayn proa-<u>blaym</u>. zer <u>li</u>-khern om feer uwr op yer buw-<u>roa</u>
	Okay, no problem. They will be on your desk at four o'clock.

Words to Know

de koffiemachine	*der <u>ko</u>-fee-ma-shee-ner*	the coffee machine
dringend	*<u>dring</u>-ernt*	urgent
de documenten	*der doa-kuw-<u>men</u>-tern*	the documents
zich haasten	*zikh <u>haas</u>-tern*	to hurry
het bureau	*het buw-<u>roa</u>*	the desk

Part III
Dutch on the Go

'Okay, so we couldn't find the Van Gogh museum because you weren't able to ask for directions in perfect Dutch. You're not going to cut your ear off or anything, are you?'

In this part . . .

In this part you will find all the language you may need for travelling and finding your way in your residence, be it temporarley or not. It gives you the Dutch that the locals use in banks and post offices, hotels, and transport. For your safety, phrases you may need in case of emergency are included.

Chapter 10

Money, Banks, and Post Offices

· ·

In This Chapter

▶ Changing money

▶ PINs and chips

▶ Knowing what you are talking about: Die, dat, wat

▶ At the bank

▶ At the post office

· ·

*I*n this chapter, you will learn how you talk about money. Whether you are speaking to someone at the bank or a friend is explaining to you how to make your way in the Dutch financial world, a pocketful of the right expressions will make you feel at ease.

Changing Money

At the airport you'll find **wisselkantoren** (*vi-serl-kan-toa-rern*) (exchange offices) that are a specialised business to accept your **vreemde valuta** (*fraym-der faa-luw-taa*) (foreign currency) and provide you with **euro's** (*u-roas*) (euros). At most banks **geld wisselen** (*khelt-vi-ser-lern*) (to change money) will be easy.

You will usually find a board with the current **wisselkoers** (*vi-serlkoors*) (exchange rate) or the **dagkoers** (*dakh-koors*) (current rate, today's rate) displayed in a prominent location. Look for the column **aankoop** (*aan-koap*) and the bank employee **aan de balie** (*aan der baa-lee*) (at the counter) will either complete your transaction on the spot or send you on to the **kassa** (*ka-saa*) (the cash register).

Regardless of where you decide to change your money, transacting your business is not difficult. All you need are the following phrases:

- **Ik wil graag . . . in euro's wisselen.** (*ik vil khraakh . . . in u-roas vi-ser- lern*) (I would like to change . . . into euros).

- **Wat is de wisselkoers?** (*vat is der vi-serl-koors*) (What is the exchange rate?)

- **Neemt u ook munten aan?** (*naymt uw oak muhn-tern aan*) (Do you also take coins?)

When you change money, you may be asked for **een identiteitsbewijs** (*ern ee-den-tee-tayts-ber-vays*) (your ID) or **een paspoort** (*ern pas-poort*) (your passport). The teller will ask you:

Heeft u een identiteitsbewijs? (*hayft uw ern ee-den-tee-tayts-bervays*) (Do you have proof of identification?)

After you have proven that you are who you say you are the teller may ask you how you want the money:

Hoe wilt u het geld hebben? (*hoo vilt uw het khelt heh-bern*) (How would you like to have the money?)

Try out one of the following sample phrases:

- **Ik wil graag vijf bankbiljetten van 100 euro.** (*ik vil khraakh fayf bank-bil-yeh-tern fan hon-dert u-roa*) (I'd like to have five 100 euro notes.)

- **In briefjes van tien/twintig/vijftig/honderd graag.** (*in breef-yers fan teen/tvin-tikh/fayf-tikh/hon-dert khraakh*) (In bills of 10/20/50/ 100 please.)

- **. . . en de rest in kleingeld.** (*en der rest in klayn-khelt*) (. . . and the balance in small change.)

Talkin' the Talk

Kent, an American tourist in the Netherlands, heads to a bank to change money.

Kent:	**Hallo. Ik wil graag Amerikaanse dollars wisselen. Wat is de wisselkoers op dit moment?** *ha-loa. ik vil khraakh aa-may-ree-kaan-ser do-lars vi-ser-lern. vat is der vi-serl-koors op dit moa-ment* Good morning, I would like to change American dollars. What's the exchange rate, please?

Bank employee:	**Goedemorgen. Een ogenblikje alstublieft. U krijgt voor een dollar € 0,84.**
	khoo-der-mor-khern. ern oa-khern-blik-yer als-tuw-bleeft. uw kraykht foar ern do-lar akh-tern-fayr-tikh u-roa-sent
	Good morning. One moment please. For one US Dollar you get € 0.84.
Kent:	**Ik wil graag 200 dollar in euros wisselen.**
	ik vil khraakh tvay-hon-dert do-lar in u-roas vi-ser-lern
	I would like to exchange 200 dollars into euros.
Bank employee:	**Geen probleem. Heeft u een identiteisbewijs bij u?**
	khayn proa-blaym. hayft uw ern ee-den-tee-tayts-ber-vays bay uw
	No problem. Have you got an ID with you?
Kent:	**Hier is mijn paspoort.**
	heer is mayn pas-poart
	Here is my passport.
Bank employee:	**Voor 200 dollar krijgt u €168,54. Daar gaat € 2,50 aan kosten vanaf. Dat wordt dan € 166,04**
	foar tvay-hon-dert do-lar kraykht uw hondert-akh-tern-zes-tikh u-roa feer-ern-fayf-tikh. daar khaat tvay u-roa fayf-tikh aan kos-tern fa-naf. dat vort dan hon-dert-zes-ernzes- tikh u-roa en feer sent
	For 200 dollars you get € 168.54, less € 2.50 costs, so that's € 166.04.
Kent:	**Dank u.**
	dank uw
	Thanks.

Words to Know

Amerikaanse dollar	a-mer-ree-kahn-ser dol-lar	US Dollar
een ogenblikje	ern oa-khen-blik-jer	one moment
alstublieft	als-tuw-bleeft	please
een probleem	ern proa-bleym	a problem

Decimal notation

The Dutch use commas to denote a decimal point. In amounts of more than 1000 the Dutch use full stops to denote the thousand column, so one thousand and sixty-six euros and four cents would be written as € 1.066,04.

PINs and Chips

All banks issue **een pinpas** (*ern pin-pas*) or **betaalpas** (*ber-taal-pas*) (debit card).

The **pinpas** allows you to withdraw money directly from your **bankrekening** (*bank-ray-ker-ning*) (checking account). **Geldautomaten** (*khelt-ow- toa-maa-tern*) (Automatic Teller Machines) in order to **geld opnemen** (*khelt-op-nay-mern*) (to withdraw money) are everywhere: outside banks, inside banks, near railway stations, shopping centres, and post offices. A popular expression for **geld opnemen** is **geld uit de muur trekken** (*khelt oait der muwr treh-kern*) (to 'pull money from the wall', withdraw money at an ATM) when you use de **geldautomaat**. **Geldautomaten** will handle cards of **de Postbank** (*der post-bank*) (the Dutch Post Office Bank) and bank systems, plus the main international banks. However, your withdrawal limit may be lower than that of your own bank and there can be **extra kosten** (*eks-traa kos-tern*) (an extra service charge).

Just look for your card symbol on the machine to ensure that it takes your type of card.

If you're lucky, the ATM will give you a choice of languages to communicate in, but just in case Dutch is your only option, you want to be prepared. A typical run-through of prompts might look like this:

- **Voer uw pas in.** (*foor uw pas in*) (Insert card.)

- **Kies uw taal.** (*kees uw taal*) (Choose your language.)

- **Voer uw pincode in.** (*foor uw pin-koa-der in*) (Enter your PIN code.)

- **Voer het bedrag in.** (*foor het ber-drakh in*) (Enter the amount of money.)

- **Bevestig het bedrag.** (*ber-fes-tikh het ber-drakh*) (Confirm the amount of money.)

- **Neem uw pas terug.** (*naym uw pas ter-ruhkh*) (Take out your card.)

- **Neem uw geld uit.** (*naym uw khelt oait*) (Take out your money.)

Transaction completed! You should now be flush with **contant geld** (*kon-tant khelt*) (cash), unless something went wrong. The machine might be out of order, in which case you'll see the following message:

> **Buiten gebruik.** (*boai-tern kher-broaik*) (Out of order.)

The machine might spit out your card without parting with any of its bounty. In this case, you might receive the message:

> **Uw pas is ongeldig.** (*uw pas is on-khel-dikh*) (Your card is not valid.)

In case the machine accepts the card, but nothing happens after you have entered your PIN code, the message could be:

> **Ongeldige pincode.** (*on-khel-di-kher pin-koa-der*) (Invalid PIN code.)

In a worst-case scenario: The machine swallows your card and holds it with only this message for consolation:

> **Storing. Bel . . .** (*stoa-ring. bel*) (Error. Please call . . .)

Depending on the bank the machine will tell you the maximum amount of money you can withdraw.

Pins and chips everywhere

Contante betaling (*kon-tan-ter ber-taa-ling*) (cash payment), **pinnen** (*pi-nern*) (to pay by PIN or switch/debit card) en **chippen** (*chi-pern*) (to pay with a quick transaction card) are used for most transactions. Credit cards can be used in most of the larger chain stores but are still not as widely accepted as in the US or UK.

When you open a bank or post office account in the Netherlands, you will receive your card with **een persoonlijke viercijferige code** (*ern persoan- ler-ker feer-say-fer-er-ker koa-der*) (a personal four-digit number) that is used for all **geldopnames** (*khelt-op-naa-mers*) (withdrawals) and **banktransacties** (*bank-trans-ak-sees*) (bank transactions). In almost all cases, this number will be randomly chosen for you.

The Dutch use debit cards for paying. Each debit card has its own PIN (Personal Identification Number) code consisting of four numbers. Credit cards are less popular. People use credit cards in parking garages, restaurants and to pay things they buy on the Net.

Depending on its type, your bank card may be coupled with **een creditcard** (*ern kreh-dit-kart*) (a credit card). The card belongs to **een privérekening** (*ern* pree-*fay*-ray-ker-ning) or een **particuliere rekening** (*ern par-tee-kuw-lee-rer ray-ker-ning*) (a personal account). Unless coupled to a credit card account, the value of the transaction is immediately **afgeschreven** (*af-kher-skhray-fern*) (deducted) from your account. The same card, or in some cases a separate one, can be used as an electronic wallet that you can **opladen** (*op-laa-dern*) (to charge) and used for quick transactions (**chippen**) (*chi-pern*).

Fewer and fewer people pay cash, especially in towns where carrying cash is dangerous. Shopkeepers prefer to have as little cash in their register as possible and invest in **pinautomaten** (*pin-ow-toa-maa-tern*) (cash machines). You will see the blue and white boards with the word **PIN** in almost all shops and even at the marketplace. In some parts of the larger towns **parkeerautomaten** (*par-kayr-ow-toa-maa-tern*) (car park ticket machines) do not accept coins, just a transaction by **chip card** (*chip-kart*).

Knowing What You Are Talking about: 'Die', 'dat', 'wat'

You are now entering the area of the relative pronouns. Just like conjunctions, relative pronouns connect two parts of the sentence. Unlike a conjunction, the pronoun belongs to a word in the first part of the sentence. This word in the first part of the sentence is called **antecedent** (*an-ter-ser-dent*) (antecedent). In the first sample sentence the word **die** (*dee*) (that) is the relative pronoun of the antecedent **de creditcard**. 'De' words, i.e. antecedents that have the article **de**, always have the relative pronoun **die**. Check the following examples:

- ✔ **de creditcard die gestolen is** (*der kreh-dit-kart dee kher-stoa-lern is*) (the credit card that has been stolen)

- ✔ **een creditcard die gestolen is** (*ern kreh-dit-kart dee kher-stoa-lern is*) (a credit card that has been stolen)

- ✔ **de geldautomaat die gerepareerd is** (*der khelt-ow-toa-maat die kher-ray-pa-rayrt is*) (the ATM that has been fixed)

- ✔ **een geldautomaat die gerepareerd is** (*ern khelt-ow-toa-maat die kher-ray-pa-rayrt is*) (an ATM that has been fixed)

- ✔ **de man die kaal is** (*der man dee kaal is*) (the man who is bald)

- ✔ **de mannen die kaal zijn** (*der ma-nern dee kaal zayn*) (the men who are bald)

- ✔ **de jongen die verliefd is** (*der yong-ern dee fer-leeft is*) (the boy who is in love)

- ✔ **de jongens die verliefd zijn** (*der yong-erns dee fer-leeft zayn*) (the boys who are in love)

For **het** words the relative pronoun is **dat.**

- ✔ **het kind dat geboren is** (*het kint dat kher-<u>boa</u>-rern is*) (the child that has been born)

- ✔ **een kind dat geboren is** (*ern kint dat kher-<u>boa</u>-rern is*) (a child that has been born)

- ✔ **het meisje dat gevallen is** (*het <u>mays</u>-yer dat kher-<u>fa</u>-lern vas*) (the girl who has fallen down)

- ✔ **een meisje dat gevallen is** (*het <u>mays</u>-yer dat kher-<u>fa</u>-lern vas*) (a girl who has fallen down)

Plurals, including those of **het** words, always have **de. De** has the relative **die.** Check the following examples:

- ✔ **het boek dat verkocht is** (*het book dat fer-<u>kokht</u> is*) (the book that has been sold)

- ✔ **de boeken die verkocht zijn** (*der <u>boo</u>-kern dee fer-<u>kokht</u> zayn*) (the books that have been sold)

- ✔ **het ei dat gebroken is** (*het ay dat kher-<u>broa</u>-kern is*) (the egg that is broken)

- ✔ **de eieren die gebroken zijn** (*der <u>ay</u>-er-ern dee kher-<u>broa</u>-kern zayn*) (the eggs that are broken)

If you don't refer to one word, but to a whole sentence, you use the relative pronoun **wat.**

> **De bank is 's avonds gesloten, wat ik niet handig vind.** (*de bank is <u>saa</u>-fonts kher-<u>sloa</u>-tern vat ik neet <u>han</u>-dikh fint*) (The bank is closed in the evening, which I find inconvenient.)

In order to find out what the antecedent exactly is in this sentence, you can turn the second part of the sentence into a question, like this:

'What do you find inconvenient?' 'The fact that the bank is closed in the evening.'

The answer (the fact that the bank is closed in the evening) is the antecedent of the second part of the sentence.

- ✔ **Ik kreeg een fles wijn, wat een verrassing voor me was.** (*ik kraykh ern fles vayn vat ern fer-<u>ra</u>-sing foar mer vas*) (I received a bottle of wine, which was a surprise for me.)

  'What was a surprise for you?' 'The fact that I received a bottle of wine.'

✔ **Mijn fiets ging kapot, wat nogal vervelend was.** (*mayn feets khing kaa-pot vat no-khal fer-fay-lernt vas*) (My bike broke down, which was pretty annoying.)

'What was pretty annoying?' 'The fact that my bike broke down.'

The relative pronoun **wat** is also used with the antecedents **alles, iets, weinig, niets, veel**. See the following sentences:

✔ **Alles wat je over wisselkoersen wilt weten, kun je vinden op internet.** (*a-lers vat yer oa-fer vi-serl-koor-sern vilt vay-tern kuhn yer fin-dern op in-ter-net*) (Everything you want to know about exchange rates can be found on the Internet.)

✔ **Dat is iets wat ik altijd nog eens wil leren.** (*dat is eets vat ik al-tayt nokh erns vil lay-rern*) (This is something that I would like to learn.)

✔ **Er is weinig wat hij niet heeft.** (*ehr is vay-nikh vat hay neet hayft*) (There is hardly anything that he does not possess.)

✔ **Er is niets wat ik meer haat dan in de rij staan.** (*ehr is neets vat ik mayr haat dan in der ray staan*) (There is nothing that I hate more than queuing.)

✔ **Veel van wat je niet weet, kun je vinden op internet.** (*fayl fan vat yer neet vayt kuhn yer fin-dern op in-ter-net*) (Much of what you don't know can be found on the Internet.)

At the Bank

If you want to open **een bankrekening** (*ern bank-ray-ker-ning*) (a bank account) with a Dutch bank, you need to show a lot of documents: a passport, of course, but also proof of residency from **de Gemeentelijke Basisadministratie Persoonsgegevens** (*der kher-mayn-ter-ler-ker baa-sisat- mee-nee-straa-tsee per-soans-kher-khay-ferns*) (the GBA, which handles all registration and paperwork for your local government) and proof of income as well as your **sofinummer** (*soa-fee-nuh-mer*) (your social-fiscal/insurance/Social Security number). Non-European Union citizens require even more papers.

Internet banking

In the Netherlands 37% of the population conduct (part of) their banking on the Internet, **internetbankieren** (*in-ter-net-ban-kee-rern*). All the banks offer Internet banking facilities. They allow you to monitor and manage your **rekening-courant** (*ray-ker-ning koo-rant*) (current account), open **een spaarrekening** (*ern spaar-ray-ker-ning*) (a savings account) and **geld overmaken** (*khelt oa-fern-maa-kern*) (to transfer money). You can have a look at your **tegoed** (*ter-khoot*) (credit) any time.

'Acceptgiro' and 'automatische overschrijving'

De acceptgiro (*der ak-sept-khee-roa*) (bank transfer) is giving way to forms of payment by Internet. For the use of utilities and monthly services, companies will send you a bill with an **acceptgiro**, which you sign, and post to your bank. You fill out the number of your **girorekening** (*khee-roa-ray-ker-ning*) (Post Office Bank account) or **bankrekening** (*bank-ray-ker-ning*) (an account with a commercial bank such as ABN AMRO, ING, Rabobank or Fortis). All banks charge money for each **acceptgiro** they handle, so many people prefer to save costs by paying the acceptgiro electronically. Providers of utilities and renters/lessors prefer **een automatische overschrijving** (*ern ow-toa-maa-tee-ser oa-fer-skhray-fing*) (a direct debit).To do so you must get **een formulier** (*ern for-muw-leer*) (a form) from the company you want to pay, not the bank. It is usually a two-part form, with the second part held back in case you want to cancel **de afschrijvingen** (*der af-skhray-fing-ern*) (the withdrawals). After filling out the form, you post it back. It can take up to one month to process your request.

Geld opnemen (*khelt-op-nay-mern*) (to withdraw money) at the counter in a bank is still possible but will cost you some extra money. The next phrases might be helpful:

- ✔ **Ik wil graag . . . opnemen.** (*ik vil khraakh . . . u-roa op-nay-mern*) (I would like to withdraw . . .)

- ✔ **Mag ik uw paspoort/betaalpas zien?** (*makh ik uw pas-poart/ber-taal- pas zeen*) (May I see your passport/banker's card?)

- ✔ **Wilt u hier tekenen?** (*vilt uw heer tay-ker-nern*) (Sign here, please)

- ✔ **Waar moet ik tekenen?** (*vaar moot ik tay-ker-nern*) (Where do I sign?)

- ✔ **U kunt het geld krijgen bij de kas.** (*uw kuhnt het khelt kray-khern bay der kas*) (You can collect the money from the cashier.)

At the Post Office

E-mail has taken over part of the traditional **brief** (*breef*) (letter). However, **de postbode** (*der post-boa-der*) (the postman) brings us on a daily base **zakelijke post** (*zaa-ker-ler-ker post*) (business mailings), **pakjes** (*pak-yers*) (parcels), **verjaardagskaarten** (*fer-yaar-dakhs-kaar-tern*) (birthday cards), and **kerstkaarten** (*kerst-kaar-tern*) (Christmas cards).

If you want to send something to your beloved, the next phrases might help you:

Waar is een brievenbus? (*vaar is ern <u>bree</u>-fern-buhs*) (Where can I find a postbox/mailbox?)

When you find the box it may read:

De volgende lichting is om 17.00 uur. (*der <u>fol</u>-khen-der <u>likh</u>-ting is om fayf uwr*) (The next collection is at 5 p.m.)

or

Lichting 2 is geschied. (*<u>likh</u>-ting tvay is kher-<u>skheet</u>*) (Collection 2, the Monday collection, has been done.)

If you need to be at the post office you can ask:

  ✔ **Waar is het dichtstbijzijnde postkantoor?** (*vaar is het <u>dikhst</u>-bay-zayn-der <u>post</u>-kan-toar*) (Where is the nearest post office?)

  ✔ **Wat zijn de openingstijden van het postkantoor?** (*vat zayn der <u>oa</u>-per-nings-tay- dern fan het <u>post</u>-kan-toar*) (What are the opening hours of the post office?)

Some Dutch post offices have **balies** (*<u>baa</u>-lees*) (open counters) and some have **loketten** (*loa-<u>keh</u>-tern*) (closed counters). When it's crowded, it's important to queue for the right counter. The counters will have the following notices:

  ✔ **alle lokethandelingen** (*<u>a</u>-ler loa-<u>ket</u>-han-der-ling-ern*) (all services)

  ✔ **Postbank** (*<u>post</u>-bank*) (Post Office Bank/Girobank)

  ✔ **postpakketten** (*<u>post</u>-pa-keh-tern*) (parcel post)

  ✔ **uitbetalingen** (*<u>oait</u>-ber-taa-ling-ern*) (payments)

  ✔ **aangetekende stukken** (*<u>aan</u>-kher-tay-ken-der <u>stuh</u>-kern*) (registered mail)

  ✔ **zegelverkoop** (*<u>zay</u>-kherl-fer-koap*) (stamps)

  ✔ **telefoon** (*tay-ler-<u>foan</u>*) (telephone)

When it's your turn, you can ask the post office employee:

  ✔ **Hoeveel moet er op een briefkaart/ansichtkaart?** (*<u>hoo</u>-fayl moot er op ern <u>breef</u>-kaart/<u>an</u>-sikht-kaart*) (How much is a stamp for a postcard?)

  ✔ **Hoeveel moet er op drukwerk?** (*<u>hoo</u>-fayl moot er op <u>druhk</u>-verk*) (How much is a stamp for printed matter?)

  ✔ **Moet dit per pakketpost?** (*moot dit pehr pa-<u>ket</u>-post*) (Are you going to send this by parcel post?)

✔ **Hoeveel moet er op een brief/briefkaart naar Engeland/Amerika?**
(*hoo-fayl moot er op ern* <u>*breef*</u>/*breef-kaart naar* <u>*eng*</u>*-erlant/aa-*<u>*may*</u>*-ree-kaa*)
(How much is a stamp for a letter/postcard to Britain/America?)

When ordering something, you could say:

Drie postzegels van . . . cent alstublieft. (*dree* <u>*post*</u>*-zay-kherls fan . . . sent al-stuw-*<u>*bleeft*</u>) (Three stamps for . . . cents, please.)

In case you are a lover of **filatelie** (*fee-laa-ter-*<u>*lee*</u>) (philately) try the next phrases:

✔ **Heeft u ook bijzondere postzegels?** (*hayft uw ook bee-*<u>*zon*</u>*-der-er zay-kherls*) (Do you have any special stamps?)

✔ **Ik wil graag deze serie.** (*ik vil khraakh* <u>*day*</u>*-zer* <u>*si*</u>*-ree*) (I'd like to have this series.)

Of course, you know how to address a letter. On **de envelop** (*der en-fer-*<u>*lop*</u>) (the envelope) should be: **de geadresseerde** (*der kher-a-dreh-*<u>*sayr*</u>*-der*) (the addressee), **de straat** (*der straat*) (the street) and **het huisnummer** (*het* <u>*hoais*</u>*-nuh-mer*) (the number) or the **postbus** (<u>*post*</u>*-buhs*) (the PO box), **de postcode** (*der* <u>*post*</u>*-koa-der*) (postal code), **de stad** (*der stat*) (the town) and, when outside the Netherlands, **het land** (*het lant*) (the country). It should also carry **een postzegel** (*ern* <u>*post*</u>*-zay-kherl*) (a stamp) and the name of **de afzender** (*der* <u>*af*</u>*-zen-der*) (the sender). You could send your letter **aangetekend** (<u>*aan*</u>*-kher-tay-kent*) (registered) or **per luchtpost** (*pehr* <u>*luhkht*</u>*-post*) (by air mail).

Talkin' the Talk

Cilla Vermeent is at the post office. She wants to buy the special December stamps that are used for Christmas cards. She has been queuing for a long time but when it's her turn, a lady jumps the queue.

Cilla:	**Ik ben aan de beurt, ik sta al een hele tijd te wachten.**
	ik ben aan der burt ik staa al ern <u>*hay*</u>*-ler tayt ter* <u>*vakh*</u>*-tern*
	It's my turn, I have been waiting for a long time.
Lady:	**Ik heb haast.**
	ik hep haast
	I am in a hurry.
Post office employee:	**U kunt achteraansluiten.**
	(to the lady) *uw kuhnt akh-ter-*<u>*aan*</u>*-sloai-tern*
	You can queue up.

(to Cilla) **Nu bent u aan de beurt.**

nuw bent uw aan der burt

Now it's your turn.

Cilla: **Ik wil graag 30 decemberzegels.**

ik vil khraakh <u>dehr</u>-tikh day-<u>sem</u>-ber-zaykherls

I would like 30 December stamps.

Post office employee: **We verkopen ze in vellen van 20. Wilt u er 20 of 40?**

ver fer-<u>koa</u>-pern zer in <u>feh</u>-lern fan <u>tvin</u>-tikh. vilt uw er <u>tvin</u>-tikh of <u>fayr</u>-tikh

We sell them in sheets of 20. Do you want 20 or 40?

Cilla: **Geef er maar 40.**

khayf er maar <u>fayr</u>-tikh

I'll take 40.

Post office employee: **Wilt u een BTW-bon?**

vilt uw ern bay-tay-<u>vay</u>-bon

Do you want a receipt with VAT?

Cilla: **Nee, dat is niet nodig, het is privé.**

nay dat is neet <u>noa</u>-dikh het is pree-<u>vay</u>

No thank you, they are for private use.

Post office employee: **Wilt u pinnen?**

khaat uw <u>pi</u>-nern

Do you want to pay with your PIN card?

Cilla: **Ja graag.**

yaa kraakh

Yes please.

Post office employee: **De magneetstrip aan de andere kant graag. Ja, zo . . . U kunt nu uw code intoetsen.**

der makh-<u>nayt</u>-strip aan der <u>an</u>-der-er kant khraakh. yaa zoa. uw kuhnt nuw uw <u>koa</u>-der in-toot-sern

The magnetic strip on the other side please. Yes, like that . . . You can enter your PIN code now.

Alstublieft, uw bon en fijne feestdagen.

als-tuw-<u>bleeft</u> uw bon en <u>fay</u>-ner <u>fayst</u>-daa-khern

Here you are, your receipt, and Merry Christmas.

Words to Know

ik ben aan de beurt	*ik ben aan der burt*	It's my turn
achteraansluiten	*akh-ter aon-sloai-tern*	to queue up
een vel	*een fehkl*	a sheet
privé	*pree-vay*	private
pinnen	*pi-nern*	to pay by switch/ debit card
de magneetstrip	*der makh-nayt-strip*	the magnetic strip

Chapter 11

Asking for Directions

. . . .

In This Chapter

▶ Going North, South, East, and West

▶ Finding your way: **rechts, links, rechtdoor**

▶ By car, by train, by bus, or by plane: **gaan**

. . . .

*T*he key to getting around is to know how to get where you're going. Before you leave, it's always a good idea to find out where your desired destination is located. Being able to ask where the train station or museum is located is a good start. But of course, you also want to understand the directions you are given – behind the church, take the first street on the left – and so on. If you are afraid you might be lost, this is the chapter that will get you back on the map.

Going North, South, East, and West

Here you'll find some other useful words to find your way. Notice that **de windstreken** (*der vint-stray-kern*) (the directions) are written with small letters in Dutch!

> ✔ **het noorden** (*het noar-dern*) (the North)
>
> ✔ **het zuiden** (*het zoai-dern*) (the South)
>
> ✔ **het oosten** (*het oa-stern*) (the East)
>
> ✔ **het westen** (*het ves-tern*) (the West)

You combine these words with **in**:

> ✔ **Groningen ligt in het noorden.** (*khroa-ning-ern likht in het noar-dern*) (Groningen is in the North.)
>
> ✔ **Maastricht ligt in het zuiden.** (*maas-trikht likht in het zoai-dern*) (Maastricht is in the South.)

✔ **Den Haag ligt in het westen.** (*den-haakh* ligt in het *ves*-tern) (The Hague is in the West.)

✔ **Nijmegen ligt in het oosten.** (*nay*-may-khern likht in het *oas*-tern) (Nijmegen is in the East.)

The Dutch will not use the directions when showing you the way. If you're in the centre of Amsterdam, they will not tell you that you have to go north in order to reach Zaandam. If you travel by car, they will tell you how to find the ring road A10 and to follow the signs direction Zaandam. When you've made a mistake, and you've arrived in Hoorn (which is north of Zaandam) people will not tell you to go south. They will tell you to return and take the A7 in the direction of Amsterdam. Signposting on the Dutch main roads is based on the names of big cities. If you drive without GPS, be sure to have a look at the map and make a list of road numbers and cities you have to pass before you leave!

Asking for help with directions

Luckily, it's pretty easy to ask for directions in Dutch. The secret to finding a location is the word **waar** (*vaar*) (where). The question you want to ask starts with:

Waar is . . . ? (*vaar is*) (Where is . . . ?)

At the end of the sentence, just supply the name of the location you're looking for. You could include any of the following:

✔ **het station** (*het sta-shon*) (the train station)

✔ **de taxistandplaats** (*der tak-see-stant-plaats*) (the taxi stand)

✔ **het metrostation** (*het may-troa-sta-shon*) (the underground station)

✔ **de bushalte** (*der bus-hal-ter*) (the bus station)

✔ **het vliegveld** (*het fleekh-felt*) (the airport)

✔ **de haven** (*der haa-fern*) (the harbour)

✔ **het hotel** (*het hoa-tel*) (the hotel)

✔ **de kerk** (*der kehrk*) (the church)

✔ **het postkantoor** (*het post-kan-toar*) (the post office)

✔ **de markt** (*der markt*) (the market)

✔ **het museum** (*het muw-zay-uhm*) (the museum)

✔ **het park** (*het park*) (the park)

Of course, if you're in a large town, a very general question such as 'Where is the station?' or 'Where is the church?' may be met with a puzzled look. There may be various stations and multiple churches. You need to make your questions as specific as possible. For example, if you know the proper name of the station or the church, include it in your question. Your specified questions may sound like this:

- ✔ **Waar is het station WTC?** (*vaar is het sta-shon vay-tay-say*) (Where is the WTC station?)

- ✔ **Waar is de Sint Nicolaaskerk?** (*vaar is der sint-nee-koa-laas-kehrk*) (Where is the Saint Nicholas church?)

If you don't exactly know what the name is of the thing you are looking for, for instance a park, you could ask the way to the nearest park. Just insert **dichtstbijzijnde** (*dikhst-bay-zayn-der*) (nearest) between **de** or **het** and the name of the location you are looking for. Check out a few examples of **dichtstbijzijnde**:

- ✔ **Waar is het dichtstbijzijnde park?** (*vaar is het dikhst-bay-zayn-der park*) (Where is the nearest bus stop?)

- ✔ **Waar is het dichtstbijzijnde station?** (*vaar is het dikhst-bay-zayn-der sta-shon*) (Where is the nearest train station?)

How far is it?

In order to decide whether you want to walk to some place or take a bus or cab, you might want to find out how far away your destination is. You have a couple of options to find out if something is located in the vicinity or far away, and the key words to know are: **dichtbij** (*dikht bay*) or **vlakbij** (*flak bay*) (near) and **ver** (*fehr*) (far) or **ver weg** (*fehr vekh*) (far away).

You can ask the question:

Is . . . ver weg? (*is . . . fehr vekh*) (Is . . . far away?)

Just fill in the name of the location you're asking about. So, for example, if you were headed to the WTC station, you might ask someone.

Is het station WTC ver weg? (*is het sta-shon vay-tay-say fehr vekh*) (Is the WTC station far away?)

The answer might be:

Nee, het station WTC is niet ver weg. Het is vlakbij. (*nay het sta-shon vay-tay-say is neet fehr vekh. het is flak bay*) (No, the WTC station is not far away. It's near.)

The person you're talking to may even start to give you directions to the place you're heading for. For help in understanding directions, read the section 'Describing a Position or Location', later in this chapter.

It is also possible to say it the other way around and find out how close something is by using the word **dichtbij**. You can ask the question:

> **Is het station WTC dichtbij?** (*is het sta-<u>shon</u> vay-tay-<u>say</u> dikht bay*) (Is the WTC station nearby?)

The word **dichtbij** is used in the question and in the answer you will hear more often **vlakbij:**

> **Ja, het station WTC is vlakbij.** (*yaa het sta-<u>shon</u> vay-tay-<u>say</u> is flak bay*) (Yes, the WTC station is nearby).

When you are looking for a place, and you don't know if there is a place like that nearby at all, you might use the following question:

> **Is er een station in de buurt?** (*is er ern sta-<u>shon</u> in der buwrt*) (Is there a train station nearby?)

In order to say you don't know your way around you can say:

> **Ik ben hier niet bekend.** (*ik ben heer neet ber-<u>kent</u>*) (I don't know my way around here.)

If you want to be more polite, you can say:

> **Het spijt me, ik ben hier niet bekend.** (*het spayt mer ik ben heer neet ber-<u>kent</u>*) (Sorry, I don't know my way around here.)

Going 'hier' and 'daar'

The words **hier** (*heer*) (here) and **daar** (*daar*) (there) often play an important part in communicating directions. They make directions just a little more specific. Look at the following sentences to see how **hier** and **daar** work in directions:

- ✔ **Het station is hier niet ver vandaan.** (*het saa-<u>shon</u> is heer neet fehr fan-<u>daan</u>*) (The train station is not far from here.)

- ✔ **De bushalte Rembrandtstraat is hier niet ver vandaan.** (*der <u>buhs</u>-hal-ter <u>rem</u>-brant-straat is heer neet fehr fan-<u>daan</u>*) (The bus stop Rembrandtstraat is not far from here.)

Common expressions you might hear are:

> ✔ **Dat is hier.** (*dat is heer*) (That's right here.)
>
> ✔ **Dat is daar.** (*dat is daar*) (That's right over there.)

Other possible combinations are:

> ✔ **Dat is hier recht tegenover.** (*dat is heer rekht tay-kern-oa-fer*) (that's right across the street.)
>
> ✔ **Dat is daar recht tegenover.** (*dat is daar rekht tay-kern-oa-fer*) (It's just opposite.)

Asking how to get there

When you want to ask 'How do I get there?' you use the verb **komen** (*koa-mern*) (to come), which means both 'to come' and when used with a preposition 'to get there'.

You conjugate **komen** like this:

Conjugation	Pronunciation
ik kom	*ik kom*
jij komt	*yay komt*
u komt	*uw komt*
hij/zij/het komt	*hay/zay/het komt*
wij komen	*vay koa-mern*
jullie komen	*yuw-lee koa-mern*
zij komen	*zay koa-mern*

The basic form of the question (How do I get to?) is:

> **Hoe kom ik . . .** (*hoo kom ik*) (How do I get to . . .)

To finish the rest of the sentence, you need to use a proposition, like **in**:

> **Hoe kom ik in het centrum?** (*hoo kom ik in het sen-truhm*) (How do I get to the centre?)

or

> **Hoe kom ik in Zaandam?** (*hoo kom ik in zaan-dam*) (How do I get to Zaandam?)

Describing a Position or a Location

After you ask for directions, you must be ready to understand the possible answers. Is very common to express location of place in relation to a well-known landmark or location. In this case your helper will use one of the following prepositions:

- ✔ **voor** (*foar*) (before)
- ✔ **na** (*naa*) (after)
- ✔ **bij** (*bay*) (by)
- ✔ **op** (*op*) (on)
- ✔ **in** (*in*) (in)

You might hear one of the following sentences:

- ✔ **U gaat voor het park rechtsaf.** (*uw khaat foar het park rekht- af*) (Before the park turn to the right.)
- ✔ **U gaat na het park rechtsaf.** (*uw khaat naa het park rekhts-af*) (After the park turn to the right.)
- ✔ **U gaat bij het eerste stoplicht rechtsaf.** (*uw khaat bay het ayr-ster stop-likht rekhts-af*) (At the first traffic lights you turn to the right.)
- ✔ **U rijdt dan op de A7.** (*uw rayt dan op der aa zay-fern*) (You are then driving on the A7.)
- ✔ **U bent dan al in Zaandam.** (*uw bent dan al in zaan-dam*) (Then you have arrived at Zaandam.)

The preposition "to"

You use the preposition **naar** (*naar*) (to) when talking about a direction.

- ✔ **Hoe kom ik naar het Centaal Station?** (*hoo kom ik naar het sen-traal sta-shon*) (How do I get to the Central Station?)
- ✔ **Ik probeer naar het Centraal Station te komen.** (*ik pro-bayr naar het sen-traal sta-shon ter koa-mern*) (I'm trying to get to the Central Station.)
- ✔ **Morgen ga ik naar het strand.** (*mor-khern khaa ik naar der stat*) (Tomorrow I'm going to the beach.)
- ✔ **Laten we naar Den Haag gaan.** (*laa-tern ver naar den-haakh khaan*) (Let's go to The Hague.)

You'll find more information about prepositions in Chapter 2.

Talkin' the Talk

 Raymond van Dieren is on a business trip to Utrecht. As both planned business meetings are in the centre of town, he took the train. The first meeting is in the morning and the other one in the afternoon. After his first meeting, he is talking to the receptionist of the company he visited. He asks her if she knows a good restaurant nearby.

Raymond: **Mag ik u vragen: weet u een goed restaurant in de buurt? Ik heb vanavond een afspraak in het centrum.**
makh ik uw <u>fraa</u>-khern vayt uw ern khoot restoa-<u>rant</u> in der buwrt. ik hep fa-<u>naa</u>-font ern <u>af</u>-spraak in het <u>sen</u>-truhm
Would you know a good restaurant nearby for tonight? I am meeting someone in the centre.

Receptionist: **Op de Oude Gracht zijn veel restaurants.**
op der <u>ow</u>-der khrakht zayn fayl res-toa-<u>rants</u>
On the Oude Gracht are a lot of restaurants.

Raymond: **Ik ben hier niet bekend. Hoe kom ik daar?**
ik ben heer neet ber-<u>kent</u>. hoo kom ik daar
I don't know my way around, how do I get there?

Receptionist: **Ziet u die kerk daar? Na de kerk gaat u links. U komt dan op een plein.**
zeet uw dee kehrk daar. naa der kehrk khaat uw links. uw komt dan op ern playn
Do you see that church over there? After the church you go to the left. You arrive at a square.
U loopt een smal straatje door en dan bent u op de Oude Gracht.
uw loapt ern smal <u>straa</u>-tyer doar en dan bent uw op der <u>ow</u>-der khrakht
You walk through a narrow street and then you are on the Oude Gracht.

Raymond: **Dus na de kerk links en na het plein moet ik door een nauw straatje. Kunt u mij misschien een restaurant aanbevelen?**
duhs na der kehrk links en naa het playn moot ik doar ern now <u>straa</u>-tyer. kuhnt uw may mis-<u>kheen</u> ern res-toa-<u>rant</u> aan-ber-<u>fay</u>-lern
So after the church to the left and after the square I have to follow a narrow street. Could you recommend me a restaurant please?

Receptionist: **Restaurant 'De Dom' op het Domplein is erg goed.**
res-toa-<u>rant</u> der dom op het <u>dom</u>-playn is erkh khoot
Restaurant 'De Dom' on the Domplein is very good.

Raymond: **Hoe kom ik op het Domplein?**
hoo kom ik op het <u>dom</u>-playn
How do I get at the Domplein?

Receptionist: **Dat is het plein bij de kerk.**
dat is het playn bay der kehrk
That's the place near the church.
Raymond: **OK, bedankt.**
oa-kay ber-dankt
Okay thank you.
Receptionist: **Graag gedaan en eet smakelijk vanavond!**
khraakh kher-daan en ayt smaa-ker-lerk fa-naa-font
You are welcome, and enjoy your meal tonight!

Finding Your Way: 'Rechts', 'links', 'rechtdoor'

Unless you tackle the words for the various directions, such as left and right, you will forever get into trouble when asking people to show you the way. Here are the words you need to understand the various directions.

Left and right

When it comes to asking or giving directions, there's no way to get around the key words **links** (*links*) (left), **rechts** (*rekhts*) (right), and **rechtdoor** (*rekht-doar*) (straight on).

If you want to express that something is located to the left or right of something else, you add the preposition **van,** making the following:

✔ **Links van** (*links fan*) (to the left of), for example:

De kerk is links van het museum. (*der kehrk is links fan het muw-zay-uhm*) (The church is to the left of the museum.)

Words to Know

het plein	het playn	the place
het is erg goed	het is erkh khoot	it is very good
eet smakelijk	ayt smaa-ker-lerk	enjoy your meal
de straat	der straht	the street

✔ **Rechts van** (*rekhts fan*) (to the right of), for example:

Het museum is rechts van de kerk. (*het muw-zay-uhm is rekhts fan der kehrk*) (The museum is at the right of the church.)

You might also hear the words **aan uw linkerhand** (*aan uw lin-ker hant*) (at your left hand) which means the same as **aan de linkerkant** (*aan der lin-ker kant*) (at the left side) or simply **links** (*links*) (on the left):

✔ **De kerk is aan uw linkerhand** (*der kehrk is aan uw lin-ker hant*) (The church is at your left hand), or **De kerk is aan de linkerkant** (*der kehrk is aan der lin-ker kant*) (The church is at the left side) or **De kerk is links** (*der kehrk is links*) (The church is on the left).

✔ **Het museum is aan uw rechterhand** (*het muw-zay-uhm is aan uw rekh-ter hant*) (The Museum is at your right hand), **Het museum is aan de rechterkant** (*het muw-zay-uhm is aan der rekh-ter kant*) (The Museum is at the right side), or **Het museum is rechts** (*het muw-zay-uhm is rekhts*) (The Museum is on the right).

Some other expressions that come in handy:

✔ **Sla linksaf.** (*slaa links-af*) (Turn to the left.) and, more usual

Na het museum linksaf. (*naa het muw-zay-uhm links-af*) (After the museum go to the left.)

✔ **Sla rechtsaf** (*slaa rekhts-af*) (Turn to the right) and

Na de kerk rechtsaf. (*naa der kehrk rekhts-af*) (After the church turn to the right.)

Na de kerk gaat u rechtsaf. (*naa der kehrk khaat uw rekhts-af*) (After the church you go to the right.)

✔ **U loopt rechtdoor tot u een kerk ziet.** (*uw loapt rekht-doar tot uw ern kehrk zeet*) (You walk straight on until you see a church.)

Travelling by car

Walking and driving are two different things. Part of the vocabulary that you find in this chapter can be used for both ways of getting to where you want to get. However, travelling by car brings some different terms with it. You will pass **knooppunten** (*knoa-puhn-tern*) (interchanges), **rotondes** (*roa-ton-ders*) (roundabouts), **kruispunten** (*kroais-puhn-tern*) (junctions) and you will have to leave the highway at **afslag 32** (*af-slakh tvay-ern-dehr-tikh*) (exit 32) or some other number, **richting . . .** (*rikh-ting*) (direction . . .). If you don't use GPS, but prefer to print some Dutch **routeplanner** (*roo-ter-pleh-ner*) (itinary planner) that you can find on the Internet, you might read one of the following phrases:

- ✔ **U neemt de rotonde driekwart.** (*uw naymt der roa-ton-der dree kvart*) (You take the roundabout for three quarters.)

- ✔ **Op de rotonde neemt u de eerste rechts.** (*op der roa-ton-der naymt uw der ayr-ster rekhts*) (At the roundabout you take the first on the right.)

- ✔ **Vervolgens neemt u bij knooppunt de Nieuwe Meer de A10 West richting Zaanstad-Leeuwarden.** (*fer-fol-kherns naymt uw bay knoa-puhnt der nee-wer mayr der aa-teen vest rikhting zaan-stat lay-war-dern*) (After that you take at the interchange Nieuwe Meer the A10-West direction Zaandam-Leeuwarden.)

- ✔ **U gaat onder het viaduct door.** (*uw khaat on-der het fee-aa-duhkt doar*) (You pass under the cross-over.)

- ✔ **Over de brug rechtsaf.** (*oa-fer der bruhkh rekhts-af*) (Across the bridge to the right.)

Understanding where to cross and turn

When somebody is helping you to find your way, you will hear some specific verbs. **Afslaan** (*af-slaan*) (to turn) is always combined with **links** or **rechts.** As **afslaan** is a separable verb, it is separated into two parts in the present and the words **rechts** and **links** are stuck to the separated part **af**: **u slaat rechtsaf** (*uw slaat rekhts-af*) (you turn to the right) and **u slaat linksaf** (*uw slaat links-af*) (you turn to the left).

- ✔ **Na de kerk slaat u rechtsaf.** (*naa der kehrk slaat uw rekhts-af*) (After the church you turn to the right.)

- ✔ **Bij de manege slaat u linksaf.** (*bay der ma-nay-zher slaat uw linkhs-af*) (At the riding school you turn to the left.)

Often you will have to **oversteken** (*oa-fer-stay-kern*) (to cross). If you are on foot you may get the instruction **Steek de straat over** (*stayk der straat oa-fer*) (cross the street) or **Steek het plein over** (*stayk het playn oa-fer*) (cross the square). Also you will be advised: **Steek de brug over** (*stayk der bruhkh oa-fer*) (cross the bridge). In combination with the bridge you might also hear: **Ga de brug over** (*khaa der bruhkh oa-fer*) (Go over the bridge). If you are going or driving in the wrong direction, you will be told **U moet terug** (*uw moot ter-ruhkh*) (you have to turn).

Doing first things first: 'eerst', 'dan', 'daarna'

If you want to find your way it's important to do the things in the right order. The words you need for this: **eerst** (*ayrst*) (first), **dan** (*dan*) or **vervolgens** (*fer-fol-kherns*) (then), and **daarna** (*daar-naa*) (after that). Check the following example:

✔ **U gaat eerst rechtdoor** (*uw khaat ayrst rekht-doar*) (first you go straight ahead), **dan neemt u de eerste straat rechts** (*dan naymt uw der ayr-ster straat rekhts*) (then you take first street on the right) **en daarna steekt u de brug over** (*en daar-naa staykt uw der brukh oa-fer*) (and after that you cross the bridge).

Talkin' the Talk

Cilla is going to see Raymond who is in Utrecht for business. They will meet in a bar near the station. Cilla knows the name of the street and she knows that it's in the centre, but she does not know where exactly it is. She went to Utrecht by train and when leaving the station, she has to ask.

Cilla:	**Bent u hier bekend?**
	bent uw heer ber-kent
	Excuse me, do you know your way around?
Man:	**Ja, dat ben ik.**
	yaa dat ben ik
	Yes, I do.
Cilla:	**Kunt u me vertellen waar de Lange Nieuwstraat is?**
	kuhnt uw mer fer-teh-lern vaar der lang-er neew-straat is
	Could you tell me where the Lange Nieuwstraat is?
Man:	**Ja, die is vlakbij. Als u het station uitkomt, gaat u rechtsaf. Dan steekt u over en neemt de eerste straat links.**
	yaa dee is flak bay. als uw het staa-shon oait-komt khaat uw rekhts-af. dan staykt uw oa-fer en naymt der ayr-ster straat links
	Yes, that's quite near. When you leave the station, go to the right. Then you cross the street and take the first street left.
Cilla:	**Hoe heet die straat?**
	hoo hayt dee straat
	What's the name of the street?

Man:	**Dat weet ik niet. Maar hij gaat naar het centrum en je kunt hem niet missen. Daarna kruist u een gracht, dat is de Oude Gracht.**
	dat vayt ik neet. maar hay khaat naar het <u>sen</u>-truhm en yer kuhnt hem neet <u>mi</u>-sern. d<u>aar</u>-na kroaist uw ern khrakht dat is der <u>ow</u>-der khrakht
	I don't know, but it goes to the centre and you can't miss it. After that you cross a canal, that's the Oude Gracht.
Cilla:	**O ja, die gracht ken ik. Daar zijn allemaal terrasjes.**
	oa yaa dee khrakht ken ik. daar zayn <u>a</u>-lermaal ter-<u>ras</u>-yers
	Yes, I do know that canal. There are a lot of outdoor cafés.
Man:	**Als u dan nog even rechtdoor loopt, komt u in de Lange Nieuwstraat.**
	als uw dan nokh <u>ay</u>-fern rekht-<u>doar</u> loapt komt uw in der <u>lang</u>-er <u>neew</u>-straat
	If you go straight on for a while, you'll arrive at the Lange Nieuwstraat.
Cilla:	**Hartelijk bedankt.**
	<u>har</u>-ter-lerk ber-<u>dankt</u>
	Thank you very much.

Words to Know

Ik weet het niet	ik vayt het neet	I don't know
Je kunt hem niet missen	yer kuhnt hem neet <u>mi</u>-sern	you can't miss it
de terrasjes	der ter-<u>ras</u>-yers	the outdoor cafés

Coming into action

When you have asked somebody for directions, you might very well get the answer **U neemt . . .** (*uw naymt*) (You take . . .). Notice that the Dutch generally use the present tense when giving directions: **U neemt . . .** (*uw naymt*) (You take. . .), **U gaat** (*uw khaat*) (You go), and **U slaat linksaf** (*uw slaat links-af*) (You turn to the left). You will hardly ever hear imperatives like in English: take, go or turn to the left. In written instructions sometimes infinitives are used: **bij het stoplicht rechtdoor rijden** (*bay het stop-likht rekht-doar ray-dern*) (at the traffic light drive straight on), **over de brug de eerste rechts nemen** (*oa-fer der bruhkh der ayr-ster rekhts nay-mern*) (over the bridge take the first on the right).

Words such as **de eerste** (*der ayr-ster*) (the first), **de tweede** (*der tvay-der*) (the second), and **de derde** (*der dehr-der*) (the third) are called ordinal numbers. They refer to a specific number in a series and answer the question: Which one? For example, to the question 'Which street?' you might use an ordinal to answer: 'The first on the left'. Find more about ordinals in Chapter 3.

Are you afraid of losing your way? No matter where are you drive or walk, the next sentence is always useful:

Ik ben de weg kwijt. (*ik ben der vekh kvayt*) (I have lost my way.)

By Car, Train, Bus, or Plane: 'Gaan'

In Dutch you can use the verb **gaan** (*khaan*) (to go) for a lot of things. First, you'll find here all the forms of the present. Like almost all **veelgebruikte werkwoorden** (*fayl-kher-broaik-ter vehrk-voar-dern*) (verbs that are employed a lot) the conjugation of the verb **gaan** is very irregular.

Conjugation	Pronunciation
ik ga	*ik khaa*
jij gaat	*yay khaat*
u gaat	*uw khaat*
hij/zij/het gaat	*hay/zay/het khaat*
wij gaan	*vay khaan*
jullie gaan	*yuw-lee khaan*
zij gaan	*zay khaan*

This verb serves you to indicate movement in a lot of situations. Here are some examples:

- ✔ **Ik ga vanmiddag naar Den Haag.** (*ik khaa fan-mi-dakh naar den-haakh*) (I am going to The Hague this afternoon.)

- ✔ **Mijn dochter gaat naar school.** (*mayn dokh-ter khaat naar skhoal*) (My daughter goes to school.)

- ✔ **Ik ga vanmiddag naar de supermarkt.** (*ik khaa fan-mi-dakh naar der suw-per-markt*) (I am going to the supermarket this afternoon.)

You can use this 'to go' for any way of moving: you could go to The Hague by car, by train, by bus, by tram, by bike and even, when you live nearby, walking. The same is valid for the other two examples. If you want to say *how* you go, all you have to do is add some words.

- ✔ **Ik ga vanmiddag met de auto naar Den Haag.** (*ik khaa fan-mi-dakh met der ow-toa naar den-haakh*) (I'm going to The Hague by car this afternoon.)

- ✔ **Mijn dochter gaat met de bus naar school.** (*mayn dokh-ter khaat met der buhs naar skhoal*) (My daughter goes to school by bus.)

- ✔ **Ik ga met de fiets naar de supermarkt.** (*ik khaa met der feets naar der suw-per-markt*) (I am going to the supermarket on my bike.)

In English, when you take the car, you use the verb to drive. You can use it in Dutch, but only when you want to mention explicitly that you are driving.

- ✔ **Vanmiddag rijd ik naar Den Haag.** (*fan-mi-dakh rayt ik naar den-haakh*) (I'm driving to The Hague this afternoon.)

- ✔ **Mijn dochter rijdt naar school.** (*mayn dokh-ter rayt naar skhoal*) (My daughter drives to school.)

- ✔ **Ik rijd vanmiddag naar de supermarkt.** (*ik rayt fan-mi-dakh naar der suw-per-markt*) (I'm driving to the supermarket this afternoon.)

Even when you're going by plane to some place, you can use the word 'to go'. You might say:

- ✔ **Volgend jaar gaan we naar Cuba.** (*fol-khernt yaar khaan ver naar kuw-baa*) (Next year we will go to Cuba.)

- ✔ **Volgende maand ga ik naar New York.** (*fol-khern-der maant khaa ik naar noo-york*) (I am going to New York next month.)

- ✔ **Ik ga naar Londen.** (*ik khaa naar lon-dern*) (I am going to London.)

When you want to make clear that you're going by plane and that you will not drive nor take the train or boat the word **vliegen** (*flee-khern*) (to fly) will come in handy.

- **Volgende week vlieg ik naar Madrid.** (*fol-khern-der vayk fleekh ik naar ma-drit*) (I am flying to Madrid next week.)

- **Volgende maand vlieg ik naar Londen.** (*fol-khern-der maant fleekh ik naar lon-dern*) (I am flying to London next month.)

Talkin' the Talk

Cilla Vermeent goes to visit a friend for the weekend who is on holiday in a small village in Zeeland. It's Friday night and Cilla is nearly there but she has lost her way. She stops at a petrol station in order to ask where exactly it is.

Cilla: **Sorry, kunt u me de weg wijzen naar Oude Tonge?**
so-ree kuhnt uw mer der vekh vay-zern naar ow-der tong-er
I'm sorry, can you tell me the way to Oude Tonge?

Employee: **Komt u van de A15?**
komt uw fan der aa fayf-teen
Are you coming from the A15?

Cilla: **Ja, maar ik denk dat ik de weg kwijt ben.**
yaa maar ik denk dat ik der vekh kvayt ben
Yes, but I think I have lost my way.

Employee: **U heeft de verkeerde afslag genomen. Dit is afslag 33.**
uw hayft der fer-kayr-der af-slakh kher-noa-mern. dit is af-slakh dree-ern-dehr-tikh
You've taken the wrong exit. This is exit 33. You have to go back to the A 15 direction Hoogvliet.
U moet terug naar de A15 richting Hoogvliet. Als u weer op de A15 bent, neemt u afslag 34 richting Zierikzee
uw moot ter-rukh naar der aa fay-teen rikh-ting hoakh-fleet. als uw vayr op der aa fayf-teen bent naymt uw af-slakh feer-ern-dehr-tikh rikh-ting zee-rik-zay
When you are on the A15 again, take exit 34, direction Zierikzee.

Cilla: **Maar ik moet naar Oude Tonge.**
maar ik moot naar ow-der tong-er
But I have to go to Oude Tonge.

Employee:	**Ja, als u afslag 34 heeft genomen, rijdt u alsmaar richting Zierikzee. U ziet dan borden met Oude Tonge en het volgende dorp is Oude Tonge.**
	yaa als uw <u>af</u>-slakh feer-ern-<u>dehr</u>-tikh hayft kher-<u>noa</u>-mern rayt uw <u>als</u>-maar <u>rikh</u>-ting zee-rik-<u>zay</u>. uw zeet dan <u>bor</u>-dern met <u>ow</u>-der <u>tong</u>-er en het <u>fol</u>-khen-der dorp is <u>ow</u>-der <u>tong</u>-er
	Yes, after taking exit 34, you drive on in the direction of Zierikzee. First you see the signs for Oude Tonge and the next village will be Oude Tonge.
Cilla:	**OK, ik hoop dat ik het nu vind. Hartelijk bedankt.**
	oa-<u>kay</u> ik hoap dat ik het nuw fint.<u>har</u>-ter-lerk ber-<u>dankt</u>
	Ok, I hope I'll find it now. Thank you very much!
Employee:	**Graag gedaan en nog een fijne avond!**
	khraakh kher-<u>daan</u> en nokh ern <u>fay</u>-ner <u>aa</u>-font
	You are welcome and have a nice evening!

Words to Know

Ik ben de weg kwijt	ik ben der vekh kvayt	I have lost my way
de afslag	der <u>af</u>-slakh	the exit
de borden	der <u>bor</u>-dern	the signs

Chapter 12

Staying in a Hotel

*R*egardless of whether you are travelling for business or leisure, you have to sleep somewhere. In this chapter you'll find the words and sentences that you need in order to find a hotel or a Bed and Breakfast, to make reservations, inquire about the facilities of the hotel as well as check in and out.

Looking for a Hotel

If you need assistance in finding a hotel you might want to buy a hotel guide in the bookshop. If you have the possibility, surf the Net! Of course you can find information about hotels in the tourist information, **de VVV** (*der vay-vay-vay*). Some of them offer the possibility to go online.

Perhaps you want to ask somebody you know, or persons who you meet, if they can recommend a hotel. In this case you would ask:

> **Kunt u een hotel aanbevelen?** (*kuhnt uw ern hoa-tel aan-ber-faylern*) (Could/can you recommend a hotel?)

The basic word for hotel in Dutch is **het hotel** (*het hoa-tel*) (the hotel).There are many kinds of hotels that all have their own atmosphere and level of service. Some of them are not exactly hotels and are labeled differently. **Motels** (*moa-tels*) (motels) are generally near the highway/motorway. For those who intend to stay for a longer period, **een apartementenhotel** (*ern a-par-ter-men-tern-hoa-tel*) (hotel with apartments) may offer a good solution. More adventurous people might enjoy **een Bed and Breakfast** (*ern bet en brek-ferst*) (a Bed and Breakfast): a more personal accommodation than a hotel. **Een jeugdherberg** (ern *yukht-hehr-berkh*) (a youth hostel) is cheap and offers great opportunities for meeting other persons, but no luxury. Outside town you'll find lots of **vakantiehuisjes** (*faa-kan-see-hoais-yers*) (holiday cottages) that have to be reserved in advance. **Vakantiehuisjes** are generally built in parks and sometimes share accommodations like a swimming pool and a restaurant.

Reserving the room

Try to reserve your room in advance, especially during high season or when special events take place. All hotels might be fully booked! If you haven't made a reservation and you cannot find a room, you'll have a better chance outside of towns and city centres! Ask for assistance at **de VVV** (Tourist Office).

If necessary see Chapter 9 about telephoning before making the call for a reservation. When the hotel desk clerk picks up the phone you can say the following in order to make clear what you are calling for:

> **Ik wil graag een kamer reserveren.** (*ik vil khraakh ern kaa-mer ray-ser-fayr-ern*) (I would like to reserve a room).

If you want to reserve more than one room, you just have to add the number (and use the plural):

> **Ik wil graag twee kamers reserveren.** (*ik vil khraakh tvay kaa-mers ray-ser-fayr-ern*) (I would like to reserve two rooms.)

Telling when you arrive and how long you want to stay

The person who made your reservation will probably ask you a number of questions in order to complete your reservation. You'll need numbers and dates now, so you may want to read Chapter 3. One of the first questions could be:

> **Voor wanneer wilt u een kamer reserveren?** (*foar va-nayr vilt uw ern kaa-mer ray-ser-fayr-ern*) (For when would you like to reserve a room?)

or

> **Van wanneer tot wanneer wilt u een kamer reserveren?** (*foar va-nayr tot va-nayr vilt uw ern kaa-mer ray-ser-fayr-ern*) (For what dates would you like to reserve a room?)

In order to specify how many nights you intend to stay or for what date you want to reserve, you could say either of the following:

✔ **Ik wil een kamer reserveren voor . . . nachten.** (*ik vil ern <u>kaa</u>-mer ray-ser-<u>fayr</u>-ern foar <u>nakh</u>-tern*) (I would like to reserve a room for. . . nights.)

✔ **Ik wil graag een kamer reserveren van 2 tot 4 september.** (*ik vil khraakh ern <u>kaa</u>-mer ray-ser-<u>fayr</u>-ern fan tvay tot feer sep-<u>tem</u>-ber*) (I would like to reserve a room from the 2nd to the 4th of September.)

Telling what kind of room you want

The person who takes your reservation will probably ask you what kind of room you would like. He or she can ask, for example:

Wat voor soort kamer wilt u hebben? (*vat foar soart <u>kaa</u>-mer vilt uw <u>heh</u>-bern*) (What kind of a room would you like?)

You can take the initiative and state what kind of room you want with the phrase:

✔ **Ik wil graag . . .** (*ik vil khraakh. . .*) (I would like to have . . .)

- **een eenpersoonskamer** (*ern ayn-per-<u>soans</u>-kaa-mer*) (a single room)

- **een tweepersoonskamer** (*ern tvay-per-<u>soans</u>-kaa-mer*) (a double room)

- **een rookvrije kamer** (*ern <u>roak</u>-fray-er <u>kaa</u>-mer*) (a non-smoking room)

- **een kamer op de eerste verdieping** (*ern <u>kaa</u>-mer op der <u>ayr</u>-ster fer-<u>dee</u>-ping*) (a room on the first floor, American: second floor)

✔ **Ik wil graag een kamer met . . .** (*ik vil khraakh ern <u>kaa</u>-mer met*) (I would like to have a room with . . .)

- **douche** (*doosh*) (a shower)

- **bad** (*bat*) (a bath)

- **een tweepersoonsbed** (*ern tvay-per-<u>soans</u>-bet*) (a double bed)

- **twee eenpersoonsbedden** (*tvay ayn-per-<u>soans</u>-beh-dern*) (two single beds)

Wat voor een? (*vat foar ern*) (What kind of?). These three little words may be used by the person who is helping you, either in the hotel, in Tourist Information or in other places. This type of question helps people find out exactly what it is that you want. For example:

- ✔ **Wat voor een kamer wilt u?** (*vat foar ern kaa-mer vilt uw*) (What kind of room do you want?)

- ✔ **Wat voor een hotel zoekt u?** (*vat foar ern hoa-tel zookt uw*) (What kind of hotel are you looking for?)

- ✔ **Wat voor een wijn wilt u? Witte of rode?** (*vat foar ern vayn vilt uw.vi-ter of roa-der*) (What kind of wine do you wish? White or red?)

Asking the price

You also might want to find out how much the hotel room costs. There are several options to do this. You can ask what the basic price is, but you can also ask for the price with other features included.

- ✔ **Hoeveel kost de kamer per nacht?** (*hoo-fayl kost der kaa-mer pehr nakht*) (What does the room cost per night?)

- ✔ **Hoeveel is één overnachting met ontbijt?** (*hoo-fayl is ayn oa-fer-nakh- ting met ont-bayt*) (How much is accommodation including breakfast?)

- ✔ **Hoeveel is een kamer met volpension?** (*hoo-fayl is ern kaa-mer met fol-pen-shon*) (What does a room with full board cost?)

- ✔ **Hoeveel is een kamer met halfpension?** (*hoo-fayl is ern kaa-mer met half-pen-shon*) (How much is a room with half board?)

Finalising the reservation

When you want to confirm the deal, you can say:

Wilt u de kamer voor mij reserveren? (*vilt uw der kaa-mer foar mer ray-ser-fayr-ern*) (Could you reserve the room for me, please?)

Talkin' the Talk

Cilla Vermeent and her partner Rob plan to go for a long weekend to the isle of Vlieland. Cilla calls one of the hotels.

Receptionist: **Hotel De Meeuw, goedemorgen, Ellen de Haan.**
hoa-tel der mayw khoo-der-mor-khern el-leun der haan
Hotel De Meeuw, good morning, Ellen de Haan speaking.

Cilla: **Goedemorgen, met Cilla Vermeent. Heeft u een kamer vrij voor het eerste weekend van september, dus 3 en 4 september?**
khoo-der-mor-khern met si-laa fer-maynt.hayft uw ern kaa-mer fray foar het ayr-ster vee-kent fan sep-tem-ber duhs dree en feer sep-tem-ber
Good morning, Cilla Vermeent, have you got any rooms free for the first weekend of September, so the 3rd and 4th of September?

Receptionist: **Eens even kijken. Wat voor kamer wilt u reserveren?**
erns ay-fern kay-kern. vat foar kaa-mer vilt uw ray-ser-fayr-ern
Let me see. For how many persons would you like to reserve?

Cilla: **Ik wil een tweepersoonskamer reserveren.**
ik vil ern tvay-per-soans-kaa-mer ray-ser-fayr-ern
I would like to reserve a double room.

Receptionist: **U boft. We hebben precies één tweepersoonskamer over.**
uw boft. ver heh-bern prer-sees ayn tvay-per-soans-kaa-mer oa-fer
You're lucky, we have just one double room left.

Cilla: **Is dat een kamer met bad?**
is dat ern kaa-mer met bat
Does the room have a bath?

Receptionist: **Het is een kamer met een tweepersoonsbed en met een douche. Er is geen bad. Is dat een probleem?**
het is ern kaa-mer met ern tvay-per-soans-bet en met ern doosh. ehr is khayn bat. is dat ern proa-blaym
It's a room with a double bed and a shower. It does not have a bath. Is this a problem?

Cilla: **Dat hangt er vanaf. Wat is de prijs voor twee nachten?**
dat hangt er-fan-af. vat is der prays foar tvay nakh-tern
It depends. What's the price for two nights?

Receptionist: **Voor een weekend van twee nachten is het €227,50 per persoon**
foar ern vee-kent fan tvay nakh-tern is het tvay-hon-dert zay-fern-ern-tvin-tikh u-roa fayf-tikh pehr per-soan.
For a weekend of two nights it comes to €227.50 per person

Cilla:	**O, dat is veel duurder dan ik dacht.**
	oa dat is fayl <u>duwr</u>-der dan ik dakht
	Oh, that's much more expensive than I expected.
Receptionist:	**We zitten nog in het hoogseizoen.**
	ver <u>zi</u>-tern nokh in het <u>hoakh</u>-say-zoon
	It's still the high season.
Cilla:	**OK, maar ik wil eerst met mijn partner overleggen.**
	oa-<u>kay</u> maar ik vil ayrst met mayn <u>part</u>-ner oafer-<u>leh</u>-khern
	Okay, but I first want to consult my partner.
Receptionist:	**Wacht niet te lang als u wilt boeken. Vanwege het mooie weer krijgen we veel telefoontjes.**
	vakht neet ter lang als uw vilt <u>boo</u>-kern.fan-<u>vay</u>-khern het <u>moay</u>-er vayr <u>kray</u>-khern ver fayl tay-ler-<u>foan</u>-tyers
	Because of the nice weather many people are calling to book, so don't wait too long if you want to book.
Cilla:	**Ik bel u over een halfuur terug. In ieder geval bedankt voor de informatie.**
	ik bel uw <u>oa</u>-fer ern <u>half</u>-uwr ter-<u>rukh</u>. in <u>ee</u>-der kher-<u>fal</u> ber-<u>dankt</u> foar der in-for-<u>maa</u>-tsee
	I'll call you back within half an hour. Anyhow, thanks for the information.
Receptionist:	**Graag gedaan. Fijne dag nog.**
	khraakh kher-<u>daan</u>.<u>fay</u>-ner dakh nokh
	My pleasure. Have a nice day.
Cilla:	**Ja, hetzelfde.**
	yaa het-<u>zelf</u>-der
	Same to you.

Words to Know

boffen	*<u>bof</u>-fern*	being lucky
duur	*durwr*	expensive
het hoogseizoen	*het <u>hoakh</u>-say-zoon*	the high season
de partner	*der <u>part</u>-ner*	the partner
overleggen	*oa-fer-<u>leh</u>-khern*	to consult
boeken	*<u>boo</u>-kern*	to book
de informatie	*der in-for-<u>maa</u>-tsee*	the information

Checking In

When you arrive at your hotel, you have to check in at **de receptie** (*der rer-<u>sep</u>-see*) (the reception desk). In order to let the receptionist know that you have reserved you say:

✔ **Ik heb een kamer gereserveerd.** (*ik hep ern <u>kaa</u>-mer kher-ray-ser-<u>fayrt</u>*) (I have reserved a room.)

✔ **Mijn naam is . . .** (*mayn naam is*) (My name is . . .)

How long are you staying?

When you haven't reserved or when the receptionist wants to check how long you'll stay, you might hear the question:

Hoeveel nachten blijft u? (*<u>hoo</u>-fayl <u>nakh</u>-tern blayft uw*) (How many nights are you going to stay with us?)

You can reply to the question how long you intend to stay with the phrase:

✔ **Ik blijf . . .** (*ik blayf*) (I am going to stay . . .)

• **maar één nacht** (*maar ayn nakht*) (just one night)

• **drie nachten** (*dree <u>nakh</u>-tern*) (three nights)

• **een week** (*ern vayk*) (one week)

• **tot de 28e** (*tot der akh-tern-<u>tvin</u>-tikh-ster*) (until the 28th)

Filling in the registration form

You might have to fill out **een formulier** (*ern for-muw-<u>leer</u>*) (a form) at the reception desk as part of the registration process. The receptionist will hand you the form, saying something like the following:

Wilt u alstublieft dit formulier invullen? (*vilt uw al-stuw-<u>bleeft</u> dit for-muw-<u>leer</u> in-fuh-lern*) (Please fill out this form.)

What you have to put on the form varies. Sometimes names and addresses are sufficient, sometimes you have to fill out the following items:

✔ **naam** (*naam*) (surname)

✔ **voornamen** (*<u>foar</u>-naa-mern*) (first names)

✔ **straat en huisnummer** (*straat en <u>hoais</u>-nuh-mer*) (street and number)

✔ **postcode** (*post-koa-der*) (postal code)

✔ **woonplaats** (*voan-plaats*) (place of residence)

✔ **geboortedatum** (*kher-boar-ter-daa-tuhm*) (date of birth)

✔ **geboorteplaats** (*kher-boar-ter-plaats*) (place of birth)

✔ **nationaliteit** (*na-shoa-naa-lee-tayt*) (nationality)

✔ **beroep** (*ber-roop*) (occupation)

✔ **paspoortnummer** (*pas-paort-nuh-mer*) (passport number)

✔ **kenteken auto** (*ken-tay-kern ow-toa*) (license plate number)

✔ **plaats en datum** (*plaats en daa-tuhm*) (place and date)

✔ **handtekening** (*hant-tay-ker-ning*) (signature)

When you have checked in the receptionist will let you know which room number you have:

> **U heeft kamer nummer 25.** (*uw hafy kaa-mer nuh-mer fayf-ern-tvin- tikh*) (You have room number 25.)

You will receive either an electronic 'key' (a smartcard to enter your room) or a traditional key with a hanger and the number of the room on it.

In hotels with traditional keys you have to hand over the key to the reception desk when you leave the hotel. When you come back in the hotel you obviously need the key to your room. You can ask for it with one of the following sentences:

> ✔ **Mag ik mijn sleutel hebben? Nummer 25.** (*makh ik mayn slu-tel heh-bern. nuh-mer fayf-ern-tvin-tikh*) (Could I have my key? Number 25.)
>
> ✔ **De sleutel van kamer 25 alstublieft.** (*der slu-tel fan kaa-mer fayf-ern-tvin-tikh al-stuw-bleeft*) (The key to room 25 please.)

You will probably carry luggage with you, such as **een koffer** (*ern ko-fer*) (a suitcase) or even **een paar koffers** (*ern paar ko-fers*) (several suitcases). In order to mention it all you use the word **de bagage** (*der ba-khaa-zher*) (the luggage). If you need help with your luggage the following question might be helpful:

> **Kan iemand mij met mijn bagage helpen?** (*kan ee-mant may met mayn ba-khaa-zher hel-pern*) (Could anybody help me with my luggage?)

Possessive pronouns: 'mijn', 'jouw', and the rest

Possessive pronouns tell us who owns something:

- ✔ **Ik heb bagage. Dat is mijn bagage.**

  ik hep ba-<u>khaa</u>-zher. dat is mayn ba-<u>khaa</u>-zher

  I've got luggage. That is my luggage.

- ✔ **Jij hebt bagage. Dat is jouw bagage.**

  yay hept ba-<u>khaa</u>-zher. dat is yow ba-<u>khaa</u>-zher

  You've got luggage. That is your luggage.

- ✔ **Hij heeft bagage. Dat is zijn bagage.**

  hay hayft ba-<u>khaa</u>-zher. dat is zayn ba-<u>khaa</u>-zher

  He's got luggage. That is his luggage.

- ✔ **Zij heeft bagage. Dat is haar bagage.**

  xay hayft ba-<u>khaa</u>-zher. dat is haar ba-<u>khaa</u>-zher

  She's got luggage. That is her luggage.

- ✔ **U heeft bagage. Dat is uw bagage.**

  uw hayft ba-<u>khaa</u>-zher. dat is uw ba-<u>khaa</u>-zher

  You've got luggage. That is your luggage.

- ✔ **Wij hebben bagage. Dat is onze bagage.**

  vay <u>heh</u>-bern ba-<u>khaa</u>-zher. dat is on-zer ba-<u>khaa</u>-zher

  We've got luggage. This is our luggage.

- ✔ **Jullie hebben bagage Dat is jullie bagage.**

  <u>yuw</u>-lee <u>heh</u>-bern ba-<u>khaa</u>-zher. dat is <u>yuw</u>-lee ba-<u>khaa</u>-zher

  You've got luggage. That is your luggage.

- ✔ **Zij hebben bagage. Dat is hun bagage.**

  zay <u>heh</u>-bern ba-<u>khaa</u>-zher. dat is huhn ba-<u>khaa</u>-zher

  They've got luggage. That is their luggage.

So:

Personal Pronouns	Possessive Pronouns
ik	*mijn/m'n*
jij/je	*jouw/je*
u	*uw*
hij	*zijn*
zij/ze	*haar*
wij/we	*ons/onze*
jullie	*jullie/je*
zij/ze	*hun*

Note that **mijn** is written with an **n**! You use **m'n** only in spoken language. **Jouw** ends with a **w**, as does **uw**. In written Dutch people will use **jouw**: **Dank voor jouw mail** (*dank for yow mail*) (Thanks for your email). In spoken and informal Dutch it is common to use **je: Ik heb je mailtje gelezen** (*ik hep yer mayl-tyer kher-lay-zern*) (I've read your email). The same happens to **jullie/je**: in written Dutch it's correct to write: **Hoe was jullie vakantie?** (*hoo vas yuw-lee fa-kan-see*) (How was your holiday?).When you're speaking to two or more people it's quite common to say: **Hoe was je vakantie?** (*hoo vas yer fa-kan-see*) (How was your holiday?).

The personal pronoun **wij** has two possessive pronouns: **ons** and **onze**. In order to use them correctly, you need to know whether you're using a **de**-word or a **het**-word. **De**-words get onze while **het**-words get ons:

- ✔ **de vakantie** → **onze vakantie**

    der fa-kan-see → *on-zer fa-kan-see*

    the holiday → our holiday

- ✔ **de sleutel** → **onze sleutel**

    der slu-tel → *on-zer slu-tel*

    the key → our key

- ✔ **het bad** → **ons bad**

    het bat → *ons bat*

    the bath → our bath

- ✔ **het uitzicht** → **ons uitzicht**

    het oait-zikht → *ons oait-zikht*

    the view → our view

Extras and facilities

You might also want to find out what kind of facilities the hotel offers. Does your room have a minibar? Can you use the Internet? Does the hotel have a laundry service?

When you want to ask about specific features of your room, start with the phrase:

✔ **Heeft de kamer . . .?** (*hayft der <u>kaa</u>-mer*) (Does the room have . . .)

- **kabeltelevisie** (*<u>kaa</u>-berl-tay-ler-fee-see*) (cable TV)

- **satelliettelevisie** (*sa-ter-<u>leet</u>-tay-ler-fee-see*) (satellite TV)

- **een minibar** (*ern <u>mee</u>-nee-bar*) (a minibar)

- **internet** (*<u>in</u>-ter-net*) (Internet)

- **airco** (*<u>ehr</u>-koa*) (air conditioning)

- **uitzicht op zee** (*<u>oait</u>-zikht op zay*) (a view of the sea)

If you just wish to sleep without being disturbed, search your room for the sign with the following message:

Niet storen (*neet <u>stoa</u>-rern*) (Do not disturb)

The hotel

Many hotels offer extra services. Usually these services are outlined in a pamphlet or menu that you find in your room. If you don't find any written information about the services, you can call the reception and ask:

Heeft het hotel . . .? (*hayft het hoa-<u>tel</u>*) (Does the hotel have . . .)

You can ask for one of the following services by finishing the sentence with one of the words:

✔ **een sauna** (*ern <u>sow</u>-naa*) (a sauna)

✔ **een zwembad** (*ern <u>zwem</u>-bat*) (a swimming pool)

✔ **een fitnesszaal** (*ern <u>fit</u>-ners-zaal*) (a gym)

✔ **een wasservice** (*ern <u>vas</u>-ser-fis*) (laundry service)

The following questions might come in handy for inquiring about breakfast and room service:

- ✔ **Hoe laat is het ontbijt?** (*hoo laat is het ont-bayt*) (At what time is breakfast served?)

- ✔ **Kan ik roomservice krijgen?** (*kan ik room-ser-fis kray-khern*) (Do you offer room service?)

It might be very useful if somebody can leave a message for you at the hotel. If you want to know if there are any messages for you, you ask:

Heeft iemand een boodschap voor mij achtergelaten? (*hayft eemant ern boat-skhap foar mer akh-ter-kher-laa-tern*) (Has anybody left a message for me?)

Talkin' the Talk

Cilla Vermeent and her partner Rob are arriving at their hotel in Vlieland. They go to the reception in order to check in.

Cilla: **Goedenavond, ik ben Cilla Vermeent. Wij hebben een tweepersoonskamer gereserveerd.**
khoo-dern-aa-font ik ben si-laa fer-maynt. vay heh-bern ern tvay-per-soans-kaa-mer kher-ray-ser-fayrt
Good evening, I'm Cilla Vermeent. We have reserved a double room.

Receptionist: **Goedenavond. U heeft een tweepersoonskamer met bad gereserveerd voor twee nachten.**
khoo-dern-aa-font. uw hayft ern tvay-per-soans- kaa-mer met bat kher-ray-ser-fayrt foar tvay nakh-tern.
Good evening, you reserved a double room with bath for two nights.

Cilla: **Dat klopt.**
dat klopt
That's right.

Receptionist: **Wilt u dit formulier invullen?**
vilt uw dit for-muw-leer in-fuh-lern
Please fill out this form.

Cilla: **Morgen willen we gaan fietsen. Moeten we de fiet-sen nu reserveren?**
mor-khern vi-lern ver khaan feet-sern. moo-tern ver der feet-sern nuw ray-ser-fayr-ern
Tomorrow we want to go biking. Should we reserve the bikes now?

Receptionist: **Ik reserveer nu twee fietsen voor u. U vindt ze morgen aan de achterkant van het hotel.**
ik ray-ser-<u>fayr</u> nuw tvay <u>feet</u>-sern foar uw. Uw fint zer <u>mor</u>-khern aan der <u>akh</u>-ter-kant fan het hoa-<u>tel</u>
I'll reserve two bikes for you now. You'll find them tomorrow behind the hotel.

Cilla: **Mooi, dank u.**
mooy dank uw
Okay, thank you.

Receptionist: **Hier is de sleutel van uw kamer, nummer 25. De kamer is op de eerste verdieping, met uitzicht op zee.**
heer is der <u>slu</u>-tel fan uw <u>kaa</u>-mer <u>nu</u>-mer fayf-ern-<u>tvin</u>-tikh.der <u>kaa</u>-mer is op der <u>ayr</u>-ster fer-<u>dee</u>-ping met <u>oait</u>-zicht op zay
Here is the key to your room, number 25. The room is on the first floor with a view of the sea.

Cilla: **Hoe laat is het het ontbijt?**
hoo laat is het ont-<u>bayt</u>
What time do you serve breakfast?

Receptionist: **Van zeven tot tien.**
fan <u>zay</u>-fern tot teen
From 7 until 10 o'clock.

Cilla: **Dank u.**
dank uw
Thank you.

Receptionist: **Graag gedaan.**
khraakh kher-<u>daan</u>
You're welcome.

Words to Know

het formulier	het for-muw-<u>leer</u>	the form
de fiets	der feets	the bike
de sleutel	der <u>slu</u>-tel	the key
de zee	der zay	the sea

Checking Out and Paying the Bill

Dutch doesn't have a word for 'checking out'. It uses the semi-English word **uitchecken** (*oait-cheh-kern*). For more information about English verbs with a Dutch conjugation, see chapter 8. So if you want to know the time you have to leave the room, you ask:

> **Hoe laat moeten we uit de kamer zijn?** (*hoo laat moo-tern ver oait der kaa-mer sayn*) (At what time should we have left the room?)

To ask for the bill

When the moment has come to check out, you generally use the verb **vertrekken** (*fer-treh-kern*) (to leave). When you want to leave, you hand in your key at the reception and say:

> **Ik vertrek/wij vertrekken** (*ik fer-trek/vay fer-treh-kern*) (I'm leaving/ we are leaving)

After you have said this sentence, the receptionist probably will prepare your bill. And if this is not the case you can ask for the bill using the following sentence:

> **Mag ik de rekening alstublieft?** (*makh ik der ray-ker-ning als-tuw-bleeft*) (Can I have the bill please?)

Asking about special charges

Of course you have to pay extra for any special services that you have used. You might want to know how much the laundry service was. On the other hand you might want to let a receptionist know that you've taken something from the minibar. Here's how you do it:

- **Hoeveel is de wasservice?** (*hoo-fayl is der vas-ser-fis*) (How much is the laundry service?)
- **Ik heb . . . uit de minibar genomen.** (*ik hep . . . oait der mee-nee-bar kher-noa-mern*) (I have taken . . . from the minibar.)

Using separable verbs in the perfect and the past

Dutch has a lot of verbs that separate in two parts. They often start with a preposition such as **achter-**, **in-** or **uit-**:

- ✔ **achterlaten** (*akh-ter-laa-tern*) (to leave (behind))
- ✔ **invullen** (*in-fuh-lern*) (to fill out)
- ✔ **uitchecken** (*oit-cheh-kern*) (to check out)

Not all Dutch verbs that start with a preposition or another prefix are separable verbs, for instance **voorkomen** (*for-koa-mern*) (to prevent). The separable verbs are easy to recognise because they always start with a stressed syllable. Find out more about prepositions in chapter 3.

Note: these so-called separable verbs don't always separate! They do separate in the present:

- ✔ **Ik laat een boodschap achter.** (*ik laat ern boat-skhap akh-ter*) (I'm leaving a message.)
- ✔ **Ik vul het formulier in.** (*ik fuhl het for-muw-leer in*) (I'm filling out the form.)
- ✔ **Wij checken uit.** (*vay cheh-kern oait*) (We're checking out.)

Separable verbs don't separate in the perfect tense: the past participle, which you always need in order to make the perfect, consists of just one word. The following examples show you how the past participle of separable verbs is formed:

- ✔ **achterlaten → achtergelaten**

  Ik heb een boodschap achtergelaten. (*ik hep ern boat-skhap akh-ter-kher-laa-tern*) (I have left a message.)
- ✔ **invullen → ingevuld**

  Ik heb het formulier ingevuld. (*ik hep het for-muw-leer in-kher-fuhlt*) (I have filled out the form.)
- ✔ **uitchecken → uitgechekt**

  Wij hebben uitgecheckt. (*ver heh-bern oait-kher-chekt*) (We have checked out.)

So, you start with a preposition such as **achter-**, **in-**, **uit-**, after which follows the syllable that is typical for a Dutch past participle: **ge**. After **ge** follows the rest. This is different from a 'normal' past participle. A 'normal' past participle starts with **ge-**:

- ✔ **werken** → **gewerkt**

   Ik heb gewerkt. (*ik hep kher-verkt*) (I have worked.)

- ✔ **studeren** → **gestudeerd**

   Ik heb gestudeerd. (*ik hep kher-stuw-dayrt*) (I have studied.)

Separable verbs also separate in the simple past, like they do in the present:

- ✔ **Ik laat een boodschap achter.** (*ik laat ern boat-skhap akh-ter*) (I leave a message.)

- ✔ **Ik liet een boodschap achter.** (*ik leet ern boat-skhap akh-ter*) (I left a message.)

- ✔ **Ik vul het formulier in.** (*ik fuhl het for-muw-leer in*) (I fill out the form.)

- ✔ **Ik vulde het formulier in.** (*ik fuhl-der het for-muw-leer in*) (I filled out the form.)

- ✔ **Wij checken uit.** (*vay chehk-ken oait*) (We are checking out.)

- ✔ **Wij checkten uit.** (*vay chek-tern oait*) (We checked out.)

Leaving

If you have to check out of the hotel before you continue your trip, you might want to leave your luggage at the hotel for a few hours. Most hotels have no problems with this. You might need the following phrase:

> **Kan ik hier de bagage achterlaten tot . . . uur?** (*kan ik heer der ba-khaa-zher akh-ter-laa-tern tot . . . uwr*) (Could I leave the luggage here until . . . o'clock?)

When you return later for your luggage you can say:

- ✔ **Mag ik alstublieft mijn bagage?** (*makh ik als-tuw-bleeft mayn ba-khaa-zher*) (Could I have my luggage please?)

- ✔ **Mogen wij alstublieft onze bagage?** (*moa-khern vay als-tuw-bleeft on-zer ba-khaa-zher*) (Could we have our luggage please?)

When you're ready to go to the airport or the train station and you want the receptionist to call for a taxi, you ask:

> **Kunt u alstublieft een taxi bellen?** (*kuhnt uw als-tuw-bleeft ern tak-see beh-lern*) (Could you ask for a taxi please?)

The receptionist will need to know where you are going to before he or she can order a taxi. So, make sure you have the name of your destination at hand! The receptionist might ask you:

> **Waar moet u naartoe?** (*vaar moot uw naar-too*) (Where are you going to?)

Talkin' the Talk

 Cilla and Rob are leaving hotel De Meeuw. They go to the reception to check out.

Cilla: **Goedemorgen! Wij gaan vertrekken. Mag ik misschien de rekening?**
khoo-der-mor-khern. vay khaan fer-treh-kern makh ik mi-skheen der ray-ker-ning.
Good morning! We are leaving now. Can I have the bill please?

Receptionist: **Natuurlijk, een ogenblikje alstublieft. Heeft u het naar uw zin gehad?**
na-tuwr-lerk ern oa-khern-blik-yer als-tuw-bleeft. hayft uw het naar uw zin kher-hat?
Certainly, one moment please. Did you enjoy your stay?

Cilla: **Jazeker. We waren erg blij met de fietsen vanwege het prachtige weer.**
yaa-zay-ker. ver vaa-rern erkh blay met der feet-sern fan-vay-kher het prakh-ti-kher vayr
Yes, we did. We were very happy with the bikes because of the beautiful weather.

Receptionist: **Ja, u heeft geluk gehad met het weer. Heeft u nog iets uit de minibar genomen?**
yaa uw hayft kher-luhk kher-hat met het vayr. hayft uw nokh eets oait der mee-nee-bar kher-noa-mern
Yes, you have been lucky with the weather. Did you take anything from the minibar?

Cilla: **Nee, maar we hebben wel extra wijn genomen bij het eten.**
nay maar ver heh-bern vel ek-stra vayn kher-noa- mern bay het ay-tern
No, but we ordered some extra wine during dinner.

Receptionist: **Ja, dat heb ik doorgekregen van het restaurant. Alstublieft, hier is de rekening.**
yaa dat hep ik doar-kher-khray-khern fan het res-tow-rant. als-tuw-bleeft heer is der ray-ker-ning
Yes, I got that through from the restaurant. Here is the bill.

Cilla: **Hoeveel is de huur van de fietsen?**
hoo-fayl is der huwr fan der feet-sern
How much is the rent for the bikes?

Receptionist: **De fietsen waren inbegrepen.**
der feet-sern vaa-rern in-ber-khray-pern
The bikes were included.

Cilla: **Alstublieft.**
als-tuw-bleeft
Here you are.

Receptionist: **Wilt u hier tekenen? Dank u en goede reis terug!**
vilt uw heer tay-ker-nern. dank uw en ern khoo-der rays ter-rukh
Please sign here. Thank you and have a good trip home!

Cilla: **Tot ziens!**
tot zeens
Goodbye!

Chapter 13

Using Transport

. . . .

In This Chapter

▶ At the airport

▶ Travelling by car

▶ Travelling by train

▶ Travelling by bus, tram, metro, or taxi

. . . .

*I*n this chapter you are travelling by plane, train, bus, metro, tram, and taxi. After reading this chapter you will be able to communicate with desk assistants, customs officers, car rental employees, and train and bus personnel.

At the Airport

Being at the airport, means standing in line. It starts with buying or collecting your ticket until having your luggage checked. Even when an eticket saves you the trouble of collecting your ticket, you still have to check in your luggage. In this chapter you will find the expressions for asking whether you're in the right line, at what time you leave and which is your gate.

Most airport workers speak several languages, so you can use English in case you are not going to stay long in the Netherlands. In your hand you've got **het ticket** (*het ti-ket*) (the ticket) and probably **het retourticket** (*het rer-toor-ti-ket*) (the return ticket) for **de retourvlucht** (*der rer-toor-fluhkht*) (the flight back). When you check in you receive your **instapkaart** (*in-stap-kaart*) (boarding card).

Getting your ticket

Unless you have printed your e-ticket yourself or received your ticket in advance by post, you'll have to collect your ticket at the airport. First you have to find the right desk. If you cannot find it, ask someone of Information:

> **Waar is de ticketbalie?** (*vaar is der ti-ket-baa-lee*) (Where is the ticket office/ ticket agent?)

When you have arrived at the ticket counter, you can use the following phrases:

> **Ik kom mijn ticket ophalen.** (*ik kom mayn ti-ket op-haa-lern*) (I have come to collect my ticket.)

After you have collected your tickets, you may want to ask: **Hoe laat kan ik inchecken?** (*hoo laat kan ik in-cheh-kern*) (At what time can I check in?). You could also ask: **Hoeveel mag ik meenemen?** (*hoo-fayl makh ik may-nay-mern*) (How much can I carry?) or **Hoeveel kilo is toegestaan?** (*hoo-fayl kee-loa is too-kher-staan*) (How many kilos are allowed?) to confirm how much luggage you're allowed to take on the plane.

Checking in

When you check in, **het grondpersoneel** (*het khront-pehr-soa-nayl*) (the ground staff) will ask you some of the following questions:

- ✔ **Heeft u bagage?** (*hayft uw ba-khaa-zher*) (Do you have any luggage?)
- ✔ **Wilt u uw bagage op de band zetten?** (*vilt uw uw ba-khaa-zher op der bant zeh-tern*) (please put your luggage on the belt.)
- ✔ **Is dit uw handbagage?** (*is dit uw hant-ba-khaa-zher*) (Is this your hand luggage?)

When the ground staff have weighed your luggage, you could hear one of the following phrases:

- ✔ **Uw overbagage is twee kilo.** (*uw oa-fer-ba-khaa-zher is tvay kee-loa*) (Your excess baggage is two kilos.)
- ✔ **Uw overbagagetarief is 50 euro.** (*uw oa-fer-ba-khaa-zher taa-reef is fayf-tikh u-roa*) (The excess baggage charge is 50 euros.)

When the ground staff is preparing your boarding card, you might be asked the following question:

> **Wilt u bij het raam zitten of bij het gangpad?** (*vilt uw bay het raam zi-tern of bay het khang-pat*) (Do you want a window seat or an aisle seat?)

In response to the question you can respond simply **bij het raam** (*bay het raam*) (near the window) or **bij het gangpad** (*bay het khang-pat*) (on the aisle), according to your preference.

You might also want to ask the following to get some details about the flight:

⮕ **Hoe lang duurt de vlucht?** (*hoo lang duwrt der fluhkht*) (How long is the flight?)

⮕ **Wanneer vertrekt het vliegtuig?** (*va-nayr fer-trekt het fleekh-toaikh*) (When does the plane leave?)

If you're at the airport to meet somebody who is arriving on another plane, you can ask:

Wanneer komt het vliegtuig uit Edinburgh aan? (*va-nayr komt het fleekh-toaikh oait eh-din-buhrkh aan*) (What time does the plane from Edinburgh arrive?)

In case you're waiting longer than you expected, you could ask:

Heeft het vliegtuig vertraging? (*hayft het fleekh-toaikh fer-traa-khing*) (Is the plane delayed?)

Talkin' the Talk

Hans van der Jagt of Lease Consult is flying on business to Edinburgh. In the departure hall, he walks straight to the KLM counter in order to pick up his ticket.

Hans:	**Goedemorgen, ik kom mijn ticket ophalen.**
	khoo-der-mor-khern ik kom mayn ti-ket op-haa-lern
	Good morning, I would like to pick up my ticket.
Desk assistant:	**Uw naam alstublieft.**
	uw naam als-tuw-bleeft
	Your name, please.
Hans:	**Van der Jagt**
	fan der yakht
	Van der Jagt
Desk assistant:	**Alstublieft, meneer Van der Jagt, uw ticket naar Edinburgh, vlucht KL128. U kunt doorlopen naar de check-in balie.**
	als-tuw-bleeft mer-nayr fan der yakht uw ti-ket naar eh-din-burkh fluhkht kaa-el hondert-akh-tern-tvin-tikh. uw kuhnt doar-loapern naar der chek-in-baa-lee
	Here you are, Mr Van der Jagt, your ticket to Edinburgh, flight KL128. You can go to the check-in desk now.
	Hans arrives at the check-in desk.

Ground crew:	**Goedemorgen, heeft u bagage?**
	khoo-der-mor-kher hayft uw ba-khaa-zher
	Good morning, do you have any luggage?
Hans:	**Ik heb deze laptop als handbagage.**
	ik hep day-zer lep-top als hant-ba-khaa-zher
	I'm taking this laptop as hand luggage.
Ground crew:	**Wilt u een plaats bij het raam of bij het gangpad?**
	vilt uw ern plaats bay het raam of bay het khang-pat
	Do you want a window seat or an aisle seat?
Hans:	**Bij het raam graag.**
	bay het raam khraakh
	A window seat please.
Ground crew:	**Hier is uw instapkaart. U heeft stoel B158, bij het raam.**
	heer is uw in-stap-kaart. uw hayft stool bay hon-dert-akh-tern-fayf-tikh bay het raam
	Here is your boarding card. You have seat B158, a window seat.
Hans:	**Is de vlucht op tijd?**
	is der fluhkht op tayt
	Is the flight on time?
Ground crew:	**Ja, hij is op tijd. U vertrekt om 11:20 u. precies. U kunt nu meteen doorlopen naar gate 10.**
	Goede reis!
	yaa hay is op tayt. uw fer-trekt om teen foar half tvaalf prer-sees. uw kuhnt nuw mer-tayn doar-loa-pern naar gayt teen.khoo-der rays
	Yes, it is. You leave at 11.20 exactly. You can pro-ceed directly to gate 10. Have a pleasant journey!
Hans:	**Dank u.**
	dank uw
	Thank you.

CULTURAL WISDOM

Passing borders

When you travel by car or train through Europe, customs clearance is totally different from the customs clearance at the airport, in particular when you arrive at the border between two countries of the **Europese Unie** (u-roa-*pay*-ser *uw-nee*) (European Union). The members of the European Union decided to do away with passport control between their internal borders and to abolish restrictions of imports inside the European Union. So it may happen that when you pass a border between two EU countries, you'll hardly notice it! However, you will see signs about the speed limit and different traffic signs.

Going through passport control

When you have arrived at your destination, you'll have to go through **de paspoortcontrole** (*der pas-poart-kon-tro-ler*) (the passport check).

Generally there are two lines: one for **EU-onderdanen** (*ay-uw-on-der-daanern*) (EU citizens) and one for **niet-EU-onderdanen** (*neet-ay-uw-on-derdaa- nern*) (non EU citizens). When you have passed the passport check you get your luggage and you pass through **douaneafhandeling** (*doow-aa- ner-af-han-der-ling*) (customs clearance). Your luggage can be checked here.

After having arrived at the airport of your destination, you'll naturally want to leave the airport as soon as possible. Here are some words to help you when you're going through **de pascontrole** (*der pas-kon-tro-ler*) (immigration):

- ✔ **het paspoort** (*het pas-poart*) (the passport)

- ✔ **onderdaan van de Europese Unie** (*on-der-daan fan der u-roa-pay-ser uw-nee*) (citizen of a country of the European Union)

- ✔ **andere nationaliteiten** (*an-der-er na-shoa-naa-lee-tay-tern*) (other nationalities)

The customs officer may ask you how long you're going to stay as well as the purpose of your journey with one of the following questions:

- ✔ **Hoe lang blijft u in Nederland?** (*hoo lang blayft uw in nay-derlant*) (How long do you intend to stay in Holland?)

- ✔ **Bent u hier als toerist of voor zaken?** (*bent uw heer als too-rist of foar zaa-kern*) (Are you here for business or pleasure?)

You might answer with one of the following phrases:

- ✔ **Ik ben hier voor een vakantie.** (*ik ben heer foar ern fa-kan-see*) (I'm here for a holiday.)

- ✔ **Ik ben hier voor zaken.** (*ik ben heer foar zaa-kern*) (I'm here on business.)

- ✔ **Ik ben op doorreis naar Amerika.** (*ik ben op doar-rays naar aa-may- ree-kaa*) (I am a transfer passenger to America.)

Going through customs

After going through passport control, you claim your baggage and go through **de douane** (*der doow-aa-ner*) (customs), where you may have to open your bags for inspection. You can generally choose one of two options: either you queue in the line **Aangifte** (*aan-khif-ter*) (anything to declare), or you pick the line **Niets aan te geven** (*neets aan ter khay-fern*) (nothing to declare).

The customs officer might ask you:

> **Heeft u iets aan te geven?** (*hayft uw eets aan ter khay-fern*) (Do you have anything to declare?)

You could you give the following answer:

> **Ik wil dit graag aangeven.** (*ik vil dit khraakh aan-khay-fern*) (I would like to declare this.)

The customs officer might ask you to open your luggage:

> **Wilt u deze koffer/deze tas openmaken?** (*vilt uw day-zer ko-fer/day-zer tas oa-pern-maa-kern*) (Please open this suitcase/this bag.)

When the customs officer asks you what you're going to do with something you have bought you can answer:

- ✔ **Het is voor persoonlijk gebruik.** (*het is foar per-soan-lerk kher-broaik*) (It is for personal use.)
- ✔ **Het is een cadeautje.** (*het is ern ka-doa-tyer*) (It is a gift.)

If the custom officer does not agree with something he finds in your suitcase, he might say:

- ✔ **U mag dit niet invoeren.** (*uw makh dit neet in-foo-rern*) (It's not allowed to import this.)
- ✔ **U mag dit niet uitvoeren.** (*uw makh dit neet oait-foo-rern*) (It's not allowed to export this.)
- ✔ **U moet hiervoor invoerrechten betalen.** (*uw moot heer-foar oait-foor-rekh-tern ber-taa-lern*) (You have to pay duty on this.)

You could answer him with the question:

> **Hoeveel moet ik betalen?** (*hoo-fayl moot ik ber-taa-lern*) (How much do I owe you?)

When you have paid your duties and you've been cleared, the customs officer will tell you: **U mag doorlopen** (*uw makh doar-loa-pern*) (You may go through).

Travelling by Car

When you are going to travel internationally in a car, make sure that you have the right driving license. You can find information on www.rdw.nl or at your local town, city or district hall.

The most important roads are called **snelwegen** (*snel-vay-khern*) (highways/ motorways). Even though these highways have four to six **rijbanen** (*ray-baa-nern*) (lanes), you'll come across many **files** (*fee-lers*) (traffic jams). You will be in them **in het spitsuur** (*in het spits-uwr*) (during rush hours) which may last until nine o'clock in the morning and start after three o'clock in the afternoon. Whenever something special takes place: **een ongeluk** (*ern on-kher-luhk*) (an accident), **regen** (*ray-khern*) (rain), **mist** (*mist*) (fog), or **sneeuw** (*snayw*) (snow), you may **in de file staan** (*in der fee-ler staan*) (to be in a traffic jam). **Wegwerkzaamheden** (*vekh-verk-zaam-hay-dern*) (road works), especially **onderhoud** (*on-der-howt*) (maintenance), generally take place in summer, during the night and weekends. Even then, you are not sure if you can **doorrijden** (*doar-ray-dern*) (drive on).

Some important highways are:

   ✔ **de A1** (*der aa-ayn*), which goes from West to East, from Amsterdam passing through Enschede to Germany.

   ✔ **de A2** (*der aa-tvay*), which goes from North to South, from Amsterdam to Maastricht.

   ✔ **de A4** (*der aa-feer*), which goes from Amsterdam via Den Haag to Rotterdam.

If you want to see more of the country you can take a smaller road. **Provinciale wegen** (*proa-fin-shaa-ler vay-khern*) (provincial roads) have numbers and generally have two to four lanes. When you take them in order to avoid **verkeersopstoppingen** (*fer-kayrs-op-sto-ping-ern*) (traffic jams), you may find hundreds of cars trying a shortcut: it won't save you time. Are you driving for leisure? Try to travel between nine in the morning and three o'clock in the afternoon!

Renting a car

If you've decided to rent a car you need to make your way to **een autover huurbedrijf** (*ern ow-toa-fer-huwr-ber-drayf*) (a car rental agency). Here are some useful sentences once you have arrived:

   Ik wil graag een auto huren. (*ik vil khraakh ern ow-toa huw-rern*) (I would like to rent a car.)

The attendant will ask you what kind of car you want, saying something like:

Wat voor soort auto wilt u huren? (*vat faor soart ow-toa vilt uw huw-rern*) (What kind of car would you like to rent?)

To which you can respond with any of the following:

- **Een personenwagen** (*ern per-soa-nern-vaa-khern*) (a private car)
- **Een busje** (*ern buhs-yer*) (a van)
- **Een stationcar** (*ern stay-shern-kar*) (a station wagon)
- **Een automaat** (*ern ow-toa-maat*) (a car with automatic transmission)
- **Een diesel** (*ern dee-serl*) (a diesel car)

Generally the cars are divided into price classes. The following extras might be offered:

- **Een kinderzitje** (*ern kin-der-zi-tyer*) (a children's seat)
- **Handbediening rechts** (*hant-ber-dee-ning rekhts*) (manual service right)
- **Handbediening links** (*hant-ber-dee-ning links*) (manual service left)
- **Een bagagerek** (*ern ba-khaa-zher-rek*) (a luggage rack)
- **Een mobiele telefoon** (*ern moa-bee-ler tay-ler-foan*) (a cellular phone)
- **Een navigatiesysteem** (*ern na-fee-khaa-tsee-see-staym*) (GPS)

The following questions might be asked:

- **Voor hoe lang wilt u de auto huren?** (*foar hoo lang vilt uw der ow-toa huw-rern*) (For how long would you like to rent the car?)
- **Tot wanneer wilt u de auto huren?** (*tot va-nayr vilt uw der ow-toa huw-rern*) (Until when would you like to rent the car?)
- **Wanneer brengt u de auto terug?** (*va-nayr brengt uw der ow-toa ter-rukh*) (When would you like to return the car?)

And you could answer:

- **Ik heb de auto op 30 december nodig.** (*ik hep der ow-toa der dehr-tikh-ster day-sem-ber noa-dikh*) (I need the car for the 30th of December.)
- **Ik wil graag een auto huren vanaf 30 december.** (*ik vil khraakh ern ow-toa huw-rern fa-naf dehr-tikh day-sem-ber*) (I would like to rent a car from the 30th of December.)

✔ **Ik wil graag een auto huren tot 10 januari.** (*ik vil khraakh ern <u>ow</u>-toa <u>huw</u>-rern tot teen ya-nuw-<u>aa</u>-ree*) (I would like to rent a car until the 10th of January.)

✔ **Ik breng de auto terug op 10 januari.** (*ik breng der <u>ow</u>-toa ter-<u>ruhkh</u> op teen ya-nuw-<u>aa</u>-ree*) (I will return the car on January 10.)

When you arrange the details you could hear the following words:

✔ **de verzekering** (*der fer-<u>zay</u>-ker-ring*) (the insurance)

✔ **een schadeverzekering** (*ern <u>skhaa</u>-der-fer-zay-ker-ring*) (indemnity insurance)

✔ **een verzekering tegen diefstal** (*ern fer-<u>zay</u>-ker-ring <u>tay</u>-khern <u>deef</u>-stal*) (theft insurance)

✔ **een aansprakelijkheidsverzekering** (*een aan-<u>spraa</u>-ker-lerk-haytsfer-zay-ker-ring*) (third party insurance)

✔ **inclusief** (*in-kluw-<u>seef</u>*) (included)

✔ **plaatselijke belastingen** (*<u>plaat</u>-ser-ler-ker ber-<u>las</u>-ting-ern*) (local taxes)

✔ **het rijbewijs** (*het <u>ray</u>-ber-vays*) (the driving licence)

✔ **zonder kilometerbeperking** (*<u>zon</u>-der <u>kee</u>-loa-may-ter-ber-pehrking*) (unlimited mileage)

Talkin' the Talk

Marc Lambinet has just arrived from Brussels at Schiphol Airport. When he has gone through customs, he goes to a car rental agency. He is talking to the desk assistant.

Marc: **Goedemorgen, ik wil een auto huren.**
khoo-der-<u>mor</u>-khern ik vil ern <u>ow</u>-toa <u>huw</u>-rern
Good morning. I would like to rent a car.

Attendant: **Wat voor type auto wilt u?**
vat foar <u>tee</u>-per <u>ow</u>-toa vilt uw
What type of car would you like?

Marc: **Een personenwagen klasse F. Kan ik die in Brussel afleveren?**
ern per-<u>soa</u>-nern-vaa-khern <u>kla</u>-ser ef. kan ik dee in <u>bruh</u>-serl <u>af</u>-lay-fer-ern
A private car Class F. Can I leave the car in Brussels?

Attendant: **Dat kan. Voor hoe lang wilt u de autohuren?**
dat kan. foar hoo lang vilt uw der <u>ow</u>-toa <u>huw</u>-rern
Yes. For how long would you like to rent the car?

Marc: **Voor twee dagen. Ik lever hem af op 2 januari.**
foar tvay daa-khern. ik lay-fer hem af op tvay jan-uw-aa-ree
For two days. I'll deliver the car the 2nd of January.

Attendant: **We kunnen u een Mercedes C320-CDI meegeven. Dat is een erg sportieve wagen.**
ver kuh-nern uw ern mehr-say-des say dreehon-dert-tvin-tikh say-day-ee may-khay-fern.dat is ern erkh spor-tee-fer vaa-khern
We can offer you the Mercedes C320-CDI. That's a very sporty car.

Marc: **Wat is bij de prijs inbegrepen?**
vat is bay der prays in-ber-khray-pern
What's included in the price?

Attendant: **Belastingen, u heeft een schadeverzekering met een eigen risico van € 750, en het aantal kilometers is onbeperkt.**
ber-las-ting-ern uw hayft een skhaa-der-ferkhoo-ding met ern ay-khern ree-see-koa fan zay-fern-hon-dert-fayf-tikh u-roa en het aan-tal kee-loa-may-ters is on-ber-pehrkt
Taxes, you have an indemnity insurance with a € 750 excess/deductible and unlimited mileage.
Het totaalbedrag komt op € 515,13. Heeft u een creditcard?
het toa-taal-ber-drakh komt op fayf-hondert-fayf-teen u-roa dehr-teen. hayft uw ern kreh-dit-kart
The total comes to € 515.13. Do you have a credit card?

Marc: **Ik reken toch af na afloop?**
ik ray-kern tokh af naa af-loap
I'll pay afterwards, won't I?

Attendant: **Wij schrijven de gemaakte kosten af van uw credit-card. Daarom willen wij graag uw credit-cardgegevens.**
vay skhray-fern der kher-maak-ter kos-tern af fan uw kreh-dit-kart.daa-rom vi-lern vay khraakh uw kreh-dit-kart-kher-khay-ferns
We'll debit the costs to your credit card. That's why we require your credit card data.

Marc: **Heeft de auto een navigatiesysteem?**
hayft der ow-toa ern na-fee-khaa-tsee-see-staym
Does the car have GPS?

Attendant: **Ja, maar dat is dan € 10, per dag extra.**
yaa maar dat is dan teen u-roa pehr dakh ekstraa
Yes, but it is € 10 extra per day.

Marc: **Dat wil ik er graag bij. Ik ben niet bekend in Nederland.**
dat vil ik er khraakh bay.ik ben neet ber-kent in nay-der-lant
So please include this for me. I don't know my way around in the Netherlands.

Attendant: **Doen we. Mag ik uw creditcard?**
doon ver. makh ik uw kreh-dit-kart
We'll do this. Can I have your credit card?

Marc: **Natuurlijk. Ik zie dat de auto op 2 januari om 9.00 u terug moet zijn. Dan sta ik in de file bij Brussel!**
na-tuwr-lerk. ik zee dat de ow-toa op tvay januw-aa-ree om nay-khern uwr ter-ruhkh moot zayn. dan staat ik in de fee-ler bay bruh-serl
Of course. I see the car has to be back at nine o'clock on the second of January. I'll be in a traffic jam near Brussels then!

Attendant: **U kunt de auto op elk gewenst moment afleveren, ook 's nachts als u wilt.**
uw kuhnt der ow-toa op elk kher-venst moa-ment af-lay-fer-ern oak snakhts als uw vilt
You can deliver the car at any moment, also during the night, if you like.

Words to Know

sportief	spor-teef	sporty
het eigen risico	het ay-khern ree-see-koa	own risk
onbeperkt	on-ber-pehrkt	unlimited
na afloop	aa af-loap	afterwards
de kosten	der kos-tern	the costs
natuurlijk	na-tuwr-lerk	of course

Understanding maps and road signs

Even when you have GPS, it's useful to understand maps. A good map tells you where you are, how to get there and how far you have to go. Maps are very visual and you don't need to understand a lot of Dutch in order to be able to read one. You might like to know the following words for different kind of maps, in case you need to ask for one:

- ✔ **de wegenkaart** (*der vay-khern-kaart*) (the road map)
- ✔ **de stadsplattegrond** (*der stats-pla-ter-khront*) (the city plan).

On a road map you'll find, among other things:

- ✔ **autosnelwegen** ((*ow-toa-snel-vay-khern*) (highways/motorways) e.g. highway **A1**.
- ✔ **nationale hoofdwegen** (*na-shoa-naa-ler hoaft-vay-khern*) (national roads) e.g. national road **N31**.
- ✔ **provinciale wegen** (*proa-vin-shaa-ler vay-khern*) (secondary roads) e.g. secondary road **N266**
- ✔ **genummerde afritten** (*kher-nuh-mer-der af-ri-tern*) (exits with numbers) e.g. exit **23**
- ✔ **viaducten** (*fee-yaa-duhk-tern*) (fly-overs/overpasses)
- ✔ **tankstations met nachtservices** (*tank-staa-shons met nakht-ser-fis*) (filling stations that are open day and night)

Dutch pride: the water household

On the map you may also find the icons for **gemaal** (*kher-maal*) (pumping station) and **sluis** (*sloais*) (lock). Both words are connected to the enormous water household of the Netherlands. Ages ago the name of the western part of the Netherlands was **de Lage Landen** (*der laa-kher lan-dern*) (the Lowlands). Big parts of the lowlands consisted of water. Perhaps you arrived at Schiphol Airport by plane. In this case, you landed below sea-level on the bottom of a former (man-made) lake, now called **polder** (*pol-der*) (polder). The **Cruquius Gemaal** (*kruw-kee-yuhs kher-maal*) (the pumping station named after its engineer Cruquius) pumped for three years to get the **Haarlemmermeer** (*haar-leh-mer-mayr*) (Haarlem lake), where Schiphol is, free from water. The pumping station is an industrial monument now. Nowadays every **polder** has an electric **gemaal** to keep it dry.

Pleasure yachts that are sailing on the Dutch **binnenwateren** (*bi-nern-vaa-terern*) (waterways) have to pass a lot of **sluizen** (*sloai-zern*) (locks) that help to overcome differences of 3 or 4 meters in levels between the water of the **ringvaarten** (*ring-faar-tern*) (ring canals, the canals that surround a polder) and the water in the low-lying polders. Whenever you see some locks at work, make the most of your opportunity to stay a while and see how they function!

When you're driving for leisure and if you're interested in seeing special things, the icons on the map might help you to find **bezienswaardigheden** (*ber-zeens-vaar-dikh-hay-dern*) (places of interest) like **kastelen** (*kas-tay-lern*) (castles) and **ruïnes** (*ruw-vee-ners*) (ruins). In case you're going for a hike, you'll find **duinen** (*doai-nern*) (dunes), **heide** (*hay-der*) (heath) and **bos** (*bos*) (wooded area).

For those who are on business trips: **industrieterreinen** (*in-duhs-tree-tray-nern*) (industrial areas) are well indicated.

City maps

If you want to know a town, start by buying a city map. A city map shows you not only **straten** (*straa-tern*) (streets) and **pleinen** (*play-nern*) (squares), but also:

- **het stadhuis** (*het stat-hoais*) (the town hall/city hall)
- **het postkantoor** (*het post-kan-toar*) (the post office)
- **het politiebureau** (*het poa-lee-tsee-buw-roa*) (the police station)

The city map will tell you that the **centrum** (*sen-truhm*) (centre) of town consists of a **voetgangerszone** (*foot-khang-ers-zo-ner*) (pedestrian area). When you visit such a centre, leave your car on a **parkeerplaats** (*par-kayr- plaats*) (a parking lot) or in a **parkeergarage** (*par-kayr-kha-raa-zher*) (parking garage) at the edge of the centre. The town will reveal its details while you are strolling through the centre.

In smaller towns it's possible to park your car in the centre and you'll find **parkeermeters** (*par-kayr-may-ters*) (parking meters) in which you have to **geld inwerpen** (*khelt-in-ver-pern*) (insert some coins). The **inworp per uur** (*in-vorp pehr uwr*) (insertion per hour) differs from 1 to 5 **op werkdagen tot 18:00** (*op vehrk-daa-khern tot zes uwr*) (until 6 o'clock on working days) **met uitzondering van feestdagen** (*met oait-zon-der-ring fan fayst-daa-khern*) (with the exception of public holidays).

After your stroll through the centre and when you have left the parking garage, you will soon see a sign telling you: **alle richtingen** (*a-ler rikh-ting-ern*) (all directions). It brings you to **de rondweg** (*der ront-vekh*) (the ring road/ beltway) or **de ring** (*der ring*) (the ring): the road that goes around the town. It has junctions with main roads in all directions.

Large towns with historic and crowded centres will surprise you with hidden private garages even in the narrowest streets. Don't park your car on places where you see the small round red and white sign with the words **uitrit vrijlaten** (*oait-rit fray-laa-tern*) (keep exit clear).

The signs

✔ **Verboden toegang** (*fer-boa-dern too-khang*) (no entry)

and

✔ **Verboden toegang voor onbevoegden** (*fer-boa-dern too-khang foar on-ber-fookh-dern*) (no trespassing) are universal. You'll find them anywhere.

Talkin' the Talk

Raymond van Dieren needs a haircut. He tries to make an appointment with his hairdresser in **de Pijp** (*der payp*) (an area of Amsterdam, literally 'the Tube') where Raymond used to live. The hairdresser's is in one of the narrow streets near the famous daily market **Albert Cuyp** (*al-bert koaip*).

Raymond:	**Hallo Ilse, ik wil graag morgenochtend geknipt worden.**
	ha-loa il-ser ik vil khraakh mor-khern-okh-ternt kher-knipt vor-dern
	Hello Ilse, I would like to have a haircut tomorrow morning.
Ilse:	**Morgenochtend heb ik nog één plekje over, om 11:00 u 's ochtends, is dat goed?**
	mor-khern-okh-ternt hep ik nokh ayn plek-yer oa-fer om elf uwr sokh-terns is dat khoot
	Tomorrow I only have space left at eleven o'clock in the morning, is that all right?
Raymond:	**Nou, ik moet om 12:30 bij een collega zijn in Amstelveen. Halen we dat?**
	now ik moot om half ayn bay ern ko-lay-khaa zayn in am-stel-fayn.haa-lern ver dat
	Well, I have to visit a colleague in Amstelveen at 12.30. Could we manage that?
Ilse:	**Dus dan kom je met de auto?**
	duhs dan kom yer met der ow-toa
	So you are coming by car?
Raymond:	**Ja, denk je dat ik een parkeerplaats vind?**
	yaa denk yer dat ik ern par-kayr-plaats fint
	Yes, do you think I will find a parking place?
Ilse:	**Op zaterdag is het altijd erg druk op de markt.**
	op zaa-ter-dakh is het al-tayt erkh druhk op der markt
	On Saturdays the market is very crowded.

Raymond:	**OK, zaterdag kunnen we dus wel vergeten. Wat denk je van maandag 10:00 u?**
	oa-kay zaa-ter-dakh kuh-nern ver duhs vel fer-khay-tern. vat denk yer fan maan-dakh teen uwr
	Well, forget about Saturday. What about Monday, 10 o'clock?
Ilse:	**Je weet dat ik op maandag niet werk.**
	yer vayt dat ik op maan-dakh neet verk
	You know I don't work Mondays.
Raymond:	**Ben je op dinsdag open?**
	ben yer op dins-dakh oa-pern
	Are you open on Tuesdays?
Ilse:	**Ja, je kunt dan de eerste zijn, om 10:00 u. Op dat tijd-stip vind je ook wel een parkeermeter langs de Amstel, vlakbij.**
	yaa yer kuhnt dan der ayr-ster zayn om teen uwr. op dat tayt-stip fint yer oak vel ern par-kayr-may-ter langs der am-sterl flak-bay
	Yes, then you can be the first, at ten o'clock. At that point of time you will find a parking meter at the Amstel river, nearby.
Raymond:	**Afgesproken, dinsdag 10.00 u.**
	af-kher-sproa-kern dins-dakh teen uwr
	Deal then, Tuesday ten o'clock.

Words to Know

de markt	der markt	the market
druk	druhk	crowded
werken	verk-ern	to work
het tijdstip	het tayt-stip	the point of

Road signs

You don't want to get stopped for speeding down a one-way street going in the wrong direction. Road signs are generally visual and universal, yet some are verbal. Here are some signs that mean you shouldn't drive on, but turn back:

- **afgesloten** (*af-kher-sloa-tern*) (closed)
- **afgesloten voor** (*af-kher-sloa-tern foar*) (closed to)
- **gesloten** (*kher-sloa-tern*) (closed)
- **doodlopende weg** (*doat-loa-pern-der vekh*) (dead end)
- **geen doorgaand verkeer** (*khayn doar-khaant fer-kayr*) (no through traffic)
- **doorgaand rijverkeer gestremd** (*doar-khaant ray-fer-kayr kher-stremt*) (no thoroughfare)
- **eenrichtingsverkeer** (*ayn-rikh-tings-fer-kayr*) (one-way traffic)

In **de bebouwde kom** (*der ber-bow-der kom*) (the built-up area) de **maximum-snelheid** (*mak-see-muhm-snel-hayt*) (maximum speed limit) is 50 kilometers. Many small villages which you pass through when driving on a secondary road, have **flitspalen** (*flits-paa-lern*) (flash poles), small grey boxes on a pole that photograph you when you are speeding or jumping the lights. Six weeks later, you'll receive an **acceptgiro** (*ak-sept-khee-roa*) (a bank transfer) fining you for every kilometer that you drove too fast. In case you drove 30 km too fast **binnen de bebouwde kom** (*bi-nern der ber-bow-der kom*) (inside the built-up area), you'll have to pay € 170, and for speeding by 30 km on the highway, the fine will be € 160.

Breaking the rules

When you are on the motorway and guilty of **te snel rijden** (*ter snel ray-dern*) (speeding), **geen richting aangeven** (*khayn rikh-ting aan-khay-fern*) (failing to indicate a change of direction) or **verkeerd inhalen** (*fer-kayrt in-haa-lern*) (unauthorised overtaking) the police will fine you when they catch you doing so. The police will first pursue you and then they will overtake you and force you to stop, lighting up a sign on the car: **Stop, politie** (*stop poa-lee-tsee*) (stop, police). If you don't open the door of your car for the policeman, he will do it for you and he will sit on the sill of your car telling you what you did wrong and even when you say sorry, or tell him you didn't see the road sign, the story will end with a fine in excess of € 100.

The motorway

When you're driving on some secondary road and approach the motorway, you might meet the sign **Ga terug** (*khaa ter-ruhkh*) (go back!). You will see this sign at the end of exits of the highway that are parallel to the entrance of the highway. It's meant to protect sleepy drivers who might take the exit instead of the entrance. These **spookrijders** *(spoak-ray-ders)* (motorists driving against the traffic) would meet unexpected **tegenliggers** (*tay-khern-li-khers*) (on coming traffic)!

When you're on the highway you are lucky when you see light boxes with texts like **A1 filevrij** (*aa-ayn fee-ler-fray*) (no tailback). It's more likely that you will read the text: **A1 tot knooppunt Hoevelaken 8 kilometer file.** (*aa-ayn tot knoa-punt hoo-fer-laa-kern akht kee-loa-may-ter fee-ler*) (A1 until interchange Hoevelaken eight kilometers tailback).

When you're in **een opstopping** (*ern op-sto-ping*) (a traffic jam) and you'll have to **van richting veranderen** (*fan rikh-ting fer-an-der-ern*) (change direction) it is more important than ever to **invoegen** (*in-foo-khern*) (join the traffic) in time, though you have to **langzaam rijden** (*lang-zaam ray-dern*) (drive slowly). Let's hope that you won't meet **een omleiding** (*ern om-lay-ding*) (diversion)! In this case, it will help you to know that **volg route nummer 1** (*folkh roo-ter nuh-mer ayn*) means: follow route number one.

Are you overtaken by bad weather? In case of **hagel** (*haa-kherl*) (hail): **Lichten ontsteken** (*likh-tern ont-stay-kern*) (switch on lights) and drive carefully because of **slipgevaar** (*slip-kher-faar*) (slippery road)!

Talkin' the Talk

 Raymond van Dieren is talking to his wife, Renate. He has had a tough day.

Renate:	**Hoe was je dag vandaag?**
	hoo vas yer dakh fan-daakh
	How was your day today?
Raymond:	**Een ramp.**
	ern ramp
	A disaster.
Renate:	**Hoe dat zo?**
	hoo dat zoa
	How come?

Raymond: **Het verkeer was erger dan ooit. Ik moest om 11.00 u in Amersfoort zijn maar bij knooppunt Diemen zat ik al vast.**
het fer-kayr vas ehr-kher dan ooyt. ik moost om elf uwr in aa-mers-foart zayn maar bay knoa-punt dee-mern zat ik al fast
Traffic was worse than ever. This afternoon I had to be in Amersfoort at eleven o'clock but at junction Diemen I already got stuck.

Renate: **Zo vroeg al! Wat was er aan de hand?**
zoa frookh al. vat vas er aan der hant
That early! What happened?

Raymond: **Er was een omleiding want er zat een vrachtwagen vast onder een viaduct. Je kon alleen maar heel langzaam rijden.**
ehr vas ern om-lay-ding vant er zat ern frakht-vaa-khern fast onder ern fee-aa-duhkt. yer kon a-layn maar hayl lang-zaam ray-dern
There was a diversion, because a truck got stuck under a fly-over. You could only drive very slowly.

Renate: **Waarom ben je niet met de trein naar Amersfoort gegaan?**
vaa-rom ben yer neet met der trayn naar aa-mers-foart kher-gaan
Why did you not take the train to Amersfoort?

Raymond: **Ik wist niet dat er zó vroeg een opstopping zou zijn! Op de terugweg had ik gelukkig geen problemen.**
ik vist neet dat er zoa frookh ern op-sto-ping zow zayn. op de truhkh-vekh hat ik kher-luh-kikh khayn proa-blay-mern
I didn't know that there would be a traffic jam that early! Fortunately, I had no problems on my way back.

Renate: **Hebben jullie wel eens aan een teleconferentie gedacht?**
heh-bern yuw-lee vel erns aan ern tay-lercon-fer-en-tsee kher-dakht
Did you ever consider a teleconference?

Raymond: **Daar hebben we het wel eens over gehad, maar nu moeten we er maar eens werk van maken . . .**
daar heh-bern ver het vel erns oa-fer kher-hat maar nuw moo-tern ver er maar erns vehrk fan maa-kern
We have been talking about this, but now we should do something about it . . .

Words to Know

de ramp	der ramp	the disaster
vroeg	frookh	early
de vrachtwagen	der <u>frakht</u>-vaa-khern	the truck
het viaduct	het fee-aa-<u>duhkt</u>	the fly-over
de problemen	der proa-<u>blay</u>-mern	the problems

Verbs in the past tense: some irregular ones

Dutch-speaking people don't use the past tense as much as English-speaking people do. Dutch-speaking people use it when describing something, when talking about habits or when enumerating a chain of facts. The story of Raymond, on his way to Amersfoort is a chain of facts, and that's why he tells most of it in the past tense: **was, moest, zat, kon, wist,** and **had.** Raymond uses some irregular verbs. Dutch has a lot of them and, as they are irregular, they hardly follow any rules and are difficult to learn. You'll first learn the ones that are used most, just by hearing other people use them.

Let's first see how the regular past tense works. To make the past tense, take the I-form or the stem of a verb and add **–de** or **–te:**

stem + de/te

Most verbs add **–de.** But verbs that have a stem ending in the letters t, k, f, s, ch or p add **–te**. See the following examples:

Verb	Stem	Past Tense	Meaning
wonen	woon	woon**de**	to live
bloeden	bloed	bloed**de**	to bleed
gooien	gooi	gooi**de**	to throw
zeilen	zeil	zeil**de**	to sail
klagen	klaag	klaag**de**	to complain
praten	praat	praat**te**	to talk
hakken	hak	hak**te**	to chop

Verb	Stem	Past Tense	Meaning
blaffen	blaf	blaf**te**	to bark
eisen	eis	eis**te**	to claim
lachen	lach	lach**te**	to laugh
stappen	stap	stap**te**	to step

A popular trick in order to remember which letters cause the verb to end in **–te** is the word **'T KoFSCHiP**. As this word might be difficult to remember and pronounce, most English-speaking people prefer **SoFT KeTCHuP** as a memory aid.

Irregular verbs, however, don't follow these rules. There is no other solution than learning them by heart. Here are some frequently used verbs with an irregular past tense:

Zijn (to be)

Conjugation	Pronunciation
ik was	*ik vas*
jij was	*yay vas*
u was	*uw was*
hij was	*hay vas*
zij was	*zay vas*
het was	*het vas*
wij waren	*vay vaa-rern*
jullie waren	*yuw-lee vaa-rern*
zij waren	*zay vaa-rern*

Moeten (to have to)

Conjugation	Pronunciation
ik moest	*ik moost*
jij moest	*yay moost*
u moest	*uw moost*
hij moest	*hay moost*
zij moest	*zay moost*
het moest	*het moost*
wij moesten	*vay moos-tern*
jullie moesten	*yuw-lee moos-tern*
zij moesten	*zay moos-tern*

Zitten (to sit)

Conjugation	Pronunciation
ik zat	*ik zat*
jij zat	*yay zat*
u zat	*uw zat*
hij zat	*hay zat*
zij zat	*zay zat*
het zat	*het zat*
wij zaten	*vay zaa-tern*
jullie zaten	*yuw-lee zaa-tern*
zij zaten	*zay zaa-tern*

Kunnen (to be able to/can)

Conjugation	Pronunciation
ik kon	*ik kon*
jij kon	*yay kon*
u kon	*uw kon*
hij kon	*hay kon*
zij kon	*zay kon*
het kon	*het kon*
wij konden	*vay kon-dern*
jullie konden	*yuw-lee kon-dern*
zij konden	*zay kon-dern*

Weten (to know)

Conjugation	Pronunciation
ik wist	*ik vist*
jij wist	*yay vist*
u wist	*uw vist*
hij wist	*hay vist*
zij wist	*zay vist*
het wist	*het vist*
wij wisten	*vay vis-tern*
jullie wisten	*yuw-lee vis-tern*
zij wisten	*zay vis-tern*

Hebben (to have)

Conjugation	Pronunciation
ik had	*ik hat*
jij had	*yay hat*
u had	*uw hat*
hij had	*hay hat*
zij had	*zay hat*
het had	*het hat*
wij hadden	*vay ha-dern*
jullie hadden	*yuw-lee ha-dern*
zij hadden	*zay ha-dern*

Getting to work

60% of the Dutch travel to work **met de auto** (*met der ow-tow*) (by car), 10% **neemt de trein** (*naymt der trayn*) (take the train) or some other kind of **openbaar vervoer** (*oa-pern-baar fer-foor*) (public transport), 25% **gaat op de fiets** (*khaat op der feets*) (take the bike), and only 5% of them walk. The **fietsers** (*feet-sers*) (cyclists) arrive first at work: they need only 15 minutes on average. **Fietsen** (*feet-sern*) (cycling) is popular in towns and other places where distances are short. In towns cars have to wait for streams of cyclists passing by.

When you take part in Dutch traffic, you may get the impression that the majority of bikers are seriously suicidal. Although they are pretty vulnerable, many of them will not yield to a car, possibly as a matter of principle. Bikers have to indicate their direction by holding out their right or left hand, but only elderly bikers do. Jumping traffic lights is also common.

Car drivers in large towns need eyes everywhere: especially when getting out of their cars. Beware when you are driving in a narrow street: bikes will pass you left and right! Look carefully before you turn to the right: cyclists can reach speeds of more than 20 km per hour and you might have missed one when you were looking in your right wing mirror.

Racefietsers (*rays-feet-sers*) (racing cyclists) prefer **fietspaden** (*feets-paa-dern*) (cycle tracks) along provincial roads. Car drivers might meet groups of them on summer evenings, Saturdays, and Sundays. The sign **Fietsers oversteken** (*feet-sers oa-fer-stay-kern*) (cyclists' crossing) warns cylists that they have to cross the road because the **fietspad** continues at the other side of the road. Car drivers, be alert!

A company bike keeps you fit

Absence as a result of illness is every employer's nightmare. Dutch employers have to continue paying salary during two years when an employee falls ill. Employers want their employees to be healthy, and that's why **de baas** (*der baas*) (the boss) likes it when employees go for a **lunchwandeling** (*luhnsh-vander-ling*) (lunch walk). Big companies offer **stoelmassage** (*stool-ma-saa-zher*) (a massage when sitting in the working chair) or a reduction for the fitness-club (*fit-ners-klup*) (the fitness club). The law allows employers to give their employees **een bedrijfsfiets** (*ern ber-drayfs-feets*) (a company bike) tax-free worth € 750 every three years. It's even possible to lease a **bedrijfsfiets**!

Mopeds and scooters

Young people from the age of 16 drive **bromfietsen** (*brom-feet-sern*) (mopeds) and **scooters** (*skoo-ters*) (which have a higher capacity than mopeds) especially for longer distances. In towns **fietsers** and **bromfietsers** sometimes drive on the road, sometimes on **het fietspad**. **Brommers** (*bro-mers*) (this is the most common word for mopeds) sometimes are, and sometimes aren't, allowed to drive on the same **fietspad**.

To drive a moped is rather risky: every year 75 people are killed and 2000 seriously wounded. To wear a helmet is obligatory. To wear a helmet is not compulsory for bikers. **Racefietsers** and **mountainbikers** (*mown-tern-bai-kers*) (cyclists on racing or mountain bikes) often do wear one. It may save their life in case of a crash.

Talkin' the Talk

Marcel Westendorp, the sales rep of Biz Accountants, has a meeting with his colleague, the bookkeeper Petra Harskamp, at nine o'clock in the morning. As usual, Marcel is late.

Marcel: **Hallo Petra, heb je op mij gewacht?**
ha-loa pay-traa hep yer op may kher-vakht
Hello Petra, have you been waiting for me?

Petra: **Ik ben alvast begonnen, maar je weet dat ik een paar dingen met je moet bespreken.**
ik ben al-fast ber-kho-nern maar yer vayt dat ik ern paar ding-ern met yer moot ber-spray-kern
I have started already, but you know that I have to discuss a few things with you.

Marcel: **Sorry, ik stond in de file.**
so-ree ik stont in der fee-ler
I'm sorry, but I was stuck in the traffic.

Petra: **Je staat elke ochtend in de file. Waarom neem je de metro niet?**
yer staat el-ker okh-ternt in de fee-ler.vaa-rom naym yer der may-troa neet
You're stuck in the traffic every morning. Why don't you take the metro?

Marcel: **Dan moet ik daarna een kwartier lopen.**
dan moot ik daar-naa ern kvar-teer loa-pern
After that I have to walk for fifteen minutes.

Petra: **Dat is niet verkeerd. Er moeten meer redenen zijn waarom je altijd de auto neemt.**
dat is neet fer-kayrt.her moo-tern mayr ray-der- nern zayn vaa-rom yer al-tayt de ow-toa naymt
I can't see anything wrong with this. But there must be more reasons why you always take the car.

Marcel: **Zoals je weet moet ik vaak klanten bezoeken en dan heb ik een auto nodig.**
zoa-als yer vayt moot ik faak klan-tern ber-zoo-kern en dan hep ik ern ow-toa noa-dikh
As you know, I often have to visit clients and then I need a car.

Petra: **Die bezoeken kan je wat beter plannen en op de andere dagen kom je dan met het openbaar vervoer.**
dee ber-zoo-kern kan yer vat bay-ter pleh-nern en op der an-der-er daa-khern kom yer dan met het oa-pern-baar fer-foor
You could plan these visits better and on other days you use public transport.

Marcel: **Je hebt gelijk, ik heb genoeg van de A10. Ik wou dat ik net zoals jij op de fiets naar mijn werk kon!**
yer hept kher-layk ik hep kher-nookh fan der aa-teen. ik vow dat ik net zoa-als yay op der feets naar mern vehrk kon
You are right, I'm fed up with the A10. I wish I could come to work on my bike, like you!

Petra: **Ja en als het regent, ga ik met de bus.**
yaa en als het ray-khernt khaa ik met der buhs
Yes, and when it rains, I take the bus.

Words to Know

bespreken	ber-<u>spray</u>-kern	to discuss
de metro	der <u>may</u>-troa	the metro/subway/ underground
bezoeken	ber-<u>zoo</u>-kern	to visit
de klant	der klant	the client
de bus	der buhs	the bus
genoeg hebben van . . .	kher-<u>nookh</u> heb-bern fan	being fed up with . . .

The Train Station

Travelling by train can be comfortable. However, defects, accidents, falling leaves in autumn, and snow in winter may cause delays of some hours. **De Intercities** (*der in-ter-<u>si</u>-tees*) are good for large distances as they're fast and comfortable. **De sneltrein** (*der <u>snel</u>-trayn*) stops at more stations but is slower and less comfortable. From its name we may deduce that **de stoptrein** (*der <u>stop</u>-trayn*) stops at a lot of stations, the smaller ones included. During the night **de nachtnettrein** (*der <u>nakht</u>-nettrayn*) connects cities in the Randstad as well as Schiphol Airport. International trains stop at the main train stations.

Buying tickets

If you want to buy a ticket for a trip inside the Netherlands you can go directly to the station. However, it will save you a lot of time if you first study the site of the **Nederlandse Spoorwegen** (*<u>nay</u>-der-lant-ser <u>spoar</u>-vay- khern*) (Dutch Railways), abbreviated **de NS** (*der en-<u>es</u>*). Only the large stations sell tickets all day long and provide you with the necessary information. At the smaller stations you'll find no personnel or just during rush hours. Instead, every station has two or more ticket vending machines. If you don't know where to go, how to go there and have never used the machine before, better prepare your trip behind your PC!

Supposing you know where to go and you're standing at the counter, the following phrases might be useful:

- **een enkeltje naar Zutphen** (*ern en-kerl-tyer naar zuht-fern*) (a single/one-way ticket to Zutphen)
- **een retourtje Wijchen** (*ern rer-toor-tyer vee-khern*) (a return ticket to Wijchen)

It's not necessary to specify when you want to travel second class: if you don't specify anything you'll automatically get a second-class ticket. In case you want some more room, rest and luxury, you need to travel first class. You can specify this by adding:

eerste klas (*ayr-ster klas*) (first class)

De NS offers a broad range of reductions. In case you travel more often by train than occasionally it might be worthwhile to request further information. As many people travel with some form of reduction, the ticket vendor may ask you, after you have ordered your ticket:

- **Heeft u een kortingskaart?** (*hayft uw ern kor-tings-kaart*) (Have you got a reduced-fare pass?)
- **Met korting of de volle prijs?** (*met kor-ting of der fo-ler prays*) (With reduction or full price?)

Your answer might be:

- **zonder korting** (*zon-der kor-ting*) (without reduction)
- **met korting** (*met kor-ting*) (with reduction)
- **Ik heb een kortingskaart** (*ik hep ern kor-tings-kaart*) (I have a reduced-fare card)

Some train travellers who travel on a regular base, or who are preparing a complicated trip, prefer to buy their tickets in advance. This is the reason why the ticket seller might ask you, when you have ordered your ticket:

- **Reist u vandaag?** (*rayst uw fan-daakh*) (Are you travelling today?)
- **Wanneer reist u?** (*va-nayr rayst uw*) (When are you travelling?)

If you want to know what the price of the ticket is before ordering it, you ask:

Hoeveel kost een enkeltje naar Almere? (*hoo-fayl kost ern en-kerl-tyer naar al-may-rer*) (What is the price of a single to Almere?)

Be sure to arrive on time at the train station if you still have to buy your ticket. If the ticket office is not open, people may be queuing for the ticket machines. It's not possible to buy tickets on the train and you will be fined 35 plus the price for the ride if the conductor finds out that you've got no ticket, whatever the reason may be. On trips of one hour or longer, you may expect to be checked several times.

International trains and paying extra

In case you are going to make use of international trains, you can either go to a main train station or study them online. The stations also sell the paper timetable called **het spoorboekje** (*het spoar-book-yer*). It opens with a map of all the railway lines in the Netherlands and it ends with a map with the other forms of transportation after you leave the train station. The booklet also offers you a lot of other information you may need.

You have to pay **een toeslag** (*ern too-slakh*) (a surcharge) for international trains. In that case you will find the word **toeslag** on the signs with the **aankomsttijd** (*aan-koms-tayt*) (time of arrival) and **vertrektijd** (*fer-trek-tayt*) (time of departure) of the trains. In case you want to know if you need to pay extra, you could use the phrase:

Moet ik toeslag betalen voor de trein naar Keulen?(*moot ik too-slakh ber-taa-lern foar de trayn naar ku-lern*) (Do I have to pay a surcharge for the train to Cologne?)

The ticket vending machines

The Dutch railways use two kinds of ticket vending machines. You can pay either with a debit card, a smartcard, a maestro card or coins. The old model, which is getting out of use, is in Dutch only. The new model has a touch screen and four languages are available: Dutch, English, German, and French. The machine does not accept notes.

The ticket machine may seem complicated when you use it for the first time. Ask somebody to help you! You might also try it out in the quietness of your home or hotel: you'll find a demonstration version of the multi-lingual machine on the English part of the Web site www.ns.nl.

The NS website also has a very handy train planner: just provide the station of departure, the station of arrival and either the time of departure or the time at which you want to arrive. The planner will provide you with a scheme of arrival and departure times. The numbers of the platforms where you find the trains and all changes of trains are included.

The desk assistant could answer:

Ja, u moet toeslag betalen. (*yaa uw moot <u>too</u>-slakh ber-<u>taa</u>-lern*) (Yes, you have to pay a surcharge.)

or

Nee, u hoeft geen toeslag te betalen. (*nay uw hoeft kheen <u>too</u>-slakh ter ber-<u>taa</u>-lern*) (No, you don't have to pay a surcharge.)

Talkin' the Talk

 Marcel is in Amsterdam Central Station. He's buying the tickets for a complicated trip the week after. He has to join in a sales training meeting in the centre of The Hague, on Friday morning. After the training session, he is going to visit a friend in Enschede in the eastern part of the country. He's going to stay there for the weekend and will return to Amsterdam on Sunday night. Marcel decided to take the train because the road to The Hague will be very crowded on Friday morning.

Marcel:	**Volgende week ga ik een ingewikkelde reis maken en ik wil nu alvast de kaartjes kopen.**
	fol-khern-der vayk khaa ik ern in-kher-vi-kerlder rays maa-kern en ik vil nuw al-fast der kaar-tyers koa-pern
	I'm going to make a complicated trip next week and I want to buy the tickets now.
Ticket vendor:	**OK, waar gaat de reis naartoe?**
	oa-kay vaar khaat der rays naar-too
	Okay, where are you going to travel to?
Marcel:	**Op vrijdagochtend moet ik om 9.00 uur in het centrum van Den Haag zijn. Aan het eind van de middag ga ik door naar Enschede.**
	op fray-dakh-okh-ternt moot ik om nay-khern uwr in het sen-truhm fan den-haakh zayn. Aan het aynt fan der mi-dakh khaa ik door naar en-skher-day
	On Friday morning I have to be in the centre of The Hague at nine o'clock. At the end of the afternoon I'll continue to Enschede.
Ticket vendor:	**Gaat u diezelfde dag nog terug?**
	khaat uw dee-zelf-der dakh vayr ter-ruhkh
	Will you travel back that same day?
Marcel:	**Nee, ik blijf in Enschede tot zondagavond. Dan reis ik terug naar Amsterdam.**
	nay ik blayf in en-skher-day tot zon-dakh-aa-font.dan rays ik ter-ruhkh naar am-ster-dam
	Now, I'm staying in Enschede until Sunday night Then I will travel back to Amsterdam.

Ticket vendor: **Dus een enkeltje Amsterdam Centraal-Den Haag Centraal. Dan een enkeltje Den Haag Centraal-Enschede. Ten slotte nog een enkeltje Enschede-Amsterdam Centraal.**

duhs ern en-kerl-tyer am-ster-dam den-haakh sen-traal. dan ern en-kerl-tyer den-haakh sen-traal en-skher-day.ten slo-ter nokh ern en-kerltyer en-skher-day am-ster-dam sen-traal

So that's a single/one-way ticket from Amsterdam Central Station to The Hague Central Station. Then another single from The Hague Central Station to Enschede. Finally a single from Enschede to Amsterdam Central Station.

Ik maak ze zonder datum, dan kunt u ze op de dag zelf afstempelen. Met of zonder korting?

ik maak zer zon-der daa-tuhm dan kuhnt uw zer op der dakh zelf af-stem-per-lern. met of zon-der kor-ting

I'll issue them without dates: you can stamp them on the day itself. With or without reduction?

Marcel: **Zonder. Hoeveel keer moet ik overstappen?**

zon-der. hoo-fayl kayr moot ik oa-fer-sta-pern

Without. How many times do I have to change trains?

Ticket vendor: **Ik maak eerst dit af, dan maak ik een reisplan voor u. Dat is dan 38,50 bij elkaar.**

ik maak ayrst dit af dan maak ik ern rays-plan foar uw. dat is dan akh-tern-dehr-tikh u-roa fayf-tikh bay el-kaar

I'll first finish the payment and then plan the route for you. That will be †38.50 altogether.

Marcel: **OK.**

oa-kay

OK.

Ticket vendor: **Hier is uw reisplan, met alle vertrek- en aankomst-tijden, de perrons en de overstappen.**

heer is uw rays-plan met al-ler fer-trek en aan-komst-tay-dern der per-rons en der oa-fer-stapern

Here's your route plan, with all the times of departure and arrival, the platforms and the transfers.

Marcel: **OK, bedankt.**

oa-kay ber-dankt

OK, thanks.

Ticket vendor: **Goede reis!**

khoo-der rays

Have a good trip!

Words to Know

ingewikkeld	in-kher-_vi_-kerl-der	complicated
de datum	der _daa_-tuhm	the date
afstempelen	_af_-stem-per-lern	to stamp
overstappen	_oa_-fer-sta-pern	to change
de overstap	der _oa_-fer-stap	the transfer
afmaken	_af_-maa-kern	to finish
het perron	het per-_ron_	the platform

Reading timetables

At every station, you'll find notice boards with **de vertrektijden** (_der fer-_trek_-tay-dern_) (the times of departure of all the trains that stop at the station). If you don't know your way around them, the boards might be difficult to understand. It's easier if you know the meaning of the following words:

- **het vertrek** (_het fer-_trek_) (the depature)
- **de aankomst** (_der _aan_-komst_) (the arrival)
- **via** (_vee_-yaa) (by way of)
- **op werkdagen** (_op _vehrk_-daa-khern_) (working days)
- **doorgaande trein** (_doar_-khaan-der trayn_) (direct train)
- **overstappen** (_oa_-fer-sta-pern_) (to change trains/transfer)
- **zon- en feestdagen** (_zon en _fayst_-daa-khern_) (Sundays and public holidays)

You'll also find boards with the times of arrival of the international trains with the numbers of the platforms.

Asking for information

If you want to ask about the train that you wish to take, you could ask the ticket vendor or a conductor on the platform. You might use one of the following questions:

- ✔ **Van welk perron/Van welk spoor vertrekt de trein naar Groningen?** (*fan velk per-ron/fan velk spoor fer-trekt der trayn naar khroa-ning- ern*) (From which platform does the train to Groningen leave?)

- ✔ **Op welk perron/Op welk spoor komt de trein uit Rotterdam aan?** (*op velk per-ron/op velk spoor komt der trayn oait ro-ter-dam aan*) (At which platform does the train from Rotterdam arrive?)

- ✔ **Heeft de trein vertraging?** (*hayft der trayn fer-traa-khing*) (Is the train delayed?)

- ✔ **Gaat er een doorgaande trein van Nijmegen naar Leiden?** (*khaat er ern doar-khaan-der trayn fan nay-may-khern naar lay-dern*) (Is there a direct train from Nijmegen to Leiden?)

The answer to most of the questions will be a time are a number. An answer to the last question may be that there are no direct trains:

> **Nee, u moet overstappen in Duivendrecht.** (*nay uw moot oa-fer-sta-pern in doai-fern-drekht*) (No, you have to change trains in Duivendrecht.)

Going by Bus, Tram, Metro, or Taxi

In the larger towns there are generally plenty of public service vehicles. Metro and interliners to and from the suburbs take you to the centre where buses and trams take you to the place you want to be.

Taking the bus or tram

If you need help to find the right bus or tram, you could ask **de buschauffeur** (*der buhs-show-fur*) (the bus driver) or **tramconducteur** (*tram-kon-duhk-tur*) (tram conductor). You can also try to study the map which you may find in **het bushokje** (*het buhs-hok-yer*) (the bus shelter), if there is any. **De bushalte** (*der buhs-hal-ter*) (the bus stop) is often nothing more than a pole with the number of the bus on it. Sometimes the pole has a timetable that you can understand. **De tramhalte** (*der tram-hal-ter*) (the tram stop) might also offer some information. If not, you could ask a passerby in the street or somebody who's waiting for a tram or bus one of the following questions:

- **Welke bus gaat naar het centrum?** (*vel-ker buhs khaat naar het sen-truhm*) (Which bus goes to the centre?)

- **Is dit de goede tram naar het station?** (*is dit der khoo-der tram naar het staa-shon*) (Is this the right tram to the station?)

- **Stopt deze bus bij het Amstelstation?** (*stopt day-zer buhs bay het am-stel-staa-shon*) (Does this bus stop at the Amstel station?)

- **Waar moet ik overstappen?** (*vaar moot ik oa-fer-sta-pern*) (Where do I have to change buses?)

Talkin' the Talk

Cilla wants to take the bus, but she doesn't know exactly which one to take. So she asks a lady who's waiting at the bus stop.

Cilla: **Weet u ook of lijn 148 hier stopt?**
vayt uw oak of layn hon-dert-akh-tern-fayr-tikh heer stopt
Excuse me, do you know if bus number 148 stops here?

Lady: **Nee, hier komt alleen lijn 149. Waar wil je naartoe?**
nay heer komt a-layn layn hon-dert-nay-khern-ern-fayr-tikh
No, only number 149 comes here. Where do you want to go to?

Cilla: **Naar het Centraal Station.**
naar het sen-traal staa-shon
To the Central Station.

Lady: **Je kunt lijn 149 naar het Amstelstation nemen. Daar stap je over op lijn 56 naar het Centraal Station.**
yer kuhnt layn hon-dert-nay-khern-ern-fayrtikh naar het am-stel-staa-shon nay-mern. daar stap yer oa-fer op layn zes-ern-fayf-tikh naar het sen-traal staa-shon
You can take bus nr 149 to the Amstel station. There you make a transfer and take bus nr 56 or some other bus to the Central Station.

Cilla: **Weet u ook hoe laat bus 149 komt?**
vayt uw oak hoo laat layn hon-dert-nay-kern-ern-fayr-tikh komt
Do you know what time the number 149 arrives?

Lady: **Over een paar minuten.**
oa-fer ern paar mee-nuw-tern
In a few minutes.

Cilla: **En is het dan nog ver naar het Centraal Station?**
en is het dan nokh fehr naar het sen-traal sta-shon
Is it still far to the Central Station?

Lady: **Nee, misschien tien minuten. Er gaan veel bussen naar het Centraal Station, dus je hoeft niet lang te wachten.**
nay mi-skheen teen mee-nuw-tern. ehr khaan fayl buh-sern naat het sen-traal sta-shon dus yer hooft neet lang ter vakh-tern
No, some 10 minutes. A lot of buses go to the Central Station, so you won't have to wait long.

Cilla: **Bedankt voor uw hulp.**
ber-dankt foar uw huhlp
Thanks for your help.

Words to Know

de lijn	der layn	the bus number
stoppen	stop-pern	to stop
nemen	nay-mern	to take
hoe laat?	hoo laat	at what time?
over een paar minuten	oa-fer ern paar mee-nuw-tern	in a few minutes
lang wachten	lang vakh-tern	to wait a long time

Buying tickets

Strippenkaarten (<u>stri</u>-pern-kaar-tern) (public transport cards) are good for all the trams, buses, metros, ferries and short-distance suburban train routes. The ticket is divided into a number of strips, each of which represents one public transport zone. The entire country is divided into these zones and theoretically you could travel from one end of the country to the other using strip tickets. You can buy a four-strip **strippenkaart** in the bus or the tram, but the more economical one of 45 strips can be purchased in tobacco shops, newsstands, train stations, post offices and transport kiosks. **Strippenkaarten** work by stamping the card, either yourself (in the small yellow machines) or more often by a conductor or driver, at the beginning of the journey. You stamp the card for the number of zones through which you're travelling plus one additional strip. You may also stamp for more than one person on a single card. To find out how many zones you will be crossing, consult the route map and zone details posted on tram and bus shelters. You can also ask drivers or conductors for zone details.

Taking a taxi

Those who are used to hailing a taxi when they see an empty one driving, will have to adapt to different circumstances. Dutch taxis only take people when they are waiting for you at a **taxistandplaats** (<u>tak</u>-see-stantplaats) (taxi stands). You'll find them near train stations, entertainment centres and hotels. In case none are waiting outside the hotel or bar, you can ask the receptionist to call you a taxi. As many **taxicentrales** (<u>tak</u>-see-sen-traa-lers) (taxi offices) try to plan their rides, the receptionist might ask you before he makes the call, where you're going to. Once you're in the taxi, **de taxichauffeur** (der <u>tak</u>-see-show-fur) (the taxi driver), will start the meter. When you arrive, you pay the amount that the meter indicates plus tip.

When you want to know where the nearest taxi stand is, you can use the following phrases:

> **Waar is de dichtstbijzijnde taxistandplaats?** (vaar is der <u>dikhst</u>-bay-zayn-der <u>tak</u>-see-stant-plaats) (Where is the nearest taxi stand?)

After getting in, the taxi driver might ask:

> **Waar wilt u naartoe?** (vaar vilt uw naar-<u>too</u>) (Where would you like to go?)

Chapter 14

Coping with Emergencies

· ·

In This Chapter

▶ Asking for help in case of accidents and emergencies

▶ Talking to a doctor

▶ Going to the dentist

▶ Talking to the police

· ·

*L*et's hope that you'll never need the information in this chapter! The words and sentences included in this chapter are useful in case you have to talk to the police or in other cases of emergency and it may be helpful to read them. What to do when you get really hurt? This chapter assists you in dealing with all kinds of emergency situations, from visiting the doctor to reporting a theft.

Asking for Help in Case of Accidents and Emergencies

In case of emergency the most difficult thing is keeping your head cool in order to be able to tell the police, a doctor or a nurse what the problem is. So don't panic. Your English will be very helpful, but some Dutch words may save you.

Crying for help

The following expressions are very useful in case you have to cry for help:

Help! (*help*) (Help!)

In case of fire you shout:

Brand! (*brant*) (Fire!)

All members of the EU have the same, free, emergency, number 112, no matter whether you need police, ambulance, the fire brigade or a doctor. You will be answered in the language of the country, but the telephone operator will be able to help you in English. The operator asks the caller which emergency service is required and connects the caller to the control room of the service requested in the callers geographic region.

When you want someone to call the emergency number, just use this phrase:

> **Bel 112!** (*bel ayn-ayn-tvay*) (Dial 112!)

When you are panicking and have forgotten the number, you could also shout:

- **Bel de politie!** (*bel der poa-lee-tsee*) (Call the police!)
- **Bel een ambulance!** (*bel ern am-buw-lans*) (Call an ambulance!)
- **Bel de brandweer!** (*bel der brant-vayr*) (Call the fire brigade!)
- **Haal een dokter!** (*haal ern dok-ter*) (Get a doctor!)

Reporting a problem

When you have to report an accident or have to let people know that you or others are hurt, these basic sentences can help you:

- **Er is een ongeluk gebeurd.** (*ehr is ern on-kher-luhk kher-burt*) (An accident has occurred.)
- **Er is een ongeluk gebeurd op de A10.** (*ehr is ern on-kher-luhk kher-burt op der aa-teen*) (An accident has occurred on the A 10.)
- **Ik ben gewond.** (*ik ben kher-vont*) (I'm hurt.)
- **Er zijn gewonden.** (*ehr zayn kher-von-dern*) (People are injured.)

You have to be prepared for other emergencies, such as robbery or theft:

- **Ik wil aangifte doen van diefstal.** (*ik vil aan-khif-ter doon fan deef-stal*) (I want to report a robbery/theft.)
- **Houd de dief!** (*howt der deef*) (Stop thief!)

Asking for help in your own language

If you're panicking too much to be able to speak any other language than your own, this is what you say to find out if there is anybody around who speaks your language:

- ✔ **Spreekt er iemand Duits?** (*spraykt er ee-mant doaits*) (Does anybody speak German?)
- ✔ **Spreekt er iemand Engels?** (*spraykt er ee-mant eng-erls*) (Does anybody speak English?)
- ✔ **Spreekt er iemand Frans?** (*spraykt er ee-mant frans*) (Does anybody speak French?)

Solving a problem on the road

Though most of us have mobile phones, when your are on the highway you can use one of the yellow **praatpalen** (*praat-paa-lern*) (emergency telephones). They're very simple to use: just press the only knob there is and the operator of the **Alarmcentrale** (*aa-larm-sen-traa-ler*) (emergency centre) will ask you where you need help.Though she can see on her screen from which **praatpaal** you're calling, you'll have to specify the place where help is needed, so it might help to have a look around and think it over before you call. Then she will ask you what the problem is. When you need police, an ambulance or the fire brigade, the operator will put you through with the regional service in question. The service operator will ask the same questions again.

In case you have a problem with your car, the **Alarmcentrale** operator will ask you for the license number of the car as well as your name, and whether you are a member of the **ANWB** (*aa-en-vay-bay*) (the Dutch Automobile Association). Even when you're not a member, the road patrol will come to help you. Members pay less, or even nothing, if the problem can be solved easily.

After the question about the membership the operator will tell you how long you'll have to wait before the road patrol arrives. She will ask for your mobile number and advise you to stay out of your car and wait behind the crash barrier. The emergency phones are also meant for reporting an accident or a dangerous situation. The road patrol has a **verkeerd getankt-installatie** (*ferkayrt kher-tankt-in-staa-laa-tsee*) (a wrong-fuel installation) in order to empty your tank in case you tanked the wrong fuel at the filling station.

Talking to a Doctor

Most probably your doctor will understand and speak English. However, the following words are very useful when you're not feeling well:

- **de huisarts** (*der hoais-arts*) (the family doctor/general practitioner)
- **de arts** (*der arts*) (the doctor)
- **het ziekenhuis** (*het zee-kern-hoais*) (the hospital)
- **de spoedopname** (*der spoot-op-naa-mer*) (the emergency admission)
- **de artsenpraktijk** (*der art-sern-prak-tayk*) (the doctor's office)

If you need medical assistance, you can ask for a doctor or inquire where the nearest hospital or first aid is, by saying:

- **Kunt u een ambulance voor me bellen?** (*kuhnt uw ern am-buw-foar mer beh-lern*) (Could you call an ambulance for me?)
- **Ik moet snel naar een ziekenhuis.** (*ik moot snel naar het zee-kern-hoais*) (I have to get to a hospital quickly.)
- **Ik heb een arts nodig.** (*ik hep ern arts noa-dikh*) (I need a doctor.)
- **Waar is de dichtstbijzijnde EHBO-post?** (*vaar is der dikhst-bay-zayn-der ay-haa-bay-oa-post*) (Where is the nearest first aid post?)
- **Waar is het dichtstbijzijnde ziekenhuis?** (*vaar is het dikhst-bay-zayn-der zee-kern-hoais*) (Where is the nearest hospital?)
- **Waar is de polikliniek?** (*vaar is der poa-lee-klee-neek*) (Where is the out-patients' department?)

If assistance is less urgent, you can ask:

Waar is de dichtsbijzijnde artsenpraktijk? (*vaar is der dikhst-bay-zayn-der art-sern-prak-tayk*) (Where is the nearest doctor's office?)

Describing what's wrong with you

A belly pain? A pain in the neck? As sick as a dog? You will be happy that you have found this chapter! Here is what you say if you want to express that you aren't feeling well and where it hurts. The doctor might ask you the following question:

Wat scheelt er aan? (*vat skhaylt er-aan*) (What seems to be the matter?)

You could answer using one of the following phrases:

- ✔ **Ik voel me niet lekker.** (*ik fool mer neet <u>leh</u>-ker*) (I don't feel well.)

- ✔ **Ik ben ziek.** (*ik ben zeek*) (I'm ill.)

- ✔ **Ik heb koorts.** (*ik hep koarts*) (I have a fever.)

- ✔ **Ik heb last van misselijkheid.** (*ik hep last fan <u>mi</u>-ser-lerk-hayt*) (I'm suffering from nausea.)

- ✔ **Ik kan mijn arm niet bewegen.** (*ik kan mern arm neet ber-<u>vay</u>-khern*) (I can't move my arm.)

- ✔ **Ik ben gebeten door een hond.** (*ik ben kher-<u>bay</u>-tern doar ern hont*) (I have been bitten by a dog.)

Doctors and dentists

In the Netherlands people have **een huisarts** (*ern <u>hoais</u>-arts*) (a family doctor, a general practitioner). People who are new to a town or village ask their **verzekeringsmaatschappij** (*fer-<u>zay</u>-kerrings-maat-skha-pay*) (insurance company) for a list of doctors in their zip code area. However, you may have to settle for one further away as many doctors have a full list of patients already. Ask neighbours, friends and colleagues for help in tracking down a good and available doctor. Doctors work almost exclusively from their **spreekkamers** (*<u>spray</u>-kaa-mers)* (surgeries), but the idea is that they can get to your home within 10 minutes, in case of an emergency. You can call the doctor's office in order to make an appointment for **het spreekuur** (*<u>het</u> sprayk-<u>uwr</u>*) (the consultation hour), generally either in the early morning or late afternoon. The doctor takes 10 minutes for each patient. If you think you need more time, ask for a 'double appointment'! Doctors only come to your home when you've had a high fever during several days or are otherwise unable to come. When your doctor is not on call, a recorded message on his or her telephone will tell you of the nearest on-call doctor. You'll find a dentist in the same way that you find a doctor: by asking your insurance company a list of **tandartsen** (*<u>tant</u>-art-sern*) (dentists) or better: asking neighbours, friends and colleagues for recommendations. Dentists generally work with well-planned agendas and waiting lists, leaving some room for people with urgent problems. As soon as you are on the agenda, it will cost you money if you don't show up.

In case you have a pain somewhere, just start by saying:

- **Ik heb pijn in . . .** (*ik hep payn in*) (I have a pain in . . .)
    - **mijn nek** (*myan nek*) (the neck)
    - **mijn buik** (*mayn boaik*) (the belly)
    - **mijn rug** (*mayn ruhkh*) (my back)
    - **mijn keel** (*mayn kayl*) (my throat)
    - **mijn hoofd** (*mayn hoaft*) (the head)
- **Ik heb erge pijn in . . .** (*ik hep ehr-kher payn in*) (I have a bad pain in . . .)

When the doctor asks 'Where does it hurt?' you can mention one of the following parts of the body:

- **de arm** (*der arm*) (the arm)
- **het been** (*het bayn*) (the leg)
- **de borstkas** (*der borst-kas*) (the chest)
- **de borst** (*der borst*) (the breast)
- **de duim** (*der doaim*) (the thumb)
- **de dij** (*der day*) (the thigh)
- **de elleboog** (*der eh-ler-boakh*) (the elbow)
- **de enkel** (*der eng-kerl*) (the ankle)
- **het gezicht** (*het kher-zikht*) (the face)
- **de hand** (*der hant*) (the hand)
- **de heup** (*der hup*) (the hip)
- **het hoofd** (*het hoaft*) (the head)
- **de kin** (*der kin*) (the chin)
- **de knie** (*der knee*) (the knee)
- **de kuit** (*der koait*) (the calf)
- **de mond** (*der mont*) (the mouth)
- **de neus** (*der noais*) (the nose)
- **de nek** (*der nek*) (the neck)
- **het oog** (*het oakh*) (the eye)
- **het oor** (*het oar*) (the ear)
- **de rug** (*der ruhkh*) (the back)

- **de schouder** (*der skhow-der*) (the shoulder)
- **de teen** (*der tayn*) (the toe)
- **de vinger** (*der fing-er*) (the finger)
- **de voet** (*der foot*) (the foot)

Internal organs are:

- **de blinde darm** (*der blin-der darm*) (the appendix)
- **de darmen** (*der dar-mern*) (the bowels)
- **het hart** (*het hart*) (the heart)
- **de keel** (*der kayl*) (the throat)
- **de lever** (*der lay-fer*) (the liver)
- **de maag** (*der maakh*) (the stomach)
- **de nier** (*der neer*) (the kidney)
- **de tong** (*der tong*) (the tongue)

Announcing any special conditions

An important part of getting treatment is to let a doctor or dentist know if you're allergic to something or if you have any medical conditions. To do so, start out by saying:

- **Ik ben . . .** (*ik ben*) (I am . . .)
  - **zwanger** (*zwang-er*) (pregnant)
  - **diabeet** (*dee-aa-bayt*) (a diabetic)
  - **allergisch voor pollen** (*a-lehr-khees foar po-lern*) (allergic to pollen)
- **Ik heb . . .** (*ik hep*) (I have . . .)
  - **een hartprobleem** (*ern hart-proa-blaym*) (a heart condition)
  - **hoge bloeddruk** (*hoa-kher bloot-druhk*) (a high blood pressure)
  - **astma** (*ast-maa*) (asthma)
  - **epilepsie** (*ay-pee-lep-see*) (epilepsy)

The following supplementary phrases might also be useful:

✔ **Ik ben er al eerder voor behandeld.** (*ik ben er als ayr-der foar ber-han-delt*) (I've been treated for it before.)

✔ **Ik ben er al eerder aan geopereerd.** (*ik ben er al ayr-der aan kher-oa-per-rayrt*) (I've been operated for it before.)

The present perfect of verbs that start with ont-, be-, ge-, her-, ver-, and er-

Some Dutch verbs are separable verbs. Separable verbs start with a prefix, generally a preposition such as **in-** or **aan-**, and in separable verbs this little word is stressed. If you don't remember what a separable verb is, you'll find more information in Chapter 6. There also are Dutch verbs that start with an unstressed prefix. Inseparable verbs start with the unstressed syllable **ont-**, **be-**, **ge-**, **her-**, **ver-**, or **er-**. Examples of these verbs are:

✔ **ontmoeten** (*ont-moo-tern*) (to meet)

✔ **behandelen** (*ber-han-der-lern*) (to treat)

✔ **gebruiken** (*kher-broai-kern*) (to use)

✔ **herinneren** (*heh-ri-ner-ern*) (to remember)

✔ **vertellen** (*fer-teh-lern*) (to tell)

✔ **ervaren** (*ehr-faa-rern*) (to experience)

These verbs are called inseparable verbs. Whenever the prefix in the first syllable is unstressed, the verb is an inseparable verb!

Separable verbs split into two parts both in the present and in the past, but inseparable verbs never split (yes, that's why they are called inseparable). Compare the separable verb **opstaan** with the inseparable verb **ontmoeten**:

✔ **opstaan** (*op-staan*) (to get up)

  • **Ik sta op.** (*ik sta op*) (I get up.)

  • **Ik stond op.** (*ik stont op*) (I got up.)

✔ **ontmoeten** (*ont-moo-tern*) (to meet)

  • **Ik ontmoet . . .** (*ik ont-moot*) (I meet . . .)

  • **Ik ontmoette . . .** (*ik ont-moo-ter*) (I met . . .)

The past participle of a separable verb is made with the grammatical element **ge** which is placed between the prefix and the rest of the verb:

✔ **opstaan** → **op-ge-staan**

> **Ik ben laat opgestaan.** (*ik ben laat op-kher-staan*) (I got up late.)

The past participles of inseparable verbs are much easier to make. There is no **ge** inside of them.

✔ **ontmoeten** → **ontmoet**

> **Ik heb hem nooit ontmoet.** (*ik hep hem nooyt ont-moot*) (I've never met him.)

See the following examples of inseparable verbs.

✔ **De dokter heeft mij goed behandeld.** (*der dok-ter hayft mer khoot ber-han-derlt*) (The doctor treated me well.)

✔ **Ik heb geen medicijnen gebruikt.** (*ik hep khaayn may-dee-say-nern kher-broikt*) (I have not used medication.)

✔ **Mijn vrouw heeft me aan de afspraak herinnerd.** (*mayn frow hayft mer aan der af-spraak heh-ri-nert*) (My wife reminded me of the appointment.)

✔ **Ik heb de dokter alles verteld.** (*ik hep der dok-ter a-lers fer-telt*) (I have told the doctor everything.)

✔ **Ik heb dat niet zo ervaren.** (*ik hep dat neet zoa ehr-faa-rern*) (I did not experience it like this.)

Being examined

After arriving in the surgery, you want to make sure you understand the doctor's questions and instructions and leave with the right advice and medication. Here are some questions that the doctor might ask you when examining you:

✔ **Wat zijn uw klachten?** (*vat zayn uw klakh-tern*) (What complaints do you have?)

✔ **Heeft u pijn?** (*hayft uw payn*) (Are you in pain?)

✔ **Waar doet het pijn?** (*vaar doot het payn*) (Where does it hurt?)

✔ **Doet dit pijn?** (*doot dit payn*) (Does this hurt?)

✔ **Hoe lang heeft u hier al last van?** (*hoo-lang hayft uw heer al last fan*) (How long have you been suffering from this?)

✔ **Gebruikt u medicijnen?** (*kher-broaikt uw may-dee-say-nern*) (Do you use any medication?)

✔ **Bent u ergens allergisch voor?** (*bent uw ehr-kherns a-lehr-khees foar*) (Are you allergic to anything?)

And here are some instructions the doctor may give you:

- **Wilt u alstublieft uw mouw oprollen?** (*vilt uw als-tuw-<u>bleeft</u> uw mow <u>op</u>-ro-lern*) (Please roll up your sleeve.)
- **Wilt u alstublieft uw trui uitdoen?** (*vilt uw als-tuw-<u>bleeft</u> uw troai <u>oait</u>-doon*) (Please take off your pullover.)
- **Wilt u gaan liggen?** (*vilt uw khaan <u>li</u>-khern*) (Please lay down.)
- **Wilt u uw mond opendoen?** (*vilt uw uw mont <u>oa</u>-pern-doon*) (Please open your mouth.)
- **Zucht eens diep.** (*zuhkht erns deep*) (Take a deep breath.)

Understanding the diagnosis

After the examination, the doctor will tell you his **diagnose** (*dee-akh-<u>noa</u>- zer*) (diagnosis). While he's doing this, you might want to understand what's wrong with you.

You will be relieved in case the doctor says:

- **U heeft kou gevat.** (*uw hayft kow kher-<u>fat</u>*) (You've got a cold.)

or:

- **Het is niets ernstigs.** (*het is neets <u>ehrns</u>-terkhs*) (It's nothing serious.)

The doctor could also say::

- **U heeft . . .** (*uw hayft*) (You have . . .)
  - **griep** (*khreep*) (the flu)
  - **een hersenschudding** (*ern <u>hehr</u>-sern-skhuh-ding*) (a concussion)
  - **een ontsteking** (*ern ont-<u>stay</u>-king*) (an inflammation)
  - **een infectie** (*ern in-<u>fek</u>-see*) (an infection)
  - **een blindedarmontsteking** (*ern blin-der-<u>darm</u>-ont-stay-king*) (appendicitis)
  - **een longontsteking** (*ern <u>long</u>-ont-stay-king*) (pneumonia)
  - **ontstoken amandelen** (*ont-<u>stoa</u>-kern aa-<u>man</u>-der-lern*) (tonsilitis)
  - **een voedselvergiftiging** (*ern <u>foot</u>-serl-fer-khif-ter-khing*) (food poisoning)

The doctor might also say:

✔ **Uw bot . . .** (*uw bot*) (Your bone . . .)

- **is gebroken** (*is kher-<u>broa</u>-kern*) (has been fractured)

- **is gescheurd** (*is kher-<u>skhurt</u>*) (has been cracked)

- **is gekneusd** (*is kher-<u>knust</u>*) (has been injured)

✔ **U heeft een spier gescheurd.** (*uw hayft ern speer kher-<u>skhurt</u>*) (You have torn a muscle.)

✔ **U heeft een spier verrekt.** (*uw haft ern speer fer-<u>rekt</u>*) (You have pulled a muscle.)

Talkin' the Talk

Cilla Vermeent has stumbled over the stairs at work. Her right ankle hurts terribly and it is very thick. Her colleague takes her to the first aid in the hospital.

Nurse:	**Goedemiddag, wat zijn de klachten?**
	khoo-der-mi-dakh vat zayn der klakh-tern
	Good afternoon, what seems to be the matter?
Cilla:	**Ik ben gestruikeld op het werk.**
	ik ben kher-stroai-kerlt op het vehrk
	I stumbled at work.
Nurse:	**Ik zie het, je enkel is erg dik. Kun je eropstaan?**
	ik zee het yer en-kerl is ehrkh dik. kuhn yer ehr op staan
	So I see, your ankle is very thick. Can you stand on it?
Cilla:	**Ja, maar het doet erg pijn en hij wordt steeds dikker. We houden hem koel met ijs en natte handdoeken.**
	yaa maat het doot ehrkh payn en hay vort stayts di-ker. ver how-dern hem kool met ays en na-ter han-doo-kern
	Yes, but it hurts a lot and it's getting thicker and thicker. We are keeping it cool with ice and wet towels.
Nurse:	**Doet het hier pijn?**
	doot her heer payn
	Does it hurt here?
Cilla:	**Au, ja!**
	ow yaa
	Ouch, yes!
Nurse:	**Je enkel is verstuikt. Het klinkt vreemd, maar je moet hem toch zoveel mogelijk bewegen.**
	yer en-kerl is fer-stoaikt. het klinkt fraymt maar yer moot hem tokh zoa-fayl moa-kherlerk ber-vay-khern

Your ankle is strained. It sounds strange, but you have to move it as much as possible.

Probeer vanaf morgen weer een beetje te lopen en beweeg als je zit de voet af en toe.

proa-bayr fa-naf mor-khern vayr ern bay-tyer ter loa-pern en ber-vaykh als yer zit af en too yer foot

Starting tomorrow, try to walk a bit and when you're sitting, move it sometimes.

Cilla: **Kan ik autorijden?**

kan ik ow-toa-ray-dern

Will I be able to drive?

Nurse: **Dat zal erg pijn doen. Vraag je collega om je naar huis te brengen.**

dat zal ehrkh payn doon. fraakh yer ko-laykhaa om yer nar hoais ter breng-ern

It will hurt a lot. Ask your colleague to drive you home.

Cilla: **Hoe lang gaat het duren voordat ik weer gewoon kan lopen?**

hoo lang khaat het duw-rern foar-dat ik vayr kher-voan kan loa-pern

How long will it take before I can walk normally?

Nurse: **Dat hangt er vanaf. Je kunt het lopen langzaam opvoeren en met een week kun je weer naar je werk, als je zittend werk doet.**

dat hangt er fan-af. yer kuhnt het loa-pern lang-zaam op-foo-rern en met ern vayk kuhn yer vayr naar yer vehrk als yer zi-ternt vehrk doot

It depends. You can slowly increase the walking and after one week, you'll be able to go to work if you have sedentary work.

Ga naar de huisarts als de pijn na vier dagen nog niet minder wordt.

khaa naar de hoais-arts als der payn naa feer daa-khern nokh neet min-der vort

Please see your doctor if the pain hasn't diminished after four days.

Cilla: **Komt het weer helemaal goed?**

komt het vayr hay-ler-maal khoot

Will it completely recover?

Nurse: **De meeste mensen kunnen weer alles doen, maar bij te zware belasting kan de enkel weer pijn gaan doen.**

der mays-ter men-sern kuh-nern vayr a-lers doon maar bay ter svaa-rer ber-las-ting kan der en-kerl vayr payn khaan doon

Most people can do all the things they did before, but when you stress it too much, the ankle may hurt again.

Words to Know

struikelen	_stroai_-ke-lern	to stumble
het ijs	het ays	the ice
de handdoek	der _han_-dook	the towel

Getting treatment

After the doctor has told you what's wrong, he will tell you which steps have to be taken:

✔ **Ik schrijf u . . . voor** (*ik skhrayf uw . . . foar*) (I'm prescribing you . . .)

- **een pijnstiller** (*ern payn-sti-ler*) (a painkiller)
- **een kalmerend middel** (*ern kal-may-rernt mi-derl*) (a sedative)
- **een slaapmiddel** (*ern slaap-mi-derl*) (sleeping pills)
- **antibiotica** (*an-tee-bee-oa-tee-kaa*) (antibiotics)

Or the doctor could refer you to someone else:

✔ **U moet een röntgenfoto laten maken.** (*uw moot ern ruhnt-khernfoa-toa laa-tern maa-kern*) (You should have an X-ray taken.)

✔ **Ik moet u naar een specialist verwijzen.** (*ik moot uw naar ern spay-shaa-list fer-vay-zern*) (I have to refer you to a specialist.)

The doctor will give you **een recept** (*ern rer-sept*) (a prescription) that you should take to **een apotheek** (*ern a-poa-tayk*) (a pharmacy) in order to get your **medicijnen** (*may-dee-say-nern*) (prescription drugs).

The following expressions will help you to understand when and how often you are supposed to take your medication:

✔ **U moet een tablet nemen . . .** (*uw moot ern ta-blet nay-mern*) (you must take a tablet . . .):

- **drie keer per dag** (*dree kayr pehr dakh*) (three times a day)
- **na elke maaltijd** (*naa el-ker maal-tayt*) (after each meal)
- **met wat water** (*met vat vaa-ter*) (with some water)
- **voor het slapengaan** (*foar het slaa-pern-khaan*) (before you go to bed)

Some medications, such as aspirin, paracetamol, and cough syrup are non-prescriptive. You don't need a prescription, and you can get them at the **drogisterij** (*der droa-khis-ter-ray*) (the chemist's/drugstore). These are commonly part of a **winkelketen** (*vin-kerl-kay-tern*) (chain of shops) and their products range from toothpaste to beauty products and anything to make housekeeping easier.

For prescription drugs, however, you'll have to go to the **apotheek** (*apoa- tayk*) pharmacy). **Apothekers** (*a-poa-tay-kers*) (pharmacists) will only sell you prescription drugs when you hand them over the prescription. They will add extensive written information to the drug or inform you orally. They will keep a list of medicines sold to you in the computer and check whether your new medicine makes a good combination with your other medicines. Dutch doctors are very sparing on medicines: don't be amazed when they send you home without any prescription, saying: 'You will be better in a week.' Some doctors are very strict on sleeping pills: they will not prescribe you more than five or ten at one time.

Going to the Dentist

When you want to speak Dutch to your dentist, here are some useful sentences.

Before seating you in his **tandartsstoel** (*tant-arts-stool*) (dentist chair), the dentist might ask you:

> **Wat is het probleem?** (*vat is het proa-blaym*) (What seems to be the matter?)

You could use one of the following answers:

- ✔ **Ik heb kiespijn.** (*ik hep kees-payn*) (I have a toothache.)

- ✔ **Ik heb mijn vulling verloren.** (*ik hep mayn fuh-ling fer-loa-rern*) (I lost a filling.)

- ✔ **Ik heb mijn kunstgebit gebroken.** (*ik hep mayn kuhnst-kher-bit kher-broa-kern*) (I broke my dentures.)

Understanding the diagnosis

In order to tell you what's wrong the dentist might use one of the following phrases:

- ✔ **U heeft . . .** (*uw hayft*) (you have)
  - **een gaatje** (*ern khaa-tyer*) (caries)
  - **een zenuwontsteking** (*ern zay-nuw-ont-stay-king*) (neuritis)

Understanding what the dentist is going to do

You might hear one of the following phrases when the dentist tells you what he is going to do:

- ✔ **Ik geef u een . . .** (*ik khayf uw ern*) (I'll give you a . . .)
  - **noodvulling** (*noat-fuh-ling*) (temporary filling)
  - **wortelkanaalbehandeling** (*vor-terl-ka-naal-ber-han-der-ling*) (root canal treatment)
  - **zenuwbehandeling** (*zay-nuw-ber-han-der-ling*) (root canal work)
- ✔ **Ik moet deze kies trekken.** (*ik moot day-zer kees treh-kern*) (I have to pull this tooth.)
- ✔ **Ik moet deze kies vullen.** (*ik moot day-zer kees fuh-lern*) (I have to fill this tooth.)

Talking to the Police

You have just discovered that your flat has been burgled. A lot has been stolen, but the burglar left your copy of *Dutch For Dummies*. You've been lucky!

You can use these sentences in order to solve the problem:

> **Waar is het politiebureau?** (*vaar is het poa-lee-tsee-buw-roa*) (Where is the police station?)

When you are going to report something, you can say:

- ✔ **Ik wil aangifte doen van . . .** (*ik wil aan-khif-ter doon fan*) (I'd like to report . . .)
  - **diefstal** (*deef-stal*) (robbery/theft)
  - **zakkenrollerij** (*za-kern-ro-ler-ray*) (pickpocketing)
  - **inbraak** (*in-braak*) (breaking and entering)
  - **het openbreken van mijn auto** (*het oa-pern-bray-kern fan mern ow-toa*) (that my car has been broken into)
  - **vernieling** (*fer-nee-ling*) (vandalism)
  - **verlies** (*fer-lees*) (loss)

For burglary the police officer will talk to you personally. You may have to wait a long time before it's your turn but the case will be given attention. The police officer might write your story down in a **proces-verbaal** (*proa-ses fer-baal*) (an official report). For small crimes, like the theft of a bike, the officer will ask you to fill out a form yourself, in Dutch. In that case, the police officer will ask you:

> **Wilt u dit formulier invullen?** (*vilt uw dit for-muw-leer in-fuh-lern*) (Would you fill out this form?)

Though you may think that it's of no use to report small crimes such as the theft of your laptop from your car or your car itself or that of a moped, the police will work on it, as this kind of crimes is often the work of gangs and sometimes can be solved. The more details you can give of the stolen object, the greater the chance it will be found one day.

Describing what has been stolen

To report something has been stolen you say:

✔ **Mijn . . . is gestolen.** (*mayn . . . is kher-stoa-lern*) (My . . . has been stolen)
- **portefeuille** (*por-ter-fu-yer*) (wallet)
- **portemonnee** (*por-ter-mo-nay*) (purse)
- **handtas** (*han-tas*) (handbag)
- **tas** (*tas*) (bag)
- **digitale camera** (*dee-khee-taa-ler kaa-mer-raa*) (digital camera)
- **videocamera** (*fee-dee-yoa-kaa-mer-raa*) (video camera)
- **mobiele telefoon** (*moa-bee-ler tay-ler-foan*) (cell phone)
- **geld** (*khelt*) (money)
- **pinpas** (*pin-pas*) (bank card)
- **creditcard** (*kreh-dit-kart*) (credit card)
- **reisdocumenten** (*rays-doa-kuw-men-tern*) (travel documents)
- **paspoort** (*pas-paort*) (passport)
- **baggage** (*ba-khaa-zher*) (luggage)
- **auto** (*ow-toa*) (car)

As soon as you know enough Dutch to be able to fill out a form, you can report small crimes, such as pickpocketing and bagsnatching online. The site of the Dutch police, www.politie.nl, has a small part in English, but for **aangifte doen** (*aan-khif-ter doon*) (to report a crime) one will have to go to the Dutch part of the site, where you first have to check whether the police in a region the crime took place, prefers you to come to the police office or to report online. You can also make a phone call (0900–8844). The operator will speak English.

Answering questions of the police

You've had a good look at the thief. You may have shouted: **Help! Houd de dief!** (*help howt der deef*) (Help, catch the thief!). After sitting down to make a statement the police officer will ask you for a lot of details. Was he or she tall or small, fat or thin, hairy or bald? The police might ask you:

Kunt u de persoon beschrijven? (*kuhnt uw der per-soan ber-skhray-fern*) (Could you describe the person?)

Starting the description you say:

- ✔ **De persoon had . . .** (*der per-soan hat*) (the person had . . .)

    - **blond haar** (*blont haar*) (blond haar)

    - **zwart haar** (*svart haar*) (black hair)

    - **rood haar** (*roat haar*) (red hair)

    - **grijs haar** (*khrays haar*) (grey hair)

    - **een baard** (*ern baart*) (a beard)

    - **geen baard** (*khayn baart*) (no beard)

    - **een snor** (*ern snor*) (a moustache)

    - **geen snor** (*khayn snor*) (no moustache)

    - **een kaal hoofd** (*ern kaal hoaft*) (a bald head)

    - **een bril** (*ern bril*) (a pair of glasses)

Or you could say:

- ✔ **De persoon was . . .** (*der per-soan vas*) (the person was . . .)

    - **groot** (*khroat*) (tall)

    - **klein** (*klayn*) (small)

    - **ongeveer 1,80 m groot** (*on-kher-fayr ayn may-ter takh-tikh khroat*) (about 1.80 meter/6 feet tall)

    - **ongeveer 20 jaar oud** (*on-kher-fayr tvin-tikh yaar owt*) (about 20 years old)

The police might ask you when and where it happened, using the following phrases:

- **Wanneer is dit gebeurd?** (*va-nayr is het kher-burt*) (When did this happen?)
- **Waar was u op dat moment?** (*vaar vas uw op dat moa-ment*) (Where were you at that moment?)

Protecting your rights abroad

When you get into trouble, you don't know anything about legal matters and you need help, here are two very important phrases that you should know:

- **Ik heb een advocaat nodig.** (*ik hep ern at-foa-kaat noa-dikh*) (I need a lawyer.)
- **Ik wil graag de ambassade bellen.** (*ik vil khraakh der am-ba-saa-der beh-lern*) (I would like to call the embassy.)

Talkin' the Talk

Raymond van Dieren has to take some documents to one of his clients. He parks his car in front of the office and enters the building. When he comes back half an hour later, his car has been broken into and his laptop has been stolen. He goes to the nearest police station.

Raymond:	**Goedemiddag, ik wil aangifte doen van diefstal. Mijn auto is opengebroken en mijn laptop is gestolen.** *khoo-der-mi-dakh ik vil aan-khif-ter doon fan deef-stal. mayn ow-toa is oa-pern-kher-broakern en mayn lep-top is kher-stoa-lern* Good afternoon I want to report a theft. My car has been broken into and my laptop computer has been stolen.
Policeman:	**Wanneer is dat gebeurd?** *va-nayr is dat kher-burt* When did this happen?
Raymond:	**Tussen 11:00 en 11:30 vanochtend.** *tuh-sern elf uwr en half tvaalf fa-nokh-ternt* Between 11 and half past 11 this morning.
Policeman:	**Waar is dat gebeurd?** *vaar is dat kher-burt* Where did it happen?
Raymond:	**Hier vlakbij, op de Felsersplaats.** *heer flak-bay op der fel-ser-plaats* Quite near here, at the Felserplaats.

Policeman:	**Was uw laptop van buitenaf zichtbaar?**
	vas uw <u>lep</u>-top fan <u>boai</u>-tern-af <u>zikht</u>-baar
	Could your laptop be seen from outside?
Raymond:	**Nee, natuurlijk niet, hij lag in de achterbak, uit het zicht. Ik laat mijn laptop nooit op de bank liggen.**
	nay na-<u>tuwr</u>-lerk neet hay lakh in der <u>akh</u>-ter-bak oait het zikht. ik laat mayn <u>lep</u>-top nooyt op de bank <u>li</u>-khern
	No, of course not, as it was in the boot, out of sight. I never leave my laptop on the back seat.
Policeman:	**Hoe kon de dief dan weten dat er iets waardevols in uw achterbak zat?**
	hoo kon der deef dan <u>vay</u>-tern dat er eets <u>vaar</u>-der-fols in uw <u>akh</u>-ter-bak zat
	How could the thief tell that there was an object of value in your boot?
Raymond:	**Misschien heeft iemand gezien dat ik hem erin legde. Ik moest bij een bedrijf naast de sportschool zijn en daar stonden een paar mensen buiten met elkaar te praten.**
	mi-<u>skheen</u> hayft <u>ee</u>-mant kher-<u>zeen</u> dat ik hem ehr-<u>rin</u> <u>lekh</u>-der. ik moost bay ern ber-<u>drayf</u> naast der <u>sport</u>-skhoal zayn en daar <u>ston</u>-dern ern paar <u>men</u>-sern <u>boai</u>-tern met el-<u>kaar</u> ter <u>praa</u>-tern
	Perhaps somebody noticed I put it there. I had to visit a company next to the gym and some people there were talking outside.
Policeman:	**Waarom heeft u de laptop niet mee naar binnen genomen?**
	<u>vaa</u>-rom hayft uw der <u>lep</u>-top neet may naar <u>bi</u>-nern kher-<u>noa</u>-mern
	Why did not you take the laptop inside?
Raymond:	**Ik dacht dat het vijf minuten zou duren, maar ik moest binnen wachten.**
	ik dakht dat het fayf mee-<u>nuw</u>-tern zow <u>duw</u>-rern maar ik moost <u>bi</u>-nern <u>vakh</u>-tern
	I thought it would take five minutes, but I had to wait inside.
Policeman:	**Heeft u uw auto goed afgesloten?**
	hayft uw uw <u>ow</u>-toa khoot <u>af</u>-kher-sloa-tern
	Did you lock your car properly?
Raymond:	**Ja, dat doe ik altijd. De auto is opengebroken.**
	jaa, dat doo ik al-<u>tayt</u>. der <u>ow</u>-toa is <u>oa</u>-pernkher-broa-kern
	I always do. The car has been broken into.
Policeman:	**Vult u dit formulier maar in.**
	fuhlt uw dit for-muw-<u>leer</u> maar in
	Please fill out this form.

Words to Know

de diefstal	der *deef*-stal	the theft
de dief	der deef	the thief
de laptop	der *lep*-top	the laptop
van buitenaf	fan *boai*-tern-af	from outside
de achterbak	der *akh*-ter-bak	the boot
het bedrijf	het ber-*drayf*	the company
de sportschool	der *sport*-skhoal	the gym

Part IV
The Part of Tens

The 5th Wave   By Rich Tennant

'I'd speak more Dutch if I were confident enough, but I'm afraid I'll put my wooden clog in my mouth.'

In this part . . .

If you are looking for very practical tips about Dutch and how to use it, this is the part for you. Here you'll find ten ways to learn Dutch quickly, discover more about ten public holidays, get the low-down on how to sound professional at work, and more.

Chapter 15

Ten Ways to Pick Up Dutch Quickly

• •

*W*hether you are preparing your stay in the Netherlands or you're already there, you are interested in Dutch. In this chapter you'll find tips on how to improve your Dutch in a playful way.

Learning Dutch in the Street

As soon as you arrive in the Netherlands, you'll start picking up Dutch. You'll read words and phrases everywhere: at the airport, in the streets, and in the supermarket. At the airport, you will hear and see a lot of English along with the Dutch translation.

In the streets you'll see advertisings and traffic signs and some will puzzle you. You'll find the explanation of part of the written signs in Chapter 13 of this book. Road maps and the Internet will help you to find explanations of other traffic signs.

The supermarket supplies you not only with food but also with lots of information: You'll read important words about food on the signs indicating the groups of products and on the products themselves.

A good way to test yourself is to start writing your shopping lists in Dutch.

Looking Things Up in the Dictionary

As soon as the learning process has started, words will puzzle you. Get out your dictionary or use the dictionary at the end of this book and look up the word. It helps to remember words when you try to learn not only the word itself but a sentence with the word in it. Look for a sentence that appeals to you and forget the ones that you don't need.

Writing Your Own Dictionary

After looking up a word or a phrase in the dictionary, write it down in your own dictionary. Linguists tell us that we have to handle words seven times before they are 'ours'. The handling may consist of hearing it, writing it and saying it.

Emotion plays a role in remembering and forgetting: you may get irritated when you notice that you are looking up the same word for the fifth time. When you find you're getting annoyed at yourself it will help you to remember the word by saying it aloud several times to yourself and writing it down in your own dictionary. Some words will be important to you, as you want to use them a lot. Other words may be of no interest: don't write them down.

Buy a little notebook in order to write down the words you want to remember. You can write them down in the order that they come to you, but, in order to be able to find them back, it's better to write them in alphabetical order. A notebook for telephone numbers is already alphabetised. Reread the booklet during lost moments: on the plane, on the train and when waiting somewhere. You'll be happy to notice later that you have mastered most words!

Verbs in Your Pocket

Verbs are the materials of a language. When you learn a language, you generally start talking in infinitives or 'whole verbs': **ik spreken een beetje Nederlands** (I to speak a little bit Dutch). Using infinitives is a functional way of communicating, but you will sound much better when you conjugate your verbs, that is, use the right forms for every person: **ik spreek een beetje Nederlands** (*ik sprayk ern bay-tyer nay-der-lants*) (I speak a little bit Dutch). You'll need some discipline to do this from the beginning, but the effort you made will be rewarded later: it is easier to acquire something than to get out of a bad habit!

Start learning the conjugation of regular verbs and check yourself on the crib sheet that you've written for yourself and keep in your pocket. You can glance at it at any moment: on the plane, on the train, when you're waiting and, most important of all, when you're puzzled and curious. Make a new crib sheet for yourself every week, continuing with the important irregular verbs in the present, like **hebben** (*heh-bern*) (to have) and **zijn** (*zayn*) (to be). Continue this process as long as you like.

Using the CD of This Book

The language CD of this book offers a lot of valuable dialogues, as you will hear them in real life. Listen to it as much as you can: when cooking or driving your car. As the CD accompanies the book, it's most effective to use both simultaneously. Unlike most other CDs, however, this CD can be listened to without needing to answer questions from an exercise book, as is usual in other language methods.

Listening to Dutch Radio and TV

When in your car or at home, you might be able to listen to some Dutch radio stations. Even if you prefer a music station, you'll hear spoken Dutch in between. It will take you a lot of time before you can really understand radio programs that offer a lot of spoken words and information, so it will be frustrating trying to understand what they are saying. Listening to them for five or ten minutes every day might help you just to get used to the Dutch intonation and accent. After some time, you'll recognise a word once in a while, and later on you might understand a sentence here and there. It's easier to understand people who are speaking to you face-to-face.

Watching Dutch TV might be more rewarding than listening to the radio. Start looking at the dozens of English spoken series and films are screened every week that are subtitled in Dutch! You'll learn a lot of words in a playful way, enjoying yourself with a series you like. Just browse, and watch several times a week!

Advanced learners might enjoy watching **het Jeugdjournaal** (*het yukht-joor-naal*) (the news for young people) early in the evening. Have you got children? Watch it together with them: it informs you very well about Dutch life and events in clear, simple and correct language.

Celebrating a Dutch Hour

You can also organise a 'Dutch hour' at home. Designate an hour when you try to phrase in Dutch the little things you do as you go along, such as **Ik ga naar de keuken** (*ik khaa naar der ku-kern*) (I'm going to the kitchen) and **Ik doe de glazen in de afwasmachine** (*ik doo der khlaa-zern in der af-vas-ma-shee-ner*) (I'm putting the glasses into the dishwasher).

In case you have a Dutch-speaking partner, take the Dutch hour together! Don't be too hard on yourself, and start with a quarter of an hour a day. Talk in Dutch, starting with the basic things: the items on the table, in a room, in the house etc. In the next phase, you might tell your partner what both of you are doing: **Ik drink water** (*ik drink <u>vaa</u>-ter*) (I am drinking water), **jij drinkt wijn** (*yay drinkt vayn*) (you are drinking wine). As soon as you've mastered the present tense, you could ask your partner to say in Dutch how his day was, using the perfect tense. Of course you needn't be as systematic as that, try it your own way.

Asking the Dutch to Explain

Get in touch with Dutch people. After all, that's why you're learning Dutch! They will appreciate it very much that you are trying to learn Dutch. For first and superficial contacts many Dutch people will start talking back in English to you. They like to practice their English. When you see people more often, you can ask them to speak Dutch to you or to speak Dutch part of the time. Ask them to explain if you don't understand. You might also ask them to listen to you speaking Dutch. It will cost you a lot of energy and the listener a lot of patience in the beginning, so don't try to it all the time: start with a quarter of an hour.

Have you got Dutch-speaking colleagues? You'll feel much more at ease when you understand some of their conversation at moments of relaxation: at the coffee machine, when entering and when leaving. Ask questions when you don't understand! Don't make too high demands on yourself: don't expect yourself to understand them when they're joking in Dutch!

Reading the Free Papers

Are you travelling by train or by bus? Browse the free papers that you find in the public transport. You'll find the most important international and Dutch news in them and you might be able to read some headlines or subcaptions to photographs when you follow the news at home in your own language. The papers will give you good subjects for social talk with your colleagues and friends. Asking them questions about things you don't understand will help you find your way in Dutch society.

Surfing the Net

Many Dutch websites are written in Dutch and have English parts. As most information on the net is written in short and clear language, you can learn words and sentences looking up information you need on the Internet. First try to read the Dutch part and then check whether you understood the information well, by reading the English part.

Chapter 16

Five Things You Should Never Say

● ●

*T*his chapter aims at saving you from embarrassment. You may have heard foreign visitors saying things that make you hold your breath. Well, here are some pointers to help you prevent saying things that will make you want to bite your tongue!

Nice Car, How Much Did It Cost?

Though some Dutch people talk a lot about money and are proud when they've made a good deal, people generally don't like you to ask how much they paid for something. If they want to tell you the price of something, they will, if they don't, don't ask for it.

Give Me a Cup of Coffee!

Foreigners should be warned that Dutch service is not the same as, for instance, American service. A certain notion of equality is essential to Dutch society, and most Dutch people believe that even if you happen to be the Queen of the United Kingdom, you still have to treat the waitress as a peer. If you give the impression of 'bossing around', you will bring out the very worst in a Dutchman. Always, always add **alsjeblieft** or **graag**.

I Couldn't Sleep at All Last Night

Dutch people don't appreciate to hear very personal things about your health if you're not very close friends. Be sure not to complain about everyday things such as indigestion, sleeplessness, obesity, hot flushes, etcetera if you do not know people intimately. The other person will be either uncomfortable or bored. Be sure to keep these things away from work, unless you are feeling really unwell.

How Much Money Do You Make?

Your salary is a point of discussion between you and your superior. Your boss should tell you how the salary system of your company works. Don't ask your colleagues, neighbours, or friends about their salaries unless they tell you spontaneously what their income is. You might ask questions about the salary system, but don't get too personal.

The Dutch Are Boring!

As soon as you meet the Dutch, you will be forming stereotypes like: **Nederlanders zijn saai** (_nay-der-lan-ders zayn saay_) (The Dutch are boring), **Nederlanders zijn gierig** (_nay-der-lan-ders zayn khee-rikh_) (The Dutch are stingy), **Nederlanders kunnen geen feest vieren** (_nay-der-landers kuh-nern khayn fayst fee-rern_) (The Dutch don't know how to party) etcetera. But be careful: for all their tolerance, many Dutch people take great pride in their country, and harsh criticism will surely anger and offend them. When you're puzzled about certain things you notice, ask questions! Good friends will admit weak points and you might have a good laugh.

The Dutch might say things about you or your countrymen that hurt you. They are generally stereotypes. Clear the air by saying: **Iedereen is anders, zelfs mensen uit hetzelfde land** (_ee-der-ayn is an-ders zelfs men-sern oait het-zelf-der lant_) (Everybody's different, even people from the same country.).

Chapter 17

Ten Favourite Dutch Expressions

• •

*O*nce you get tuned in to Dutch a little, you may suddenly hear people using these Dutch expressions that seem to slip out at any given moment. You may have heard some of them already in informal settings and now it's time to use them yourself among friends!

We bellen hè?

(*ver beh-lern heh*)

The literal translation is: 'We will call, won't we'? You can use this phrase to say goodbye to friends. It means that you will see each other, but that you don't know when.

Ik ga het niet redden

(*Ik gaa het neet rehd-dern*)

This expression means: 'I am not going to make it'. You can use it anywhere when you are unable to finish something or to arrive on time: in daily life as well as in work situations.

Niet te geloven

(*neet ter kher-loa-fern*)

When somebody is telling a story and you don't know what to say, you can lengthen your reaction time by this phrase, which means: 'Is that really true'? The other person will react by elaborating, giving you time to think of another response. The literal translation is: you couldn't believe it.

The expression **echt waar?** (*ekht vaar*) is another good way to express amazement, and means: 'Really?'.

The phrase **Nee toch** (*nay tokh*) also means something like: 'No, it isn't true, is it?' and is another expression that you can use when somebody tells you an amazing story. The expressions **Niet te geloven**, **echt waar** and **nee toch** are especially used when the other person is telling a negative story.

Tjonge jonge

(*tshonger yonger*)

These two words can be translated by 'Well, well'. This response to an amazing story may sound slightly cynical, but can be neutralised by a conclusion like: **Wie had dat ooit gedacht** (*vee hat dat ooyt kher-dakht*) ('Who would have thought that?').

Mij niet gezien

(*may neet kher-zeen*)

People who imagine themselves in a situation the other person is telling about, use this reaction, which means something like: 'I wouldn't like it'. You could use it when your friend is telling you: **Ik heb vanmorgen om zes uur gezwommen** (*ik hep fan-mor-khern om zes uwr kher-svo-mern*) (I had a swim at six o'clock this morning).

Echt niet!

(*ekht neet*)

You can use this expression, which means 'Really not!', as a reinforcement of the expression **mij niet gezien**. Both expressions indicate that you are not willing to do the thing you are talking about. The expressions **echt niet** and **mij niet gezien** are only used informally: you may very well infuriate your boss if you react like this to one of his requests.

Maakt niet uit

(*maakt neet oait*)

The translation of this phrase is: 'Never mind'. When a friend breaks one of your precious wine glasses, it is a good moment for you to try this phrase. Of course, if you are less cool-headed about the accident, you could also say: **Wat doe je nou**! (*vat doo yer now*) (What are you doing!).

Niet verkeerd

(*neet ver-kehrt*)

The Dutch use the word **niet** (*neet*) a lot. It's rather difficult for them to be really very enthusiastic. The typical Dutch expression **niet verkeerd** literally means 'Not really wrong' but may indicate some enthusiasm, depending on the tone in which it is said. It means you like something.

Wat leuk!

(*vat luk*)

When someone tells you something upbeat, you might react with this phrase, which means 'How nice!' Watch your tone when using it: when you're not enthusiastic enough, it might sound sarcastic.

Ik ga ervoor

(*ik khaa er-foar*)

This sentence means: I'm going for it, and shows that you're enthusiastic and willing to reach a goal.

Chapter 18

Ten Public Holidays to Remember

∙ ∙

*S*ome of the following holidays may not be familiar to you, or at least, you may not be familiar with the way people in the Netherlands celebrate them.

Oudejaarsavond en Nieuwjaarsdag

When **Oudejaarsavond** (*ow-der-yaars-aa-font*) (New Year's Eve) is on a weekday, shops and banks are open until four o'clock. After that everybody goes home, to family or to friends to pass the evening together until 12 o'clock. It's traditional to have **oliebollen** (*oa-lee-bo-lern*) (doughnuts) or the old-fashioned **appelflappen** (*a-perl-fla-pern*) (apple turnovers) before 12 o'clock. Television has special New Year's Eve programmes. Shortly before midnight, people open a bottle of champagne to make a toast. Immediately after midnight the fireworks start. Now it's time to leave the house, either to join in the fireworks or to watch them, wishing your neighbours a happy New Year. Some neighbours will invite you to come and join them in more drinks, snacks or a light meal. Young people make use of New Year's Eve to join (several) parties that last all night.

Nieuwjaarsdag (*neew-yaars-dakh*) (New Year's Day), is the day after: people sleep late or visit their parents or in-laws.

In business, in early January New Year's receptions and New Year's dinners are held. Business life returns to its normal pace in the last week of January.

Carnaval

The northern part of the Netherlands is mostly **protestant** (*proa-ter-stant*) (Protestant) and the southern part **katholiek** (*ka-toa-leek*) (Catholic). In the 1960s, however, a secularisation wave took place. In addition more and more people from other countries came to live in the Netherlands, introducing other religions. The southern part of the Netherlands **onder de rivieren** (*on-der der ree-fee-rern*) (below the rivers) did continue the tradition of celebrating **Carnaval** (*kar-ner-fal*) (carnival), which has its roots in Catholic religion.

The preparations for this great celebration start as early as November, on the 11th of the 11th, with the election of **Prins Carnaval** (*prins kar-ner- fal*) (Prince Carnival) in every town and village. At the end of February or the beginning of March, the festivities open on Monday with parades and parties for which people dress up in fancy costumes. **Aswoensdag** (*as-voons-dakh*) (Ash Wednesday) marks the end of carnival and the beginning of the **Vastentijd** (*fas-tern-tayt*) (Lent), the 40-day period before Easter.

Some bars in the northern part of the Netherlands try to imitate the southern atmosphere of Carnival. All Dutch schools are out during the week of Carnival, and many people use this **krokusvakantie** (*kroa-kuhsfa- kan-see*) (named for the crocuses that start flowering in this period) to go on winter sports: **op wintersport gaan** (*op vin-ter-sport khaan*). Sometimes the weather gods have some ice in store for those who stay in the Netherlands.

Pasen

Pasen (*paa-sern*) (Easter) is a Christian feast and for those who are not religious or have a different religion, Easter just means a nice long weekend in March or April. For those who go to school or work in the public arena it starts on **Goede Vrijdag** (*khoo-der fray-dakh*) (Good Friday). Banks, shops and companies continue work until five. Breakfast on Easter Sunday, should be festive: the table is traditionally decorated with yellow ribbons or flowers, painted eggs, currant bread and Easter bunnies. Easter Monday is for visiting relatives or shopping.

Koninginnedag

Koninginnedag (*koa-ning-i-ner-dakh*) (Queen's Birthday) is the Dutch national holiday, on the 30th of April (in fact the previous queen's birthday). It is usually the start of a school holiday of one or two weeks: **de meivakantie** (*der may-fa-kan-see*). As this season often has sunny days **de meivakantie** is very popular for all kinds of outings, though it may freeze during the nights. Preparations for **Koninginnedag** start a long time ahead: many people keep things or grow plants which they want to sell at **de vrijmarkt** (*der fray-markt*) (street market). Over 24 hours, starting the night before Queen's Birthday, everybody, children included, is allowed to sell their junk, books, and plants, or to play music and give a show for some money. Amsterdam gets very crowded on this day, and as people just leave anything they don't sell, this invariably results in a mess at the end of the day.

Every year the Queen and her family visit another region of the Netherlands for a show of folklore, mingling as much as possible with **het gewone volk** (*het kher-voa-ner folk*) (the common people).

Dodenherdenking en Bevrijdingsdag

Dodenherdenking (*doa-dern-hehr-denk-ing*) (Commemoration of the Dead) and **Bevrijdingsdag** (*ber-fray-dings-dakh*) (Liberation day) go together on the 4th and 5th of May.

On the evening of the 4th of May the Queen lays **een krans** (*ern krans*) (a wreath) at **het Nationale Monument op de Dam** (*het na-shoa-naa-ler moa-nuw-ment op der dam*) (the National Monument on the Dam square) in Amsterdam. Immediately after this, at eight o'clock exactly, people all over the Netherlands keep two minutes of silence in order to commemorate the dead of World War II. The next day, **Bevrijdingsdag** (*ber-fray-dings-dakh*) offers festivities in many towns, but is only an official holiday once every five years.

Hemelvaartsdag

Hemelvaartsdag (*hay-merl-faarts-dakh*) (Ascension Day), is 40 days after Easter and always on a Thursday, generally in May or early June. Many people take the next day off for a long weekend.

Pinksteren

Pinksteren (*pink-ster-ern*) (Whitsun) is nine days later and means another long weekend. It starts on Saturday morning with **Luilak** (*loai-lak*) ('Lazybones'). This old tradition of children getting up very early in order to wake up **luilakken** (*loai-la-kern*) (lazybones), dragging pots and pans behind their bikes, has now disappeared. The tradition of **belletje trekken** (*beh-ler-tyer treh-kern*) (ring the doorbell and run away) was, in some regions, accompanied by drawing on the windows with candles. As fun later on changed to vandalism, nowadays community centres organise parties for the kids, starting the night before.

Sint-Maarten

Sint-Maarten (*sint maar-tern*) (Martinmas) is on the 11th of November and has its origins in the legend of St Martin, who tore his coat in two to share it with a poor man who was shivering in the cold. Some northern towns and regions continue the tradition and children in the ages six to nine make lanterns at school. As soon as it's dark, around six o'clock, the children head out in groups with their lanterns, often accompanied by an adult. They ring the doors and when the door is opened, the children sing variations on the Martinmas song, which is always funny and ends with the request: please, give us some sweets. When the song is finished, the children expect to receive a handful of sweets in their plastic bags. For those adults who wait in the dark until the children have passed by, the kids sing a special song which is not very complimentary.

Sinterklaas

Sinterklaas (*sin-ter-klaas*) (St Nicholas) is, like Martinmas, a holiday for the children. Some weeks before the 5th of December Saint Nicholas arrives on a steam ship, so to speak, sitting on his white horse and accompanied by his black knight **Zwarte Piet** (*svar-ter peet*) (Black Peter). At night, when all children are asleep, **Sint en Piet** (*sint en peet*) (St Nicholas and Peter) tour the rooftops in order to throw little presents through the chimneys in the shoes of of the sleeping children. On the 5th of December, all family members offer each other presents and traditionally, every present should be accompanied by a funny poem that tells something about the receiver of the present. If the fifth is a weekday, the celebration is generally held in the weekend.

Some people regard **Sinterklaas** as the quintessential Dutch festivity. Although more and more people give each other presents on Christmas Day, many others continue to celebrate Sinterklaas, considering Christmas 'too American'. Of course some people can't choose and celebrate both festivities – to the great satisfaction of their children.

Kerstmis

Kerstmis (*kehrst-mis*) (Christmas) is the most important public holiday of the year. Everybody is off on **Eerste Kerstdag** (*ayr-ster kehrst-dakh*) (Christmas Day) and **Tweede Kerstdag** (*tvay-der kehrst-dakh*) (Boxing Day). All schools have two-week holidays and a lot of companies are closed for the holidays until the second of January. Preparations for Christmas start on the 6th of December: on that day, the first **kerstkaart** (*kehrst-kaart*) (Christmas card) may arrive. Companies and private persons send out Christmas cards wishing each other **prettige feestdagen** (_preh-ti-kher fayst-daa-khern_) (Merry Christmas and a Happy New Year). The first Christmas card announces a busy month ahead at work, things to be finished before the end of the year, a **kerstviering** (_kehrst-fee-ring_) (a Christmas service) or a **kerstdiner** (_kehrst-dee-nay_) (Christmas dinner) and the traditional **kerstpakket** (_kehrst-pa-ket_) (Christmas hamper): a present that the boss offers to his employees in appreciation of their work.

When the 24th of December is a weekday, work ends at four o'clock, and everybody hurries home for **Kerstavond** (_kehrst-aa-font_) (Christmas Eve). Some people go to church, others just try to unwind or make preparations for the most important day: Christmas Day. Christmas dinner is held in the evening of Christmas Day, generally with family, and sometimes with some good friends. Boxing Day is for family visits, a walk or some other outing.

Chapter 19

Ten Phrases That Make You Sound Professional

• •

*T*his chapter provides you with some typical Dutch expressions that will serve you well when working with managers and bosses or when you are a one of them yourself. They are very Dutch and give you the opportunity to stay polite and keep your options open. You'll surprise your colleagues when you use them.

Komt het gelegen?

(*komt het kher-lay-khern*)

This question means: 'Is it convenient?' and is a very gentle way of opening a conversation with somebody who is busy. A variation is: **Komt het uit?** (*komt het oait*). The other person might answer: **Waar gaat het over?** (*vaar khaat het oa-fer*) (What is it about?) and then decide whether to talk the subject over immediately or make an appointment for some other moment.

Stoor ik?

(*stoar ik*)

You are very polite when you ask this question, which means 'Am I disturbing you?', when two or more people are talking and you have to interrupt. You might also say: **Mag ik even storen?** (*makh ik ey-vern stoarern*) (I'm sorry to disturb you, but can I talk to you for a moment?). People will answer **Zeg het maar** (*zekh het maar*) (go ahead) or **We zijn bijna klaar** (*ver zayn bay-naa klaar*) (We're almost ready).

Je hebt gelijk!

(yer hept kher-_layk_)

In order to express a belief that the other person is right you can say informally **Je hebt gelijk!** (yer hept kher-_layk_) (You're right!) or more formal: **U heeft gelijk** (uw hayft kher-_layk_). Admitting this first gives you an opening to modify the other person's opinion, adding your own arguments, introducing them like this: **Je hebt gelijk, maar . . .** (yer hept kher-_layk, maar_) (You're right, but . . .).

Afgesproken

(_af_-kher-sproa-kern)

This is the Dutch word for a saying 'It's a deal!'. In business people use it when they have made a serious deal in which both parties' commitment is needed. This kind of deal is often followed by a written contract, but the word **afgesproken** or **ik ga akkoord** (ik gaa ahk-_koart_) (I agree) is worth almost as much as the contract.

Ik hoor het graag

(ik hoar het khraakh)

Many people use this sentence, which literally means 'I'd like to hear it', to finish an e-mail, when they want you to give a reply. You can also use it in a conversation when the person you want to do something needs some time to prepare or think it over.

Klopt dat?

(klopt dat)

This expression means: 'Is that right?' and is the end of a carefully worded assumption like: **Ik hoor dat je een andere baan zoekt, klopt dat?** (ik hoar dat yer ern _an_-der-er baan zookt, klopt dat) (I've heard you are looking for another job, is that right?). Many people will end a question with this expression in order not to insult the other person in case the assumption is not right.

Wat is er aan de hand?

(*vat is er aan der hant*)

This very open and neutral question means: 'What's the matter?'

Daar word ik niet blij van

(*daar vort ik niet blij van*)

Executives and all other persons who need to express themselves very diplomatically, without hurting anybody, use this euphemistic phrase to express that they don't really agree with a situation or what the other person is telling them. It means: 'I'm not getting any kicks out of it'.

Daar zitten wij niet op te wachten

(*daar zi-tern vay neet op ter vakh-tern*)

When you use this sentence, in reaction to what somebody tells you, the other person will probably look for another solution. The phrase literally means: 'We are not waiting for this' and implies that you're definitely not happy with it. It is similar to the last phrase.

Dat is koffiedik kijken

(*dat is ko-fee-dik kay-kern*)

This expression will help you to reject a plan or a proposal that makes you feel uncertain. It literally means: 'This is like studying coffee grounds'. In English you would say: 'I haven't got a crystal ball'.

Part V
Appendixes

The 5th Wave   By Rich Tennant

'You're absolutely certain the concierge said this was the tulip boat tour around Amsterdam?'

In this part . . .

These appendixes will come in quite handy. The verb tables show regular and irregular verbs, and you can find the word you are looking for by using the minidictionaries. A list of the tracks on the CD that goes with the book is also included. You can use this list to look up the dialogues when you want to read them while listening.

Appendix A
Dutch Verbs

Regular Verbs

Regular Verbs (e.g. *werken* – to work)
Past Participle: *gewerkt* (worked)

	Present	Past	Past Participle
ik (I)	werk	werkte	
jij (you) (informal, singular)	werkt	werkte	gewerkt
u (you) (formal, singular and plural)	werkt	werkte	(hebben)
hij/zij/het (he/she/it)	werkt	werkte	
wij (we)	werken	werkten	
jullie (you)(informal, plural)	werken	werkten	
zij (they)	werken	werkten	

Separable verbs

Separable Verbs (e.g. *afhalen* – to take away)

	Present	Past	Past Participle
ik (I)	haal af	haalde af	
jij (you)	haalt af	haalde af	afgehaald
u (you)	haalt af	haalde af	(hebben)
hij/zij/het (he/she/it)	haalt af	haalde af	
wij (we)	halen af	haalden af	
jullie (you)	halen af	haalden af	
zij (they)	halen af	haalden af	

Reflexive verbs

Reflexive Verbs (e.g. *zich vergissen* – to make a mistake)

	Present	Past	Past Participle
ik (I)	vergis me	vergiste me	
jij (you)	vergist je	vergiste je	vergist
u (you)	vergist *u*/zich	vergiste *u*/zich	(hebben)
hij/zij/het (he/she/it)	vergist zich	vergiste zich	
wij (we)	vergissen ons	vergisten ons	
jullie (you)	vergissen je	vergisten je	
zij (they)	vergissen zich	vergisten zich	

Irregular Dutch Verbs

hebben (to have)
Past Participle: *gehad* (had)

	Present	Past	Past Participle
ik (I)	heb	had	
jij (you)	hebt	had	gehad
u (you)	hebt/heeft	had	(hebben)
hij/zij/het (he/she/it)	heeft	had	
wij (we)	hebben	hadden	
jullie (you)	hebben	hadden	
zij (they)	hebben	hadden	

zijn (to be)
Past Participle: *geweest* (been)

	Present	Past	Past Participle
ik (I)	ben	was	
jij (you)	bent	was	geweest
u (you)	bent	was	(zijn)
hij/zij/het (he/she/it)	is	was	
wij (we)	zijn	waren	
jullie (you)	zijn	waren	
zij (they)	zijn	waren	

beginnen (to begin)

	Present	Past	Past Participle
ik	begin	begon	
jij	begint	begon	begonnen
u	begint	begon	(zijn)
hij/zij/het	begint	begon	
wij	beginnen	begonnen	
jullie	beginnen	begonnen	
zij	beginnen	begonnen	

begrijpen (to understand)

	Present	Past	Past Participle
ik	begrijp	begreep	
jij	begrijpt	begreep	begrepen
u	begrijpt	begreep	(hebben)
hij/zij/het	begrijpt	begreep	
wij	begrijpen	begrepen	
jullie	begrijpen	begrepen	
zij	begrijpen	begrepen	

blijven (to stay)

	Present	Past	Past Participle
ik	blijf	bleef	
jij	blijft	bleef	gebleven
u	blijft	bleef	(zijn)
hij/zij/het	blijft	bleef	
wij	blijven	bleven	
jullie	blijven	bleven	
zij	blijven	bleven	

brengen (to bring)

	Present	Past	Past Participle
ik	breng	bracht	
jij	brengt	bracht	gebracht
u	brengt	bracht	(hebben)
hij/zij/het	brengt	bracht	
wij	brengen	brachten	
jullie	brengen	brachten	
zij	brengen	brachten	

denken (to think)

	Present	Past	Past Participle
ik	denk	dacht	
jij	denkt	dacht	gedacht
u	denkt	dacht	
hij/zij/het	denkt	dacht	(hebben)
wij	denken	dachten	
jullie	denken	dachten	
zij	denken	dachten	

doen (to do)

	Present	Past	Past Participle
ik	doe	deed	
jij	doet	deed	gedaan
u	doet	deed	(hebben)
hij/zij/het	doet	deed	
wij	doen	deden	
jullie	doen	deden	
zij	doen	deden	

drinken (to drink)

	Present	Past	Past Participle
ik	drink	dronk	
jij	drinkt	dronk	gedronken
u	drinkt	dronk	(hebben)
hij/zij/het	drinkt	dronk	
wij	drinken	dronken	
jullie	drinken	dronken	
zij	drinken	dronken	

eten (to eat)

	Present	Past	Past Participle
ik	eet	at	
jij	eet	at	gegeten
u	eet	at	(hebben)
hij/zij/het	eet	at	
wij	eten	aten	
jullie	eten	aten	
zij	eten	aten	

gaan (to go)

	Present	Past	Past Participle
ik	ga	ging	
jij	gaat	ging	gegaan
u	gaat	ging	(zijn)
hij/zij/het	gaat	ging	
wij	gaan	gingen	
jullie	gaan	gingen	
zij	gaan	gingen	

geven (to give)

	Present	Past	Past Participle
ik	geef	gaf	
jij	geeft	gaf	gegeven
u	geeft	gaf	(hebben)
hij/zij/het	geeft	gaf	
wij	geven	gaven	
jullie	geven	gaven	
zij	geven	gaven	

helpen (to help)

	Present	Past	Past Participle
ik	help	hielp	
jij	helpt	hielp	geholpen
u	helpt	hielp	(hebben)
hij/zij/het	helpt	hielp	
wij	helpen	hielpen	
jullie	helpen	hielpen	
zij	helpen	hielpen	

kijken (to watch)

	Present	Past	Past Participle
ik	kijk	keek	
jij	kijkt	keek	gekeken
u	kijkt	keek	(hebben)
hij/zij/het	kijkt	keek	
wij	kijken	keken	
jullie	kijken	keken	
zij	kijken	keken	

komen (to come)

	Present	Past	Past Participle
ik	kom	kwam	
jij	komt	kwam	gekomen
u	komt	kwam	(zijn)
hij/zij/het	komt	kwam	
wij	komen	kwamen	
jullie	komen	kwamen	
zij	komen	kwamen	

kopen (to buy)

	Present	Past	Past Participle
ik	koop	kocht	
jij	koopt	kocht	gekocht
u	koopt	kocht	(hebben)
hij/zij/het	koopt	kocht	
wij	kopen	kochten	
jullie	kopen	kochten	
zij	kopen	kochten	

krijgen (to get)

	Present	Past	Past Participle
ik	krijg	kreeg	
jij	krijgt	kreeg	gekregen
u	krijgt	kreeg	(hebben)
hij/zij/het	krijgt	kreeg	
wij	krijgen	kregen	
jullie	krijgen	kregen	
zij	krijgen	kregen	

kunnen (can)

	Present	Past	Past Participle
ik	kan	kon	
jij	kunt/kan	kon	gekund
u	kunt	kon	(hebben)
hij/zij/het	kan	kon	
wij	kunnen	konden	
jullie	kunnen	konden	
zij	kunnen	konden	

laten (to let, to leave)

	Present	Past	Past Participle
ik	laat	liet	
jij	laat	liet	gelaten
u	laat	liet	(hebben)
hij/zij/het	laat	liet	
wij	laten	lieten	
jullie	laten	lieten	
zij	laten	lieten	

lezen (to read)

	Present	Past	Past Participle
ik	lees	las	
jij	leest	las	gelezen
u	leest	las	(hebben)
hij/zij/het	leest	las	
wij	lezen	lazen	
jullie	lezen	lazen	
zij	lezen	lazen	

liggen (to lie)

	Present	Past	Past Participle
ik	lig	lag	
jij	ligt	lag	gelegen
u	ligt	lag	(hebben)
hij/zij/het	ligt	lag	
wij	liggen	lagen	
jullie	liggen	lagen	
zij	liggen	lagen	

lopen (to walk)

	Present	Past	Past Participle
ik	loop	liep	
jij	loopt	liep	gelopen
u	loopt	liep	(hebben)
hij/zij/het	loopt	liep	
wij	lopen	liepen	
jullie	lopen	liepen	
zij	lopen	liepen	

moeten (to have to, must)

	Present	Past	Past Participle
ik	moet	moest	
jij	moet	moest	gemoeten
u	moet	moest	(hebben)
hij/zij/het	moet	moest	
wij	moeten	moesten	
jullie	moeten	moesten	
zij	moeten	moesten	

mogen (to be allowed to, to like)

	Present	Past	Past Participle
ik	mag	mocht	
jij	mag	mocht	gemogen
u	mag	mocht	(hebben)
hij/zij/het	mag	mocht	
wij	mogen	mochten	
jullie	mogen	mochten	
zij	mogen	mochten	

nemen (to take)

	Present	Past	Past Participle
ik	neem	nam	
jij	neemt	nam	genomen
u	neemt	nam	(hebben)
hij/zij/het	neemt	nam	
wij	nemen	namen	
jullie	nemen	namen	
zij	nemen	namen	

rijden (to drive, to ride)

	Present	Past	Past Participle
ik	rijd	reed	
jij	rijdt	reed	gereden
u	rijdt	reed	(hebben)
hij/zij/het	rijdt	reed	
wij	rijden	reden	
jullie	rijden	reden	
zij	rijden	reden	

slapen (to sleep)

	Present	Past	Past Participle
ik	slaap	sliep	
jij	slaapt	sliep	geslapen
u	slaapt	sliep	(hebben)
hij/zij/het	slaapt	sliep	
wij	slapen	sliepen	
jullie	slapen	sliepen	
zij	slapen	sliepen	

spreken (to speak)

	Present	Past	Past Participle
ik	spreek	sprak	
jij	spreekt	sprak	gesproken
u	spreekt	sprak	(hebben)
hij/zij/het	spreekt	sprak	
wij	spreken	spraken	
jullie	spreken	spraken	
zij	spreken	spraken	

staan (to stand)

	Present	Past	Past Participle
ik	sta	stond	
jij	staat	stond	gestaan
u	staat	stond	(hebben)
hij/zij/het	staat	stond	
wij	staan	stonden	
jullie	staan	stonden	
zij	staan	stonden	

zitten (to sit)

	Present	Past	Past Participle
ik	zit	zat	
jij	zit	zat	gezeten
u	zit	zat	(hebben)
hij/zij/het	zit	zat	
wij	zitten	zaten	
jullie	zitten	zaten	
zij	zitten	zaten	

zoeken (to seek)

	Present	Past	Past Participle
ik	zoek	zocht	
jij	zoekt	zocht	gezocht
u	zoekt	zocht	(hebben)
hij/zij/het	zoekt	zocht	
wij	zoeken	zochten	
jullie	zoeken	zochten	
zij	zoeken	zochten	

zullen (shall/will)

	Present	Past	Past Participle
ik	zal	zou	
jij	zult/zal	zou	(no auxiliary)
u	zult	zou	
hij/zij/het	zal	zou	
wij	zullen	zouden	
jullie	zullen	zouden	
zij	zullen	zouden	

Minidictionary

Dutch – English

A

aangifte doen: to report a crime
aankomst (de): arrival (the)
achterlaten: to leave
advocaat (de): lawyer (the)
afslag (de): exit (the)
afspraak (de): appointment (the)
airco (de): air conditioning (the)
allergisch: allergic
alles: everything
ambassade (de): embassy (the)
ambulance (de): ambulance (the)
antibiotica (de): antibiotics (the)
antwoord (het): answer/response (the)
april: April
architectuur (de): architecture (the)
augustus: August
auto (de): car (the)
autosnelweg (de): highway/motorway (the)
avond (de): evening (the)

B

baan (de): job (the)
baas (de): boss (the)
bagage (de): luggage/baggage (the)

bakker (de): baker (the)
balpen (de): ballpoint (the)
bank (de): bank (the)
bankrekening (de): checking account (the)
banktransactie (de): bank transaction (the)
bebouwde kom (de): built-in area (the)
bedrijf (het): company (the)
beeldhouwkunst (de): sculpture (the)
begin (het): beginning (the)
bellen: to call
bericht (het): message (the)
beroep (het): occupation (the)
bespreking (de): meeting (the)
bier (het): beer (the)
bij: by
bikini (de): bikini (the)
bioscoop (de): cinema (the)
boek (het): book (the)
bord (het): plate (the)
bos (het): wood (the)
boter (de): butter (the)
brand (de): fire (the)
brandweer (de): fire brigade (the)
brief (de): letter (the)
brievenbus (de): letter box (the)
brood (het): bread (the)
buiten gebruik: out of order
bureau (het): desk (the)
bus (de): bus (the)
bushalte (de): bus station/bus stop (the)

C

cadeau (het): gift

café (het): bar: pub (the)

centrum (het): centre (the)

collega (de): colleague (the)

computer (de): computer (the)

concerthal (de): concert hall (the)

contant: cash

D

daar: there

dag (de): day (the)

dagkoers (de): current rate/today's rate (the)

dans (de): dance (the)

das (de): tie (the)

de heer: Mr

december: December

denken: to think

deur (de): door (the)

diagnose (de): diagnosis (the)

dichtbij: nearby

dichtstbijzijnd: nearest

diefstal (de): robbery: theft (the)

digitale camera (de): digital camera (the)

dinsdag: Tuesday

directeur (de): director (the)

docent (de): teacher (the)

document: bestand (het): document (the)

doelpunt (het): goal (the)

doen: to do

dokter (de): doctor (the)

donderdag: Thursday

douane (de): customs (the)

douche (de): shower (the)

drinken: to drink

drogisterij (de): chemist's/drugstore

E

eergisteren: the day before yesterday

eerste klas (de): first class (the)

enkeltje (het): single ticket (the)

eten: to eat

euro (de): euro (the)

Europese Unie (de): European Union (the)

evenement (het): event (the)

excuus (het): excuse (the)

F

familie (de): family: relatives (the)

fantastisch: fantastic

februari: February

feest (het): party (the)

festival (het): festival (the)

fiets (de): bike (the)

fietsen: to cycle

fietspaden (de): bicycle tracks (the)

film (de): film (the)

finale (de): finals (the)

fooi (de): tip (the)

formulier (het): form (the)

foto (de): photograph (the)

G

gaan: to go

gebruiken: to use

geld (het): money (the)

geldautomaat (de): Automatic Teller Machine (ATM)/cash dispenser

gesloten: closed

geven: to give

gewond: injured

gezin (het): family (the)

girorekening (de): Post Office bank account: giro account (the)

gisteren: yesterday

glas (het): glass (the)

goed: good

goedemiddag: good afternoon

goedemorgen: good morning

goedenavond: good evening

golf: golf

groenteboer (de): greengrocer (the)

groeten: regards

groot: large: big

H

halfpension: half board

hallo: hello

handtekening (de): signature (the)

haven (de): harbour (the)

hebben: to have

helpen: to help

herhalen: to repeat

hier: here

hoe: how

hotel (het): hotel (the)

huren: to rent

I

identiteitsbewijs (de): ID (the)

iets: something

in: in

industrieterrein (het): industial area (the)

infectie (de): infection (the)

instapkaart (de): boarding card (the)

interessant: interesting

internet (het): Internet (the)

inzicht (het): insight (the)

J

ja: yes

jaar (het): year (the)

januari: January

jas (de): coat (the)

joggen: to jog

jongen (de): boy (the)

juli: July

juni: June

K

kaartjes (de): tickets (the)

kantoor (het): office (the)

kassa (de): cash register (the)

kennis (de): acquaintance (the)

kerk (de): church (the)

kinderen (de): children (the)

klacht (de): complaint (the)

klein: small: little

knooppunt (het): interchange (the)

koffer (de): suitcase (the)

koffie (de): coffee (the)

koken: to cook

komen: to come

kopje (het): cup (the)

koud: cold

kruispunt (het): junction/crossing (the)

kunnen: can: to be able to

kunst (de): art (the)

L

land (het): country (the)
lepel (de): spoon (the)
leren: to learn
leuk: nice
lift (de): lift: elevator (the)
links: left
luchtpost (de): air mail (the)
luisteren: to listen

M

maand (de): month (the)
maandag: Monday
maart: March
maat (de): size (the)
maken: to make
makkelijk: easy
man (de): man (the)
map (de): file (the)
markt (de): market (the)
maximumsnelheid (de): speed limit (the)
medicijnen (de): Medicine (the)
mei: May
meisje (het): girl (the)
melk (de): milk (the)
meneer: mijnheer (de): sir (the): Mr
mes (het): knife (the)
met: with
metrostation (het): underground/subway
   station (the)
mevrouw: Mrs
middag (de): afternoon (the)
mobieltje (het): cell phone (the)
moeilijk: difficult
mooi: beautiful: pretty

morgen: tomorrow
museum (het): museum (the)
musical (de): musical (the)
muziek (de): music (the)

N

na: after
naam (de): name: surname (the)
naar: to
naast: next to
nationaliteit (de): nationality (the)
natuurlijk: of course
navigatiesysteem (het): navigation
   system/GPS (the)
nee: no
nemen: to take
niet storen: do not disturb
nietmachine (de): stapler (the)
niets: nothing
noorden (het): North (the)
november: November

O

ochtend (de): morning (the)
oktober: October
omleiding (de): diversion (the)
ondertekenen: to sign
ongeluk (het): accident (the)
ontbijt (het): breakfast (the)
ontsteking (de): inflammation (the)
ontwerper (de): designer (the)
oosten (het): East (the)
op: on
open: open
openbaar vervoer (het): public transport
   (the)

openbaar: open to the public
opera (de): opera (the)
ouders (de): parents (the)
overeenkomst (de): agreement (the)
overhemd (het): shirt (the)
overmorgen: the day after tomorrow
oversteken: to cross

P

pak, mantelpak (het): suit (the)
pakje (het): package: parcel (the)
park (het): park (the)
parkeerautomaat (de): car park ticket machine (the)
parkeerplaats (de): parking (the)
parterre (de): ground floor (the)
partner (de): partner (the)
paspoort (het): passport (the)
perron: spoor (het): platform (the)
persoon (de): person (the)
pinpas: betaalpas (de): debit card
politie (de): police (the)
portemonnee (de): purse (the)
postkantoor (het): post office (the)
postzegel (de): stamp (the)
potlood (het): pencil (the)
praten: to talk
pretpark (het): amusement park (the)
printer (de): printing machine (the)
proces verbaal (het): official report (the)
publiek (het): public (the)

R

receptie (de): reception (the)
rechtdoor: straight on
rechts: right
reddingsbrigade (de): lifeguards (the)

reisdocument (het): travel document (the)
reizen: to travel
rekening (de): bill: check (the)
reserveren: to reserve
restaurant (het): restaurant (the)
retourticket: retourtje (het): return ticket (the)
richting (de): direction (the)
rijbewijs (het): driving licence (the)
roken: to smoke
roltrap (de): escalator (the)
rotonde (de): roundabout (the)
routeplanner (de): itinerary planner (the)

S

saai: dull
sap (het): juice (the)
sauna (de): sauna (the)
schaatsen: to skate
schip (het): ship (the)
schoenenzaak (de): shoe shop (the)
schouwburg (de): theater (the)
secretaris (de): secretary (the)
september: September
slager (de): butcher (the)
slapen: to sleep
slecht: bad
sleutel (de): key (the)
slijterij (de): liquor store (the)
snel: fast
soep (de): soup (the)
souterrain (het): basement (the)
spaarrekening (de): savings account (the)
sparen: verzamelen: to collect
spitsuur (het): rush hour (the)
sportschool (de): gym (the)
spreekuur (het): consultation hour (the)
spreken: to speak

staan: to stand

stad (de): town (the)

stadhuis (het): town hall: city hall (the)

station (het): train station (the)

sterkte: all the best

strand (het): beach (the)

strippenkaart (de): bus and tram card (the)

student (de): student (the)

studie (de): studies (the)

supermarket (de): supermarket (the)

surfen: wave surfing

T

tandarts (de): dentist (the)

tankstation (het): filling station (the)

taxi (de): taxi (the)

taxistandplaats (de): taxi stand (the)

tegenliggers (de): oncoming traffic (the)

telefoon (de): telephone (the)

telefoonwinkel (de): telephone shop (the)

teleurstellend: disappointing

tennis (het): tennis (the)

theater (het): theatre (the)

thee (de): tea (the)

ticket (het): ticket (the)

toast (de): toast (the)

toeslag (de): surcharge (the)

toilet (het): toilet (the)

toneelstuk (het): play (the)

tot horens: I'll hear from you

tot ziens: goodbye

toerist (de): tourist (the)

tramhalte (de): tram stop (the)

trein (the): train (the)

tweeverdieners (de): two-earner: double-income household (the)

U

uitchecken: to check out

uitgaan: to go out

uitnodiging (de): invitation (the)

uitstekend: excellent

uitverkocht: sold out

V

vakantie (de): holiday (the)

vakantiehuis (het): holiday cottage (the)

vandaag: today

varen: boating

veel: much: many

verboden toegang: no entry

vergadering (de): meeting (the)

verjaardag (de): birthday (the)

verkeer (het): traffic (the)

verkeersopstopping (de): traffic jam (the)

verkopen: to sell

verleden tijd (de): past (the)

verliezen: to lose

vermoeiend: exhausting

verpleegkundige (de): nurse (the)

vertraging (de): delay (the)

vertrek (het): departure (the)

vertrekken: to leave

verzekering (de): insurance (the)

verzekeringsmaatschappij (de): insurance company (the)

videocamera (de): video camera (the)

vliegen: to fly

vliegtuig (het): plane (the)

vliegveld (het): airport (the)

vlucht (de): flight (the)

voetbalstadion (het): football stadium (the)
volpension: full board
voltooide tijd (de): perfect (the)
voor: in front of: before
voornaam (de): first name (the)
voorschrijven: to prescribe
voorstellen: to introduce
voorstelling (de): show (the)
vork (de): fork (the)
vragen: to ask
vreemde valuta (de): foreign currency (the)
vriend (de): friend (the)
vrijdag: Friday
vrouw (de): woman (the)

W

waar: where
waarom: why
wachten: to wait
wanneer: when
warm: warm
wat: what
wedstrijd (de): match (the)
week (de): week (the)
weekend (het): weekend (the)
wegenkaart (de): road map (the)
wegwerkzaamheden (de): road works (the)
werken: to work
westen (het): West (the)
wie: who
wijn (de): wine (the)
winnen: to win

wisselkantoor (het): exchange office (the)
wisselkoers (de): exchange rate (the)
woensdag: Wednesday

Z

zaken (de): business (the)
zakenreis (de): business trip (the)
zaterdag: Saturday
zee (de): sea (the)
zeilen: sailing
zelfbediening (de): self-service (the)
zich bemoeien met: to meddle in
zich gedragen: to behave oneself
zich herinneren: to remember
zich vergissen: to make a mistake
zich vervelen: to be bored
ziek: ill
ziekenhuis (het): hospital (the)
zijn: to be
zondag: Sunday
zonnebaden: to take a sunbath
zonnebrandcreme (de): suntan cream (the)
zuiden (het): South (the)
zullen: shall: will
zwembad (het): swimming pool (the)
zwembroek (de): swimming trunks (the)
zwemmen: to swim

English – Dutch

A

accident (the): **ongeluk (het)**

acquaintance (the): **kennis (de)**

after: **na**

afternoon (the): **middag (de)**

agreement (the): **overeenkomst (de)**

air conditioning (the): **airco (de)**

air mail (the): **luchtpost (de)**

airport (the): **vliegveld (het)**

all the best: **sterkte**

allergic: **allergisch**

ambulance (the): **ambulance (de)**

amusement park (the): **pretpark (het)**

answer: reaction (the): **antwoord (het)**

antibiotics (the): **antibiotica (de)**

appointment (the): **afspraak (de)**

April: **april**

architecture (the): **architectuur (de)**

arrival (the): **aankomst (de)**

art (the): **kunst (de)**

August: **augustus**

Automatic Teller Machines (ATM):
    geldautomaat (de)

B

bad: **slecht**

baker (the): **bakker (de)**

ballpoint (the): **balpen (de)**

bank (the): **bank (de)**

bank transaction (the): **banktransactie (de)**

bar (the): **café (het)**

basement (the): **souterrain (het)**

beach (the): **strand (het)**

beautiful: pretty: **mooi**

beer (the): **bier (het)**

beginning (the): **begin (het)**

bicycle tracks (the): **fietspaden (de)**

bike (the): **fiets (de)**

bikini (the): **bikini (de)**

bill (the): **rekening (de)**

birthday (the): **verjaardag (de)**

boarding card (the): **instapkaart (de)**

boating: **varen**

book (the): **boek (het)**

boss (the): **baas (de)**

boy (the): **jongen (de)**

bread (the): **brood (het)**

breakfast (the): **ontbijt (het)**

built-in area (the): **bebouwde kom (de)**

bus (the): **bus (de)**

bus station: bus stop (the): **bushalte (de)**

bus and tram card (the): **strippenkaart (de)**

business (the): **zaken (de)**

business trip (the): **zakenreis (de)**

butcher (the): **slager (de)**

butter (the): **boter (de)**

by: **bij: door: via: tegen**

C

can: **kunnen**

car (the): **auto (de)**

car park ticket machine (the): **parkeer-automaat (de)**

cash register (the): **kassa (de)**

cash: **contant**

centre (the): **centrum (het)**

checking account (the): **bankrekening (de)**

chemist (the): **drogisterij (de)**

children (the): **kinderen (de)**
church (the): **kerk (de)**
cinema (the): **bioscoop (de)**
closed: **gesloten**
coat (the): **jas (de)**
coffee (the): **koffie (de)**
cold: **koud**
colleague (the): **collega (de)**
company (the): **bedrijf (het)**
complaint (the): **klacht (de)**
computer (the): **computer (de)**
concert hall (the): **concerthal (de)**
consultation hour (the): **spreekuur (het)**
country (the): **land (het)**:
cup (the): **kopje (het)**
current rate: today's rate (the):
   dagkoers (de)
customs (the): **douane (de)**

D

dance (the): **dans (de)**
day (the): **dag (de)**
debit card: **pinpas: betaalpas (de)**
December: **december**
delay (the): **vertraging (de)**
dentist (the): **tandarts (de)**
departure (the): **vertrek (het)**
designer (the): **ontwerper (de)**
desk (the): **bureau (het)**
diagnosis (the): **diagnose (de)**
difficult: **moeilijk**
digital camera (the): **digitale camera(de)**
direction (the): **richting (de)**
director (the): **directeur (de)**
disappointing: **teleurstellend**
dish, plate (the): **bord (het)**
diversion (the): **omleiding (de)**

doctor (the): **dokter (de)**
document (the): **document (het)**
do not disturb: **niet storen**
door (the): **deur (de)**
driving licence (the): **rijbewijs (het)**
dull: **saai**

E

East (the): **oosten (het)**
easy: **makkelijk**
elevator (the): **lift (de)**
embassy (the): **ambassade (de)**
escalator (the): **roltrap (de)**
euro (the): **euro (de)**
European Union (the): **Europese Unie (de)**
evening (the): **avond (de)**
event (the): **evenement (het)**
everything: **alles**
excellent: **uitstekend**
exchange office (the): **wisselkantoor (het)**
exchange rate (the): **wisselkoers (de)**
excuse (the): **excuus (het)**
exhausting: **vermoeiend**
exit (the): **afslag (de)**

F

family (the): **gezin (het)**
family: relatives (the): **familie (de)**
fantastic: **fantastisch**
fast: **snel**
February: **februari**
festival (the): **festival (het)**
file (the): **map (de)**
filling station (the): **tankstation (het)**
film (the): **film (de)**

finals (the): **finale (de)**
fire (the): **brand (de)**
fire brigade (the): **brandweer (de)**
first class (the): **eerste klas (de)**
first name (the): **voornaam (de)**
flight (the): **vlucht (de)**
football: **voetbal (het)**
football stadium (the): **voetbalstadion(het)**
foreign currency (the): **vreemde valuta(de)**
fork (the): **vork (de)**
form (the): **formulier (het)**
Friday: **vrijdag**
friend (the): **vriend (de)**
full board: **volpension**

G

gift: **cadeau (het)**
girl (the): **meisje (het)**
glass (the): **glas (het)**
goal (the): **doelpunt (het)**
going out: **uitgaan**
golf: **golf**
good afternoon: **goedemiddag**
good evening: **goedenavond**
good morning: **goedemorgen**
good: **goed**
goodbye: **tot ziens**
GPS (the): **navigatiesysteem (het)**
greengrocer (the): **groenteboer (de)**
ground floor (the): **parterre (de)**
gym (the): **sportschool (de)**

H

half board: **halfpension**
harbour (the): **haven (de)**
hello: **hallo**
help: **help**

here: **hier**
highway (the): **autosnelweg (de)**
hobby (the): **hobby (de)**
hockey: **hockey**
holiday (the): **vakantie (de)**
holiday cottage (the): **vakantiehuis (het)**
hospital (the): **ziekenhuis (het)**
hotel (the): **hotel (het)**
how: **hoe**

I

I'll hear from you: **tot horens: we bellen**
ID (the): **identiteitsbewijs (de)**
ill: **ziek**
in front of: before: **voor**
in: **in**
industial area (the): **industrieterrein (het)**
infection (the): **infectie (de)**
inflammation (the): **ontsteking (de)**
injured: **gewond**
insight (the): **inzicht (het)**
insurance (the): **verzekering (de)**
insurance company (the): **verzekerings-maatschappij (de)**
interchange (the): **knooppunt (het)**
interesting: **interessant**
internet (the): **internet (het)**
invitation (the): **uitnodiging (de)**
itinerary planner (the): **routeplanner (de)**

J

January: **januari**
job (the): **baan (de)**
juice (the): **sap (het)**
July: **juli**
junction (the): **kruispunt (het)**
June: **juni**

K

key (the): **sleutel (de)**
knife (the): **mes (het)**

L

large: big: **groot**
lawyer (the): **advocaat (de)**
left: **links**
letter (the): **brief (de)**
letter box (the): **brievenbus (de)**
lifeguards (the): **reddingsbrigade (de)**
liquor store (the): **slijterij (de)**
luggage (the): **bagage (de)**

M

man (the): **man (de)**
March: **maart**
market (the): **markt (de)**
match (the): **wedstrijd (de)**
May: **mei**
medicine (the): **medicijnen (de)**
meeting (the): **bespreking (de)**
meeting (the): **vergadering (de)**
message (the): **bericht (het)**
milk (the): **melk (de)**
mobile phone (the): **mobieltje (het)**
Monday: **maandag**
money (the): **geld (het)**
month (the): **maand (de)**
morning (the): **ochtend (de)**
Mr: **de heer**
Mrs: **mevrouw**
much: many: **veel**
museum (the): **museum (het)**

music (the): **muziek (de)**
musical (the): **musical (de)**

N

name: surname (the): **naam (de)**
nationality (the): **nationaliteit (de)**
nearby: **dichtbij**
nearest: **dichtstbijzijnd**
next to: **naast**
nice: **leuk**
no entry: **verboden toegang**
no: **nee**
North (the): **noorden (het)**
nothing: **niets**
November: **november**
nurse (the): **verpleegkundige (de)**

O

occupation (the): **beroep (het)**
October: **oktober**
of course: **natuurlijk**
office (the): **kantoor (het)**
official report (the): **proces verbaal (het)**
on: **op**
oncoming traffic (the): **tegenliggers (de)**
open to the public: **openbaar**
open: **open**
opera (the): **opera (de)**
out of order: **buiten gebruik**

P

package (the): **pakje (het)**
parents (the): **ouders (de)**
park (the): **park (het)**

parking (the): **parkeerplaats (de)**
partner (the): **partner (de)**
party (the): **feest (het)**
passport (the): **paspoort (het)**
past (the): **verleden tijd (de)**
pencil (the): **potlood (het)**
perfect (the): **voltooide tijd (de)**
person (the): **persoon (de)**
photograph (the): **foto (de)**
plane (the): **vliegtuig (het)**
platform (the): **perron: spoor (het)**
play (the): **toneelstuk (het)**
police (the): **politie (de)**
post office (the): **postkantoor (het)**
Post Office Bank : Girobank account (the):
  girorekening (de)
printing machine (the): **printer (de)**
public (the): **publiek (het)**
public transport (the): **openbaar
  vervoer (het)**
purse (the): **portemonnee (de)**

R

reception (the): **receptie (de)**
regards: **groeten**
restaurant (the): **restaurant (het)**
return ticket (the): **retourticket:
  retourtje (het)**
right: **rechts**
road map (the): **wegenkaart (de)**
road works (the): **wegwerkzaamheden (de)**
robbery: theft (the): **diefstal (de)**
roundabout (the): **rotonde (de)**
rush hour (the): **spitsuur (het)**

S

sailing: **zeilen**
Saturday: **zaterdag**
sauna (the): **sauna (de)**
savings account (the): **spaarrekening (de)**
sculpture (the): **beeldhouwkunst (de)**
sea (the): **zee (de)**
secretary (the): **secretaris (de)**
self-service (the): **zelfbediening (de)**
September: **september**
shall: will: **zullen**
ship (the): **schip (het)**
shirt (the): **overhemd (het)**
shoe shop (the): **schoenenzaak (de)**
show (the): **voorstelling (de)**
shower (the): **douche (de)**
signature (the): **handtekening (de)**
single ticket (the): **enkeltje (het)**
size (the): **maat (de)**
small: little: **klein**
sold out: **uitverkocht**
something: **iets**
soup (the): **soep (de)**
South (the): **zuiden (het)**
speed limit (the): **maximumsnelheid (de)**
spoon (the): **lepel (de)**
stamp (the): **postzegel (de)**
stapler (the): **nietmachine (de)**
straight on: **rechtdoor**
student (the): **student (de)**
studies (the): **studie (de)**
suit (the): **pak, mantelpak (het)**
suitcase (the): **koffer (de)**
Sunday: **zondag**

suntan cream (the): **zonnebrandcreme (de)**
supermarket (the): **supermarket (de)**
surcharge (the): **toeslag (de)**
swimming pool (the): **zwembad (het)**
swimming trunks (the): **zwembroek (de)**

T

taking a sunbath: **zonnebaden**
taxi (the): **taxi (de)**
taxi stand (the): **taxistandplaats (de)**
tea (the): **thee (de)**
teacher (the): **docent (de)**
telephone (the): **telefoon (de)**
telephone shop (the): **telefoonwinkel (de)**
tennis: **tennis (het)**
the day after tomorrow: **overmorgen**
the day before yesterday: **eergisteren**
theatre (the): **schouwburg (de): theater (het)**
there: **daar**
Thursday: **donderdag**
ticket (the): **ticket (het)**
tickets (the): **kaartjes (de)**
tie (the): **das (de)**
tip (the): **fooi (de)**
to ask: **vragen**
to be able to: **kunnen**
to be bored: **zich vervelen**
to be: **zijn**
to behave oneself: **zich gedragen**
to call: **bellen**
to check out: **uitchecken**
to collect: **sparen: verzamelen**
to come: **komen**
to cook: **koken**

to cross: **oversteken**
to cycle: **fietsen**
to do: **doen**
to drink: **drinken**
to eat: **eten**
to fly: **vliegen**
to give: **geven**
to go: **gaan**
to have: **hebben**
to help: **helpen**
to introduce: **voorstellen**
to jog: **joggen**
to learn: **leren**
to leave: **achterlaten: vertrekken**
to listen: **luisteren**
to lose: **verliezen**
to make: **maken**
to make a mistake: **zich vergissen**
to meddle in: **zich bemoeien met**
to prescribe: **voorschrijven**
to remember: **(zich) herinneren**
to rent: **huren**
to repeat: **herhalen**
to report a crime: **aangifte doen**
to reserve: **reserveren**
to sell: **verkopen**
to sign: **ondertekenen**
to skate: **schaatsen**
to sleep: **slapen**
to smoke: **roken**
to speak: **spreken**
to stand: **staan**
to swim: **zwemmen**
to take: **nemen**
to talk: **praten**
to think: **denken**

to travel: **reizen**

to use: **gebruiken**

to wait: **wachten**

to win: **winnen**

to work: **werken**

to: **naar**

toast (the): **toast (de)**

today: **vandaag**

toilet (the): **toilet (het)**

tomorrow: **morgen**

tourist (the): **tourist (de)**

town (the): **stad (de)**

town hall: city hall (the): **stadhuis (het)**

traffic (the): **verkeer (het)**

traffic jam (the): **verkeersopstopping (de)**

train (the): **trein (the)**

train station (the): **station (het)**

tram stop (the): **tramhalte (de)**

travel document (the): **reisdocument (het)**

Tuesday: **dinsdag**

two-earner: double-income household (the): **tweeverdieners (de)**

U

underground: subway station (the): **metrostation (het)**

V

video camera (the): **videocamera (de)**

volleyball: **volleybal**

W

warm: **warm**

wave surfing: **surfen**

Wednesday: **woensdag**

week (the): **week (de)**

weekend (the): **weekend (het)**

West (the): **westen (het)**

what: **wat**

when: **wanneer**

where: **waar**

who: **wie**

why: **waarom**

wine (the): **wijn (de)**

with: **met**

woman (the): **vrouw (de)**

wood (the): **bos (het)**

Y

year (the): **jaar (het)**

yes: **ja**

yesterday: **gisteren**

Appendix C

About the CD

*F*ollowing is a list of the tracks that appear on this book's audio CD, which you can find inside the back cover. Note that this is an audio-only CD – just pop it into your stereo (or whatever you use to listen to your regular music CDs).

Table A-1	The Tracks on the Audio CD		
Track	*Title*	*Chapter*	*Page*
1	The Dutch alphabet	1	15
2	Formal greeting	4	71
3	Informal greeting	4	72
4	Meeting for the first time	4	73
5	Introducing someone formally	4	75
6	Saying goodbye	4	76
7	Asking where someone is from	4	79
8	Talking about languages	4	82
9	Talking about family	5	93
10	Making a reservation	6	109
11	Entering a restaurant	6	110
12	Taking your order	6	117
13	Getting the bill and tipping	6	120
14	Buying food at the market	6	127
15	Getting help from the shop assistant	7	138

(continued)

Table A-1 *(continued)*

Track	Title	Chapter	Page
16	Trying something on	7	144
17	Buying clothes	7	146
18	Making a date to go to the movies	8	154
19	Making an appointment	9	182
20	Leaving a message 1	9	185
21	Leaving a message 2	9	186
22	Office talk	9	197
23	Changing money	10	202
24	Finding a restaurant	11	221
25	Asking directions 1	11	225
26	Asking directions 2	11	229
27	Reserving a room	12	235
28	Checking into a hotel	12	242
29	Checking out	12	247
30	Picking up a ticket at the airport	13	251
31	Renting a car	13	257
32	On the road	13	265
33	Being late for work	13	271
34	Buying train tickets	13	276
35	Going by bus	13	280
36	Reporting a burglary	14	300

Index

FOR DUMMIES®

Do Anything. Just Add Dummies

UK editions

SELF HELP

978-0-470-51291-3

978-0-470-03135-3

978-0-470-51501-3

BUSINESS

978-0-7645-7018-6

978-0-7645-7056-8

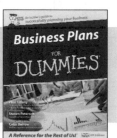

978-0-7645-7026-1

PERSONAL FINANCE

978-0-7645-7023-0

978-0-470-51510-5

978-0-470-05815-2

Answering Tough Interview Questions For Dummies
(978-0-470-01903-0)

Being the Best Man For Dummies
(978-0-470-02657-1)

British History For Dummies
(978-0-470-03536-8)

Buying a Home on a Budget For Dummies
(978-0-7645-7035-3)

Buying a Property in Spain For Dummies
(978-0-470-51235-77)

Buying & Selling a Home For Dummies
(978-0-7645-7027-8)

Buying a Property in Eastern Europe For Dummies
(978-0-7645-7047-6)

Cognitive Behavioural Therapy For Dummies
(978-0-470-01838-5)

Cricket For Dummies
(978-0-470-03454-5)

CVs For Dummies
(978-0-7645-7017-9)

Detox For Dummies
(978-0-470-01908-5)

Diabetes For Dummies
(978-0-470-05810-7)

Divorce For Dummies
(978-0-7645-7030-8)

DJing For Dummies
(978-0-470-03275-6)

eBay.co.uk For Dummies
(978-0-7645-7059-9)

Economics For Dummies
(978-0-470-05795-7)

English Grammar For Dummies
(978-0-470-05752-0)

Gardening For Dummies
(978-0-470-01843-9)

Genealogy Online For Dummies
(978-0-7645-7061-2)

Green Living For Dummies
(978-0-470-06038-4)

Hypnotherapy For Dummies
(978-0-470-01930-6)

Neuro-linguistic Programming For Dummies
(978-0-7645-7028-5)

Parenting For Dummies
(978-0-470-02714-1)

Pregnancy For Dummies
(978-0-7645-7042-1)

Renting out your Property For Dummies
(978-0-470-02921-3)

Retiring Wealthy For Dummies
(978-0-470-02632-8)

Self Build and Renovation For Dummies
(978-0-470-02586-4)

Selling For Dummies
(978-0-470-51259-3)

Sorting Out Your Finances For Dummies
(978-0-7645-7039-1)

Starting a Business on eBay.co.uk For Dummies
(978-0-470-02666-3)

Starting and Running an Online Business For Dummies
(978-0-470-05768-1)

The Romans For Dummies
(978-0-470-03077-6)

UK Law and Your Rights For Dummies
(978-0-470-02796-7)

Writing a Novel & Getting Published For Dummies
(978-0-470-05910-4)

FOR DUMMIES®

Do Anything. Just Add Dummies

HOBBIES

978-0-7645-5232-8

978-0-7645-5395-0

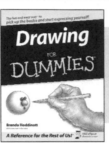

978-0-7645-5476-6

Also available:

Art For Dummies
(978-0-7645-5104-8)

Aromatherapy For Dummies
(978-0-7645-5171-0)

Bridge For Dummies
(978-0-471-92426-5)

Card Games For Dummies
(978-0-7645-9910-1)

Chess For Dummies
(978-0-7645-8404-6)

Improving Your Memory
For Dummies
(978-0-7645-5435-3)

Massage For Dummies
(978-0-7645-5172-7)

Meditation For Dummies
(978-0-471-77774-8)

Photography For Dummies
(978-0-7645-4116-2)

Quilting For Dummies
(978-0-7645-9799-2)

EDUCATION

978-0-7645-5434-6

978-0-7645-5581-7

978-0-7645-5422-3

Also available:

Algebra For Dummies
(978-0-7645-5325-7)

Astronomy For Dummies
(978-0-7645-8465-7)

Buddhism For Dummies
(978-0-7645-5359-2)

Calculus For Dummies
(978-0-7645-2498-1)

Cooking Basics For Dummies
(978-0-7645-7206-7)

Forensics For Dummies
(978-0-7645-5580-0)

Islam For Dummies
(978-0-7645-5503-9)

Philosophy For Dummies
(978-0-7645-5153-6)

Religion For Dummies
(978-0-7645-5264-9)

Trigonometry For Dummies
(978-0-7645-6903-6)

PETS

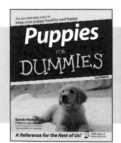

978-0-470-03717-1

978-0-7645-8418-3

978-0-7645-5275-5

Also available:

Aquariums For Dummies
(978-0-7645-5156-7)

Birds For Dummies
(978-0-7645-5139-0)

Dogs For Dummies
(978-0-7645-5274-8)

Ferrets For Dummies
(978-0-7645-5259-5)

Golden Retrievers
For Dummies
(978-0-7645-5267-0)

Horses For Dummies
(978-0-7645-9797-8)

Jack Russell Terriers
For Dummies
(978-0-7645-5268-7)

Labrador Retrievers
For Dummies
(978-0-7645-5281-6)

Puppies Raising & Training
Diary For Dummies
(978-0-7645-0876-9)

FOR DUMMIES®

The easy way to get more done and have more fun

LANGUAGES

978-0-7645-5193-2

978-0-7645-5193-2

978-0-7645-5196-3

Also available:

Chinese For Dummies
(978-0-471-78897-3)

Chinese Phrases
For Dummies
(978-0-7645-8477-0)

French Phrases For Dummies
(978-0-7645-7202-9)

German For Dummies
(978-0-7645-5195-6)

Italian Phrases For Dummies
(978-0-7645-7203-6)

Japanese For Dummies
(978-0-7645-5429-2)

Latin For Dummies
(978-0-7645-5431-5)

Spanish Phrases
For Dummies
(978-0-7645-7204-3)

Spanish Verbs For Dummies
(978-0-471-76872-2)

Hebrew For Dummies
(978-0-7645-5489-6)

MUSIC AND FILM

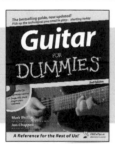

978-0-7645-9904-0

978-0-7645-2476-9

978-0-7645-5105-5

Also available:

Bass Guitar For Dummies
(978-0-7645-2487-5)

Blues For Dummies
(978-0-7645-5080-5)

Classical Music For Dummies
(978-0-7645-5009-6)

Drums For Dummies
(978-0-471-79411-0)

Jazz For Dummies
(978-0-471-76844-9)

Opera For Dummies
(978-0-7645-5010-2)

Rock Guitar For Dummies
(978-0-7645-5356-1)

Screenwriting For Dummies
(978-0-7645-5486-5)

Songwriting For Dummies
(978-0-7645-5404-9)

Singing For Dummies
(978-0-7645-2475-2)

HEALTH, SPORTS & FITNESS

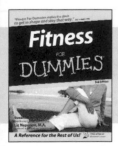

978-0-7645-7851-9

978-0-7645-5623-4

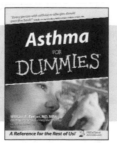

978-0-7645-4233-6

Also available:

Controlling Cholesterol
For Dummies
(978-0-7645-5440-7)

Diabetes For Dummies
(978-0-470-05810-7)

High Blood Pressure
For Dummies
(978-0-7645-5424-7)

Martial Arts For Dummies
(978-0-7645-5358-5)

Menopause FD
(978-0-470-061008)

Pilates For Dummies
(978-0-7645-5397-4)

Weight Training
For Dummies
(978-0-471-76845-6)

Yoga For Dummies
(978-0-7645-5117-8)

FOR DUMMIES®

Helping you expand your horizons and achieve your potential

INTERNET

The Internet FOR DUMMIES
John R. Levine
Margaret Levine Young
Carol Baroudi

978-0-470-12174-0

Search Engine Optimization FOR DUMMIES
Peter Kent

978-0-471-97998-2

Creating Web Pages FOR DUMMIES
Bud E. Smith
Arthur Bebak

978-0-470-08030-6

Also available:

Blogging For Dummies
For Dummies, 2nd Edition
(978-0-470-23017-6)

Building a Web Site For
Dummies, 3rd Edition
(978-0-470-14928-7)

Creating Web Pages
All-in-One Desk Reference
For Dummies, 3rd Edition
(978-0-470-09629-1)

eBay.co.uk
For Dummies
(978-0-7645-7059-9)

Video Blogging FD
(978-0-471-97177-1)

Web Analysis For Dummies
(978-0-470-09824-0)

Web Design For Dummies,
2nd Edition
(978-0-471-78117-2)

DIGITAL MEDIA

Digital Photography FOR DUMMIES
Julie Adair King

978-0-7645-9802-9

iPod & iTunes FOR DUMMIES

978-0-470-17474-6

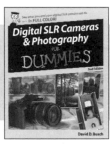

Digital SLR Cameras & Photography FOR DUMMIES
David D. Busch

978-0-470-14927-0

Also available:

BlackBerry For Dummies,
2nd Edition
(978-0-470-18079-2)

Digital Photography
All-In-One Desk Reference
For Dummies
(978-0-470-03743-0)

Digital Photo Projects
For Dummies
(978-0-470-12101-6)

iPhone For Dummies
(978-0-470-17469-2)

Photoshop CS3 For Dummies
(978-0-470-11193-2)

Podcasting
For Dummies
(978-0-471-74898-4)

COMPUTER BASICS

PCs FOR DUMMIES
Dan Gookin

978-0-470-13728-4

Laptops FOR DUMMIES
Dan Gookin

978-0-470-05432-1

Windows Vista ALL-IN-ONE DESK REFERENCE FOR DUMMIES
Woody Leonhard

978-0-471-74941-7

Also available:

Macs For Dummies,
9th Edition
(978-0-470-04849-8)

Office 2007 All-in-One Desk
Reference For Dummies
(978-0-471-78279-7)

PCs All-in-One Desk
Reference For Dummies,
4th Edition
(978-0-470-22338-3)

Upgrading & Fixing PCs
For Dummies, 7th Edition
(978-0-470-12102-3)

Windows XP For Dummies,
2nd Edition
(978-0-7645-7326-2)